JOWITT'S
DICTIONARY OF ENGLISH LAW

SECOND CUMULATIVE SUPPLEMENT
TO THE
SECOND EDITION

AUSTRALIA AND NEW ZEALAND
The Law Book Company Ltd.
Sydney : Melbourne : Perth

CANADA AND U.S.A.
The Carswell Company Ltd.
Agincourt, Ontario

INDIA
N.M. Tripathi Private Ltd.
Bombay
and
Eastern Law House Private Ltd.
Calcutta and Delhi
M.P.P. House
Bangalore

ISRAEL
Steimatzky's Agency Ltd.
Jerusalem : Tel Aviv : Haifa

MALAYSIA : SINGAPORE : BRUNEI
Malayan Law Journal (Pte.) Ltd.
Singapore

PAKISTAN
Pakistan Law House
Karachi

JOWITT'S
DICTIONARY
OF
ENGLISH LAW

SECOND CUMULATIVE SUPPLEMENT
TO THE
SECOND EDITION

BY
EMLYN WILLIAMS, LL.B.
of Lincoln's Inn, Barrister

LONDON
SWEET & MAXWELL
1985

First edition 1959
Second impression 1965
Third impression 1972
Fourth impression 1974
Second edition 1977
Second impression 1978
Third impression 1980
Fourth impression 1981
First supplement 1981
Second cumulative supplement 1985

Published by
Sweet & Maxwell Ltd. of
11 New Fetter Lane, London.
Computertypeset by Burgess & Son (Abingdon) Ltd.
Printed in Great Britain by
Page Bros. (Norwich) Ltd.

British Library Cataloguing in Publication Data

Jowitt, William Allen Jowitt, *Earl*
Jowitt's dictionary of English law.—2nd ed.
2nd suppl.
1. Law—England—Dictionaries
I. Title II. Walsh, Clifford III. Burke,
John, *1896-1980* IV. Williams, Emlyn, *1946-*
344.208′6 KD313

ISBN 0–421–29370–5

PREFACE

The compilation of further notices of the developments in the last four years which affect so extensive a text as the Dictionary has proved increasingly difficult. As time and the accumulation of new law bring us nearer to the Third Edition, I have preferred to concentrate on the amendments which affect the "core" of the law. The necessary restriction of the size of this new Supplement has also encouraged me to leave out of account significant number of items which, though interesting, cannot justify preference to changes which affect, for example, the constitutions of the Supreme Court (the Supreme Court Act 1981), the county courts (the County Court Rules 1981 and the County Courts Act 1984), and the magistrates' courts (the Magistrates' Courts Rules 1981 and the Magistrates' Courts Act 1980).

The increasing use of delayed commencements has made a coherent account of the law more difficult than one might wish. I have taken little, if any, account of provisions where the commencement date is in doubt. As a result, I have not included any extensive notes about, for example, the Matrimonial and Family Proceedings Act 1984, Parts III and V.

In 1976 the Editor of the Second Edition, the late John Burke, wrote "The common law has taken a beating." My reading over the four years since the First Supplement leaves me wondering how he could possibly express the effects of the changes since he wrote; "grievous bodily harm" seems hardly adequate! There is no intention to oppose all change; much of it is not only necessary but also beneficial. The rationalisation (in due course) of the distribution of family law matters is in prospect (though omitted from this particular volume, as noted above), and new provisions to deal with computer software and other technological innovations are essential. Once a problem is identified, however, there seems to be a tendency "to have a law against it," not necessarily with any substantial prospect of solving the problem or of integrating the new provisions into the earlier law.

As before, I must disclaim any pretence to omniscience: again quoting my learned predecessor, "It is not possible in a work whose ambit is the whole of English law to avoid error but I have the poor satisfaction of knowing that any error is wholly my own." I have attempted to cover developments up to the end of 1984, and have avoided making further up-dating amendments during the course of proofs, preferring to complete this project and to move on towards the next edition.

Both the publishers and I are aware of the value of comments from readers. If any of the material in this Supplement, or any omission committed there, provokes a strong (indeed, any) reaction which a reader wishes to pass on, correspondence should be sent to the publishers' office in London.

Emlyn Williams
West Malling

Dictionary of English Law

A

Abatement of civil proceedings. See also R.S.C., Ord. 28, r. 11, and Ord. 34, r. 9. Proceedings by and against the Crown are not affected by the demise of the Crown (Crown Proceedings Act 1947, s. 32); proceedings brought under the Crown Proceedings Act 1947, Part II, are not affected by any change in the person holding the office of Attorney General (*q.v.*) or in the person or body of persons constituting the department concerned in the proceedings (Crown Proceedings Act 1947, s. 17(5)).

Abatement of criminal proceedings. The Magistrates' Courts Act 1952, s. 101, has been repealed and replaced by the Magistrates' Courts Act 1980, s. 124, without change of effect.

Abatement of customs and excise duties. The Customs and Excise Act 1952, s. 263, has been repealed and replaced by the Customs and Excise Management Act 1979, s. 130, and the Alcoholic Liquor Duties Act 1979, s. 46.

Abatement of false lights and signals. The penalty for failure to comply with a notice under the Merchant Shipping Act 1894, s. 667, was prospectively increased to £1,000 by the Merchant Shipping Act 1979, s. 42, Sched. 6, Part VI, para. 10.

Abduction. The Representation of the People Act 1949, s. 101, has been repealed and replaced by the Representation of the People Act 1983, s. 115, without change of effect.

See also the Child Abduction Act 1984.

Able-bodied seaman. The Merchant Shipping Act 1970, s. 43, was brought into operation on December 19, 1975, by the Merchant Shipping Act 1970 (Commencement No. 4) Order 1975 (S.I. 1975 No. 2156). Orders made under s. 43 include the Merchant Shipping (Certification of Deck Officers) Regulations 1977 S.I. 1977 No. 1152 as amended by S.I. 1978 No. 430, and the Merchant Shipping (Certification of Marine Engineer Officers) Regulations 1977 (S.I. 1977 No. 2072, as amended by S.I. 1979 No. 599). The scope of s. 43 has been amended by the Merchant Shipping Act 1979, s. 37.

Absence beyond the seas. The Limitation Acts 1939 and 1963 and subsequent legislation have been repealed and replaced by the Limitation Act 1980.

Absence of accused. The Magistrates' Courts Act 1952, ss. 4(3) and 15, and the Act of 1957, s. 1, have been repealed and replaced by the Magistrates' Courts Act 1980, ss. 4(3), 11 and 13, and 12 respectively, without change of effect.

Abusing children. The reasoning in *R.* v. *Tyrrel* [1894] 1 Q.B. 710, was followed in *R.* v. *Whitehouse* [1978] Q.B. 868, C.A. For the creation of new offences relating to photographing children see the Protection of Children Act 1978.

Acceptance of goods. The Sale of Goods Act 1893, ss. 34, 35, have been repealed and replaced by the Sale of Goods Act 1979, ss. 34, 35, without change of effect; the Misrepresentation Act 1967, s. 4(2), has been incorporated in the Act of 1979, s. 35.

Acceptance of service. The provisions relating to entry of an appearance have been replaced by similar rules relating to acknowledgment of service and notice of intention to defend (Rules of the Supreme Court (Writ and Appearance) 1979 (S.I. 1979 No. 1716)).

Access to children. Special provision has been made for rights of access to children (Health and Social Services and Social Security Adjudications Act 1983 (adding Part IA to the Child Care Act 1980); see also CARE AND PROTECTION.

Accessory or **Accessary.** The Accessories

and Abettors Act 1861, s. 8, has been amended by the Criminal Law Act 1977, Sched. 12, so as to apply to indictable offences instead of to misdemeanours.

The Magistrates' Courts Act 1952, s. 35, has been repealed and replaced by the Magistrates' Courts Act 1980, s. 44, without change of effect.

Accident. The Judicature Act 1925, s. 36, has been repealed and replaced by the Supreme Court Act 1981, s. 49, without change of effect.

Accidents, Notice of. See also the Notification of Accidents and Dangerous Occurrences Regulations 1980 (S.I. 1980 No. 804), made under the Health and Safety at Work, etc., Act 1974, s. 15.

Road Accidents. Penalties under the Road Traffic Act 1972, s. 25, Sched. 4, were substantially increased (the maximum fine, for example, to £1,000) by the Transport Act 1981, s. 25.

Accommodation works. The Transport Act 1947, s. 14, was repealed by the Statute Law (Repeals) Act 1974, Sched., Part VI.

Account or **Accompt.** The Companies Act 1948, ss. 147, 148 153(3), 410, have been repealed by the Companies Act 1976, s. 42(2), Sched. 3; and s. 150 of the 1948 Act has been amended by s. 8 of the 1976 Act. The time allowed for laying and delivering accounts is now prescribed by the 1976 Act, ss. 6–7 (U.K. companies) and ss. 9–10 (overseas companies).

The Companies Act 1948, s. 149 and Sched. 8, have been renumbered as s. 149A and Sched. 8A, and a substitute s. 149 and Sched. 8 have been inserted (Companies Act 1981, s. 1(2), Sched. 1). The original provisions apply only to the companies not affected by the accounting rules of the 1981 Act (*i.e.*, banking, insurances and shipping companies: see the Act of 1981, Sched. 2, para. 8); the new rules are stricter than the original 1948 provisions.

Detailed provisions for the contents of company accounts are contained in regulations from time to time (see, *e.g.* the Companies (Accounts and Audit Regulations 1984 (S.I. 1984 No. 1659) and the Companies (Accounts) Regulations 1984 (S.I. 1984 No. 1659)).

The Judicature 1925, s. 56, has been repealed and replaced by the Supreme Court Act 1981, s. 61, without change of effect. The Limitation Act 1939, s. 2(2), related to the obsolete common law action for an account; this procedure was abolished by the Limitation Amendment Act 1980, s. 13, Scheds. 1 and 2. The current equivalent provision for actions for an account is the Limitation Act 1980, s. 23, which provides that the appropriate period is the limitation period for the claim in relation to which the duty to account arises. See also *Tito* v. *Waddell* (*No. 2*), *Tito* v. *A.-G.* [1973] Ch. 106, per Megarry V.-C., for a discussion of the relation of common law and equitable claims for an account.

Account duty. The Customs and Inland Revenue Act 1881, ss. 38, 39, were repealed by the Finance Act 1975, s. 59, Sched. 13, Part I, in connection with the replacement of estate duty by capital transfer tax.

Accountable. For the repeal of the Law of Property Act 1925, ss. 16–18, in connection with the replacement of estate duty by capital transfer tax see the Finance Act 1975, s. 59, Sched. 13, Part I.

Accountable receipt. The Forgery Act 1913, s. 2(2)(*a*), has been repealed and replaced by the Forgery and Counterfeiting Act 1981, ss. 1, 8, without significant change of effect despite substantial changes of terminology.

Accountant-General or **Accomptant-General.** The Supreme Court Pay Office was renamed the Court Funds Office by the Supreme Court Funds Rules 1975 (S.I. 1975 No. 1803), r. 3.

The Judicature Act 1925, s. 133, and the Administration of Justice Act 1965, have been repealed and replaced by the Supreme Court Act 1981, s. 97, without change of effect.

Accountant to the Crown. The provisions formerly set out in the Land Charges Act 1925, s. 25, are now contained in the Land Charges Act 1972, s. 15; Sched. 3 to the 1972 Act contained provisions relating to local land charges, and these now appear in the Local Land Charges Act 1975.

Accounts and inquiries. The references to entry of an appearance should be read as references to acknowledgment of service: see the Rules of the Supreme Court (Writ and Appearance) 1979 (S.I. 1979 No. 1716).

Accusation. The common law offence of conspiracy has been abolished (with exceptions) and replaced by a statutory offence

(Criminal Law Act 1977, ss. 1–5).

Accused, Statement of. The Magistrates' Courts Rules 1968, r. 4, has been revoked and replaced by the Magistrates' Courts Rules 1981, r. 7, without change of effect.

Acknowledgment. Although the period of limitation begins to run afresh from each new acknowledgment (or part payment), and may therefore be repeatedly extended, an acknowledgment made after the expiration of the statutory period will no longer revive the debt or obligation (Limitation Act 1980, s. 29(7), replacing the Limitation Act 1939, s. 23(5) (added by the Limitation Amendment Act 1980, s. 6)).

The Limitation Act 1939 has been repealed by the Limitation Act 1980 (which consolidates the Limitation Acts 1939, 1963, 1975 and the Limitation Amendment Act 1980).

The original version of the Wills Act 1837, s. 9, has been replaced by a revised text inserted by the Administration of Justice Act 1982, s. 18; this rationalises the signing and authentication of wills. See also ATTESTATION CLAUSE.

Acquittance. The Forgery Act 1913, ss. 2(2)(a), 18, have been repealed and replaced by the Forgery and Counterfeiting Act 1981, ss. 1, 8, without change of effect.

Act of bankruptcy. The minimum debt to support a bankruptcy petition was increased to £200 (Insolvency Act 1976, s. 1, Sched. 1, Part I), and was then further increased to £750 (Insolvency Proceedings (Increase of Monetary Limits) Regulations (S.I. 1984 No. 1199)).

The Administration of Justice Act 1965, s. 21, and the Attachment of Earnings Act 1971, s. 4(3), have been repealed (Insolvency Act 1976, ss. 13, 14, Sched. 3), so that the initiation of attachment of earnings proceedings in the county court no longer amounts to an act of bankruptcy.

Applications to county courts for administration orders are now made under the County Courts Act 1984, ss. 112 *et seq.*, which replace the repealed provisions of the 1959 Act.

Act of Parliament. The commencement of an Act is now governed by the Interpretation Act 1978, s. 4. The Interpretation Act 1889, s. 9, has been replaced by the Interpretation Act 1978, s. 3, without change of effect.

Act of Settlement. The Judicature Act 1925, s. 12, has been repealed and replaced by the Supreme Court Act 1981, s. 11, without change of effect.

Act of State. See also the State Immunity Act 1978.

Actio personalis moritur cum persona. The Fatal Accidents Acts 1846 to 1908, have been consolidated into the Fatal Accidents Act 1976, and the Carriage by Air Act 1932, has been replaced by the Carriage by Air Act 1961.

Actions and matters in the High Court. The Judicature Act 1925, s. 225, has been repealed and replaced by the Supreme Court Act 1981, s. 151, in which the legislative terms have been modified but without significant change of effect.

Actual bodily harm. The procedure for a matrimonial order consequent upon a s. 47 assault no longer obtains, the jurisdiction of magistrates having been revised by the Domestic Proceedings and Magistrates' Courts Act 1978.

Address for service. Though the filing of a memorandum of appearance has been replaced by the procedure for acknowledgment of service (S.I. 1979 No. 1716), the defendant is still required to state an address for service.

Adjournment. The C.C.R. 1936, Ord. 13, r. 4, has been revoked and replaced by the C.C.R. 1981, Ord. 13, r. 3. The Magistrates' Courts Act 1952, ss. 14–17, 46–49, 105, and the Magistrates' Courts Act 1957, s. 4, have been repealed and replaced by the Magistrates' Courts Act 1980, ss. 10, 11, 13, 15 and 16 (criminal cases) and ss. 54–57 (civil cases), without change of effect.

Adjustment of a loss. The latest revision of the York-Antwerp Rules was in 1974.

Administration action or matter. The Judicature Act 1925, s. 56, has been repealed and replaced by the Supreme Court Act 1981, s. 61, without change of effect.

Administration bond. The Judicature Act 1925, s. 167 (as revised in 1971), has been repealed and replaced by the Supreme Court Act 1981, s. 120, which contains general powers to require administrators to give security for the proper performance of their duties.

Administrator. The jurisdiction of county courts under the County Courts Act 1959,

s. 52, was increased to include estates of up to £15,000 (S.I. 1977 No. 600), and then further increased to £30,000 (County Courts (Jurisdiction) Order 1981 (S.I. 1981 No. 1123)). The Act of 1959, s. 52, has now been repealed and replaced by the County Courts Act 1984, s. 23, without change of effect.

The jurisdiction of county courts to assume the administration of the estate of a debtor has been increased to include cases not involving more than £2,000 of indebtedness. The Administration of Justice Act 1965, s. 21, has been repealed (Insolvency Act 1976, ss. 13, 14, Sched. 3). The limit was then increased to £5,000, and is now regulated by the County Courts Act 1984, ss. 112–117 (replacing the Act of 1959, ss. 148–156).

The Judicature Act 1925, s. 56(3), has been repealed and replaced by the Supreme Court Act 1981, s. 61, Sched. 1, para. 3, without change of effect. The definition from the Act of 1925, s. 175, has been repeated in the Act of 1981, s. 128. The Act of 1925, ss. 160, 162, have been repealed and replaced by the Act of 1981, ss. 114, 116, the new s. 114 incorporating an amendment so that it is no longer essential for two persons to act, the court having a discretion to appoint "one or more additional personal representatives" in minority and life interest cases.

Admiralty. The Interpretation Act 1889, s. 12(4), has been repealed by the Interpretation Act 1978 s. 25(1), Sched. 3, without change of effect.

Admiralty Court. The jurisdiction of county courts in admiralty matters has been extended (Administration of Justice Act 1977, s. 15, and S.I. 1977 No. 600 and S.I. 1981 No. 1123). The list of courts with admiralty jurisdiction has been revised (see the Civil Courts Order 1983 (S.I. 1983 No. 713)). The County Courts Act 1959, ss. 56–61, have been repealed and replaced by the County Courts Act 1984, ss. 26–31, without change of effect.

The Administration of Justice Act 1956, ss. 1–4, have been repealed and replaced by the Supreme Court Act 1981, ss. 20–22; in consolidating the 1956 provisions a modification has been made to put a charterer by demise in the same position as an owner; therefore, if the person who would be liable *in personam* is the demise charterer of the ship in question, the action may be brought against the ship (even if there has been a change of ownership since the cause of action arose).

The Judicature Act 1925, ss. 4, 27, have been repealed and replaced by the Supreme Court Act 1981, ss. 5, 16, without change of effect.

Adoption of children. The Administration of Justice Act 1970, s. 1(1), Sched. 1, have been repealed and replaced by the Supreme Court Act 1981, s. 61, Sched. 1, para. 3, without change of effect.

A complex code of procedure for adoption cases (under the Adoption Acts 1958, 1969 and the Children Act 1975, Part I, applies in High Court and county court proceedings (Adoption Rules 1984 (S.I. 1984 No. 265). See also the Adoption Agencies Regulations 1984 (S.I. 1984 No. 1984)). In magistrates' courts the procedure is governed by a separate set of rules which have been recently amended to deal with applications for freeing for adoption under the Children Act 1975, ss. 14–16 (see S.I. 1984 No. 611).

Adoption of transaction. The Sale of Goods Act 1893, s. 18, has been repealed and replaced by the Sale of Goods Act 1979, s. 18, without change of effect.

Adulteration. The provisions relating to the adulteration of beer are now contained in the Alcoholic Liquor Duties Act 1979, s. 72. The special provisions concerning adulteration of tea were repealed by the Finance Act 1962, s. 34(7), Sched. 11, Part II, so that tea was then dealt with under the general provisions of the Food and Drugs Act 1955.

The Food and Drugs Act 1955, s. 32, has now been repealed and replaced by the Food Act 1984, s. 36, without change of effect. The entire 1955 legislation has been consolidated into the 1984 Act.

Adverse possession. The Limitation Act 1939, ss. 4, 9, 10, have been repealed and replaced by the Limitation Act 1980, s. 15, Sched. 1. These provisions incorporate amendments first enacted in the Limitation Amendment Act 1980, s. 4.

Advertisement. The Town and Country Planning (Control of Advertisements) Regulations 1969, have been further amended by S.I. 1975 No. 898.

The Local Government Act 1933, s. 289, was repealed by the Local Government Act 1972, s. 232, Sched. 30, without replacement; defacement of advertisements would now presumably be punished under the Criminal Damage Act 1971 (see DAMAGE, CRIMINAL).

Advisory, Conciliation and Arbitration Service. The functions of conciliation officers have been continued by the Employment Protection (Consolidation) Act 1978, s. 133.

The functions of the Advisory, Conciliation and Arbitration Service have been considered in *United Kingdom Association of Professional Engineers* v. *Advisory, Conciliation and Arbitration Service* [1980] 1 W.L.R. 302, H.L.

The provisions for recognition of unions (Employment Protection Act 1975, ss. 11–15) and the complaint procedure (s. 16), have been discontinued (Employment Act 1980, s. 19(*b*), repealing the Act of 1975, ss. 11–16), without replacement.

Advowson. For the specialised limitation period relating to claims to enforce advowsons see the Limitation Act 1980, s. 25.

The Pastoral Measure 1968, s. 16, has been repealed and replaced by the Pastoral Measure 1983, s. 17, without change of effect.

Aerodromes. See also the Civil Aviation Act 1978, which provided for the establishment of the Aviation Security Fund (*q.v.*) (ss. 1–4), and authorised the making of by-laws about noise, vibration and pollution (ss. 8 (now repealed), 9), and other matters. See also the Civil Aviation Act 1982, Part II (ss. 25–59).

The Maplin Development Act 1973, was repealed by the Maplin Development Authority (Dissolution) Act 1976, s. 3, Sched.

Affidavit. The court may now dispense with the requirement that the place of residence of the deponent be stated: deponents giving evidence in a professional, business or other occupational capacity may give a work address instead of a residential address; a deponent who is a party to the cause or matter in which the affidavit is sworn or who is employed by a party must state that fact in the affidavit (R.S.C. Ord. 41, r. 1(1)) (see S.I. 1979 No. 522).

Affiliation. The Affiliation Proceedings Act 1957, has been further amended by the Domestic Proceedings and Magistrates' Courts Act 1978 (ss. 49–53), providing, *inter alia*, that payments may be ordered to be made to the child himself, and that payments should normally continue until the child's first birthday after attaining school leaving age though not beyond the child's eighteenth birthday, as well as authorising the award of lump sums.

The Magistrates' Courts Act 1952, has been repealed and replaced by the Magistrates' Courts Act 1980. Section 65 of the 1980 Act now contains the definition of "domestic proceedings".

The Administration of Justice Act 1970, s. 1(1), Sched. 1, have been repealed and replaced by the Supreme Court Act 1981, s. 61, Sched. 1, para. 3, without change of effect. The Magistrates' Courts Act 1952, ss. 74–76, have been repealed and replaced by the Magistrates' Courts Act 1980, ss. 92–96, without change of effect.

Affirmation. The Oaths Act 1888, and the Oaths Act 1961, have been consolidated into the Oaths Act 1978.

Age. A child is now *doli incapax* up to the age of ten years (Children and Young Persons Act 1933, s. 50 (as amended by the Children and Young Persons Act 1963, s. 16)).

The Magistrates' Courts Act 1952, s. 126(5), has been repealed and replaced by the Magistrates' Courts Act 1980, s. 150(4), without change of effect. The Representation of the People Act 1969, s. 1, has been repealed and replaced by the Representation of the People Act 1983, s. 1(1), without change of effect.

Agency. For regulations under the Insurance Companies Act 1974, s. 64 (now repealed and replaced by the Insurance Companies Act 1982, s. 74), see S.I. 1976 No. 521.

Agent provocateur. The propositions mentioned were confirmed in *R.* v. *Sang* [1980] A.C. 402, H.L.

Aggravated assault. The power to make a matrimonial order on this ground no longer obtains, the jurisdiction of magistrates having been revised by the Domestic Proceedings and Magistrates' Courts Act 1978.

Agricultural holding. The main provisions relating to security of tenure of agricultural holdings have been consolidated into the Agricultural Holdings (Notices to Quit) Act 1977.

For substantial new provisions relating to the security of tenure of agricultural workers housed by their employers see the Rent (Agriculture) Act 1976. See also the Agricultural Holdings Act 1984 (especially s. 2, which provides for the repeal of the succession provisions of 1976).

Agricultural Mortgage Corporation. See also the Agriculture (Miscellaneous Provisions) Act 1976.

The Agricultural Mortgage Corporation Act 1958, was repealed by the Statute Law (Repeals) Act 1977, s. 1(1), Sched. 1, Part VIII.

Agricultural statistics. The provisions of the Acts of 1947 and 1972 have been repealed and replaced by the Agricultural Statistics Act 1979 (as amended by the Agriculture (Amendment) Act 1984), without substantial change of effect.

Agriculture. The definition which formerly appeared in the Town and Country Planning Act 1962, s. 221(1), now appears in the Town and Country Planning Act 1971, s. 290.

Agriculture, Fisheries and Food, Ministry of. The salary of the Minister is periodically revised; see, *e.g.* S.I. 1979 No. 905.

Aid and abet. Aiding and abetting an attempt is still a crime (see *R.* v. *Dunnington* [1984] Q.B. 472, C.A.).

Air corporation. See also the Civil Aviation Act 1978, establishing (by ss. 1–4) the Aviation Security Fund (*q.v.*), and amending the borrowing and other powers of the Civil Aviation Authority and the British Airways Board. The Air Corporations Act 1967, has been repealed by the Act of 1978, s. 14(2), Sched. 2.

The principal provisions relating to the British Airways Board have been consolidated in the British Airways Board Act 1977.

Air corporations. The general legislative control of civil aviation has now been consolidated in the Civil Aviation Act 1982. See also AIR NAVIGATION.

Air Force. The Air Force Act 1955, is now kept in force by orders made under the Armed Forces Act 1981, s. 1(1) (replacing the Armed Forces Act 1976, s. 1(2)). The relevant provisions of the Reserve Forces Act 1966, have been repealed and replaced by the Reserve Forces Act 1980, without significant alteration of effect.

Air navigation. The general provisions regulating air navigation now include the Civil Aviation Acts 1978 and 1982.

The Emergency Laws (Re-Enactments and Repeals) Act 1964, s. 16, has been repealed by the Statute Law (Repeals) Act 1977, s. 1(1), Sched. 1, Part XIX.

British Airways Board v. *Taylor* [1975] 1 W.L.R. 1197, has been the subject of an appeal to the House of Lords, where the reasoning set out was disapproved, but the appeal was dismissed on other grounds: [1976] 1 W.L.R. 13, H.L.

The general establishment of the Civil Aviation Authority and the overall controls of air navigation have been consolidated into the Civil Aviation Act 1982.

Air Transport Licensing Board. This body has been superseded by the Civil Aviation Authority which was established by the Civil Aviation Act 1971, ss. 1, 2; by ss. 21–25, the Civil Aviation Authority was empowered to regulate the grant, control and refusal of air transport licences which are required for carriage by air for reward or in the course of a business (s. 21).

Alibi. A defendant whose solicitors fail to observe the statutory requirements (Criminal Justice Act 1967, s. 11) will normally be granted leave to serve notice out of time, and any necessary adjournment will be granted to the prosecution (*R.* v. *Cooper* (1979) 69 Cr.App.R. 229, C.A.).

Aliquis non debet esse judex in propria causa quia non potest esse judex et pars. Specific statutory provisions exist to empower the members of tribunals and courts to determine cases where they might be thought to have some pecuniary interest; see, *e.g.* the General Rate Act 1967, s. 106, which empowers justices to deal with cases involving distess for rates even though the rates in question are due in respect of an area for which they are ratepayers.

Aliud est celare, aliud tacere. The Sale of Goods Act 1893, s. 14, and the Supply of Goods (Implied Terms) Act 1973, s. 3, have been repealed and replaced by the Sale of Goods Act 1979, s. 14, without change of effect.

Allegiance, Oath of. The British Nationality Act 1948, ss. 6, 10, Sched. 1, have been repealed and replaced by the British Nationality Act 1981, s. 42(1), Sched. 5, without change of effect.

Altar. The precise location of an altar appears not to be limited, provided that it serves the needs of the congregation (*Re All Saints', Whitstable* [1984] 1 W.L.R. 1164).

Alternative accommodation. The Rent Act 1968, s. 10, and Sched. 3, Part I, have been repealed and replaced by the Rent Act 1977, s. 98, Sched. 15, Part I.

Alternative verdict. For the power to bring in a verdict of not guilty of the offence charged in an indictment but guilty of some other offence (implicitly or expressly included within the offence charged), see the Criminal Law Act 1967, s. 6(3).

In a number of cases there is provision for the return of an alternative verdict in circumstances where the above-mentioned power would not be available (*e.g.* a verdict of careless driving (*q.v.*) may be reached in a prosecution for reckless driving (Road Traffic Act 1972, s. 93, Sched. 4, Part IV, paras. 3A, 4)).

Amalgamation. The Insurance Companies Act 1974, ss. 12, 42, 43, have been repealed and replaced by the Insurance Companies Act 1982, ss. 15, 49, 50, a consolidating Act.

Ambulance. The National Health Service Reorganisation Act 1973, s. 2, has been repealed and replaced by the National Health Service Act 1977, s. 2, without change of effect.

Amendment. The office of clerk of the peace was abolished by the Courts Act 1971, s. 44, so that the amendment of orders of courts of summary jurisdiction may be effected until they have been acted upon. For specific provision (which displaces the general rules) for criminal proceedings in magistrates' courts see the Magistrates' Courts Act 1980, s. 142 (replacing earlier provisions of a like kind).

The Magistrates' Courts Act 1952, s. 100, has been repealed and replaced by the Magistrates' Courts Act 1980, s. 123, without change of effect.

Amends, Tender of. The Lands Clauses Consolidation Act 1845, s. 135, has been repealed by the Statute Law (Repeals) Act 1978, Sched., Part III.

Ampere. S.I. 1963 No. 1354, has been revoked by S.I. 1976 No. 1674.

Analysis. The Food and Drugs Act 1955, ss. 89, 93, Sched. 7, have been repealed and replaced by the Food Act 1984, ss. 76, 80, Sched. 7, without change of effect.

Anatomy. The Anatomy Act 1832 has been (prospectively) repealed and replaced by the Anatomy Act 1984, without change of effect.

Ancient monuments. The Monuments (Metropolis) Act 1878, appears to have been repealed, so that Cleopatra's Needle is no longer the subject of specific statutory provision.

Ancient Monuments Boards. There were three corporate bodies of this name for England, Scotland and Wales respectively. They were charged with the duty to advise the Secretary of State with respect to the exercise of his functions under the Ancient Monuments and Archaeological Areas Act 1979, both generally and in specific cases (Act of 1979, s. 23, replacing the Ancient Monuments Consolidation and Amendment Act 1913, s. 15). The boards were required to send to the Secretary of State an annual report on the discharge of their functions (Act of 1979, s. 24) and the Secretary of State is required to lay that report before each House of Parliament (*ibid.*). By the National Heritage Act 1983, s. 39(2), the Boards ceased to exist, having been replaced (in effect) by the Historic Buildings and Monuments Commission for England (Act of 1983, s. 32, Sched. 3).

Ancillary relief. For the general ancillary jurisdiction of the county court see the County Courts Act 1984, s. 38, replacing the Act of 1959, s. 74. Provided a money claim of some sort is made, its value is of no importance, so that a claim of £1 damages is enough to confer the ancillary jurisdiction for the grant of injunctions, etc. (*Hatt & Co. (Bath) Ltd.* v. *Pearce* [1978] 1 W.L.R. 885, C.A.).

Animals, Diseases of. The Diseases of Animals Act 1950 and associated legislation have been repealed and replaced by the Animal Health Act 1981, without change of effect.

Animals, Liability for. The Highways Act 1959, s. 135, has been repealed and replaced by the Highways Act 1980, s. 155, without change of effect.

Annual return. The Companies Act 1948, s. 127, and the Companies Act 1967, s. 47, have been repealed by the Companies Act

1976, s. 42(2), Sched. 3. For the revised requirements see the Act of 1976, ss. 1–11; special provisions for private companies (no longer exempt) are contained in s. 6.

Answer. The Matrimonial Causes Rules 1971, r. 18, has been revoked and replaced by the Matrimonial Causes Rules 1977 (S.I. 1977 No. 2016), r. 18, without change of effect.

Anticipatory breach of contract. For an example of such a breach and a discussion of the remedies available see *Hasham* v. *Zenab* [1960] A.C. 316, P.C.

Apology. In the event of a case going to the Court of Appeal, no reference may be made to any payment into court under the Libel Act 1845, until all questions of liability to be determined on appeal have been decided (R.S.C. Ord. 59, r. 12A).

Apothecary. The Medical Act 1956, s. 30, has been repealed and replaced by the Medical Act 1978, s. 31(2), Sched. 7; the provisions of 1978 have themselves been repealed and replaced by the Medical Act 1983, s. 46.

The Medical Act 1956, s. 27, has been repealed and replaced by the Medical Act 1983, s. 46, without change of effect. Penalties on summary conviction have been increased to a fine not exceeding level five on the standard scale (£2,000) (Medical Act 1983, s. 49(1), replacing 1956, s. 31).

The Apothecaries Act 1815, ss. 20, 21, have been repealed without replacement by the Statute Law (Repeals) Act 1976, s. 1(1), Sched. 1, Part VIII. The prohibitions in question come within the general restrictions on dispensing medicines (see above).

Appeal. The procedure on civil appeals to the House of Lords is now regulated by the Directions as to Procedure promulgated in May 1977, and certain associated Standing Orders of the House of Lords. The procedure on criminal appeals to the House of Lords is now regulated by the Procedure Applicable to Criminal Appeals promulgated in November 1976, and certain associated Standing Orders.

The Judicature Act 1925, s. 27, has been repealed and replaced by the Supreme Court Act 1981, s. 61, without change of effect. The Magistrates' Courts Act 1952, s. 83, and the Courts Act 1971, s. 56, Sched. 9, have been repealed and replaced by the Magistrates' Courts Act 1980, s. 108, without change of effect. The County Courts Act 1959, s. 109, has been repealed and replaced by the County Courts Act 1984, s. 77, without change of effect.

Appearance. The procedure of entering an appearance has been abolished and replaced by filing an acknowledgment of service and notice of intention to defend (R.S.C. Ord. 12, as amended by S.I. 1979 No. 1716). The new provisions relating to default are broadly similar to the earlier ones. The acknowledgment of service must be delivered to the Central Office (or district registry) within 14 days of the service of the writ or originating summons; the court then sends a copy (bearing the court seal) to the plaintiff (R.S.C. Ord. 12, r. 4).

Appendix. The authority for the practice of the House of Lords is now the Directions as to Procedure (1977), Dir. 22(ii).

Apply, Liberty to. See also *Practice Direction* [1980] 1 W.L.R. 322 (Fam. D.).

Apposal of sheriffs. The provision referred to was repealed by the Statute Law Revision Act 1948, s. 1, Sched. 1. The modern equivalent appears to the punishment prescribed by the Sheriffs Act 1887, ss. 22, 29(1), (2).

Appropriates; Appropriation. The Sale of Goods Act 1893, s. 18, r. 5, has been repealed and replaced by the Sale of Goods Act 1979, s. 18, r. 5, without change of effect.

In the law of theft (*q.v.*) it is the dishonest appropriation of property belonging to another which constitutes the actus reus of the offence (Theft Act 1968, s. 1(1)). The 1968 Act provides that any assumption by a person of the rights of an owner amounts to appropriation, and this includes cases where he has come by the property (whether innocently or not) without stealing, and later assumes a right to keep it, whether by keeping it or by dealing with it as an owner (s. 3(1)). Where property or a right or interest in property is or purports to be transferred to a person acting in good faith, a later assumption by him of rights which he believed himself to be acquiring will not by reason of any defect in the transferor's title amount to theft of the property (s. 3(2)).

The Limitation Act 1939, has been repealed and replaced by the Limitation Act

1980.

Approval, Sale on. The Sale of Goods Act 1893, s. 18, r. 4, has been repealed and replaced by the Sale of Goods Act 1979, s. 18, r. 4, without change of effect.

Arbitration. Further provision for arbitration has been made in the Arbitration Act 1979. The new Act has repealed earlier provisions for statement of a case (Act of 1950, s. 21), and provided for judicial review of arbitration awards (Act of 1979, s. 1) and a procedure for the determination of preliminary points of law by the High Court (s. 2), as well as conferring new powers on arbitrators to make (and have enforced) interlocutory orders as if they were orders of the court (s. 5).

The County Courts Act 1959, s. 92, has been repealed and replaced by the County Courts Act 1984, s. 64, without change of effect. The Limitation Act 1939, s. 27, has been repealed and replaced by the Limitation Act 1980, s. 34, without change of effect; for actions to enforce an award where the submission is not by an instrument under seal, however, see the Limitation Act 1980, s. 7.

Archdeacon. The Pastoral Measure 1968, s. 18, has been repealed and replaced by the Pastoral Measure 1983, s. 19, without change of effect. Power has been granted to bishops to appoint persons to exercise the powers and functions of archdeacons when an archdeaconry is vacant (Church of England (Miscellaneous Provisions) Measure 1983, s. 9).

Architect. The liability of an architect for negligence was reviewed by the House of Lords in *Sutcliffe* v. *Thackrah* [1974] A.C. 727, where it was held that the negligent issue of interim certificates would render an architect liable for damages since he could not enjoy the privileges accorded to an arbitrator or other person exercising a judicial or quasi-judicial function.

Archives. Provision has been made for the preservation of parochial registers and records, requiring the deposit of older records in diocesan record offices (Parochial Registers and Records Measure 1978).

Area health authority. Part of the national health service (*q.v.*), the establishment of these bodies was provided for by the National Health Service Act 1977, ss. 8, 9, 12, Sched. 15 (which repeated the terms of earlier legislation); they were made responsible to regional health authorities (*q.v.*). The need for them was abolished by the Health Services Act 1980, which gave the minister the opportunity to replace them with district health authorities (*q.v.*) (see ss. 1, 2).

Argumentative. The provisions relating to affidavits (the former R.S.C. Ord. 38, r. 3) have been revoked without replacement.

Arma in armatos sumere juro sinunt. See now the Criminal Law Act 1967, s. 3, authorising the use of such force as is reasonable in the circumstances to prevent the commission of any crime (see ARREST).

Army. The Army Act 1955, is now renewed annually by Order in Council under the Armed Forces Act 1981, s. 1 (replacing the Armed Forces Act 1976, s. 1). See, *e.g.* the Army, Air Force and Naval Discipline Acts (Continuation) Order 1984 (S.I. 1984 No. 1147), authorising a 12 months' extension from 31 August 1984.

Array. The Courts Act 1971, s. 33, has been repealed and replaced by the Juries Act 1974, s. 12(6) (see CHALLENGE) without change of effect.

Arrest. A person who has been arrested may now require intimation of his arrest and of the place where he is being detained to be sent to one person reasonably named by him with no more delay than is essential (Criminal Law Act 1977, s. 62).

The Magistrates' Courts Act 1952, s. 15, and the Magistrates' Courts Act 1957, s. 4, have been repealed and replaced by the Magistrates' Courts Act 1980, s. 13, without change of effect.

Arson. The statutory offence under the Criminal Damage Act 1971, s. 1(3), is now triable either summarily or on indictment (Criminal Law Act 1977, s. 16(1), (2), Sched. 2, para. 29 (now itself repealed and replaced by the Magistrates' Courts Act 1980, ss. 17 *et seq.*)).

Articulated vehicle. For the definition of an articulated goods vehicle see the Road Traffic (Drivers' Ages and Hours of Work) Act 1976, s. 1, Sched. 1, para. 5. The Road Traffic Act 1972, s. 191, definition has been replaced by a new text (Transport Act 1980, s. 63); the modification legalises the charging of fares on articulated buses.

Artificers. The Employers and Workmen Act 1875, s. 10, has been repealed by the

Statute Law (Repeals) Act 1973, Sched. 1.

Artificial person. The Interpretation Act 1889, s. 19, has been repealed and replaced by the Interpretation Act 1978, s. 5, Sched. 1, which provide that, unless the contrary appears, "person" includes a body of persons corporate or unincorporate.

Ashpit. The Public Health Act 1936, s. 72, which provided for the cleansing of ashpits, was repealed by the Control of Pollution Act 1974, s. 108, Scheds. 3, 4; equivalent provision is made in general terms by the Act of 1974, ss. 12–17.

Assault. Assaults contrary to the Police Act 1964, s. 51(1), are now triable only summarily (Criminal Law Act 1977, ss. 15, 30, Sched. 1 (now repealed and replaced by the Magistrates' Courts Act 1980, ss. 17 *et seq.*)).

The procedure for a matrimonial order consequent upon an assault no longer obtains, the jurisdiction of magistrates having been revised by the Domestic Proceedings and Magistrates' Courts Act 1978.

Assessor. The use of an assessor in the county court in cases under the Pilotage Act 1983, s. 26(3) (replacing the Pilotage Act 1913, s. 28(2)), is compulsory; in the absence of the parties' agreement to the contrary, the same rule applies in cases under the Race Relations Act 1976 (see s. 67(4)).

The Judicature Act 1925, s. 98, has been repealed and replaced by the Supreme Court Act 1981, s. 70, without change of effect. The County Courts Act 1959, s. 91, and the Administration of Justice Act 1969, s. 8, have been repealed and replaced by the County Courts Act 1984, s. 63, without change of effect. The C.C.R. 1936, Ord. 31, has been revoked and replaced by the C.C.R. 1981, Ord. 13, r. 11.

Assign; Assignment. The Patents Act 1949, s. 74, has been repealed by the Patents Act 1977, s. 132, Sched. 6; the provisions governing the assignment (in broadly similar terms) are now set out in the Act of 1977, ss. 30, 36.

Assignment of action or matter. The revision of court procedures in 1982 (see the Rules of the Supreme Court (Amendment No. 2) 1982 (S.I. 1982 No. 1111)), resulted in the abolition of the Chancery Division groups.

Assignment of copyright. See COPYRIGHT.

Assise of Novel Disseisin. The abolition of this form of real action was effected by the Real Property Limitation Act 1833, s. 36.

Assistance, Writ of. The prescribed (modern) form of the writ issued to recover possession is set out at R.S.C. App. A, No. 69.

Assize. The Courts Act 1971, s. 1(2), has been repealed by the Supreme Court Act 1981, s. 152(4), Sched. 7, without replacement.

Assured tenancy. See the Housing Act 1980, ss. 56–58.

Asylum. The Mental Health Act 1959, has been repealed and replaced (almost entirely) by the Mental Health Act 1983, which consolidated the 1959 and amending legislation.

Atomic energy. Further statutory provisions for the financing of the nuclear industry are contained in the Nuclear Industry (Finance) Act 1977, which deals with the financing of British Nuclear Fuels Limited, the Radiochemical Centre Limited and the National Nuclear Corporation Limited.

By the Nuclear Safeguards and Electricity (Finance) Act 1978, provision is made for giving effect to the International Agreement for the Application of Safeguards in connection with the Treaty on the Non-Proliferation of Nuclear Weapons (made on September 6, 1976).

See also the Congenital Disabilities (Civil Liability) Act 1976, s. 3, and the Nuclear Material (Offences) Act 1983.

Attachment. County court garnishee proceedings are now conducted under the provisions of the C.C.R. 1981, Ord. 30.

Attempt. The common law relating to attempt has been abolished and replaced by the code set out in the Criminal Attempts Act 1981.

Attendance centres. The Criminal Justice Act 1948, s. 19, and associated legislation, have been repealed and replaced by the Criminal Justice Act 1982, ss. 16–19. The amendments made by the 1982 Act, however, were mostly of a procedural nature.

Attestation clause. The Wills Act 1837, s. 9, has been revised by the insertion of a new text by the Administration of Justice Act 1982, s. 17. The new provisions authorise the witnesses to sign (or acknowledge their signatures) separately if they wish, provided they do so in the presence of the testator. The requirement of signature "at the end or foot [of the will]" has been replaced by a provision which requires an intention on the part of the testator "by his signature . . . to give effect to the will."

Attorney. The Judicature Act 1925, s. 215(2), was repealed by the Solicitors Act 1932, s. 82, Sched. 4, and has not appeared in later re-enactments of either statute.

Attorney-General. The Race Relations Act 1965, s. 6, has been repealed and replaced by the Public Order Act 1936, s. 5A (inserted by the Race Relations Act 1976, s. 70), which also requires the fiat of the Attorney-General before a prosecution may be commenced.

The salary of the Attorney-General is revised from time to time (see, *e.g.* S.I. 1979 No. 905).

The proceedings in respect of which the consent or fiat of the Attorney-General is required as authority to commence or continue proceedings are as follows (in alphabetical order):

Agricultural Credits Act 1928, s. 10; Agricultural Land (Removal of Surface Soil) Act 1953, s. 3; Agriculture and Horticulture Act 1964, s. 20; Auctions (Bidding Agreements) Act 1927, s. 1; Aviation Security Act 1982, s. 8 (replacing the Hijacking Act 1971, s. 5 and the Protection of Aircraft Act 1973, s. 4); Biological Weapons Act 1974, s. 2; Cancer Act 1939, s. 4; Children and Young Person (Harmful Publications) Act 1955; Contempt of Court Act 1981, s. 8(3); Counter-Inflation Act 1973, s. 17; Criminal Justice Act 1967, s. 3; Criminal Law Act 1977, ss. 4, 9; Customs and Excise Management Act 1979, s. 147; Explosive Substances Act 1883; Genocide Act 1969, s. 1; Highways Act 1980, s. 312; Housing Act 1957, s. 85; Internationally Protected Persons Act 1978, s. 2; Law of Property Act 1925, s. 183; Legal Aid Act 1974, s. 22; Magistrates' Courts Act 1980, s. 71; Marine Insurance (Gambling Policies) Act 1909, s. 1; Mines and Quarries Act 1954, s. 164; National Health Service Act 1977, s. 124; Newspaper, Printers and Reading Room Repeal Act 1869; Official Secrets Act 1911 and 1920; Prevention of Corruption Acts 1906 and 1916; Prevention of Oil Pollution Act 1971, s. 19; Prevention of Terrorism (Temporary Provisions) Act 1984, s. 14, Sched. 3, Part II, para. 3; Public Bodies (Corrupt Practices) Act 1889; Public Health Act 1936, s. 298; Public Order Act 1936, ss. 1, 2, 5A; Public Utilities Street Works Act 1950, s. 30; Rivers (Prevention of Pollution) Act 1961, s. 11; Sexual Offences (Amendment) Act 1976, s. 5; Solicitors Act 1974, ss. 20, 42; Shipping Contracts and Commercial Documents Act 1964, s. 3; Suppression of Terrorism Act 1978, s. 4; Theatres Act 1968, s. 8.

Attornment. The Sale of Goods Act 1893, s. 45(3), has been repealed and replaced by the Sale of Goods Act 1979, s. 45(3), without change of effect.

Auction. The Sale of Goods Act 1893, s. 58(3), (4), has been repealed and replaced by the Sale of Goods Act 1979, s. 58(3), (4), without change of effect.

Audit. The auditing of company accounts has been further provided for by the Companies Act 1976, ss. 13–20. The qualifications required for appointment as an auditor are prescribed by s. 13 (see also the Insolvency Act 1976, s. 9, which relates to disqualification and qualification for appointment as an auditor). Auditors must be appointed or re-appointed annually at a general meeting at which the directors lay the accounts before the company (s. 14(1)). The requirement of special notice of a resolution at a general meeting for the appointment of auditors has been widened (see s. 15). Auditors may now communicate their reasons for resignation to members and creditors and the Registrar of Companies (ss. 16, 17).

Sections 159–160 of the Act of 1948, and s. 13 of the Act of 1967 have been repealed since they have been substantially replaced.

Fresh provision for local government audit was made by the Local Government Finance Act 1982, Part III (ss. 11–36), under which an independent Audit Commission was established. It is no longer possible for a private "approved auditor" to conduct audits of local authorities. The Local Government Act 1972, ss. 154–167, have been repealed since they have been replaced by the 1982 provisions.

The Trustee Savings Bank Act 1969, s. 74, has been repealed and replaced by the Trustee Savings Bank Act 1981, ss. 23–25.

The Administration of Justice Act 1965, ss. 1, 2, 18, have been repealed and replaced by the Administration of Justice Act 1982, ss. 38–47. By a transitional provision (1982, s. 73(8)), the position of the Public Trustee was assimilated to that of the Accountant General for certain functions related to the common investment scheme.

See also the National Audit Act 1983.

Audita querela. The Judicature Act 1925, s. 41, has been repealed by the Supreme Court Act 1981, s. 152(4), Sched. 7, without replacement; the general statutory authority is now the Act of 1981, ss. 49, 84–85, 87.

Authority. The Misrepresentation Act 1967, s. 3, has been amended so as to show that the terms "fair and reasonable" are to be interpreted in the same way as they are interpreted in the application of the Unfair Contract Terms Act 1977 (see the Act of 1977, ss. 8, 11(1), Sched. 2).

Autrefois acquit. If justices enter an acquittal, there is nevertheless a possibility that it may be set aside by judicial review if the proceedings amounted to a nullity (*R.* v. *Dorking Justices ex p. Harrington* [1984] A.C. 743, H.L.).

Autrefois convict. The Interpretation Act 1889, s. 33, has been repealed and replaced by the Interpretation Act 1978, s. 18, without change of effect.

Aviation Security Fund. This Fund was established by the Civil Aviation Act 1978, ss. 1–4, to provide money for the expenses of protecting aircraft, aerodromes and air navigation installations against acts of violence, as well as for the policing of airports. See also the Civil Aviation Act 1982.

Award. The powers of the High Court to review an award have been modified by the Arbitration Act 1979, ss. 1, 2. Exclusion agreements, preventing the reference of an award to the Court, are authorised (s. 3) subject to certain exceptions (s. 4). The provisions for statement of a special case (Act of 1950, s. 21), have been repealed and replaced by the new provisions (Act of 1979, s. 1).

B

Backing a warrant. See now the Criminal Law Act 1977, s. 38, which provides for the execution of unbacked warrants throughout the United Kingdom.

The Magistrates' Courts Act 1952, s. 102, has been repealed and replaced by the Magistrates' Courts Act 1980, s. 125, without change of effect.

Bail (in criminal proceedings). Fresh provision for the grant of bail in criminal proceedings has been made by the Bail Act 1976. The Act repeats (in revised terms) the replaced provisions of the Criminal Justice Act 1967, ss. 18 *et seq.*, which provided for a general presumption in favour of granting bail to a person before conviction as well as on certain other occasions (s. 4), so that bail may be withheld only in prescribed circumstances (specified in Sched. 1). The person granted bail cannot be required to give any recognizance for his surrender to custody (s. 3), and security may be taken only in certain cases (see s. 3(3)); the same rule applies to sureties (s. 8). The person bailed comes under a duty to surrender to custody at the expiration of the bail period (which must be notified to him under s. 5) and failure to surrender is an offence (s. 6(2)); it is the defendant's responsibility to prove that he had reasonable cause for not surrendering (s. 6(3)). A person who absconds while on bail, or who fails to comply with any conditions imposed (see s. 3), becomes liable to arrest (s. 7), whereupon he must be brought before the court for a re-consideration of the question whether bail should be again allowed (s. 7(4)–(6)). There is no such offence as "breach of bail conditions" so no punishment may be imposed for failure to observe any conditions. When the defendant comes before the court after a breach, however, the court may remand or commit him in custody instead of on bail (s. 7(5)), though it must observe the usual rules about the grant of bail in reaching its decision.

To agree to indemnify sureties in criminal proceedings constitutes an offence (s. 9) triable either way, but proceedings may be commenced only with the consent of the

Director of Public Prosecutions (s. 9).

Special provisions facilitate the grant of legal aid (*q.v.*) for the purpose of making a bail application (s. 11).

A person charged with treason may be granted bail only on the certificate of the Secretary of State or by order of a High Court judge (Magistrates' Courts Act 1980, s. 41, replacing the Magistrates' Courts Act 1952, s. 8).

In the event of an application for bail being renewed, the duty of justices is only to hear any fresh matters which may be advanced on behalf of the defendant; matters which have already been examined are not required to be re-examined every time (*R.* v. *Nottingham Justices, ex p. Davies* [1981] Q.B. 38, D.C.).

A right of appeal to the Crown Court (as an alternative to an application to the judge in chambers under the Criminal Justice Act 1967, s. 22) against the refusal of bail by magistrates was introduced by the Criminal Justice Act 1982, s. 60. This is in addition to the right to make such an application to the Crown Court in cases where an appeal to that court is in progress.

The Magistrates' Courts Act 1952, ss. 7, 8, 14–17, 20, 38, 46–49, 55, 89, 103 and 105, have been repealed and replaced by the Magistrates' Courts Act 1980, ss. 6, 41, 10–16, 24, 43, 54–57, 64, 144, 117 and 128, without change of effect. The Courts Act 1971, s. 13, has now been repealed and replaced by the Supreme Court Act 1981, s. 70, without significant change of effect. The Judicature Act 1925, s. 31(*a*), has been repealed and replaced by the Supreme Court Act 1981, s. 18(1)(*a*), without change of effect. The Criminal Justice Act 1967, s. 24, has been repealed and incorporated in the Magistrates' Courts Act 1980, ss. 1, 13, 14. The Powers of Criminal Courts Act 1973, s. 50 (the power of inspection), was repealed by the Criminal Justice Act 1982, s. 78, Sched. 16.

Bailiff. Appointments are no longer made under the County Courts Act 1959, s. 28 (which was repealed by the Courts Act 1971, s. 56(4), Sched. 11), but under the Courts Act 1971, s. 27, which contains general powers to engage court staff.

Bailment. For the imposition of liability on the theft of goods from a gratuitous bailee whose mistake has prevented the bailor collecting the goods as arranged, see *Mitchell* v. *Ealing London Borough Council* [1979] Q.B. 1.

The Disposal of Uncollected Goods Act 1952, has been repealed and replaced by the Torts (Interference with Goods) Act 1977, ss. 12, 13, Sched. 1, without substantial change of effect.

Bakehouse. The Factories Act 1961, s. 70, has been repealed and replaced by S.I. 1974 No. 1941, without specific replacement, on the coming into operation of provisions of the Health and Safety at Work, etc., Act 1974, which replace s. 70.

Ballast. Although the Coast Protection Act 1939, was repealed by the Coast Protection Act 1949, ss. 18(9), 48, Sched. 3, orders made under s. 1 of the 1939 Act were continued in force by s. 18(10) of the 1949 Act. The general prohibition of excavation or removal of any materials from the seashore was also continued by virtue of the Act of 1949, s. 18.

Ballot. The Representation of the People Act 1949, ss. 11–15, 146–164, have been repealed and replaced by the Representation of the People Act 1983, ss. 18–22, 168–186, without change of effect.

Secret postal ballots for certain trade union activities are provided for in the Employment Act 1980, ss. 1–3, and government funds have been made available in some cases (see, *e.g.* the Funds for Trade Union Ballots Regulations 1984 (S.I. 1984 No. 1654)). Ballots in respect of union membership agreements (see CLOSED SHOP) were provided for in 1980 (see the Employment Protection (Consolidation)) Act 1978, s. 58A, Employment Act 1980, s. 7). A further revision was made in 1982 (Employment Act 1982, s. 3, replacing the earlier versions of the Act of 1978, ss. 58, 58A). See also the Trade Union Act 1984, Parts I–III (ss. 1–19); these provisions include a loss of immunity for liability in the absence of ballots before industrial action (see s. 10).

Banc (or **Banco**), **Sittings in.** The Judicature Act 1925, s. 63, has been repealed and replaced by the Supreme Court Act 1981, s. 66. Since the Administration of Justice Act 1977, s. 9 (now replaced by the 1981 Act, s. 66), rules of court have been able to provide for a Divisional Court to sit with no more than two judges.

Bank. The Companies Act 1948,

ss. 429–432, have been repealed by the Banking Act 1979, s. 51(2), Sched. 7. The 1979 Act brings within the control of the Bank of England any deposit-taking institution or person (with exceptions, detailed in Sched. 1). The limit prescribed by the Act of 1948, s. 119, has also been repealed. See also BANK OF ENGLAND and DEPOSIT PROTECTION BOARD.

Bank notes, Bank bills. The Forgery Act 1913, ss. 2, 9, have been repealed and replaced by the Forgery and Counterfeiting Act 1981, ss. 14 *et seq.*

Bank of England. Additional functions have been conferred on the Bank of England by the Banking Act 1979, Part I (ss. 1–20), so that it now exercises powers of control over deposit-taking institutions by issuing and revoking licences (ss. 3–10), as well as having powers to investigate the affairs of deposit-taking institutions (ss. 16–20).

Banker. The scope of the protection afforded by the Cheques Act 1957, s. 4, has been restricted (by the Torts (Interference with Goods) Act 1977, s. 11(1)), but again modified so as to provide a defence of contributory negligence in favour of a banker (Banking Act 1979, s. 47). See CONTRIBUTORY NEGLIGENCE.

The restrictions on the number of persons in a banking partnership have been abolished (Banking Act 1979, s. 51(2), Sched. 7).

Bankers' books, Evidence of. The substitution of a new text for the Bankers' Books Evidence Act 1879, s. 9 (by the Banking Act 1979, s. 51(1), Sched. 6, Part I, para. 1), authorises the use of certified copies of the entries in the books (and other records) of a wider range of institutions than previously, now including banks (in the commonly-accepted sense), licensed institutions (under the Banking Act 1979, ss. 3–10), municipal banks, trustee savings banks (within the meaning of the Trustee Savings Bank Act 1981, s. 3), the National Savings Bank and the Post Office (when acting in the exercise of its powers to provide banking services).

The term "books" includes records of all descriptions and therefore extends to computerised and microfilmed forms of record (*Barker* v. *Wilson* [1980] 1 W.L.R. 884, D.C.).

Banker's draft. See also the Banking Act 1979, s. 47, which modifies the effect of the Torts (Interference with Goods) Act 1977, s. 11(1), providing a banker with a defence of contributory negligence on the part of the customer.

Bankruptcy. Amendments to the general law have been made by the Insolvency Act 1976. The principal changes are the increases in the monetary limits for instituting bankruptcy proceedings (s. 1, Sched. 1), the establishment of the Insolvency Services Account (*q.v.*), the introduction of a power to dispense with public examination of a debtor (s. 6), fresh provision for discharge either automatically (s. 7) or on the application of the official receiver of the bankrupt (s. 8), and miscellaneous provisions relating to administration orders (ss. 11–13).

Bankruptcy courts. The Courts Act 1971, s. 26, has been repealed and replaced by the Supreme Court Act 1981, s. 89(2), without change of effect. The Judicature Act 1925, Sched. 4, has been repealed and replaced by the Supreme Court Act 1981, Sched. 2, Part II, para. 5, without change of effect. The Taxing Master, High Court in Bankruptcy, has been abolished under the power contained in the Supreme Court Act 1981, s. 89(5).

Bankruptcy Estates Account. See INSOLVENCY SERVICES ACCOUNT.

Bankruptcy notice. The minimum debt to support a bankruptcy notice (under the Bankruptcy Act 1914, s. 4(1)(*a*)) was increased to £200 (Insolvency Act 1976, s. 1, Sched. 1, Part I), and has been further increased to £750 (Insolvency Proceedings (Increase in Monetary Limits) Regulations 1984 (S.I. 1984 No. 1199)). The time for complying with a bankruptcy notice (Act of 1914, s. 1(1)(*g*)) has been extended to 10 days (Insolvency Act 1976, s. 4).

Bar. The Limitation Act 1939 has been repealed and replaced by the Limitation Act 1980, without significant change of effect.

Barbed wire. The Highways Act 1959, s. 135, has been repealed and replaced by the Highways Act 1980, s. 164, without change of effect.

Bare licensee. The duty of care originally imposed by the Occupiers' Liability Act 1957, has been extended by the Occupiers' Liability Act 1984.

Bargain and sale. The Sale of Goods Act 1893, s. 20, has been repealed and replaced by the Sale of Goods Act 1979, s. 20, without change of effect.

Baron. The Judicature Act 1925, s. 4, has been repealed and replaced by the Supreme Court Act 1981, s. 5, without change of effect.

Barrister. The rule in *Rondel* v. *Worsley* [1969] 1 A.C. 191, H.L., has been considered in *Saif Ali* v. *Sydney Mitchell & Co.* (*P. Third Party*) [1980] A.C. 198, H.L., where it was held that counsel's immunity from suit extended only to work which was so intimately connected with the conduct of the case in court that it could properly be said to be a preliminary decision on the course to be pursued at the hearing in court.

Base fee. The Limitation Act 1939, s. 11, has been repealed and replaced by the Limitation Act 1980, s. 27, which (unlike the 1874 and earlier provisions) provides a "cure" for certain defective disentailing assurances.

Bastard. The definitions of "child" and "issue" have been widened and the effect on a will of their predecease has been modified by the introduction of a new text for the Wills Act 1837, s. 33 (Administration of Justice Act 1982, s. 19). In consequence the Family Law Reform Act 1969, s. 16, has been repealed without replacement (Act of 1982, s. 75, Sched. 9).

Bathing. The power to make by-laws under the Public Health Act 1936, s. 231, with respect to public bathing has been slightly modified (Local Government (Miscellaneous Provisions) Act 1976, s. 17) so as to extend the possible area of operation of the by-laws. For the Secretary of State's confirmation of by-laws see also the Act of 1976, s. 17(2).

For the provision of public swimming pools and other recreational facilities see the Local Government (Miscellaneous Provisions) Act 1976, s. 19.

Beer. The definition of beer in the Customs and Excise Act 1952, s. 307, has been repeated without alteration in the Alcoholic Liquor Duties Act 1979, s. 1(2). The 1952 Act, ss. 125–138, have been repealed and replaced by the Act of 1979, ss. 12, 37–43, 47–53.

Bees. The Bees Act 1980, provides for the control of pests and diseases which affect bees. The import of bees has already been extensively regulated by prohibition orders made under the Agriculture (Miscellaneous Provisions) Act 1954, s. 10 (see, *e.g.* S.I. 1979 No. 587).

Bench warrant. The Courts Act 1971, s. 13, was amended so as to bring it into accord with the new rules about the grant of bail under the Bail Act 1976 (see BAIL (IN CRIMINAL PROCEEDINGS), and appropriate amendments were made in the procedural rules. The Act of 1971, s. 13, has now been repealed and replaced by the Supreme Court Act 1981, s. 80, without significant relevant change of effect, and the Crown Court Rules 1971, have been revoked and replaced by the Crown Court Rules 1982 (S.I. 1982 No. 1109) (with amendments).

Benefice; Beneficium. The rules made under the Pastoral Measure 1968, s. 28, Sched. 4 (but see below), are the Compensation of Clergy Rules 1970 (S.I. 1970 No. 1009).

The situation where there has been a serious breakdown of the pastoral relationship between the incumbent and the parishioners, or where an incumbent is unable by reason of age or infirmity to discharge adequately the duties which attach to his benefice is governed by the Incumbents (Vacation of Benefices) Measure 1977.

The Pastoral Measure 1968, ss. 16, 69, have now been repealed and replaced by the Pastoral Measure 1983, ss. 17, 69, without significant change of effect.

Bereavement. In place of other rights a new cause of action has been introduced enabling a person who has suffered bereavement in consequence of the tortious act of another to claim a fixed sum (currently at the original statutory figure of £3,500) for the bereavement (Fatal Accidents Act 1976, s. 1A (as inserted by the Administration of Justice Act 1982, s. 3)).

Berwick-upon-Tweed. The Wales and Berwick Act 1746, s. 3, has been repealed and replaced by the Interpretation Act 1978, s. 25, Sched. 3; by s. 5, Sched. 1 of the 1978 Act, "England" is defined as the area of the counties established by the Local Government Act 1972, s. 1 (together with Greater London and the Isles of Scilly), thus including Berwick-upon-Tweed.

Beset. The Trade Union and Labour Relations Act 1974, s. 15, has been modified by the Employment Act 1980, s. 16 (so as to restrict secondary picketing) and by the

Employment Act 1982, Sched. 3 (so as to bring former employees within the protection it affords).

Betting. See also the Betting, Gaming and Lotteries (Amendment) Act 1980, and the Betting, Gaming and Lotteries (Amendment) Act 1984, ss. 1 and 3.

The Betting and Gaming Duties Act 1972, and associated legislation, have been repealed and replaced by the Betting and Gaming Duties Act 1981, without significant change of effect.

Bias. For an example of a statutory provision authorising justices to determine a case where they might be thought to be affected by their decision see the General Rate Act 1967, s. 106.

Bicycles. The offence of dangerous cycling (Road Traffic Act 1972, s. 17) has been abolished and replaced by the offence of riding recklessly (Criminal Law Act 1977, s. 50(2), substituting into the Act of 1972, s. 17, a new text, which reads "A person who rides a cycle, not being a motor vehicle, on a road recklessly, shall be guilty of an offence.") The punishment and procedural requirements have not been altered.

For the general revision of the levels of fines see FINE.

Bill of entry. The Customs and Excise Act 1952, ss. 28, 47, have been repealed and replaced by the Customs and Excise Management Act 1979, ss. 37, 52, 53, without substantial alteration.

Bill of sight. The Customs and Excise Act 1952, s. 29, has been repealed and replaced by the Customs and Excise Management Act 1979, s. 38, without change of effect.

Bill of stores. The Customs and Excise Act 1952, s. 35, has been repealed and replaced by the Customs and Excise (General Reliefs) Act 1979, s. 10, without change of effect.

Billet; Billeting. For the billeting of reserve and auxiliary naval forces of the Crown see the Reserve Forces Act 1980, s. 53.

Billiards and bagatelle. Fines under the Gaming Act 1845, have been revised under the general scheme contained in the Criminal Justice Act 1982 (see FINE).

Bind over. The Magistrates' Courts Act 1952, s. 7, has been repealed and replaced by the Magistrates' Courts Act 1980, s. 6. The Magistrates' Courts Rules 1968, s. (*sic*) 7, has been revoked and replaced by the Magistrates' Courts Rules 1981, rr. 6, 7. Defendants are no longer "bound over to appear" since (provided bail is granted) they come under a special statutory duty (Bail Act 1976, s. 3) to surrender to their bail at the Crown Court. See BAIL (IN CRIMINAL PROCEEDINGS). The Magistrates' Courts Act 1952, s. 91, has been repealed and replaced by the Magistrates' Courts Act 1980, s. 115, without change of effect.

Birds. The Protection of Birds Act 1954, s. 8(2), has been repealed and replaced by the Wildlife and Countryside Act 1981, s. 8, without significant change of effect.

The Protection of Birds Act 1954, the Protection of Birds Act 1954 (Amendment) Act 1964, the Protection of Birds Act 1967 and the Nature Conservancy Act 1973, Sched. 1 (part), have been repealed and replaced prospectively by the Wildlife and Countryside Act 1981.

Birth, Notification of. The Public Health Act 1936, s. 203, was repealed and replaced by the National Health Service Act 1977, s. 124, with the substitution of "area health authority" (*q.v.*) for "welfare authority." Proceedings in respect of the offence of failing to give notice may not, without the written consent of the Attorney-General, be taken by any person other than a party aggrieved or the area health authority concerned (s. 124(6)).

Birth, Registration of. The Parochial Registers and Records Measure 1929, has been repealed and replaced by the Parochial Registers and Records Measure 1978. See also REGISTRATION OF BIRTHS.

The Forgery Act 1913, s. 3, has been repealed and replaced by the Forgery and Counterfeiting Act 1981, s. 5.

Black list. A provision similar to the Licensing Act 1902, s. 6, is contained in the Licensed Premises (Exclusion of Certain Persons) Act 1980, under which an "exclusion order" (*q.v.*) may be made by any court by or before which any person is convicted of an offence on licensed premises if the court is satisfied that he resorted to or threatened to resort to violence. Ranging from three months to two years, such an order is enforceable by fine or imprisonment (s. 2); there is a right to expel (with police assistance if requested) from licensed premises any person suspected of being in breach of such an order (s. 3).

Blasphemy. The modern law has been generally reviewed in *R.* v. *Lemon* [1979] A.C. 617, H.L., where it was held that the defendant's intention was irrelevant to a conviction for blasphemous libel since this is an offence of strict liability.

The Blasphemy Act 1697, passed to suppress blasphemy and profanity, was repealed by the Criminal Law Act 1967, s. 13, Sched. 4, Part I.

Blind persons. Supplementary benefit is now paid under the authority of the Supplementary Benefit Act 1976, special rates still being prescribed for blind people.

The National Assistance Act 1948, s. 31, has been repealed and replaced by the Residential Homes Act 1980, ss. 8, 11, Sched. 2.

Block grant. This was an element of local authority finance and has been replaced by rate support grant under the Local Government, Planning and Land Act 1980.

Blood. The fees for blood tests are revised regularly; see, *e.g.*, the Blood Test (Evidence of Paternity) (Amendment) Regulations in 1979 (S.I. 1979 No. 1226), and in 1984 (S.I. 1984 No. 1243).

The Road Traffic Act 1972, s. 9, was replaced by revised provisions for taking specimens. See now the Road Traffic Act 1972, s. 8 (as substituted by the Transport Act 1981, s. 25, Sched. 8).

Board of Trade. The Harbour Transfer Act 1862, s. 2, was repealed by the Statute Law Revision Act 1893, and the Interpretation Act 1889, s. 12(8), has been repealed by the Interpretation Act 1978, s. 25, Sched. 3, without replacement.

Boats. The Public Health Acts Amendment Act 1907, s. 94, has been amended by the Local Government (Miscellaneous Provisions) Act 1976, s. 178, so as to increase the control exercised over licensed pleasure boats. Local authorities now have a general power to issue by-laws in respect of pleasure boats (Local Government, Planning and Land Act 1980, ss. 185, 186) (including amendments of the Act of 1907, s. 94). See also PLEASURE BOATS.

The provision of boats on ships is regulated principally by the Merchant Shipping Act 1894, s. 427 (as substituted in 1949 and variously amended). Boats may also be required to be carried in fishing vessels (see the Fishing Vessels (Safety Provisions) Act 1970, s. 2).

Boilers. For repeals of the Boiler Explosions Act 1882 and the Boiler Explosions Act 1890 see S.I. 1980 No. 804 and S.I. 1974 No. 1886.

Bollards. The Road Traffic Regulation Act 1967, ss. 69, 70, and associated legislation, have been repealed and replaced by the Road Traffic Regulation Act 1984, ss. 92–94, without change of effect.

Bomb hoax. Two statutory offences under this name have been introduced (Criminal Law Act 1977, s. 51). The sending or placing of any article or substance by way of a hoax, and the communication of any false information by way of a hoax are both proscribed. The penalties on summary conviction are a fine not exceeding £2,000 (see FINE) or imprisonment not exceeding three months or both, and, on conviction on indictment, imprisonment not exceeding five years (s. 51(4)).

Bond. The Forgery Act 1913, s. 2(1)(*b*), has been repealed and replaced by the Forgery and Counterfeiting Act 1981, s. 1. The penalty has been reduced to a maximum of ten years' imprisonment (Act of 1981, s. 6(2)).

Books of account. The Companies Act 1948, s. 147, has been repealed by the Companies Act 1976, s. 42(3), Sched. 3. In place of the earlier provisions the Act of 1976, s. 12, requires each company to keep accounting records which are sufficient to show and explain the company's transactions (s. 12(2)). In particular there are listed the following: (a) daily entries of all receipts and expenditures and the transactions to which they relate; (b) a record of all the assets and liabilities of the company; (c) where the company's business involves dealing in goods, annual statements of stockholdings and details of sales and purchases of goods (including the names and addresses of purchasers and sellers) (s. 12(4), (5)).

The books of a private company must be kept for at least three years from the time of their creation (s. 12(9)(*a*)), and those of a public company for at least six years (s. 12(9)(*b*)).

Booty of war. The Judicature Act 1925, s. 27, and the Administration of Justice Act 1956, s. 1, have been repealed and replaced by the Supreme Court Act 1981, s. 16, without change of effect.

Borough. The definition in the Interpretation Act 1889, s. 15, has been repealed without replacement by the Interpretation Act 1978, s. 25, Sched. 3.

Borstal institutions. These penal establishments have been abolished by the Criminal Justice Act 1982, s. 1(3), their place being taken by the newly devised youth custody (*q.v.*).

Bottomry bond or contract: Bottomree; Bummaree. The Administration of Justice Act 1965, s. 1(1)(*r*), has been repealed and replaced by the Supreme Court Act 1981, s. 20(2)(*r*), without change of effect.

Boundary. Powers of inspection of property which is the subject-matter of proceedings are now exercised under R.S.C. Ord. 29, r. 2.

Bounds. Powers of inspection are now exercised under R.S.C. Ord. 29, r. 2.

Boys. The Mines and Quarries Act 1954, ss. 124–131, have been amended and partly repealed by the Mines and Quarries Acts 1954 to 1971 (Repeals and Modifications) Regulations 1974 (S.I. 1974 No. 2013) to take account of the implementation of related provisions of the Health and Safety at Work, etc., Act 1974, and the establishment of the Health and Safety Executive.

Brawling. The Places of Religious Worship Act 1812, s. 12, has been repealed without replacement by the Courts Act 1971, s. 56(4), Sched. 11, Part IV. A common practice is to charge a breach of the peace under the Public Order Act 1936, s. 5. The Religious Disabilities Act 1846, s. 4, was repealed by the Statute Law (Repeals) 1977, s. 1(1), Sched. 1, Part V.

Breach of confidence. For the impact of public policy on such a breach (so as to justify what might otherwise be an improper disclosure) see *Hubbard* v. *Vosper* [1972] 2 Q.B. 84, C.A.

Breach of the peace. This offence must now be tried summarily, and the punishments available are a term of imprisonment not exceeding six months or a fine not exceeding £2,000, or both (Criminal Law Act 1977, ss. 15, 30, Sched. 1; for the general revision of the levels of fines see also FINE). The Magistrates' Courts Act 1952, s. 91, under which a civil complaint lay for an order binding the defendant over to be of good behaviour and to keep the peace, has been repealed and replaced by the Magistrates' Courts Act 1980, s. 115, without change of effect.

Breach of trust. The Limitation Act 1939, s. 19 (including subs. (1A), added by the Limitation Amendment Act 1980, s. 5), has been repealed and replaced by the Limitation Act 1980, s. 21, without further change of effect.

Bread. The Food and Drugs Act 1955, has been repealed and replaced by the Food Act 1984, without significant change of effect.

Breath specimen. First authorised by the Road Traffic Act 1972, s. 8 (as set out in the Transport Act 1981, s. 25, Sched. 8), this is a quantity of breath used to determine the blood alcohol level of a person suspected of driving or attempting to drive with blood alcohol above the prescribed limit. The machine used is commonly call an "intoximeter". See also BREATH TESTS. The printout from the machine is perfectly acceptable as evidence (see *Gaimster* v. *Marlow* [1984] Q.B. 218, D.C.).

Breath tests. The original code of procedure under the Road Traffic Act 1972, s. 8, has been repealed and replaced by a revised text of the Act of 1972, s. 7 (as substituted by the Transport Act 1981, s. 25, Sched. 8). Breath tests must be carefully distinguished from breath specimens: the former are commonly conducted as the roadside with "breathalysers" and act as a screening device; the latter require specialised "intoximeter" machines found only in police stations.

Bribe. The Representation of the People Act 1949, s. 99, has been repealed and replaced by the Representation of the People Act 1983, s. 113, without change of effect.

Bridge. The Highways Act 1959, and associated legislation have been repealed and replaced by the Highways Act 1980, without change of effect. The Road Traffic Regulation Act 1967, s. 17, was repealed by the Local Government, Planning and Land Act 1980, s. 1, Sched. 7, Part II, para. 4, thus abolishing certain ministerial controls over bridges.

Bridle-path; Horseway; Packway. The Highways Act 1959 and associated legislation have been repealed and replaced by the

Highways Act 1980, the principal relevant provisions being ss. 24–27 (construction and creation), s. 43 (maintenance) and ss. 118, 119 (stopping up and diversion).

Bristol bargain. In *A. Ketley* v. *Scott* [1981] I.C.R. 241, the borrower's application (under the Act of 1974, s. 139) to reopen a short term loan on what amounted to a 48 per cent. per annum interest rate was refused.

British America. See also the Canada Act 1982, terminating the power of the Westminster Parliament to legislate for Canada. Insofar as it is completely bi-lingual, this Act would appear to be unique in modern times.

British citizen. One who qualifies as one of the prime class of persons set out in the British Nationality Act 1981, Part I (ss. 1–14).

British Islands. The Interpretation Act 1889, s. 18(1), has been repealed and replaced by the Interpretation Act 1978, s. 5, Sched. 1, without change of effect.

British ship. The British Nationality Act 1948, Sched. 4, Part I, has been repealed without replacement by the British Nationality Act 1981, s. 52, Sched. 9. The requirement of British (or associated) nationality appears to have survived the changes wrought by the Act of 1981.

British Sugar Corporation. The Sugar Industry (Reorganisation) Act 1936, was repealed without replacement by the Sugar Act 1956: the Act of 1956 itself has been repealed by the Food Act 1984, s. 134, Sched. 11. Under s. 68 of the 1984 Act, British Sugar PLC is allocated various responsibilities in connection with education and research relating to home-grown sugar beet.

Broadcasting. The main statutory provisions in respect of the Independent Broadcasting Authority were consolidated in the Broadcasting Act 1981. The Representation of the People Act 1949, s.80, and the Act of 1969, s. 9, have been repealed and replaced by the Representation of the People Act 1983, ss. 92, 93 and 194, without change of effect.

For cable-based systems see the Cable and Broadcasting Act 1984.

Broadmoor Act. The Mental Health Act 1959, has been repealed and replaced by the Mental Health Act 1983 (with minimal exceptions). The meaning of "special hospital" for the purposes of the 1983 Act has (by virtue of s. 145(1)) the same meaning as in the National Health Service Act 1977, s. 4.

Broker. The County Courts Act 1959, s. 131, has been repealed and replaced by the County Courts Act 1984, s. 96, without change of effect.

Building. The Finance Act 1972, s. 15A, has bee repealed and replaced by the Value Added Tax Act 1983, s. 21, without change of effect.

Building Acts. Further statutory amendments of the building regulation regime are contained in the Housing and Building Control Act 1984, Parts II and III (ss. 39–62). See also the Building Act 1984 (which consolidates a number of statutes relating to building, buildings and related matters).

Building lease. The definition formerly contained in the Settled Land Act 1882, s. 1(10)(iii), has been repealed, but is repeated without change of effect in the Settled Land Act 1925, s. 117(1)(iii).

Building line. The Highways Act 1959, ss. 73–75, have been repealed and replaced by the Highways Act 1980, s. 74, without significant change of effect.

Building society. The discretionary power to pay in respect of deceased members or creditors in the absence of probate or letters of administration was in 1975 increased to £1,500 (S.I. 1975 No. 1137); and has now been further increased to £5,000 (S.I. 1984 No. 539).

The tax position has been significantly revised so that the bulk of domestic mortgages come within the "Miras" scheme under which tax relief if given automatically, only the net sum remaining payable to the building society (see generally the Finance Act 1982, s. 26, Sched. 7; qualifying lenders are listed in Orders made under the Act: S.I. 1983 No. 1807 and S.I. 1984 Nos. 93, 368 and 1907).

The £25,000 limit under the Finance Act 1974, s. 19, Sched. 1, para. 5(1), has been increased to £30,000 (Finance (No. 2) Act 1983, s. 3), and has remained there for the time being (Finance Act 1984, s. 22).

Bull. The Improvement of Live Stock (Licensing of Bulls) Act 1931, has been repealed by the Animal Health and Welfare Act 1984, s. 12, so as to remove controls on keeping bulls. The keeping of a bull on land crossed by public rights of way is prohibited (Wildlife and Countryside Act 1981, s. 59), subject on summary conviction to a fine (*q.v.*) not exceed £200.

Bullock order. The power to join parties which is referred to is now contained in R.S.C. Ord. 15, r. 4.

Burial. The Burial Act 1900, has been repealed without replacement by the Statute Law (Repeals) Act 1978, s. 1, Sched. 1, Part XVII. The general provisions of the Act of 1972, Sched. 26, still operate.

The restrictions on the use to which a disused burial ground may be put have been relaxed (Disused Burial Grounds (Amendment) Act 1981, s. 1), subject to exceptions in the case of objections (s. 1(1)(*b*)) and consecrated ground (s. 5).

Burkism. For the (prospective) repeal of the Anatomy Act 1832 see ANATOMY.

Business names. The Registration of Business Names Act 1916, has been repealed without replacement by the Companies Act 1981, s. 119, Sched. 4. In its place a very limited form of civil disability has been introduced by the Act of 1981, ss. 28–30: the principal shortcomings of the new provisions are that they depend on the institution of court proceedings and do not disable a counterclaim by a party in default of the disclosure provisions of the Act.

Business scheme. The War Damage Act 1943 has been repealed without replacement by the Statute Law (Repeals) Act 1981, s. 1(1), Sched. 1, Part XI.

By-laws; Bye-laws. The Towns Improvement Clauses Act 1847, s. 200, and the Town Police Clauses Act 1847, s. 81, have been repealed by the Statute Law (Repeals) Act 1975, s. 1(1), Sched. Part VIII. The Housing Act 1957, ss. 145, 147 and 148, have been repealed by the Local Government Act 1972, s. 272, Sched. 30. The Interpretation Act 1889, ss. 32, 37, have been repealed and replaced by the Interpretation Act 1978, ss. 12–14, without substantial change of effect.

The penalties payable under certain bylaws have been raised by the Criminal Law Act 1977, s. 31 and other legislation (see FINE).

C

Cab. See also the Transport Act 1981, s. 35, relating to charges for licensing cabs and drivers (modifying the Metropolitan Public Carriage Act 1869, s. 6, and the Town Police Clauses Act 1847, s. 37), leaving councils to determine the sum they see fit to levy for licences (compare the Local Government (Miscellaneous Provisions) Act 1976, s. 70)).

For the general revision of the levels of fines on summary conviction see FINE.

Cairns' Act. The decision in *Horsler* v. *Zorro* [1975] Ch. 302, has been overruled by the House of Lords in *Johnson* v. *Agnew* [1979] A.C. 367, where it was held that the election between specific performance and damages should be made at the trial of the action, and that if an order for specific performance were chosen (and made) but the order was not obeyed, the plaintiff might apply to the court so as to obtain a judgment sounding in damages instead. The Judicature Act 1925, s. 36, has been repealed and replaced by the Supreme Court Act 1981, s. 50, with significant change of effect.

Calling the jury. The Courts Act 1971, s. 35(1), has been repealed and replaced by the Juries Act 1974, ss. 11(1), 12(1), (3), without change of effect.

Campbell's (Lord) Act. The Limitation Act 1939, ss. 2B (together with the Limitation Act 1975, s. 1, Sched. 1, para. 1), 2C and 2D, have been repealed and replaced by the Limitation Act 1980, ss. 1 and 12(1), 13, 33, without significant change of effect. The Act of 1980, s. 33 (together with its predecessors) has occasioned massive case law on account of the discretion conferred on the court of "disapply" the (primary) limitation period set for personal injuries actions.

Camping. The Highways Act 1959, s. 127, has been repealed and replaced by the Highways Act 1980. s. 148, without change of effect. The powers of local authorities under the Housing Act 1957, s. 9, have been extended by the Housing Act 1980, s. 148. The Housing Act 1957, s. 44, was repealed without replacement by the Housing Act 1974, s. 130(4), Sched. 15. See also MOBILE HOMES.

Canada. See the Canada Act 1982, terminating the power of the Westminster Parliament to legislate for Canada. Insofar as it is completely bi-lingual, this Act would appear to be unique in modern times.

Canal. General public health provisions in relation to canal boats are contained in the Public Health (Control of Diseases) Act 1984, Part IV (ss. 49–53).

Cancel, Cancellation. The Judicature Act 1925, s. 56(1)(*b*) (which provided for cancellation etc.), has been repealed and replaced by the Supreme Court Act 1981, s. 53, without change of effect.

Cancer. Advertisements containing any offer to treat any person for cancer, or to prescribe any remedy for it, or to give any advice in connection with the treatment of it are prohibited except for special cases involving the medical profession and professions ancillary to medicine (Cancer Act 1939, s. 4; Medicines Act 1968, s. 135(2), Sched. 6).

Candidate. The Representation of the People Act 1949, s. 103, has been repealed and replaced by the Representation of the People Act 1983, s. 118, without change of effect.

Cannabis. The definition of cannabis now reads: cannabis (except in the expression "cannabis resin") means any plant of the genus Cannabis or any part of any such plant (by whatever name designated) except that it does not include cannabis resin or any of the following products after separation from the rest of the plant, namely (a) mature stalk of any such plant, (b) fibre produced from mature stalk of any such plant, and (c) seed of any such plant (Misuse of Drugs Act 1971, s. 37(1) (as substituted by the Criminal Law Act 1977, s. 52)).

Canvasser. The Representation of the People Act 1949, has been repealed and consolidated into the Representation of the People Act 1983.

Capias ad satisfaciendum. The issue of this writ having been discontinued by the Administration of Justice Act 1956, the writ itself has been abolished (Supreme Court Act 1981, s. 141).

Capital duty. See also the Finance Act 1975, s. 38(3), Sched. 7, and the Finance Act 1976, s. 128.

Capital gains tax. The legislation controlling this tax has been consolidated in the Capital Gains Tax Act 1979, and further amended, principally by the Finance Act 1984, Part II, Chapter III (ss. 63–71).

Capital transfer tax. The legislation controlling this tax has been consolidated in the Capital Transfer Tax Act 1984. The amendments of recent years include significant reductions in the top rate of tax, a ten-year cumulation period for lifetime gifts, and the introduction of indexation in line with inflation. Certain earlier provisions, however, have not been incorporated in the consolidation; see, *e.g.* the National Heritage Act 1980, Part II (ss. 8–15), which provides for the surrender of all kinds of property in place of paying capital transfer tax or any interest due on any such tax.

Caption. The Magistrates' Courts Act 1952, s. 41, has been repealed and replaced by the Magistrates' Courts Act 1980, s. 105, without change of effect. The Magistrates' Courts Rules 1968, r. 29(3), has been revoked and replaced by the Magistrates' Courts Rules 1981, r. 33, without change of effect.

Car tax. The legislation controlling this tax has been consolidated in the Car Tax Act 1983; the rate remains the same (Act of 1983, s. 1(2)). See also S.I. 1983 No. 1781.

Caravan sites. Further amendments of the Act of 1968 have been made by the Local Government, Planning and Land Act 1980, ss. 173–178.

Care and protection. Complicated provision has been made for rights of access to children who are in care (Child Care Act 1980, Part IA (inserted by the Health and Social Services and Social Security Adjudications Act 1983, s. 6, Sched. 1, Part I)).

Careless driving. The offence of dangerous driving has been abolished, the two most serious offences now being (1) causing death by reckless driving, and (2) reckless driving (Road Traffic Act 1972, ss. 1, 2 (as substituted by the Criminal Law Act 1977, s. 50)). The "alternative verdict" procedure (under the Road Traffic Act 1972, s. 93,

Sched. 4, Part IV, paras. 3A, 4) remains in operation.

Carnal knowledge. As a result of *R.* v. *Whitehouse* [1977] Q.B. 868, C.A., the Criminal Law Act 1977, s. 54, was passed, making it an offence for a man to have sexual intercourse with a girl under the age of 16 who he knows to be his granddaughter, daughter or sister. On summary conviction the punishment may be a fine (*q.v.*) up to £2,000, or six months' imprisonment or both, and on conviction on indictment the maximum penalty is imprisonment not exceeding two years (s. 54(4)).

Carriageway. The Highways Act 1959, s. 295(1), has been repealed and replaced by the Highways Act 1980, s. 329(1), without change of effect.

Carrying costs. The Judicature Act 1925, s. 50, has been repealed and replaced by the Supreme Court Act 1981, s. 51, without change of effect.

Case. The Judicature Act 1925, s. 101, has been repealed without replacement by the Supreme Court Act 1981, s. 152(4), Sched. 7; it is possible that the former procedure would still be observed.

Case stated by arbitrator. The Arbitration Act 1950, s. 21, has been repealed by the Arbitration Act 1979, ss. 1, 8. The place of the earlier procedure has been taken by (1) judicial review (Act of 1979, s. 1); and (2) reference of a preliminary point of law for the opinion of the High Court (Act of 1979, s. 2).

The new provisions permit an appeal from an arbitrator to the High Court but this may occur only in certain cases. The appeal lies solely on a point of law (s. 1(2)); the appeal must "arise out of" an award made on an arbitration agreement (s. 1(2)), and the agreement must be in writing (s. 7(1)(*e*) and the Act of 1950, s. 32); the consent of all the parties or the leave of the High Court must be obtained (leave being available only if there is no valid exclusion agreement or if the High Court considers that, having regard to all the circumstances, the determination of the relevant question of law could substantially affect the rights of one or more parties to the agreement) (Act of 1979, s. 1(3), (4)). Any grant of leave by the High Court may be made subject to conditions (s. 1(4)). In some cases an arbitrator may be required to give reasons for his award (s. 1(5), (6)).

A preliminary point of law may also be referred to the High Court for determination (s. 2).

Both the right of appeal (s. 1) and the procedure for reference of a preliminary point of law (s. 2) may be excluded by agreement (s. 3), subject to certain restrictions (s. 4).

Case stated by justices. The time for applying for the statement of a case has been extended to 21 days (Criminal Law Act 1977, s. 65, Sched. 12). This time limit will be strictly enforced (*Michael* v. *Bowland* [1977] 1 W.L.R. 296), though it has also been held that the [three months] allowed for the justices to state a case may be extended on application to the Divisional Court (*Whittingham* v. *Nattrass* [1958] 1 W.L.R. 1016).

The Magistrates' Courts Act 1952, s. 87, has been repealed and replaced by the Magistrates' Courts Act 1980, s. 111, the period in which the application may be made having been extended to 21 days. The Magistrates' Courts Rules 1968, rr. 65–68, have been revoked and replaced by the Magistrates' Courts Rules 1981, rr. 76–81, without significant change of effect.

Casting vote. The Representation of the People Act 1949, Sched. 2, r. 50, has been repealed and replaced by the Representation of the People Act 1983, Sched. 1, r. 49, without change of effect.

Catering Wages Commission. The Wages Councils Act 1959, has been repealed and replaced by the Wages Councils Act 1979, which consolidates the various previous provisions.

Cattle-grid. The Highways Act 1959, ss. 87–97, 219, have been repealed and replaced by the Highways Act 1980, ss. 82–90, 243, without change of effect. For the general revision of the levels of fines on summary conviction see FINE.

Cause of action. The Limitation Act 1939 and associated legislation have been repealed and replaced by the Limitation Act 1980, which also incorporates amendments made by the Limitation Amendment Act 1980.

Caution. The Magistrates' Courts Rules 1968, r. 4(7), has been revoked and replaced by the Magistrates' Courts Rules 1981, r. 7(7), without change of effect.

Caveat; Caveator. The Judicature Act 1925, s. 154, and the Administration of Justice Act 1970, Sched. 2, para. 12, have been repealed and replaced by the Supreme Court Act 1981, s. 108, without change of effect.

Caveat actor. The principle that a man is usually presumed to intend the probable consequences of his act is somewhat modified in the criminal law by the provision that in determining whether the defendant has committed any offence neither a judge nor a jury is bound in law to infer that he intended or foresaw a result of his actions by reason only of its being a natural and probable consequence of his actions, but must decide whether the defendant did intend or foresee that result by reference to all the evidence, drawing such inferences from the evidence as appear proper in the circumstances (Criminal Law Act 1967, s. 8).

Caveat emptor. The Sale of Goods Act 1893, ss. 12, 14 (as amended), have repealed and replaced by the Sale of Goods Act 1979, ss. 12, 14, without change of effect.

Caveat viator. The occupier of a yard in a dangerous state would now be liable to a trespasser on account of that dangerous condition in cases where he owed a "common duty of humanity" to the injured trespasser (*Herrington* v. *British Railways Board* [1972] A.C. 877, H.L., and *Pannett* v. *McGuiness & Co. Ltd.* [1972] 2 Q.B. 599, C.A.).

Cellar. The Factories Act 1961, s. 70, has been repealed by the Factories Act 1961, etc. (Repeals and Modifications) Regulations 1974 (S.I. 1974 No. 1941)); this matter now comes within the scope of the town and country planning legislation. For the general revision of the levels of fines on summary conviction see FINE.

The Highways Act 1959, ss. 131 (which contained the power to order the removal of projections from buildings), 153 and 154, have been repealed and replaced by the Highways Act 1980, ss. 151, 179, 180, without change of effect.

Census. The Licensing Act 1953, s. 165(5), was repealed by the Licensing Act 1961, s. 38(3), Sched. 9, Part II, without affecting its use as an illustration.

Census of production. For examples of the detailed requirements which have been ordered in recent censuses of production see S.I.s 1976 No. 1801; 1977 No. 1752; 1978 No. 1573; 1979 No. 1484; 1980 No. 1835 and 1981 No. 1487.

Central Arbitration Committee. The Employment Protection Act 1975, ss. 11–16, have been repealed without replacement by the Employment Act 1980 ss. 19(*a*), 20, Sched. 2.

Central Council for Agricultural and Horticultural Co-operation. This body has been dissolved and replaced by another organisation, called Food from Britain (Agricultural Marketing Act 1983).

Central Council for Nursing, Midwifery and Health Visiting. This body has been established by the Nurses, Midwives and Health Visitors Act 1979, s. 1. The Council's statutory duties make it responsible for establishing and improving the standards of training and professional conduct of nurses, midwives and health visitors, taking into account any duties and responsibilities which may be imposed by Community obligations (s. 2). The Act provides for National Boards acting within the Council (ss. 5–9), which will operate throughout the United Kingdom (s. 1(1)).

Central Criminal Court. The *Practice Direction* of 1971 ([1972] 1 W.L.R. 117) has been revoked and replaced (in due course) by *Practice Direction* [1982] 1 W.L.R. 101, without change of effect.

The Courts Act 1971, ss. 4(7), 29, Sched. 2, paras. 1, 2, have been repealed and replaced by the Supreme Court Act 1981, s. 8(3), without change of effect.

Central Housing Advisory Committee. The Housing Act 1957, s. 143, has been repealed by the Housing Rents and Subsidies Act 1975, s. 17, Sched. 6, Part IV, and by s. 13 of that Act the Committee has been abolished.

Central Midwives Board. This body was dissolved by the Nurses, Midwives and Health Visitors Act 1979, s. 21(1). The Act provides (s. 1(1)) for the establishment of the United Kingdom Central Council for Nursing, Midwifery and Health Visiting (*q.v.*). The Council is to have two Standing Committees (s. 3(1)) of which one will be the Midwifery committee, the majority of whose members must be practising midwives (s. 4(1)). Rules about midwifery practice (under s. 15) must be submitted to the Midwifery Committee before being promulgated by the Council (s. 4(3)).

Central Office. The Judicature Act 1925, ss. 104, 105, have been repealed and replaced by the Supreme Court Act 1981, s. 96, without change of effect.

Central Valuation Board. The Coal Industry Nationalisation Act 1946, s. 12, has been repealed by the Statute Law (Repeals) Act 1973, Sched. 1, Part X.

Certificate.

Accountant General.—The certificate is now given under the authority of the Supreme Court Funds Rules 1975 (S.I. 1975 No. 1803), r. 61.

Analyst.—The Food and Drugs Act 1955, s. 110, has been repealed and replaced by the Food Act 1984, ss. 79, 89, without significant change of effect.

Counsel.—Attendances are now certified under R.S.C. Ord. 63, App. 2, Part VIII, paras. 2(3), 5.

Master.—The former R.S.C. Ord. 44, rr. 21–25 have been revoked without replacement; the current procedure under Ord. 44, r. 10, requires the master to make an order.

Trading.—The Companies Act 1949, s. 109, has been repealed and replaced by the Companies Act 1980, s. 4, without significant change of effect.

Veterinary Inspector—The Diseases of Animals Act 1950, s. 73(5), has been repealed and replaced by the Animal Health Act 1981, s. 63(7), without change of effect.

For certificates of independence see CERTIFICATION OFFICER.

Certification Officer. The functions of the Certification Officer are analogous to those of a justice of the peace, planning inspector or arbitrator, so that it is undesirable for his determination on an application for a certificate of independence (Act of 1975, s. 8) to be the subject-matter of cross-examination (*Squibb United Kingdom Staff Association* v. *Certification Officer* [1979] 1 W.L.R. 523, C.A.).

Appeals lie from the Certification Officer to the Employment Appeal Tribunal in a number of cases (Employment Protection (Consolidation) Act 1978, s. 136(2), (3)).

For complaints about failures to observe the provisions relating to postal ballots see the Trade Union Act 1984, ss. 5, 6.

Certiorari. The meaning of the Tribunals and Inquiries Act 1971, s. 14, is that, even when pre-1958 legislation provides that "any order or determination shall not be called into question in any court, or any provision in such an Act which by similar words excludes any of the powers of the High Court", that will not be effective (*inter alia*) to prevent the removal of the proceedings into the High Court by order of certiorari.

The Administration of Justice (Miscellaneous Provisions) Act 1938, s. 7, has been repealed and replaced by the Supreme Court Act 1981, s. 29 (which contains a general power to make orders of certiorari); at the same time the County Courts Act 1959, s. 115, was repealed by the Act of 1981, s. 152(4), Sched. 7. The Courts Act 1971, s. 10(5), has been repealed and replaced by the Act of 1981, s. 28, without change of effect. The Administration of Justice Act 1960, s. 16, was repealed and replaced by the Act of 1981, s. 43 (which contains a slight extension of the powers formerly enjoyed by the High Court).

Challenge. The Criminal Justice Act 1948, s. 35, has been repealed and effectively replaced by the Juries Act 1974, s. 12(1)(*b*), which provides that in proceedings for the trial on indictment of any person charged with an offence any challenge for cause must be tried by the judge before whom that person is to be tried.

There is no right of challenge when the matter to be determined is whether the accused is mute of malice since at that stage the trial has not been commenced (*R.* v. *Paling* (1978) 67 Cr.App.R. 299, C.A.).

Chamber-clerks. The Supreme Court Officers (Pensions) Act 1954, s. 2, has been repealed and replaced by the Supreme Court Act 1981, s. 98, without significant change of effect. The terms now used are "clerks" and "secretaries".

Chambers. The sittings of a Queen's Bench judge outside London are now conducted under the terms of *Practice Direction* [1976] 1 W.L.R. 246.

The Judicature Act 1925, s. 18, has been repealed and replaced by the Supreme Court Act 1981, s. 19. There is also power to regulate the division of business between chambers and open court in the Act of 1981, s. 61.

The former Chancery practice of adjournment from a master to the judge was abolished in the course of implementing the reforms proposed in the report of the Oliver Committee (Cmnd. 8205); its place has been taken by an appeal to the Court of Appeal (R.S.C. Ord. 58, r. 2).

Chancellor, Lord. The salary of the Lord Chancellor is revised from time to time (see, *e.g.*, S.I. 1983 No. 1171).

County court judges have been replaced by circuit judges, who are appointed under the Courts Act 1971, ss. 16–22, and s. 24 (as substituted by the Supreme Court Act 1981, s. 146, and then amended by the Administration of Justice Act 1982, s. 59(3)). The Lord Chancellor still makes the appointments.

The Judicature Act 1925, s. 6(2), has been repealed and replaced by the Supreme Court Act 1981, s. 2(2), without change of effect.

Chancellor of the Duchy of Lancaster. County court judges have been replaced by circuit judges, who are appointed under the Courts Act 1971, ss. 16–22, and s. 24 (as substituted by the Supreme Court Act 1981, s. 146, and then amended by the Administration of Justice Act 1982, s. 59(3)). The Chancellor of the Duchy has lost his former powers of appointment (Act of 1971, s. 20(5)).

Justices of the peace in the counties of Greater Manchester, Lancashire and Merseyside continue to be appointed by the Chancellor of the Duchy (Justices of the Peace Act 1979, ss. 6(1), 68(1)).

The salary of the Chancellor is revised from time to time (see, *e.g.* S.I. 1979 No. 905).

Chancellor of the Exchequer. The salary of the Chancellor is revised from time to time (see, *e.g.* S.I. 1979 No. 905).

Chancellors of the Universities of Oxford and Cambridge. The savings provisions contained in the County Court Act 1959, s. 205(8), were repealed (Administration of Justice Act 1977, s. 32, Sched. 5 Part V), and any jurisdiction of the Court of the Chancellor or Vice-Chancellor of Oxford and of the Cambridge University's Chancellor's Court other than than which is provided for under the statutes of those universities has been expressly abolished (*ibid.* s. 23(3)).

Chancery. The business assigned to the Chancery Division was modified by the repeal of the Finance Act 1894, s. 14(2), and its replacement by the Finance Act 1975, Sched. 4 (which related to capital transfer tax (*q.v.*) (see R.S.C. Ord. 91, rr. 1,2). This Division also determines cases under the Patents Act 1977 (see R.S.C. Ord. 104).

The Supreme Court Funds Rules 1927, have been revoked and replaced by the Supreme Court Funds Rules 1975 (S.I. 1975 No. 1803); rr. 28–37C (some of which were added by S.I. 1983 No. 290) of the new rules deal with the investment and deposit of funds in court.

The Judicature Act 1925, ss. 4(4), 18 (misprinted as s. 26), 36, have been repealed and replaced by the Supreme Court Act 1981, ss. 5(5), 19, 49, without change of effect. The Administration of Justice Act 1970, s. 5, has been repealed and replaced by the Supreme Court Act 1981, s. 10, without change of effect; the Vice-Chancellor is now also an *ex officio* member of the Court of Appeal (Act of 1981, s. 2(2)).

Amendments to the constitution of the Chancery Division consequent on the Oliver Report (Cmnd. 8205) in 1982 included the abolition of the registrars and the establishment of Chancery Chambers (comparable to the Central Office (*q.v.*) in the Queen's Bench Division).

Chancery Chambers. Established following the Oliver Report (Cmnd. 8205), this is the administrative centre of the Chancery Division (R.S.C. Ord. 1, r. 4(1)); the organisation is more fully explained in *Practice Direction* [1982] 1 W.L.R. 1189.

Chancery Court of Lancaster. The Courts Act 1971, Sched. 1, has been repealed without replacement by the Supreme Court Act 1981, s. 152(4), Sched. 7, so that the position of the Vice-Chancellor, like his place in the list of precedence, seems to have "evaporated."

Channel Islands. The Interpretation Act 1889, s. 18, has been repealed and replaced by the Interpretation Act 1978, s. 5, Sched. 1, without change of effect.

Character. The rule that a defendant in criminal proceedings loses the protection from being asked any question which tends to show that he is of bad character if he gives evidence against any other person charged with the same offence (*i.e.* the Criminal Evidence Act 1898, s. 1(f)(iii)) has been repealed and replaced by a more widely-ranging provision, so that the protection is withdrawn when the accused gives evidence against any other person charged in the same proceedings (Criminal Evidence Act 1979, s. 1(1), reversing the severe restrictions imposed by the decision in *R.* v. *Hills* [1980] A.C. 26, H.L.). It has also been emphasised that using the word "mistake" cannot conceal what is really an attack on the character of a witness, thus letting the accused's character be put in evidence (*R.* v. *Britzman*; *R.* v. *Hall* (1983) 76 Cr.App.R. 134, C.A.)).

Charging order. The law relating to the enforcement of charges on land and securities has been revised in the Charging Orders Act 1979, which repeals and repeats the Administration of Justice Act 1956, s. 39, and the County Courts Act 1959, s. 141, with amendments.

The powers of the courts to make charging orders have been extended so that (*inter alia*) a beneficial interest in land held on trust for sale may be subjected to a charging order (Act of 1979, s. 2(1), reversing the decision in *Irani Finance Ltd.* v. *Singh* [1971] Ch. 59, C.A.). The making of a charging order may now in certain cases amount to a completed execution against goods or execution against land (the Bankruptcy Act 1914, s. 40(2), and the Companies Act 1948, s. 325(2), both having been newly substituted by the Act of 1979, s. 4).

The list of securities which may be made the subject of a charging order may now be revised by the Supreme Court Rules Committee and the County Court Rules Committee (s. 5(2), (3), thus reducing the need for further statutory amendments).

The procedure for making such orders in county courts is now regulated by the C.C.R. 1981, Ord. 31.

Charity. The terms "education" and "educational" in the context of charity law have been given an unusually extended meaning so as to bring a trust for the encouragement of football-playing within the special tax provisions available to charities (*I.R.C.* v. *McMullen* [1980] A.C. 1, H.L.).

Exemption from capital transfer tax in connection with gifts to charities is now afforded without limitation (Capital Transfer Tax Act 1984, s. 23, replacing the Act of 1976, Sched. 6, para. 10).

Chastisement. The Merchant Shipping Act 1894, ss. 220–228, have been repealed by the Merchant Shipping Act 1970, s. 100, Sched. 5 (see S.I. 1972 No. 1977). For general provision for discipline and offences see the Act of 1970, ss. 27–41.

Cheap Trains. On account of the special provisions required for London, the Transport Act 1962, ss. 44–49, have been repealed by the Transport (London) Act 1969, ss. 27(1), 47(2), Sched. 6. The Cheap Trains Act 1883, has been repealed by the Statute Law (Repeal) Act 1978, s. 1(1), Sched. 1, Part XV.

Cheese. The composition, description, labelling and advertisement of cheese, cheese spread, and compound products are regulated by the Cheese Regulations 1970 (S.I. 1970 No. 94, as amended), made under the Food and Drugs Act 1955, ss. 3, 4, 123 (now repealed but without affecting the validity of regulations already issued). The Food and Drugs Act 1955, s. 135, has been repealed and replaced by the Food Act 1984, s. 132(1), without change of effect. The 1984 Act completely replaced the 1955 provisions.

Cheque. The Theft Act 1968, s. 16(2)(a), has been repealed and replaced by the Theft Act 1978. Obtaining services by a deception (*e.g.*, using a worthless cheque in "payment") is specifically made an offence (Act of 1978, s. 1), and dishonestly obtaining goods by the means of a worthless cheque appears to come within the offence of obtaining property by a deception (Act of 1968, s. 15).

Chevening House. The Capital Transfer Tax Act 1984, s. 156, specifically excepts from its provisions any property held on the trusts set out in the Chevening Estate Act 1959, Sched.

Chicago Convention. The authority for giving effect to the Convention was the Civil Aviation Act 1949, s. 8; this has been repealed and replaced by the Civil Aviation Act 1982, s. 60, without change of effect.

Chief Baron of the Exchequer. The Judicature Act 1925, s. 35, has been repealed without replacement by the Supreme Court Act 1981, s. 152(4), Sched. 7.

Chief Registrar of Friendly Societies. The Chief Registrar is now appointed under the authority of the Friendly Societies Act 1974, s. 1(1).

Chief Justice of the Common Pleas. The Judicature Act 1925, s. 35, has been repealed without replacement by the Supreme Court Act 1981, s. 152(4), Sched. 7.

Chief-rent. Any annual or other periodic sum charged on land or issuing out of land (except rent reserved by a lease or tenancy or any sum payable by way of interest) constitutes a rentcharge (Rentcharges Act 1977, s. 1); the creation of new rentcharges is prohibited (s. 2) and provision has been made for the extinguishment of all rentcharges over a period of 60 years (s. 3). Fresh provision has been made for redemption of rentcharges (ss. 8–10), including a new formula for calculating the redemption price (s. 19, replacing the Law of Property Act 1925, s. 191, which has therefore been repealed).

The Limitation Act 1939, s. 4, has been repealed and replaced by the Limitation Act 1980, s. 15, without change of effect.

Child; Children. The duty to register the birth of a child now arises under the National Health Service Act 1977, s. 124.

Further provisions affecting children include the following statutes. The Congenital Disabilities (Civil Liability) Act 1976, confers on certain children born disabled a right of action for a claim for damages for personal injuries. The Adoption Act 1976, has (prospectively) consolidated many of the provisions relating to the adoption of children. The Protection of Children Act 1978, prohibits the taking of indecent photographs of children and related activities (see also ABUSING CHILDREN and the Child Abduction Act 1984). The Child Care Act 1980, has consolidated many of the provisions relating to children in care, and the Foster Children Act 1980, has consolidated many of the provisions relating to the fostering of children on a private basis (those who have been fostered into the care of statutory authorities being dealt with under the Child Care Act 1980). By the Health and Social Services and Social Security Adjudications Act 1983, s. 6, Sched. 1, Part I (which inserted Part 1A into the Child Care Act 1980), new provision was made for rights of access to children in care.

The Criminal Law Act 1977, s. 45, created a new offence of inciting a girl to have incestuous intercourse when she is under the age of 16 (see CARNAL KNOWLEDGE).

For the purposes of the law of family inheritance, the term "child" includes both legitimate and illegitimate children and a child en ventre sa mère at the death of the deceased (Inheritance (Provision for Family and Dependants) Act 1975, s. 25(1)).

Child destruction. The offence of child destruction may be found even when the accused has been acquitted of administering any noxious thing (etc.) with a view to causing an abortion (under the Offences against the Person Act 1861, s. 58). Liability for this offence is specifically preserved by the Abortion Act 1967, s. 5 (and see ABORTION).

Chimneys. The fines for setting chimneys on fire have been increased (see the Criminal Law Act 1977, s. 31(5), (6); for the general revision of the levels of fines on summary conviction see FINE).

Christianity. For further judicial comments on the relationship between Christianity and the law, see *R.* v. *Lemon* [1979] A.C. 617, H.L.

Christmas Day. The C.C.R. 1936, Ord. 1, r. 2, and Ord. 48, r. 10, have been revoked and replaced by the C.C.R. 1981, Ord. 2, r. 2, without change of effect. The former Ord. 8, r. 3, has been revoked and replaced by the 1981 Rules, Ord. 7, r. 3, without change of effect.

Church. The Pastoral Measure 1968, ss. 27–29, have been repealed and replaced by the Pastoral Measure 1983, ss. 27–29, without change of effect.

Cinematograph. The detailed provisions requiring exhibitors to show a specified quota of British films have been amended to take account of long-running films, permitting the quota requirements to be observed on an average basis over two years (Films Act 1979, s. 1, amending the Films Act 1960, s. 6).

The Films Act 1980, altered the functions of the National Film Finance Corporation, and extended the period of the levy under the Act of 1957, also extending the quota period and the requirements imposed in connection with the quota (ss. 5, 6), giving the Secretary of State the power to suspend the quota requirements (s. 7).

The Cinematograph Film Production (Special Loans) Acts 1949–1980, have been repealed and replaced by the National Film Finance Corporation Act 1981, without significant change of effect. See also NATIONAL FILM FINANCE CORPORATION.

The Cinematograph Films Acts 1957 to 1980 have been repealed and replaced by the Film Levy Finance Act 1981, without change of effect.

Circuits. The county court circuits continued in existence by the (now repealed) County Courts Act 1959, ss. 1, 2, are more commonly called districts; the areas of the current districts are delimited by the Civil Courts Order 1983 (S.I. 1983 No. 713).

The Courts Act 1971, s. 27 (which dealt with appointments of various High Court officers), has been repealed and replaced by the Supreme Court Act 1981, s. 89. The County Courts Act 1959, ss. 1, 2 have been repealed and replaced by the County Courts Act 1984, s. 1, without change of effect.

Circuity of action. For an illustration of the modern procedure in operation see *Post Office* v. *Hampshire County Council* [1980] Q.B. 124, C.A.

The Judicature Act 1925, s. 39, has been repealed without replacement by the Supreme Court Act 1981, s. 152(4), Sched. 7; the same Act, by s. 19(2)(*b*), preserves the Supreme Court's jurisdiction enjoyed under earlier legislation.

Circulars, Moneylenders'. All the statutory provisions referred to have been repealed by the Consumer Credit Act 1974, s. 193(3), Sched. 5, Part I, since an equivalent prohibition is contained in the Act of 1974, s. 50.

Circumstantial evidence. Even in homicide cases circumstantial evidence may found a conviction; the burden of proof is the same as in ordinary cases where direct evidence is available, *i.e.* proof beyond reasonable doubt (*McGreevy* v. *D.P.P.* [1973] 1 W.L.R. 276, H.L.).

Citizen of the United Kingdom and colonies. The British Nationality Act 1948 and 1958 have been repealed and replaced by the British Nationality Act 1981, with modifications.

City of London Court. The County Courts Act 1959, s. 197, has been repealed without replacement by the Supreme Court Act 1981, s. 152(4), Sched. 7. The special status of the court was preserved by the Courts Act 1971, s. 42, and this has been continued by the County Courts Act 1984, s. 1(3).

Civil employment, Reinstatement in. The provisions of the Reinstatement in Civil Employment Act 1950, have been completely repealed (Statute Law (Repeals) Act 1977, s. 1(1), Sched. 1, Part I), and the Navy, Army and Air Force Reserve Act 1954, has been repealed entirely (Statute Law (Repeals) Act 1976, s. 1, Sched. 1, Part IV). The Navy, Army and Air Force Reserve Act 1964, s. 2(6), has been repealed and replaced by the Reserve Forces Act 1980, ss. 145(1), 146(1), without change of effect.

Civil interests of service men. The provisions of the Reinstatement in Civil Employment Act 1950, have been completely repealed (Statute Law (Repeals) Act 1977, s. 1(1), Sched. 1, Part I). The Navy, Army and Air Force Reserve Act 1964, s. 2(6), has been repealed and replaced by the Reserve Forces Act 1980, ss. 145(1), 146(1), without change of effect.

Clearance area. The Housing Act 1974, s. 42, has been repealed without replacement by the Housing Act 1980, s. 152, Sched. 26.

Clerical error. For the courts' powers to correct wills which contain such faults see RECTIFICATION; RECTIFY.

Clerical subscription. The Pastoral Measure 1968, s. 75, has been repealed and replaced by the Pastoral Measure 1983, s. 75, without change of effect.

Clerk of the Chancery Lists. This is an officer of Chancery Chambers who is responsible for listing causes and matters for hearing in the Chancery Division; for the scope of the officer's work see *Practice Direction* [1983] 1 W.L.R. 436. See also CLERK OF THE LISTS.

Clerk of the Lists. This is an officer of the Central Office (*q.v.*), who is responsible for arranging the lists of cases for hearing in the Queen's Bench Division. Application may be made to him to fix a date for the trial, and for transfer between the various lists of actions which have been set down under R.S.C. Ord. 34, for trial (see *Practice Direction* [1981] 1 W.L.R. 1296). See also CLERK OF THE CHANCERY LISTS.

Clerk of the Crown in Chancery. The Judicature Act 1925, s. 133, has been repealed and replaced by the Supreme Court Act 1981, s. 97, which provides that "the office of Accountant General of the Supreme Court shall be held by the Permanent Secretary to the Lord Chancellor", without mentioning the office of the Clerk to the Crown in Chancery.

Clerk to the justices. The Justices of the Peace Act 1949, s. 20, has been repealed and replaced by the Justices of the Peace Act 1979, s. 26, without change of effect, and the Administration of Justice Act 1964, s. 15, has been repealed and replaced by the Act of 1979, ss. 25(5), 27(9), 37, 38(4), also without change of effect.

The general powers and duties of a clerk are outlined in the Act of 1979, s. 28. Though the justices are entitled to have the advice of the Clerk himself, his duties are most often carried out by assistants, who must now be qualified under the Justices' Clerks' (Qualification of Assistants) Rules 1979 (S.I. 1979 No. 570), which require the assistants to be qualified as barristers, solicitors, or under a certificate of qualification which ranks as equivalent to the professional ones.

Further rules have been made (under what is now s. 28) authorising the clerk to the justices to take a number of steps which formerly required a justice or bench of justices (see the Justices' Clerks Rules 1970 (S.I. 1970 No. 231, amended by S.I 1983 No. 527) for the list).

The principal court duties of the clerk to the justices (and his substitutes in court) have been reviewed in *Practice Direction* [1981] 1 W.L.R. 1163.

Clerks of the Indictments. The work formerly done by these officers is now done by officers of the Crown Court (established under the Courts Act 1971, s. 4, and continued under the Supreme Court Act 1981, s. 8) instead of in the Central Office (*q.v.*). The Supreme Court of Judicature (Circuit Officers) Act 1946, was repealed by the Courts Act 1971, s. 56(4), Sched. 11, Part IV, without being replaced.

Close company. The capital transfer tax provisions cited have been repealed and replaced by the Capital Transfer Tax Act 1984 (see Part II (ss. 94–102)).

Close season. The close season in respect of roe deer has been amended by the Roe Deer (Close Seasons) Act 1977, so that for roe deer bucks the dates are November 1 to March 31 inclusive (s. 1).

The "special penalties" provisions of the Protection of Birds Act 1954, Sched. 1, Part II, have been repealed and replaced by the Wildlife and Countryside Act 1981, ss. 1, 2, 4, 6, 19, 22, Sched. 1, Part II, without significant change of effect. The list in the Act of 1954, Sched. 3, has been replaced by the Act of 1981, ss. 2, 3, 22, Sched. 2, Part I.

Closed shop. This term is used to designate the situation where all the employees of a firm (or recognisable part of a firm) are required to be members of a trade union; such situations may be divided in "pre-entry" and "post-entry" classes. The legal term is "union membership agreement," which is defined as an agreement which (a) is made by or on behalf of, or otherwise exists between, one or more independent trade unions and one or more employers or employers' associations, and (b) relates to employees of an indentifiable class, and (c) has the effect in practice of requiring the employees for the time being of the class to which it relates (irrespective of whether there is a condition to that effect in their contract of employment) to be or become a member of the union or one of the unions which is or are parties to the agreement or arrangement or of another specified independent trade union (Trade Union and Labour Relations Act 1974, s. 30(1)). It was provided that the dismissal of an employee by an employer was to be regarded as fair if it was the practice in accordance with a closed shop agreement or arrangement for employees to belong to a specified trade union and the reason for dismissal was that the employee was not a member of an appropriate union or had refused or proposed to refuse to become or remain a member of that union or one of those unions (Employment Protection (Consolidation) Act 1978, s. 58(3)). An exception was provided for the case of those who, on the grounds of religious belief, genuinely objected to being a member of any trade union (Act of 1978, s. 58(3) (see also CONSCIENTIOUS OBJECTOR)). See also the Employment Protection (Consolidation) Act 1978, s. 58A (as substituted by the Employment Act 1982, s. 3), and the Employment Code of Practice (Closed Shop Agreements and Arrangements) Order 1983 (S.I. 1983

No. 584), which brought into operation the revised Code under the Employment Act 1980, s. 3.

See also the Employment Protection (Consolidation) Act 1978, ss. 76A–76C (added by the Employment Act 1980, s. 10, s. 76A having been again replaced by the Employment Act 1982, s. 7).

Union membership requirements in contracts for the supply of goods or services are prohibited and related provision is made by the Employment Act 1982, ss. 12–14.

The Trades Union Congress has a review committee which considers cases involving any person who works or seeks to work in an establishment where there is a closed shop when the worker cannot obtain or retain membership of an appropriate union and has already taken all the steps he can by way of appeal in the union he has selected.

Club. The former provisions for entering an appearance have been replaced by the requirement of acknowledging service of a writ or originating summons (R.S.C. Ord. 12, as amended by S.I. 1979 No. 1716). The acknowledgement of service must be completed by the person or persons against whom the proceedings are issued.

The decisions in *Charter* v. *Race Relations Board* [1973] A.C. 868, H.L., and *Dockers' Labour Club and Institute* v. *Race Relations Board* [1976] A.C. 285, H.L., have been overruled by the Race Relations Act 1976, s. 25. This provides that (as respects associations neither within the provisions relating to trade unions, etc., (s. 11) nor those relating to a "sector of the public") it is unlawful for an association to discriminate on racial grounds against a person who is not a member of the association in the terms on which it is prepared to offer him membership or by refusing or deliberately omitting to accept his application for membership. These provisions are limited in their operation to associations where there are more than 25 members, and where admission to membership is regulated by the constitution of the association and is so conducted that the association is not a "section of the public" (see s. 25). Where there are more than 25 members in an association, the general provisions of the Act prohibit discrimination on the ground that the association is a "sector of the public" (s. 20).

Coal. Further provision for the financing of the coal industry has been made by the National Coal Board (Finance) Act 1976, and Coal Industry Act 1977, which deals with grants to the coal industry, extends the Board's powers and authorises the provision of pensions and other benefits under the Coal Industry Nationalisation Act 1946.

Coasting trade. The Customs and Excise Act 1952, ss. 57-62, have been repealed and replaced by the Customs and Excise Management Act 1979, ss. 69–74, without change of effect.

Cock-fighting. The maximum punishment on summary conviction of this offence has been increased (see the Criminal Law Act 1977, s, 31, Sched. 6; see also FINE).

Code. The Sale of Goods Act 1893, has been repealed and replaced by the Sale of Goods Act 1979, which is also a consolidating statute.

Coin. The Coinage Offences Act 1936, has been repealed and replaced by the Forgery and Counterfeiting Act 1981, Part II (ss. 14–28), with modifications. For the modification of the requirements of fineness of the Maundy money see MAUNDY THURSDAY.

Collective agreement. In employment law a collective agreement is an agreement or arrangement made by or on behalf of one or more trade unions and one or more employers or employers' associations and relating to one or more of (a) the terms and conditions of employment; (b) the engagement or non-engagement or termination or suspension of employment of one or more workers; (c) the allocation of work between workers; (d) matters of discipline; (e) membership of a trade union; (f) facilities for trade union officials; (g) machinery for negotiation or consultation and other procedures relating to the foregoing matters (Trade Union and Labour Relations Act 1974, s. 30(1)). This definition is adopted in the Employment Protection (Consolidation) Act 1978 (see s. 153(1)). Collective agreements made before December 1971 or after July 1974 are conclusively presumed not to be legally enforceable unless they are in writing and contain an express provision stating that the parties intend the agreement to be a legally enforceable contract (Act of 1974, s. 18(1)). An agreement may be divided into parts, some of which are legally enforceable, others not being so enforceable (s. 18(3)). A collective agreement may prohibit or restrict the right of workers to engage in a strike or other industrial action, but those terms cannot form part of any contract between any worker and his employee unless the agreement is in writing and contains a statement that the restriction or prohibition clause may be incorporated in a worker's contract and it is reasonably accessible to the worker at his work-place, and the agreement is concluded exclusively with independent trade unions; further, these terms must also be incorporated in the worker's contract (whether expressly or by implication) (Act of 1974, s. 18(4)).

See also GUARANTEE PAYMENT.

Collision of ships. The current regulations under the Merchant Shipping Act 1894, s. 418, are the Collision Regulations and Distress Signals Order 1977 (S.I. 1977 No. 982). Additional powers have been conferred on Department of Trade Inspectors (Merchant Shipping Act 1979, ss. 27, 28).

Colonial development. The Colonial Development Corporation has been renamed the Commonwealth Development Corporation (Commonwealth Development Corporation Act 1963, s, 1); see also COMMONWEALTH DEVELOPMENT CORPORATION.

Colony. A British colony is now defined as any part of Her Majesty's dominions outside the British Islands except (a) countries having fully responsible status within the Commonwealth, (b) territories for whose external relations a country other than the United Kingdom is responsible, or (c) associated states; and where parts of such dominions are under both a central and a local legislature, all parts under the central legislature are deemed to be one colony (Interpretation Act 1978, s. 5, Sched. 1, replacing the Interpretation Act 1889, s. 18).

Commercial causes. The Administration of Justice Act 1970, s. 3, has been repealed and replaced by the Supreme Court Act 1981, ss. 6, 62(3), without change of effect.

Commission for examination of witnesses. For the detailed procedures to be observed in obtaining evidence under the Evidence (Proceedings in Other Jurisdictions) Act 1975, see R.S.C. Ord. 70.

The C.C.R. 1936, Ord 20, r. 18, has been revoked and replaced by the C.C.R. 1981, Ord. 20, r. 13, without change of effect. The County Courts Act 1959, s. 85, has been repealed and replaced by the County Courts Act 1984, s. 56, without change of effect.

Commission of the peace. The Administration of Justice Act 1973, s. 1(1), and the Courts Act 1971, s. 3, have been repealed and replaced by the Justices of the Peace Act 1979, ss. 1, 5(1) and 5(2), respectively, all without change of effect.

Commissioners for oaths. The fees payable on the administration of an oath by a commissioner have been increased to £3 for each oath and 75p for each exhibit (Commissioners for Oaths (Fees) Order 1984 (S.I. 1984 No. 481)).

Commissioners of Customs and Excise. The terms of appointment, duties, powers and privileges of the Commissioners are now laid down in Part II (ss. 6–18) of the Customs and Excise Management Act 1979 (replacing the Act of 1952, without change of effect).

The collection of value added tax is now conducted under the Value Added Tax Act 1983, ss. 1, 48(1); the Act of 1983 consolidated the value added tax legislation.

Commissioners of Inland Revenue. The Finance Act 1975, Sched. 4, has been repealed and replaced as part of the consolidation of the legislation relating to capital transfer tax by the Capital Transfer Tax Act 1984.

Commissioners of Patents. The Patents Act 1949, s. 83, has been repealed and replaced by the Patents 1977, s. 132, Sched. 6. See COMPTROLLER–GENERAL OF PATENTS, DESIGNS AND TRADE MARKS.

Commit; Commitment; Committal. The Magistrates' Courts Act 1952, ss. 7, 8, 28, 29, 64–67, 70(2)–(5), 73, 74–76 and 126(1), have been repealed and replaced by the Magistrates' Courts Act 1980, ss. 6, 41, 37, 38, 76–79, 83, 96, 93–95 and 150(1), respectively. The Administration of Justice Act 1970, ss. 12, 28 and 43, have been repealed and replaced by the Magistrates' Courts Act 1980, s. 92. The Criminal Justice Act 1972, s. 45, has been repealed and replaced by the Magistrates' Courts Act 1980, s. 4(4); the Criminal Justice Act 1967, ss. 1, 2, 3, 4 and

89, have been repealed and replaced by the Magistrates' Courts Act 1980, ss. 6(2), 102, 8, 6(5) and 106, respectively. These changes having been part of the consolidation of the Magistrates' Courts Act provisions, there has been only slight change in the re-enactments.

The provisions for the enforcement of maintenance orders (Administration of Justice Act 1970) have been repealed and replaced by the Supreme Court Act 1981, s. 61(1), (3), Sched. 1, para. 3, without change of effect.

Committee of inspection. The scope of the summary administration provisions of the Bankruptcy Act 1914, s. 129, has been raised from £300 to £4,000 (Insolvency Act 1976, s. 1, Sched. 1).

Common. For the impact of the revision of penalties on summary conviction on the Law of Property Act 1925, s. 193(1)(*c*), (4) see FINE.

Common fund. The Administration of Justice Act 1965, s. 1 (together with its associated provisions), has been (prospectively) repealed and replaced by the Administration of Justice Act 1982, s. 42; Part VI (ss. 38–48) of the Act of 1982 relates to the general scheme.

Common law. The Judicature Act 1925, s. 36, has been repealed and replaced by the Supreme Court Act 1981, s. 49, without change of effect beyond a slight increase in the powers of the Supreme Court Rules Committee.

Common Law Procedure Acts 1852, 1854 and 1860. The Judicature Act 1925, s. 99, has been repealed and replaced by the Supreme Court Act 1981, s. 84, without significant change of effect.

Common lodging-house. Further provisions for the control of infectious or notifiable diseases relating to common lodging-houses are contained in the Public Health (Control of Diseases) Act 1984, ss. 39–42.

Common Market. Elections for "Common Market Parliament" members were established by the European Assemblies Election Act 1978, and the salaries and other emoluments of the members provided for in the European Assembly (Pay and Pensions) Act 1979. The entry of Greece into the organisation was recognised and provided for in the European Communities (Greek Accession) Act 1979.

Commonwealth citizen. The British Nationality Act 1948, s. 1, has been repealed without replacement by the British Nationality Act 1981, s. 52(8), Sched. 9.

Commonwealth Development Corporation. Originally established as the Colonial Development Corporation under the Overseas Resources Development Act 1948, the Corporation was the subject of the Overseas Resources Development Act 1959; by the Commonwealth Development Act 1963 the name was altered to the modern one. The statutory provisions relating to the Corporation have been consolidated into the Commonwealth Development Corporation Act 1978; membership and the proceedings of the Corporation are regulated by the Commonwealth Development Corporation Regulations 1979 (S.I. 1979 No. 495). Further financial provision was made by the Commonwealth Development Corporation Act 1982.

Commorientes. The Finance Act 1975, s. 22(9), has been repealed and replaced by the Capital Transfer Tax Act 1984, ss. 4(2), 54(4), without change of effect. The definition in s. 4(2), differs from the "normal" rule (Law of Property Act 1925, s. 184), providing that "where it cannot be known which of two or more persons who have died survived the other or others they shall be assumed to have died at the same instant". This is (in most cases) more beneficial from the point of view of a potential tax-payer than the 1925 provision.

Communion, Holy. Alternative rites to the one contained in the Book of Common Prayer were authorised by the Prayer Book (Alternative and Other Services) Measure 1965, subject to a veto (s. 3) by the parochial church council (*q.v.*).

Three alternative forms of the service were promulgated under the 1965 provisions, and modified forms of these now appear in the Alternative Services Book which has been authorised for use since November 1980.

Communis error facit jus. The rule in *Baker* v. *Boulton* (1808) 1 Camp. 493, has long been obsolete, having been abrogated by the Fatal Accidents Act 1846 (now repealed and consolidated into the Fatal Accidents Act 1976). See also BEREAVEMENT.

Community bus. See the Transport Act 1978, ss. 5, 6 and the Community Bus Regulations 1978 (S.I. 1978 No. 1313).

Community homes. The Children and Young Persons Act 1969, ss. 35–42, 44–45, 47–50, have been repealed and replaced by the Child Care Act 1980, Part IV (ss. 31–44), and s. 72, without change of effect.

Community service order. Amendments to the detailed provisions of the scheme (including its extension to 16 year-old offenders) have been made by the Criminal Justice Act 1982, s. 68, Sched. 12. Reciprocal orders between the component parts of the United Kingdom and the extension of the scheme to 16 year-olds were authorised by the Criminal Justice Act 1982, s. 68, Sched. 13 (which added ss. 17A–17C to the main 1973 provisions).

Commutation. For the commutation of pensions of officers see also the Pensions Commutation Act 1882. The provisions of the 1871 Act have been repealed in so far as they apply to persons (mainly civil servants) who are within the terms of the Superannuation Act 1972 (Act of 1972, s. 29(4), Sched. 8).

Companies. The constitution and management of companies has been further regulated by the Companies Act 1980 and 1981. The Companies Act 1981 is now fully in operation (S.I. 1984 No. 684), as is the Act of 1976 (S.I. 1984 No. 683). See also the Companies (Beneficial Interests) Act 1983.

Companies Liquidation Account. See INSOLVENCY SERVICES ACCOUNT.

Compensation for improvements. The Agricultural Holdings Act 1948, s. 42, has been repealed by the Agricultural Holdings Act 1984, s. 10(2), Sched. 4.

Compensation orders. The Powers of Criminal Courts Act 1973, s. 35(5), has been repealed and replaced by the Magistrates' Courts Act 1980, s. 40 (which has itself been affected by the Criminal Penalties etc. (Increase) Order 1984 (S.I. 1984 No. 447)), so that the limit is now £2,000. The limit under this provision may now be altered to take account of any change in the value of money (Criminal Law Act 1977, s. 61(1), (2)).

Compensation orders in respect of criminal damage to monuments in the guardianship of the Secretary of State or any local authority by virtue of the Ancient Monuments and Archaeological Areas Act 1979, must be made in favour of the Secretary of State or the local authority in question (Ancient Monuments and Archaeological Areas Act 1979, s. 29). It is therefore possible for a person on whose land a monument is situated to be required to pay compensation to the Secretary of State or local authority in the event of being found guilty on a charge of criminal damage to his own property.

The principles to be observed when awarding compensation have received frequent consideration by the courts, but the Powers of Criminal Courts Act 1973, s. 35(1), (1A) (as substituted by the Criminal Justice Act 1982, s. 67), now provides for the compensation of a victim of crime to have preference over the imposition or collection of any fine, as well as authorising (for the first time) the making of a compensation order without any other penalty being imposed.

The Magistrates' Court Act 1952, s. 64, has been repealed and replaced by the Magistrates' Court Act 1980, s. 75, without change of effect.

Complaint. The Magistrates' Courts Act 1952, ss. 50–55, 73, 74, 91, 92, have been repealed and replaced by the Magistrates' Courts Act 1980, ss. 51–64 (in respect of civil proceedings) and 65–74 (in respect of domestic proceedings), 96, 93, 115, 116, respectively, subject to amendments to take account of additional jurisdictions imposed by statute (*e.g.* the Domestic Proceedings and Magistrates' Courts Act 1978), but otherwise without change of effect.

Comptroller; Controller. For fresh provisions in respect of the Comptroller and Auditor-General of the Exchequer and Audit Department see the National Audit Act 1983. See also NATIONAL AUDIT OFFICE and PUBLIC ACCOUNTS COMMISSION.

Comptroller-General of Patents, Designs and Trade Marks. This official is charged with the control and management of the register of trade marks at the Patents Office (Trade Marks Act 1938, s. 1(4)). This register was originally provided for by the Trade Marks Act 1905, s. 4 (repealed). The Comptroller also has functions under the Registered Designs Act 1949, acting as registrar (s. 44(1)) in control of the register maintained at the Patents Office (s. 17), and under the Patents Acts 1949 and 1977 (see the Act of 1977, ss. 17 *et seq.*, 72, 73, 97, 107, 108, 115, 121, 130(1)).

Compulsory pilotage. The Pilotage Act 1913, s. 15, has been repealed and replaced by the Pilotage Act 1983, s. 35. Sections 30–35 of the 1983 Act provide a general code governing compulsory pilotage. The new provisions also displace the Merchant Shipping Act 1979, s. 8, whilst repeating their effect, so that the "excepted ships" will continue to be solely Crown vessels and those specified in the by-laws of the pilotage district, all others being subject to compulsory pilotage.

Compulsory purchase. The Acquisition of Land (Authorisation Procedure) Act 1946, and associated legislation, have been repealed and replaced by the Acquisition of Land Act 1981. The Community Land Act 1975 also provided for compulsory purchase, but it has been repealed without replacement by the Local Government, Planning and Land Act 1980, s. 194, Sched. 34, Part XI.

Computer. See COPYRIGHT.

Concealment. Special limitation periods apply to cases where there has been some element of concealment which affects the knowledge of the party who sustains the loss or damage (Limitation Act 1980, s. 32). The essence of the provisions is to make the limitation period in respect of the cause of action run from the discovery of the true situation or the date when that discovery might reasonably have been made.

Concessions, Extra-statutory. For judicial disapproval (but understanding) of the practice of allowing these concessions see *Vestey* v. *Inland Revenue Commissioners* [1979] Ch. 198, where Walton J. points out that they are a modern form of a general dispensing power which it was thought had been abolished at the time of the Bill of Rights (see also the same case on appeal to the House of Lords, [1980] A.C. 1148).

Condition. In the law of contract the distinction between conditions and warranties is a matter for the court and cannot be determined by the parties (*Wickman Machines Tool Sales Ltd.* v. *L. Schuler A.G.* [1974] A.C. 235, H.L.).

Conditional sale agreements. For the revised levels of the various limits controlling the application of the Consumer Credit Act 1974, see the Consumer Credit (Increase of Monetary Amounts) Order 1983, S.I. 1983 No. 1571, and the Consumer Credit (Increase of Monetary Limits) Order 1983 (S.I. 1983 No. 1878).

Conditions of sale. The Sale of Goods Act 1893, s. 12 (together with the amendment effected by the Supply of Goods (Implied Terms) Act 1973, s. 1), has been repealed and replaced by the Sale of Goods Act 1979, s. 12, without change of effect.

Condonation. This concept has disappeared from the matrimonial law in force in magistrates' courts, the matrimonial jurisdiction of magistrates having been revised by the Domestic Proceedings and Magistrates' Courts Act 1978. Under the new Act matrimonial orders are available on broadly similar lines to those which obtain in divorce proceedings in county courts and the High Court. The repeal of the Matrimonial Causes Act 1965, s. 42, has come into operation.

Condonation also appears in military law, where it is of significance in connection with the inter-relationship of military and civil courts (Army Act 1955, s. 134; Air Force Act 1955, s. 134).

Conduct money. The Judicature Act 1925, s. 49(1), has been repealed and replaced by the Supreme Court Act 1981, s. 36(1), without change of effect.

The Courts Act 1971, s. 4(8), has been repealed and replaced by the Supreme Court Act 1981, s. 45(4), which excludes certain High Court powers in civil cases; the Crown Court has power to require the attendance of witnesses by virtue of the Criminal Procedure (Attendance of Witnesses) Act 1965, s. 2.

The County Courts Act 1959, s. 85, has been repealed and replaced by the County Courts Act 1984, s. 55, without change of effect.

The Magistrates' Courts Act 1952, s. 77, has been repealed and replaced by the Magistrates' Courts Act 1980, s. 97, without change of effect. The statute applies not only to indictable offences but also to summary criminal cases and civil proceedings. See also the Criminal Procedure (Attendance of Witnesses) Act 1965.

Confidential communications. The rule in *Hobbs* v. *Hobbs and Cousens* [1960] P. 112, has been overruled by *Waugh* v. *British Railways Board* [1980] A.C. 521, H.L.; it is of the essence of the claim to privilege that the dominant purpose behind the communication should be the conduct of litigation. In these circumstances not all internal communications of a company to and with its legal department are privileged (see *Alfred Crompton Amusement Machines Ltd.* v. *Customs and Excise Commissioners* (*No. 2*) [1974] A.C. 405, H.L.), but only those which are clearly related to litigation.

For the position of journalists see PRESS.

Further restrictions have been imposed on claims to the privilege of non-disclosure of confidential communications. Now, therefore, in proceedings for infringement of rights in respect of intellectual property and related offences, the risk of incriminating oneself or one's spouse is no longer justification for non-disclosure (Supreme Court Act 1981, s. 72, reversing the rule in *Rank Film Distributors Ltd.* v. *Video Information Centre* [1982] A.C. 380, H.L.).

It can be a defence to acclaim for breach of confidence to show that it is in the public interest to publish, and this is not confined to cases of wrong-doing by the plaintiff (*Lion Laboratories Ltd.* v. *Evans* [1984] 3 W.L.R. 539, C.A.).

Confiscation. The Criminal Justice Act 1972, s. 23(1)–(4), (6), has been repealed and replaced by the Powers of Criminal Courts Act 1973, s. 43, without change of effect, and the Act of 1972, s. 23(5), has been amended by the Act of 1973, s. 56(1), Sched. 5.

Confusion. The power granted to the Law Society under the Solicitors Act 1974, s. 32, has been exercised in the making of the Solicitors' Accounts Rules 1975, the Solicitors' Trust Account Rules 1975 and the Solicitors' Accounts (Deposit Interest) Rules 1975 (all dated April 11, 1975).

Certain difficulties arising from confusion of (*inter alia*) materials have been considered in courts dealing with retention of title clauses in contracts (*e.g. Aluminium Industrie Vaassen B.V.* v. *Romalpa Aluminium Ltd.* [1976] 1 W.L.R. 676, C.A.; *In re Bond Worth Ltd.* [1980] Ch. 228; and *Borden* (*U.K.*) *Ltd.* v. *Scottish Timber Products Ltd.* [1981] Ch. 25, C.A.).

Congenital disability. A right of action for damages for congenital disabilities is conferred in certain cases by the Congenital Disabilities (Civil Liability) Act 1976; the Act even confers this right of action on a child born with a disability which results from his mother's failure to take as much care of him (in utero) as the law imposes on her with respect to the safety of other people (s. 2), provided the disability arises out of some occurrence when the mother was the driver of a motor vehicle at a time when she knew or ought to have known that she was pregnant.

Conscientious objector. All the 1948 and 1950 provisions mentioned have been repealed by the Statute Law (Repeals) Act 1977, s. 1(1), Sched. 1, Part I.

Although there are statutory provisions (Employment Protection (Consolidation) Act 1978, s. 58(3)) to prevent an employee being dismissed (without compensation) for not belonging to a specified trade union (see CLOSED SHOP), provided his objection to membership is genuinely on grounds of religious belief, the line between religion and conscience may be an extremely fine one, especially when conscience is claimed to stem from religion (see *Saggers* v. *British Railways Board* (*No. 2*) [1978] I.C.R. 1111, E.A.T.).

Consecration. The Burial Act 1900, has been repealed without replacement by the Statute Law (Repeals) Act 1978, s. 1, Sched. 1, Part XVII.

Consent. The Judicature Act 1925, s. 31(1)(*h*) (formerly the authority for the requirement of leave), has been repealed and replaced by the Supreme Court Act 1981, s. 18(1)(*d*).

In the law of tort and medical (negligence) cases the doctrine of "informed consent" has been closely examined, but effectively rejected (*Maynard* v. *West Midlands Regional Health Authority* [1984] 1 W.L.R. 634, H.L.); see also *Siddaway* v. *Bethlem and Maudsley Hospital* [1984] 2 W.L.R. 778, C.A. (and the rejection of the plaintiff's appeal by the House of Lords). The same rule applies to the question of the consent (if any) of a prisoner to medical treatment (*Freeman* v. *Home Office* [1984] Q.B. 524, C.A.).

In the Queen's Bench Division a special procedure was introduced in 1980 (revised in 1982) for obtaining by consent various common forms of order of judgment

(R.S.C. Ord. 45, r. 5A).

The circumstances in which a consent judgment or order may be set aside were reviewed in *Siebe Gorman Ltd.* v. *Pneupac Ltd.* [1982] 1 W.L.R. 185, C.A., where a distinction was drawn between cases which were based on a real (contractual) agreement to the order or judgment (in which, therefore, the judgment or order should not readily be set aside) and those where there was simply no objection to the proposed order or judgment (in which case the judgment or order would be more readily set aside).

Consent orders in matrimonial cases may be made in magistrates' courts under the Domestic Proceedings and Magistrates' Courts Act 1978, s. 6, when the person who is to receive any money payments may make an application for the necessary order. The procedure will in due course be available on the application of either party to the case but the amendment made by the Matrimonial and Family Proceedings Act 1984, s. 10, has not yet been brought into operation.

Consolidation Acts. The Interpretation Act 1889, s. 38(1), has been repealed and replaced by the Interpretation Act 1978 (itself a consolidation Act), which, in s. 17(2)(*a*), repeats the provision quoted, and adds (s. 17(2)(*b*)) that, in the same circumstances, "in so far as any subordinate legislation made or anything done under the enactment so repealed, or having effect as if so made or done, could have been made or done under the provision re-enacted, it shall have effect as if made or done under that provision."

Although earlier provisions consolidated into a "new edition" of a statute are a proper aid to the construction of the new Act, the modern practice of making amendments and then consolidating (see, *e.g.* the Limitation Amendment Act 1980 and the Limitation Act 1980) can cause problems of an unexpected nature (see *Di Palma* v. *Victoria Square Property Co. Ltd.* [1984] 2 W.L.R. 761 and *Jones* v. *Barnett* [1984] 3 W.L.R. 333).

Consolidation of actions. Comparable arrangements for consolidation of proceedings, and for selected actions ("test cases") to be dealt with while all cases except the selected one are stayed, exist in the county court (C.C.R. 1981, Ord. 13, r. 9, replacing the C.C.R. 1936, Ord. 17). The revision of 1981 assimilated the county court procedure to that delimited by the former R.S.C. Ord. 4, r. 10, which has been renumbered r. 9.

Consols. This form of government annuity was first provided for in the National Debt Act 1751 (25 Geo. II, c. 27), which was not finally repealed until 1870.

Consortium. See also BEREAVEMENT.

Conspiracy. Subject to exceptions, the common law criminal offence of conspiracy has been abolished (Criminal Law Act 1977, s. 5(1)). The common law relating to the offence of conspiracy to defraud remains in operation, and the new provisions do not relate to any case where the agreement in question amounts to a conspiracy to defraud at common law (s. 5(2)). The common law offence still applies to cases which involve entering into an agreement to engage in conduct which tends to corrupt public morals or which outrages public decency but which would not amount to or involve the commission of an offence if carried out by a single person otherwise than in pursuance of an agreement (s. 5(3)). Incitement and attempt to commit the offence of conspiracy (of whatever kind) are no longer criminal matters (s. 5(7)). The Conspiracy and Protection of Property Act 1875, s. 3, is no longer in force (Act of 1977, s. 5(11)).

The new provisions create an offence which consists in any person agreeing with any other person or persons that a course of conduct should be pursued which, if the agreement is carried out in accordance with their intentions, either (a) will necessarily amount to or involve the commission of an offence or offences by one or more of the parties to the agreement, or (b) would do so but for the existence of facts which render the commission of the offence (or any of them) impossible (Criminal Law Act 1977, s. 1(1) (as substituted by the Criminal Attempts Act 1981, s. 5(1))). Special provisions restrict the occasions when the offence may be committed in connection with any offence of strict liability and in comparable cases (s. 1(2)), and to prevent the commission of this offence in certain cases involving trade disputes (s. 1(3)). A person cannot be guilty of the statutory offence of conspiracy when he will be the victim of the offence which it is intended should be committed (s. 2). The penalty on conviction for conspiracy is normally the same as for the offence intended to be committed, with special provision for certain cases (s. 3). Proceedings for the new offence are normally required to be brought by or with the consent of the Director of Public Prosecutions (s. 4). See *R.* v. *Duncalf* [1979] 1 W.L.R. 918, C.A.

Constituency. Provision has been made for an increase in the number of constituencies in Northern Ireland (House of Commons (Redistribution of Seats) Act 1979). The Representation of the People Act 1949, s. 1, has been repealed and replaced by the Representation of the People Act 1983 s. 1, without change of effect.

Constructive notice. The operation of the doctrine of constructive notice (under the Law of Property Act 1925, s. 199) is excluded in certain cases: a purchaser who enters into a contract to buy unregistered land which is affected by a registered land charge is not treated as having notice of any land charge of which he is not actually aware (Law of Property Act 1969, s. 24). The person entitled to the benefit of a land charge which is thus "overruled" may be entitled to compensation (see the Act of 1969, s. 25).

Consul. Fresh provision has been made for fees to be prescribed for consular acts (Consular Fees Act 1980).

Consumer. "Dealing as a consumer" (as defined in the Unfair Contract Terms Act 1977, s. 12) confers special rights in prescribed cases (see UNFAIR CONTRACT TERMS).

Consumer credit. By May 19, 1985, the Consumer Credit Act 1974 will be fully in force (Consumer Credit Act (Commencement No. 8) Order 1983 (S.I. 1983 No. 1551)).

The financial levels controlling the application of the Act have been revised (Consumer Credit (Increase of Monetary Amounts) Order 1983 (S.I. 1983 No. 1571); Consumer Credit (Increase of Monetary Limits) Order 1983 (S.I. 1983 No. 1878)).

Consumer protection. The Consumer Protection Act 1961 and 1971, have been repealed and replaced by the Consumer Protection Act 1978, which preserved the orders made under the earlier legislation.

Contagious diseases. The Health Service and Public Health Act 1968, s. 27, has been repealed by the Public Health (Control of Diseases) Act 1984, s. 78, Sched. 3. The definition of "notifiable disease" in the Act of 1984 is the same as in the Public Health Act 1936, s. 343 (which has been repealed by the same provision).

Contempt of court. By the Contempt of Court Act 1981, fresh general provision was made in respect of this offence. Of special note are: magistrates' courts now have power to deal summarily with contempt of their proceedings (s. 11); restrictions are placed on the use of tape-recorders in courts, leave of the court being the sole effective justification (s. 9). Originally the penalties available to county courts were those prescribed for "inferior courts" (*Peart* v. *Stewart* [1983] 2 A.C. 109, H.L.), but by the County Courts (Penalties for Contempt) Act 1983, they were re-grouped with the Supreme Court. See also JURY and PRESS.

The County Courts Act 1959, ss. 157–162, have been repealed and replaced by the County Courts Act 1984, ss. 118–122, without change of effect.

Continental shelf. Special provision has been made for the application of certain employment legislation connected with the exploration or exploitation of areas of the continental shelf adjacent to areas already designated under the Act of 1964 (Employment (Continental Shelf) Act 1978).

Contraceptives. The Secretary of State is charged with the duty to arrange, to such extent as he thinks necessary, to meet all reasonable requirements in England and Wales for the giving of advice on contraception, the medical examination and treatment of people who seek advice on contraceptives, and the supply of contraceptive substances and appliances (National Health Service Act 1977, s. 5(1)(*b*)).

Contract. The restriction imposed on enforcement by action of a contract for the sale of land or of an interest in land requires the written note or memorandum to be signed by (or on behalf of) the person to be charged (Law of Property Act 1925, s. 40(1)). See also CONTRACT FOR SALE OF LAND.

Restrictions have been imposed on the use in consumer contracts of clauses excluding liability for breach of contract, negligence or other breach of duty (Unfair Contract Terms Act 1977). See UNFAIR CONTRACT TERMS.

Contract for sale. The Sale of Goods Act 1893, has been repealed and replaced by the Sale of Goods Act 1979, without change of effect other than to incorporate the amendments made in 1973 and 1977.

Contract for sale of land. The restriction imposed on enforcement by action of a contract for the sale of land or of an interest in land requires the written note or memorandum to be signed by (or on behalf of) the person to be charged (Law of Property Act 1925, s. 40(1)). A letter denying the existence of a contract falling within the statutory provisions cannot itself be used as the requisite statutory "note or memorandum" (*Law* v. *Jones* [1974] Ch. 112, citing *Thirkell* v. *Cambi* [1919] 2 K.B. 590).

The use of the phrase "subject to contract" has been the subject of various judicial interpretations (see *Law* v. *Jones* [1974] Ch. 112, C.A., distinguishing and not following earlier cases), but is now generally accepted as being effective to prevent the creation of the note or memorandum required under the Act to confer enforceability on the relationship between the correspondents (see *Tiverton Estates Ltd.* v. *Wearwell Ltd.* [1975] Ch. 146, C.A.).

The authority of a solicitor who is dealing with a sale of land includes the power to arrange the exchange of the contract by telephone (*Domb* v. *Isoz* [1980] Ch. 548, C.A.).

Contract, Freedom of. Further restrictions on freedom of contract have been introduced by the Unfair Contract Terms Act 1977, which precludes the use in consumer contracts of terms which would exclude liability for breach of contract, negligence or other breach of duty (see UNFAIR CONTRACT TERMS).

Contracting out. On the joint application of the persons who are or will be the landlord and the tenant in relation to a tenancy already or to be granted for a term of years certain under Part II of the Landlord and Tenant Act 1954 (which relates to security of tenure for business, professional and certain other tenants), the courts may authorise the inclusion of a clause which prevents the tenant applying for the grant of a further tenancy under the renewal provisions of the 1954 Act (Landlord and Tenant Act 1954, s. 38(4), added by the Law of Property Act 1969, s. 5).

See also OCCUPATIONAL PENSIONS BOARD.

Contribution. New general provision has been made by the Civil Liability (Contribution) Act 1978. The basic rule is that any person liable in respect of any damage suffered by any other person may recover contribution in respect of the same damage (irrespective of whether the first person's liability is joint with the first person's liability) (Act of 1978, s. 1(1)). This rule applies even though the claimant for contribution has ceased to be liable in respect of the damage in question since the time when the damage occurred, provided he was so liable immediately before he made or was ordered to make the payment in respect of which the contribution is sought (s. 1(2)), and notwithstanding that he has ceased to be liable in respect of the damage in question since the time when it occurred (unless his liability terminated on account of the expiration of a period of limitation) (s. 1(3)). Further provisions enable claims for contribution to be made by those who have settled or compromised claims made against them (s. 1(4)), and make relevant judgments within the United Kingdom conclusive as to certain matters in subsequent contribution proceedings (s. 1(5)).

The assessment of the contribution to be paid by each party is conducted by the court, the amount recoverable being (as in previous legislation) such sum as may be found to be just and equitable having regard to (each) party's responsibility for the damage in question (s. 2(1)). The order may require the contributor to pay all or any amount of the sum in question (s. 2(2), (3)), but must take account of any deduction required to be made on account of any contributory negligence or any limit imposed by or under any enactment or by any agreement made before the damage occurred (s. 2(3)).

Judgment recovered against any person liable in respect of any debt or damage is no bar to taking or continuing proceedings against any other person who is jointly liable in respect of the same debt or damage (s 3); this extends the abolition of common law rules to debt cases, tort proceedings alone have been dealt with originally by the Law Reform (Married Women and Tortfeasors) Act 1935, s. 6(1)(*a*) (now repealed). Special provision has been made for the situation where successive actions are brought against persons who are liable for the same damage, the costs of subsequent proceedings being disallowed unless the court is of the opinion that there was reasonable ground for bringing the later proceedings (s. 4). The new provisions bind the Crown (s. 5).

Somewhat comparable provisions in employment law have been introduced by the Employment Protection (Consolidation) Act 1978, ss. 76A–76C (added by the Employment Act 1980, s. 10, and s. 76A further revised in the Employment Act 1982, s. 7). The 1982 version of s. 76A contains amendments allowing the complainant to insist of the joinder of the third party, also extending (until the time when the tribunal makes its award) the time when a joinder may be effected. For picketing (*q.v.*) cases see the Act of 1978, s. 26A (added by the Act of 1980, s. 15(4), and a revised text of which was substituted by the Employment Act 1982, s. 11).

The Limitation Act 1963, s. 4, has been repealed and replaced by the Limitation Act 1980, s. 10. The Children and Young Persons Act 1963, s. 30, has been repealed and replaced by the Child Care Act 1980, s. 51, without change of effect.

Contributory negligence. Although contributory negligence is no defence in proceedings founded on conversion (*q.v.*) or on intentional trespass to goods (Torts (Interference with Goods) Act 1977, s. 11(1)), it may be pleaded in certain cases concerning bankers: in any circumstances in which proof of absence of negligence on the part of a banker would be a defence to proceedings by reason of the Cheques Act 1957, s. 4, a defence of contributory negligence is available to a banker (notwithstanding the provisions of the 1977 Act) (Banking Act 1979, s. 47).

It has been held that a plea of contributory negligence must be specifically pleaded (*Foukes* v. *Slaytor* [1983] 1 W.L.R. 1293, C.A.).

Convention. The repeal (in part) of the Tokyo Convention Act 1967, by the Civil Aviation Act 1982, does not affect its citation here.

Conversion. The tort of conversion now includes what was formerly known as detinue (*q.v.*), which has been abolished (Torts (Interference with Goods) Act 1977, s. 2(1)); an action now lies in conversion for loss or destruction of goods which a bailee has allowed to happen in breach of his duty to his bailor (Act of 1977, s. 2(2)). The forms of judgment available in an action for conversion have been prescribed (s. 3), and interlocutory relief may be granted in certain cases (s. 4). Payment of damages for wrongful interference with goods (defined in s. 1) may extinguish the claimant's title to the goods in question (s. 5(1)), but only when the claimant is compensated for the whole of his interest in the goods (s. 5(3)).

Special provision has been made for the cases of double liability for wrongful interference with goods (Act of 1977, s. 7), for compensation where there are competing rights to goods (s. 8), and for concurrent actions (s. 9). Contributory negligence is no defence to proceedings founded on conversion (Act of 1977, s. 11(1)), but this rule has been excluded from cases involving cheques (see CONTRIBUTORY NEGLIGENCE).

The Limitation Act 1939, has been repealed and replaced by the Limitation Act 1980, ss. 2 and 3, without significant change of effect.

Conversion, Equitable. The very existence of this doctrine is convincingly doubted at 100 L.Q.R. (1984) 84.

Conveyancing counsel. The Judicature Act 1925, s. 217, has been repealed and replaced by the Supreme Court Act 1981, s. 131, without change of effect.

Conviction. A conviction of an offence in respect of which an order of discharge (whether conditional or absolute) or a probation order is made ranks as a conviction only for certain (limited) purposes (Powers of Criminal Courts Act 1973, s. 13).

Convocation. The forms of writs for summoning and dissolving Convocation (S.I. 1970 No. 821), have been amended (Crown Office (Writs for Dissolving and Summoning Convocations) (Amendment) Rules 1975 (S.I. 1975 No. 802)) so as to provide for suffragan bishops elected to the Upper Houses.

Co-operative building society. Further provisions relating to the tax position of these organisations were introduced in the Income and Corporation Taxes Act 1970, ss. 341A, 342A (inserted by the Housing Act 1974, ss. 11, 120). Some of these organisations are within the "Miras" scheme under the Finance Act 1982, s. 26, Sched. 7 (see also BUILDING SOCIETY).

Co-operative Development Agency. For the establishment of this body, its functions and financial arrangements see the Co-operative Development Agency Act 1978: see also the Co-operative Development Agency and Industrial Development Act 1984, which provides both for the extension of the functions of the Agency (s. 2) and also for its dissolution (s. 3).

Copy. The various methods by which copies of documents may now be made for use in court proceedings are now delineated by R.S.C. Ord. 66. For the certification of office copies see R.S.C. Ord. 38, r. 10.

Copyright. Fresh provision has been made for penalties for offences relating to infringing copies of sound recordings and cinema films, together with the issue and execution of search warrants related to such offences (Copyright Act 1956, ss. 21(7A)–(7D), 21A, 21B (added by the Copyright (Amendment) Act 1983 ss. 1, 2)).

In Australia it has been held that a computer program is not a literary work and is therefore not protected by normal copyright provisions (*Apple Computer Inc.* v. *Computer Edge Pty.* [1984] F.S.R. 246, Fed. Ct. of Australia).

Coram non judice. The Justices Protection Act 1848, s. 2, has been repealed and replaced by the Justices of the Peace Act 1979, s. 45, without change of effect.

Corn returns. The Corn Returns Regulations 1974, have been revoked and replaced by the Corn Returns Regulations 1976 (S.I. 1976 No. 1035, as amended by S.I. 1979 No. 607, whereby a new form of return was prescribed).

Corn sales. The references in the Corn Sales Act 1921, to imperial pounds have been converted into references to kilograms (Corn Sales Act 1921 (Amendment) Regulations 1979 (S.I. 1979 No. 357)).

Corneal grafting. The Human Tissue Act 1961, ss. 2(1), 3, have been (prospectively) repealed by the Anatomy Act 1984, s. 13(2), in connection with a limited revision of the statutory provisions in respect of the use of bodies of dead persons for research and similar activities.

Cornwall. The statutory powers of management of the Duchy of Cornwall have been widened by the Duchy of Cornwall Management Act 1982.

Coroner. A coroner's inquest touching the death of a person who came by his death by murder, manslaughter or infanticide is no longer charged with a duty to find any person guilty of murder, manslaughter or infanticide, and the power to charge a person with these offences has been abolished (Criminal Law Act 1977, s. 56(1)). The coroner is no longer bound to summon a jury in the cases already mentioned, nor where the death was caused by an accident arising out of the use of a vehicle in a street or public highway (s. 56(2)). The text of the Coroners (Amendment) Act 1926, s. 20, has been amended as to make it normal practice for a coroner's inquest to be adjourned in the event of criminal proceedings being instituted in respect of cases involving murder, manslaughter or infanticide (Criminal Law Act 1977, s. 56(3), Sched. 10).

A coroner is no longer required to hold an inquest to view a body (Coroners Act 1980, s. 1), and now has power to hold an inquest in an area other than the one where the body lies (s. 2). Fresh provision (Act of 1980, s. 4) enables a coroner to order the exhumation of bodies.

The jury for a coroner's court is now selected under the same rules as a Crown Court or county court jury (Coroners Act 1887, s. 3A (inserted by the Coroners Juries Act 1983, s. 1)).

The rules of procedure have been codified (Coroners Rules 1984, S.I. 1984 No. 552).

Corporation. The Interpretation Act 1889, s. 19, has been repealed and replaced by the Interpretation Act 1978, s. 5, Sched. 1, without change of effect.

The Magistrates' Courts Act 1952, ss. 36, 132, Scheds. 2, 6, and amending legislation, have been repealed and replaced by the Magistrates' Courts Act 1980, s. 46, Sched. 3, without change of effect.

Corpse. The Public Health Act 1936, ss. 161–163, have been repealed by the Public Health (Control of Diseases) Act 1984, s. 78, Sched. 3. The Act of 1984, Part III (ss. 46–48), contains new general provisions governing the disposal of dead bodies; the new Act also repeats (in s. 45) the power to prevent the holding of a wake over the body of a person who died while suffering from a notifiable disease.

Corroboration. The provision governing personation proceedings (the Representation of the People Act 1949, s. 146(5)) has been repealed and replaced by the Representation of the People Act 1983, s. 168(5), without change of effect. The Road Traffic Regulation Act 1967, s. 78A, has been repealed and replaced by the Road Traffic Regulation Act 1984, s. 89(2), without change of effect. See also UNUS NULLUS, ETC.

Corrupt practices. The Parliamentary Elections Act 1868, s. 3, was repealed by the Election Commissioners Act 1949, s. 21, Sched., without replacement.

The Representation of the People Act 1949, ss. 146–151 (which dealt with proceedings for corrupt and illegal practices at parliamentary elections), have been repealed and replaced by the Representation of the People Act 1983, ss. 168–173, without change of effect.

Cost of Living Index. Another index has been established under the name Tax and Price Index (*q.v.*).

Cost of work payment. The War Damage Act 1943, has been repealed without replacement by the Statute Law (Repeals) Act 1981, s. 1(1), Sched. 1, Part XI.

Costs. Cost of a litigant in person (authorised in certain cases by the Litigants in Person (Costs and Expenses) Act 1975) are taxed under a special procedure laid down in R.S.C. Ord. 62, r. 28A.

Further directions relating to the VAT element in bills of costs have been issued; the current ones are noted in the Supreme Court Practice notes to R.S.C. Ord. 62, r. 22.

The Judicature Act 1925, s. 50, has been repealed and replaced by the Supreme Court Act 1981, s. 51, without change of effect. The County Courts Act 1959, s. 47 (which dealt with the costs of cases commenced in the High Court but which could have been commenced in a county court), has been repealed and replaced by the County Courts Act 1984, s. 19, without change of effect. The County Courts Act 1959, s. 60, has been repealed and replaced by the County Courts Act 1984, s. 29. The C.C.R. 1936, Ord. 37, r. 1, has been revoked and replaced by the C.C.R. 1981, Ord. 38, r. 3; the scales are revised periodically.

Costs in criminal proceedings. The Costs in Criminal Cases (Allowances) Regulations 1975, have been revoked and replaced by S.I. 1977 No. 2069; the sums payable are revised periodically. By the Costs in Criminal Cases Act 1973, s. 17 (as amended by the Administration of Justice Act 1977, s. 2, Sched. 2, Part I), certain costs and allowances are paid out at rates which are determined administratively.

The Magistrates' Courts Act 1952, s. 55, has been repealed and replaced by the Magistrates' Courts Act 1980, s. 64, without change of effect. The Magistrates' Courts (Matrimonial Proceedings) Act 1960, has been repealed and replaced by the Domestic Proceedings and Magistrates' Courts Act 1978, by which a fresh code of matrimonial practice has been introduced.

Cotton industry. The Cotton Industry Act 1959, has been repealed by the Statute Law (Repeals) Act 1977, s. 1(1) Sched. 1, Part XIX, without replacement.

Counsel and procure. For the power of a magistrates' court to deal with a person who "aids, abets, counsels or procures the commission by another person of a summary offence" as if he were committing the same offence see the Magistrates' Courts Act 1980, ss. 44 (replacing the Magistrates' Courts Act 1952, s. 35).

Counterclaim. The C.C.R. 1936, Ord. 9, rr. 9–11, have been revoked and replaced by the C.C.R. 1981, Ord. 9, rr. 1, 2, 16, with slight modifications. The Judicature Act 1925, s. 203, has been repealed without replacement by the Supreme Court Act 1981, s. 152(4), Sched. 7; the High Court has a wide general power to control inferior courts and tribunals (see the Supreme Court Act 1981, ss. 29, 30) so that the specific provision had become otiose.

Counterfeit coin. Fresh provision has been made to punish the production and issue of counterfeit coins (Forgery and Counterfeiting Act 1981, Part II (ss. 14–28)).

County. The Administration of Justice Act 1973, s. 1(1), has been repealed and replaced by the Justices of the Peace Act 1979, s. 1(1), continuing in operation the "commission areas" established by the 1973 Act (*i.e.* every county, every London commission area and the City of London).

County associations. The Auxiliary Forces Act 1953, ss. 2–10 (and amending legislation), have been repealed and replaced by the Reserve Forces Act 1980, ss. 121–127, without change of effect.

County bridge. The Highways Act 1959, s. 23, was repealed by the Local Government Act 1972, s. 272, Sched. 30, without replacement. The bridges which were formerly designated "county bridges" became "bridges maintainable at the public expense" under the Highways Act 1959, s. 48(6) (as amended by the Local Government Act 1972, Sched. 21, Part I, para. 18(3)). The Act of 1959, s. 48(6), has now been repealed and replaced by the Highways Act 1980, s. 40(8), (9), without change of effect.

County council. The Places of Religious Worship Act 1812, was repealed (in its entirety) without replacement by the Statute Law (Repeals) Act 1977, s. 1(1), Sched. 1, Part V.

County courts. Further principal amendments to the jurisdiction and functions of county courts have been made by the Litigants in Person (Costs and Expenses) Act 1975, the Sex Discrimination Act 1975, the Domestic Violence and Matrimonial Proceedings Act 1976, the Race Relations Act 1976, the Administration of Justice Act 1977 (especially ss. 12–20), the Charging Orders Act 1979, the Contempt of Court Act 1981 (as modified by the County Courts (Penalties for Contempt Act 1983), the Supreme Court Act 1981 (which contains new provisions for the inter-relationship of county courts and the Supreme Court and for the transfer of cases between the two systems), the Administration of Justice Act 1982 (especially Part V (ss. 29–37)), and the County Courts Act 1984 (which consolidated the enactments which provide for the constitution of county courts and the general administration of the county court system). The procedural rules have been constantly under review, and a significant change was effected by the replacement of the C.C.R. 1936 by the C.C.R. 1981 (S.I. 1981 No. 1687—already heavily amended).

Qualification for appointment as a circuit judge has been modified so that a recorder of three years' standing may now be appointed (Courts Act 1971, s. 16(3); Administration of Justice Act 1977, s. 12).

The jurisdiction of county courts was increased in money value by the County Courts Jurisdiction Order 1977 (S.I. 1977 No. 600), the new limits then being £2,000 for the general common law jurisdiction and £15,000 for the equity side and probate matters. The financial limits on admiralty matters were also increased (Administration of Justice Act 1977, s. 15). The common law jurisdiction has again been increased, as has the equity side, to £5,000 and £30,000, respectively (County Courts Jurisdiction Order 1981 (S.I. 1981 No. 1123)). These revised limits have been incorporated into the County Courts Act 1984 (see s. 147(1)) and there is power (s. 145) to revise the limits of jurisdiction from time to time.

County courts now have a limited power to grant injunctions and to make declarations in respect of land (Act of 1984, s. 22, replacing the Act of 1959, s. 51A (which was added by the Administration of Justice Act 1977, s. 14). It has been held that the ancillary jurisdiction (Act of 1984, s. 38, replacing the Act of 1959, s. 74) extends to granting an injunction (not restricted to land) even though the money claim to which the claim for the injunction is linked is for a virtually nominal amount (*Hatt & Co. (Bath) Ltd.* v. *Pearce* [1978] 1 W.L.R. 885, C.A.: claim for £1 damages and an injunction).

County courts have been chosen to hear certain matters under the Sex Discrimination Act 1975 (s. 66) and under the Race Relations Act 1976 (s. 67).

Rights of audience have been extended: the Lord Chancellor has been empowered to issue Directions specifying persons in relevant legal employment who may enjoy a right of audience (Act of 1959, s. 89A. Administration of Justice Act 1977, s. 16, now both repealed and replaced by the County Courts Act 1984, s. 61), and by the County Courts (Rights of Audience) Direction 1978 this right was conferred on Fellows of the Institute of Legal Executives.

Further alterations to the detailed procedures of county courts include the following matters. References to arbitration (Act of 1984, s. 64, replacing the Act of 1959, s. 92) no longer need an order of the court, but may be made on the request of the parties (the Administration of Justice Act 1977, s. 17, introduced this). There is power for the register of judgments in future to be limited to cases involving such sum as may be specified by order, instead of a sum (currently £10) contained in an Act of Parliament (see the Act of 1984, s. 73). Registrars' duties and those of the Chief Clerk have been redistributed so as to leave the registrars free to take on more judicial work (Act of 1977, s. 19). Service of process may now be proved by certificate instead of having to be endorsed on the process in question (Act of 1984, s. 33, replacing the Act of 1977, s. 20; see SERVICE).

County courts deal with the vast majority of divorce (*q.v.*) proceedings (all the undefended suits being allocated to them): the list of courts which are designated "divorce county courts" is under constant review and is currently contained in the Civil Courts Order 1983 (S.I. 1983 No. 713).

The forms of address for judges in court are now contained in *Practice Direction* [1982] 1 W.L.R. 101 (revoking and substantially repeating earlier comparable provisions).

County elector. The Representation of the People Act 1949, has been repealed and replaced by the Representation of the People Act 1983, without significant change of effect.

County franchise. The Representation of the People Act 1949, has been repealed and replaced by the Representation of the People Act 1983, without significant change of effect.

County palatine. The Durham (County Palatine) Act 1836, was repealed without replacement by the Statute Law (Repeals) Act 1976, s. 1(1), Sched. 1, Part I.

County roads. The Highways Act 1959, ss. 21–25, were repealed by the Local Government Act 1972, s. 272, Sched. 30, without replacement. The roads which were formerly designated "county roads" became "roads maintainable at the public expense" (see COUNTY BRIDGE). For the powers of local authorities to maintain roads see the Act of 1972 ss. 187, 188.

Court. When the provisions of R.S.C. Ord. 53, were revised in 1977 (S.I. 1977 No. 1955), the rule using the expression "court or a judge" and the related definition (the former Ord. 53, r. 1(4)) was revoked without replacement. In connection with the new provisions for applications for judicial review and applications for leave to apply for such a review, however, any reference to "the court" includes a reference to a judge (Ord. 53, r. 14).

Court of Appeal. The constitution and working of the Court of Appeal (both the Criminal and Civil Divisions) have been repealed and re-enacted (in slightly modified form) by the Supreme Court Act 1981, ss. 2, 3 (judges), 15–18 (jurisdiction), and 53–60 (practice and procedure). For the most part the new Act has made minor (if any) changes, but there has been introduced a Registrar of Civil Appeals (Act of 1981, s. 88, Sched. 2) whose appointment is intended to relieve the purely judicial members of the Court of Appeal of routine administrative and similar matters. In both Divisions of the court it is now possible for two judges to constitute a full court for final judgments. The use made of time spent in hearing an appeal is intended to be improved by the use of skeleton arguments lodged before the hearing (*Practice Note* [1983] 1 W.L.R. 1055).

Court of Chancery. The Judicature Act 1925, ss. 18(2), 56(1), have been repealed and replaced by the Supreme Court Act 1981, ss. 5(1)(a), 19, 61, without change of effect.

Court of Protection. The Mental Health Act 1959, ss. 100, 115(1), 101–103, 103A, 104–107, 110, 111, have been repealed and replaced by the Mental Health Act 1983, ss. 93, 93–101, 104, 105, without significant change of effect.

Power has been granted (in the Administration of Justice Act 1982, s. 60, amending the Supreme Court Act 1981, s. 89(6)) to abolish the office of Deputy Master in the Court of Protection, and it has been exercised (S.I. 1982 No. 1755).

The procedural requirements of the Court have been consolidated into the Court of Protection Rules 1984 (S.I. 1984 No. 2035).

Court of summary jurisdiction. The Interpretation Act 1889, s, 13(11), has been repealed and replaced by the Interpretation Act 1978, s. 5, Sched. 1, without change of effect.

The Magistrates' Courts Act 1952, s. 124,

has been repealed and replaced by the Magistrates' Courts Act 1980, s. 148, without change of effect.

Courts of survey. For the (prospective) repeal of the Merchant Shipping Act 1894, ss. 289–345, and Part VI (ss. 464–491), see the Merchant Shipping Act 1970, s. 100(3), Sched. 5.

Courts of the Universities. The jurisdiction of the courts of the universities has been restricted to those matters which are referred to them by the statutes of the universities (Administration of Justice Act 1977, s. 23).

Covenant. County, district and various London councils may enter into agreements for the development of land; upon being registered as local land charges these agreements become enforceable against successors in title of the owner of the land affected, even though the agreement requires the carrying out of works (Housing Act 1974, s. 126). These agreements provide a form of exception to the usual rule that the only covenants which may be made to run with the land are those which are negative in nature.

The Limitation Act 1939, s. 2(3), has been repealed and replaced by the Limitation Act 1980, s. 8, without change of effect.

Cran. The Cran Measures Act 1908, has been repealed by the Weights and Measures Act 1979, s. 23(2), Sched. 7, without replacement.

Cream. The Food and Drugs Act 1955, ss. 47, 48, 135, have been repealed and replaced by the Food Act 1984, ss. 48, 49, 132, without change of effect.

Credit. The provisions of the Theft Act 1968, s. 16(2)(*a*), have been repealed and fresh provision has been made by the Theft Act 1978, ss. 1–3, which create specific offences of obtaining services by a deception (s. 1), evasion of liability by deception (s. 2) and making off without payment (s. 3). See DECEPTION.

Credit cards. The £30 limit mentioned has been increased to £50.

Credit-sale agreement. For the revised levels of the various limits controlling the application of the Consumer Credit Act 1974, see the Consumer Credit (Increase of Monetary Amounts) Order 1983, S.I. 1983 No. 1571, and the Consumer Credit (Increase of Monetary Limits) Order 1983, S.I. 1983 No. 1878.

Credit union. Formerly not the subject of specific legislation, credit unions were capable of registration as limited companies under the Companies Acts, or under the Industrial and Provident Societies Act 1965. The Credit Unions Act 1979, provides for their registration under the Act of 1965, but with supplementary provisions appropriate to their particular functions. They now come under the supervision of the Registrar (ss. 17–20) and are required to be insured in respect of fraud or other dishonesty (ss. 15, 16).

Creditor. The minimum debt to support a bankruptcy petition has been increased successively to £200 (Bankruptcy Act 1914, s. 4(1)(*a*) (as amended by the Insolvency Act 1976, s. 1, Sched. 1, Part I)), and then to £750 (Insolvency Proceedings (Increase in Monetary Limits) Regulations 1984 (S.I. 1984 No. 1199)). The minimum debt to service a statutory demand leading on to a winding-up petition has also been raised to £200 (Companies Act 1948, s. 223(1) (as amended by the Insolvency Act 1976, s. 1, Sched. 1, Part I))), and then £750 (Insolvency Proceedings (Increase in Monetary Limits) Regulations 1984 (S.I. 1984 No. 1199)).

Cremation. Further provisions governing the documentation authorising cremation of the remains of a person who died outside England and Wales are set out in the Cremation Regulations 1979 (S.I. 1979 No. 1138). The Human Tissue Act 1961, s. 3, has been (prospectively) repealed by the Anatomy Act 1984, s. 13(2), without replacement. The reference to cremation is not repeated, its place being taken by the expression "decent disposal" (Act of 1984, ss. 5(3), 8(1)(*a*)).

Crier. The Judicature Act 1925, s. 226(2), has been repealed without replacement by the Supreme Court Act 1981, s. 152(4), Sched. 7.

Criminal appeal. The rule in *Gelberg* v. *Miller* [1961] 1 W.L.R. 459, H.L. has been re-affirmed by *Practice Direction* [1979] 1 W.L.R. 498, in which it is advised that petitions to appeal to the House in criminal cases in respect of which no certificate has been granted by the court below under the Administration of Justice Act 1960, s. 1(2), or the Criminal Appeal Act 1968, s. 33(2), will not be received in the Judicial Office.

The constitution of the Court of Appeal (Criminal Division) has been re-enacted in the Supreme Court Act 1981, ss. 2, 3, 9–18, 53–60, which replace the earlier legislation without significant change of effect.

Criminal conversation. The abolition of the right to a claim for damages for this wrong was effected by the Law Reform (Miscellaneous Provisions) Act 1970, s. 4 (now repealed).

Criminal evidence. The rule that a defendant in criminal proceedings loses the protection from being asked any question which tends to show that he is of bad character if he gives evidence against any other person charged with the same offence (*i.e.* the Criminal Evidence Act 1898, s. 1(f)(iii)) has been repealed and replaced by a more widely-ranging provision, so that the protection is withdrawn when the accused gives evidence against any other person charged in the same proceedings (Criminal Evidence Act 1979, s. 1(1), reversing the severe restrictions imposed by the decision in *R.* v. *Hills* [1980] A.C. 26, H.L.).

For witness orders see also the Criminal Procedure (Attendance of Witnesses) Act 1965.

Criminal injuries compensation. The scheme for claiming and awarding compensation is periodically revised and certain new provisions came into force in October 1979. An important innovation at that time was the extension of the scheme to crimes of violence within the family. A three-year time limit has been put upon the making of claims, and minimum sums in respect of which an awards will be made laid down. In 1979 this was £150 in an ordinary case and £500 in cases where the injuries were caused by a member of the claimant's family. Claims may be made in respect of any crime of violence, including arson and poisoning offences. Awards may also be reduced to take account of any benefits received under the social security schemes of the United Kingdom or of any other state, or any award made under the Northern Ireland scheme, or any payments made to the claimant under insurance schemes (other than those for which the claimant has been paying the premiums).

The minimum level of payment now made (in "non-family" cases) by the Criminal Injuries Compensation Board is £400 (see [1983] C.L.Y. 601).

The Board regularly publishes lists of "sample" awards for the purpose of illustration (see, *e.g.* [1984] 6 C.L. 100a).

Criminal lunatic. The Mental Health Act 1959, has been repealed and replaced by the Mental Health Act 1983, with minimal exceptions.

Crimp. All the provisions of the Merchant Shipping Act 1894, mentioned have been (prospectively) repealed by the Merchant Shipping Act 1970, s. 100(3), Sched. 5. In the meantime the penalties under the Act of 1894, ss. 111, 112, have been (prospectively) increased to a maximum fine (*q.v.*) of £50 on summary conviction (Merchant Shipping Act 1979, s. 43, Sched. 6, Part I).

Crossed cheques. In cases where proof of absence of negligence on the part of a banker would be a defence in proceedings by virtue of the Cheques Act 1957, s. 4, a defence of contributory negligence will be available to the banker notwithstanding the provisions of the Torts (Interference with Goods) Act 1977, s. 11 (Banking Act 1979, s. 47).

Crown. The Interpretation Act 1889, s. 30, has been repealed and replaced by the Interpretation Act 1978, ss. 10, 21(1); although the Act of 1978 does not mention the Crown in the substantive provisions (s. 10), the effect of the provision is substantially the same, and all the provisions of the Act are expressly applied to the Crown (s. 21(2)).

Crown Agents for the Colonies. The Crown Agents have been re-constituted as a body corporate under the name "Crown Agents for Overseas Governments and Administrations", their duties, privileges and immunities also being provided for (Crown Agents Act 1979). Appointments to the office of Crown Agent are to be made by the Minister for Overseas Development (s. 1(2)–(4)).

Crown Court. A recorder of three years' standing may now be appointed circuit judge (Administration of Justice Act 1977, s. 12, amending the Courts Act 1971, s. 16(3)). The classes of case and division of trial lists (Supreme Court Act 1981, s. 75(1), replacing the Courts Act 1971, s. 4(5)) are now contained in the *Practice Directions*

[1971] 1 W.L.R. 1535, 1763; [1972] 1 W.L.R. 5; [1973] 1 W.L.R. 73 and [1978] 1 W.L.R. 926. These divide criminal matters into four classes of descending seriousness, requiring Class 1 cases to be heard by a High Court judge, Class 2 cases by a High Court judge except when a particular case is released by or on the authority of a presiding judge (*i.e.* a High Court judge assigned to have special responsibility for a particular circuit), Class 3 and Class 4 classes being allocated for trial by a High Court judge, or a circuit judge or a recorder.

The procedure of the Crown Court is now set out in the consolidated Crown Court Rules 1982 (S.I. 1982 No. 1109, already amended several times).

The modes of address (which remain as previously) in the Crown Court are now prescribed by *Practice Direction* [1982] 1 W.L.R. 101.

Crown Office. The Judicature Act 1925, ss. 104 *et seq.*, and the Courts Act 1971, s. 26, have been repealed and replaced by the Supreme Court Act 1981, ss. 96 *et seq.* and 89, respectively, without change of effect.

Crown privilege. In *Conway* v. *Rimmer* [1968] A.C. 910, H.L. it was ruled that the minister's claim that a document attracted Crown privilege was not necessarily conclusive of the question, and that the judge might inspect a document in respect of which the privilege was claimed. Further limitations on the use of this method of avoiding disclosure of documents may be seen in the following cases: *R.* v. *Lewes Justices, ex p. Secretary of State for the Home Department* [1973] A.C. 388, H.L. *Norwich Pharmacal Co.* v. *Customs and Excise Commissioners* [1974] A.C. 133, H.L.; *D.* v. *National Society for the Prevention of Cruelty to Children* [1978] A.C. 171, H.L. See also *Burmah Oil Co. Ltd.* v. *Bank of England* [1980] A.C. 1090, H.L., in which the House of Lords exercised the right to inspect the documents in question before making the final ruling on whether they should be ordered to be produced.

Crown proceedings. In these proceedings the Crown enjoys the benefit of specialised procedural provisions: see R.S.C. Ord. 77 and the C.C.R. 1981, Ord. 42.

Cruelty. Matrimonial orders are no longer made on this ground in magistrates' courts, their matrimonial jurisdiction having been revised by the Domestic Proceedings and Magistrates' Courts Act 1978.

Cruelty to animals. The Diseases of Animals Act 1950, has been repealed and replaced by the Animal Welfare Act 1981, without change of effect.

Cruelty to children. Reports of cruelty to children are the subject of a special form of privilege and the National Society for the Prevention of Cruelty to Children will not be ordered to disclose its sources of information (*D.* v. *National Society for the Prevention of Cruelty to Children* [1978] A.C. 171, H.L.).

The Children and Young Persons Act 1933, s. 19, was repealed and replaced by the Employment of Children Act 1973, s. 1, which authorises the Secretary of State to make regulations controlling the employment of children.

Curator bonis. English law knows of no such representative as the one who may be appointed under certain foreign systems to deal with the estates of merely missing people; in the normal case the only proper way to come before the court is as an executor or administrator (on the presumed death of the missing person) *Kamouh* v. *Associated Electrical Industries International Ltd.* [1980] Q.B. 199).

The Mental Health Act 1959, ss. 117, 152, have been repealed and replaced by the Mental Health Act 1983, s. 110, without change of effect.

Currency notes. The standards required for certain coins have been varied (Coinage Act 1971, s. 1 (as substituted by the Currency Act 1983, s. 1)), the limits on the fiduciary note issue changed (Act of 1983, s. 2), and unpresented bank notes which are no longer legal tender have been written off (Act 1983, s. 3).

Curteyn, Curtana. The sword known by this name now used at the coronation of the Kings and Queens of England first appeared at the coronation of Charles II.

Custodians of Enemy Property. All the provisions of the Enemy Property Act 1953, except ss. 4(1), (2), 16, 18, have been repealed by the Statute Law (Repeals) Act 1976, s. 1(1), Sched. 1, Part XIX.

Custody of children. The Administration of Justice Act 1970, s. 1, Sched. 1, have been repealed and replaced by the Supreme

Court Act 1981, s. 61(1), (3), Sched. 1, para. 3, without change of effect.

Customs. Substantial portions of the Customs and Excise Act 1952 (as variously amended), have been repealed and replaced by further consolidating Acts, which, however, divide into smaller portions the statute law in question: the new legislation comprises the Customs and Excise Management Act 1979, the Customs and Excise Duties (General Reliefs) Act 1979, the Alcoholic Liquor Duties Act 1979, the Hydrocarbon Oil Duties Act 1979, the Matches and Mechanical Lighters Duties Act 1979, the Tobacco Products Duties Act 1979, and the Excise Duties (Surcharges or Rebates) Act 1979. These Acts may be collectively cited as the Customs and Excise Acts 1979 (Customs and Excise Management Act 1979, s. 178(2)), and now constitute the central corpus of the law relating to customs and excise.

With minor exceptions, the Import Duties Act 1958, has been (prospectively) repealed by the European Communities Act 1972, s. 4, Sched. 3, Part I, as has the Customs Duties (Dumping and Subsidies) Act 1969.

Customs airport. The Customs and Excise Act 1952, ss. 15 *et seq.*, have been repealed and replaced by the Customs and Excise Management Act 1979, ss. 4, 21 *et seq.*, without change of effect.

Customs entries. The Customs and Excise Act 1952, s. 32, has been repealed and replaced by the Customs and Excise Management Act 1979, s. 41; the fine on failure to comply with the statutory provision was increased to £50, but otherwise the earlier provisions were repealed without change of effect (but see also FINE).

Cyanide fumigation. The Hydrogen Cyanide (Fumigation) Act 1937, ss. 3–5, Sched., have been repealed by the Hydrogen Cyanide (Fumigation) Act 1937 (Repeals and Modifications) Regulations 1974 (S.I. 1974 No. 1840), which have also amended the other provisions of the Act so as to bring the operation of the controls imposed on this form of fumigation within the terms of the Health and Safety at Work, etc. Act 1974.

Cycle track. The Highways Act 1959, ss. 66, 295(1), were repealed and replaced by the Highways Act 1980, ss. 65, 329(1), without change of effect. The Cycle Track Act 1984, s. 1(1), amends the 1980 Act, s. 329(1), so as to exclude pedal cycles which are motor vehicles within the meaning of the Road Traffic Act 1972. The new Act also regulates the construction, use and compensation in relation to cycle tracks. The detailed schemes to implement the Act include the Cycle Tracks Regulations 1984 (S.I. 1984 No. 1431). See also BICYCLE.

D

Dairies. The Food and Drugs Act 1955, ss. 28, 31, 32, 37, 38, 43–45, 47, 48, have been repealed and replaced by the Food Act 1984, ss. 32, 35, 36, 40, 41, 45, 46, 48, 49, respectively, without change of effect. The Food and Drugs (Milk) Act 1970, has been repealed and replaced by the Food Act 1984, ss. 1(1), 2, and the Agriculture (Miscellaneous Provisions) Act 1972, s. 3, has been repealed and replaced by the Animal Health Act 1981, s. 35(1), without change of effect.

Damage, Criminal. The offence of causing criminal damage by destroying or damaging property (under the Criminal Damage Act 1971, s. 1(1), (2)) is triable either way (see the Magistrates' Courts Act 1980, ss. 17 *et seq.*, replacing the Criminal Law Act 1977, ss. 16, 19 *et seq.*, for the meaning of this term and the procedures to be followed), except where the value of the damage involved is less than £200 (Magistrates' Courts Act 1980, s. 22, replacing the Criminal Law Act 1977, s. 23(1)), when the offence becomes triable only summarily (*ibid.*). For the revision of the general levels of fines on summary conviction see FINE.

Damages. The Sale of Goods Act 1893, ss. 49–51, have been repealed and replaced by the Sale of Goods Act 1979, ss. 49–51, without change of effect.

The remedy for a breach of warranty (see the Sale of Goods Act 1979, s. 14, for warranties of reasonable fitness for the purpose for which goods are sold and for warranties of reasonable quality) is a set-off against the price or an action for damages (Act of 1979, s. 53(1)). In the latter case the measure of damages is the estimated loss arising directly and naturally resulting in the ordinary course of events from the breach of warranty (s. 53(2)—stated in *Parsons* (*Livestock*) *Ltd.* v. *Uttley Ingham & Co. Ltd.* [1978] Q.B. 791, C.A., to be a statutory codification of the rule in *Hadley* v. *Baxendale* (1854) 9 Exch. 341). The rule in *Hadley* v. *Baxendale* has been further considered in *Victoria Laundries* (*Windsor*) *Ltd.* v. *Newman Industries Ltd.* [1949] 2 K.B. 528. C.A., *C. Czarnikow Ltd.* v. *Koufos* (*The Heron II*) [1969] 1 A.C. 350, H.L., and in *Parsons* (*Livestock*) *Ltd.* v. *Uttley Ingham & Co. Ltd.* (above). See MEASURE OF DAMAGES.

The rule in *Bain* v. *Fothergill* (1874) L.R. 7 H.L. 158, has been considered in *Malhotra* v. *Choudhury* [1980] Ch. 52, C.A. In that case it was held that when a defendant vendor fails to take reasonable steps to try to carry out his obligations under a contract for the sale of land, the damages should be assessed without reference to the restrictions imposed by the rule in *Bain* v. *Fothergill.* In Canada, where there is a Torrens system of registration of title to land, the rule in *Bain* v. *Fothergill* has been rejected (*A.V.B. Management Science* v. *Barwell Developments* [1979] 1 W.W.R. 330, Canadian Supreme Court).

Damages as an alternative to an order for specific performance of a contract for the sale of land or of an interest in land have been considered by the House of Lords (*Johnson* v. *Agnew* [1980] A.C. 367), and it was ruled that in the event of non-compliance with an order for specific performance the plaintiff might apply to the court for an award of damages, such an award being assessed on the normal common law principles.

Damages may also be awarded for distress and anxiety caused by breach of contract (*Jarvis* v. *Swans Tours Ltd.* [1973] Q.B. 233, C.A.; *Jackson* v. *Horizon Holidays Ltd.* [1975] 1 W.L.R. 1468, C.A.; *Heywood* v. *Wellers* [1976] Q.B. 446, C.A.).

Industrial tribunals are empowered to award damages in cases involving unfair dismissal (*q.v.*), racial discrimination or sex discrimination.

Certain foreign jurisdictions allow an award of multiple damages, and in prescribed cases the excess over the normal English award may be recovered by action in the English courts (Protection of Trading Interests Act 1980, s. 6).

The Judicature Act 1925, s. 49, has been repealed and replaced by the Supreme Court Act 1981, s. 36, without change of effect. It has been provided that a claim for exemplary damages must be specifically pleaded (R.S.C. Ord. 18, r. 8(3)).

Prospective provision has been made under which it will be possible for the court to make a provisional award of damages for personal injuries when there is proved or admitted to be a chance that at some definite or indefinite time in the future the injured person will (as a result of the act or omission which gave rise to the cause of action) develop some serious disease or suffer some serious deterioration in his physical or mental condition (Supreme Court Act 1981, s. 32A, added by the Administration of Justice Act 1982, s. 6).

Damnum sentit dominus. The Sale of Goods Act 1893, ss. 7, 21, 32, have been repealed and replaced by the Sale of Goods Act 1979, ss. 7, 21, 32, 33, without change of effect.

Dancing-house. The Public Health Acts Amendment Act 1890, s. 3, was repealed by the Local Government Act 1972, s. 272(1), Sched. 30. Section 51 of the 1890 Act was repealed by the Local Government (Miscellaneous Provisions) Act 1982, s.47, Sched. 7, Part I, as were s. 6 of the Act of 1967, and the Home Counties (Music and Dancing) Licensing Act 1926. Entertainments in public places are now regulated by local authorities (Act of 1982, s. 1).

Dangerous driving. The offence formerly provided for by the Road Traffic Act 1972, s. 2, has been abolished and replaced by the offence of reckless driving (Criminal Law Act 1977, s. 50(1), substituting into the Act of 1972, s. 2, a new text which reads: "A person who drives a motor vehicle on a road recklessly shall be guilty of an offence"). The offence of causing death by dangerous driving has been similarly abolished and replaced by the offence of causing death by reckless driving (Act of 1977, s. 10(1), substituting a new text for the Road Traffic Act 1972, s. 1). The punishments and procedural requirements have not been altered. The meaning of the term "reckless" has been considered by the Court of Appeal (see *R.* v. *Murphy* [1980] R.T.R. 145), without clarifying the mental element in the offence. (For recklessness in the general criminal law see *R.* v. *Lawrence* [1982] A.C. 510, H.L. and *R.* v. *Caldwell* [1982] A.C. 341, H.L.).

Dangerous place. The Highways Act 1959, s. 144, and the Highways Act 1971, s. 34, have been repealed and jointly replaced by the Highways Act 1980, s. 165, without change of effect.

Dangerous premises. The Occupiers' Liability Act 1957 has been modified by the provisions of the Occupiers' Liability Act 1984.

Dangerous structure. The Highways Act 1959, s. 144, and the Highways Act 1971, s. 34, have been repealed and jointly replaced by the Highways Act 1980, s. 165, without change of effect.

Dans locum contractui. This maxim has been modified by the terms of the Misrepresentation Act 1967, s. 1, which provides that where a person has entered into a contract after a misrepresentation has been made to him, and the misrepresentation has become a term of the contract or the contract has been performed (or both), if otherwise he would be entitled to rescind the contract without alleging fraud, he may rescind the contract even though the misrepresentation has become a term of the contract or the contract has been performed.

Data. For provisions relating to data protection and checks on the accuracy of records see the Data Protection Act 1984; see also COPYRIGHT.

Date. By R.S.C. Ord. 6, r. 7(3), a writ is issued on being sealed by an officer of the court office out of which it is issued; the seal shows the date on which it is applied, and so dates the issue of the writ. This is especially important in any postal application for the issue of a writ (see *Practice Direction* [1971] 1 W.L.R. 75, para. (5)).

In proceedings in the Supreme Court, the rule in *Williams* v. *Burgess* (1840) has been displaced by R.S.C. Ord. 3, r. 2(2), which is substantially the same in effect; where an act has to be done within or not less than a specified period before a given date, the period ends immediately before that date (R.S.C. Ord. 3, r. 2(3)). There are further provisions for calculating specified periods of "days" and "clear days" and for the exclusion of certain days (*e.g.* Christmas Day) (Ord. 3, r. 2(4), (5)).

The Forgery Act 1913, s. 1(2), has been repealed and replaced by the Forgery and Counterfeiting Act 1981, s. 9(1)(*g*), without significant change of effect.

Day to show cause. The procedure appears to come within the terms of R.S.C. Ord. 80, r. 2 (see note 12 to that rule).

Days of grace. The granting of days of grace on policies of insurance under the Road Traffic Act 1972, s. 143 (which relates to insurance against third-party risks or some security in respect of such risks), is not a normal practice, most policies specifically excluding such an extension of the insurer's liability.

De fide et officio judicis non recepitur quaestio; sed de scientia sive error sit juris sive facti. By virtue of the Justices of the Peace Act 1979, ss. 44–47, magistrates are afforded a protection comparable to that enjoyed by judges of superior courts. See, however, *In re McC* (*a minor*) [1984] 3 W.L.R. 1227, H.L.).

Dead ripe land. The Town and Country Planning Act 1947, s. 80, was repealed without replacement by the Town and Country Planning Act 1962, s. 223, Sched. 15.

Deaf and dumb. The Chronically Sick and Disabled Persons Act 1970, s. 25, has been repealed by the Education Act 1981, s. 21, Sched. 4. The 1981 Act enacted a new general scheme for the provision of education for children with "special educational needs" (see s. 1).

Dean. The office of dean is normally vacated at the age of 70 years, and this is normally the greatest age at which an appointment may be made; there are special provisions relating to certain posts which allow a dean to be appointed or to retain office above this age (Ecclesiastical Officers (Age Limit) Measure 1975).

Death. The Carriage by Air Act 1932, has been repealed and replaced by the Carriage by Air Act 1961, and the Carriage by Air

(Supplementary Provisions) Act 1962, the essential provisions of which are those which brought the terms of the Warsaw Convention (as amended from time to time) into English law. Further alterations to the Warsaw Convention have been made by the Protocols signed in Montreal in 1975, and those amendments are taken into account in the text of the Warsaw Convention which is appended to the Carriage by Air and Road Act 1979. (For the commencement of this Act see s. 7, and the Carriage by Air and Road Act 1979 (Commencement No. 1) Order 1980 (S.I. 1980 No. 1966).) The scheme of compensation for loss of life is basically the same as in earlier editions of the Convention, but under English law gold franks are to be replaced by special drawing rights for the purposes of assessing the compensation payable under the scheme (Act of 1979, s. 4).

The right to damages for loss of expectation of life has been abolished (Administration of Justice Act 1982, s. 1), and a claim for bereavement (*q.v.*) introduced (Fatal Accidents Act 1976, s. 1A (inserted by the Act of 1982, s. 3)).

Death duties. The Administration of Justice (Miscellaneous Provisions) Act 1933, s. 3, has been repealed by the Finance Act 1975, s. 59, Sched. 13, Part I, in connection with the abolition of estate duty and its replacement by capital transfer tax (*q.v.*). The legislation for the new tax has been consolidated (Capital Transfer Tax Act 1984).

Deathbed declarations. The Magistrates' Courts Act 1952, s. 41, has been repealed and replaced by the Magistrates' Courts Act 1980, s. 105, without change of effect. The Magistrates' Courts Rules 1968, r. 29, has been revoked and replaced by the Magistrates' Courts Rules 1981, r. 33, without change of effect.

Debt. The Limitation Act 1939, s. 2(1), (3), has been repealed and replaced by the Limitation Act 1980, ss. 5, 8, without change of effect.

The minimum debt to support a bankruptcy petition was increased to £200 (Insolvency Act 1976, s. 1, Sched. 1, Part I, amending the Bankruptcy Act 1914, s. 4(1)(*a*)), and has now been further increased to £750 (Insolvency Proceedings (Increase of Monetary Limits) Regulations 1984 (S.I. 1984 No. 1199)).

Debtor-executor. If a debtor becomes his deceased creditor's personal representative (whether executor or administrator), his debt is extinguished, but he becomes accountable to the estate for his debt in any case where he would have been so accountable if appointed executor under the deceased's will. This rule does not, however, apply if the debt was already out of time under the usual rules of limitation (Administration of Estates Act 1925, s. 21A (added by the Limitation Amendment Act 1980, s. 10)).

Deception. The scope of the criminal provisions relating to deceptions has been widened by the Theft Act 1978, which makes it an offence to obtain services by a deception (s. 1(1)), "obtaining services" being defined as a situation where another person is induced to confer a benefit by doing some act, or causing or permitting some act to be done, on the understanding that the benefit has been or will be paid for (s. 1(2)). The evasion of a liability is also proscribed (s. 2), as is making off without payment (s. 3). On conviction on indictment of an offence under ss. 1 or 2 the maximum punishment is imprisonment for not more than five years (s. 4(2)(*a*)), and for a similar conviction of an offence under s. 3 the maximum punishment is imprisonment for a period not exceeding two years (s. 4(2)(*b*)). Convictions for any of these offences when tried summarily carry a penalty of a fine (*q.v.*) not exceeding £2,000 or imprisonment for a period not exceeding six months, or both (s. 4(3)). For the purposes of ss. 1 and 2, the term "deception" means any deception (whether deliberate or reckless) by words or conduct as to fact or as to law, including a deception as to the present intentions of the person using the deception or any other person (s. 5(1)). This definition is also used in the earlier provisions of the Theft Act 1968, ss. 15, 16.

Escaping the consequences of endorsement (in a road traffic matter) by deception may lead to endorsement of a driving licence and appropriate disqualification on conviction for the offence which contains the deception (Transport Act 1981, s. 21).

Decimal currency. Further provision in respect of decimal currency is made by the

Currency Act 1983. The Currency Act 1982 provided that the word "new" might now be omitted from the expression "penny".

Declaration. The procedure under R.S.C. Ord. 15, r. 16, should not be used if criminal proceedings have been instituted in respect of the same matter (*Imperial Tobacco Ltd.* v. *A.-G.* [1981] A.C. 718, H.L.), though it would appear to be a matter for the court's discretion to grant or withhold a declaration determining the criminality (or innocence) of any particular course of action when no criminal proceedings are in train (*ibid.*).

Declaration of right. The current analogous practice of claiming against the Crown involves a petition of right (*q.v.*).

Declaratory judgment. For the restrictions on the giving of a declaratory judgment when criminal proceedings have been launched in respect of (substantially) the same matters, see *Imperial Tobacco Ltd.* v. *A.-G.* [1981] A.C. 718, H.L.

Decree. Decrees absolute of divorce may be issued six weeks after the making of the decree nisi (Matrimonial Causes (Decree Absolute) General Order 1972, the Matrimonial Causes (Decree Absolute) Order 1973). The new procedure is for the petitioner in the suit to apply for the issue of the decree (see the Matrimonial Causes Rules 1977, rr. 65, 66). In view of this reduction in the period between decree nisi and decree absolute, the procedure for expediting a decree (laid down in *Practice Direction* [1964] 1 W.L.R. 73 and *Practice Direction* [1977] 1 W.L.R. 759) is used only rarely.

The Judicature Act 1925, s. 225, has been repealed and replaced by the Supreme Court Act 1981, s. 151(1), without change of effect.

Dedication. The Highways Act 1959, ss. 33, 34, 35, 39, have been repealed and replaced by the Highways Act 1980, ss. 30, 31, 32, 37, without change of effect.

Deed. The decision in *Re Sandilands* (1871) L.R. 6 C.P. 411, was considered and approved in *First National Securities Ltd.* v. *Jones* [1978] Ch. 109, C.A.

The Judicature Act 1925, s. 55, has been repealed and replaced by the Supreme Court Act 1981, s. 61(1), (3), Sched. 1, para. 1(*g*), without change of effect.

Deed of discharge. The Finance Act 1950, s. 44(5) (as amended by the Act of 1969), has been repealed by the Finance Act 1975, s. 59, Sched. 13, Part I, in connection with the abolition of estate duty and its replacement by capital transfer tax (*q.v.*). The legislation for the new tax has been consolidated (Capital Transfer Tax Act 1984).

Deer. The penalty under the Deer Act 1963, s. 8, was increased by the Criminal Law Act 1977, s. 31, Sched. 6, to a maximum fine of £500 in any case. See also FINE.

Default summons. The C.C.R. 1936, Ord. 6, r. 2, Ord. 10 and Ord. 10, r. 2, have been revoked and replaced by the C.C.R. 1981, Ord. 3, r. 2, Ord. 9, and Ord. 9, rr. 3, 6. The expression "summary judgment" now means judgment under Ord. 9, r. 14, in a default action in respect of a claim valued at more than £500 where, despite the delivery of a defence, the plaintiff applies for judgment on the ground that there is no real defence to the claim.

Defectives. The repeal of the Mental Health Act 1959 by the Mental Health Act 1983 does not affect the context in which the 1959 Act is cited.

Defence. The provisions governing the use and form of an answer in matrimonial suits (the equivalent of a defence) are now contained in the Matrimonial Causes Rules 1977, r. 18, which substantially repeats the terms of the 1971 Rules.

The C.C.R. 1936, Ord. 9, rr. 4(1), 9(1), have been revoked and replaced by the C.C.R. 1981, Ord. 9, rr. 11 and 12, and 2, respectively, without significant change of effect.

Deferment of sentence. If the offender consents to the procedure being used, the Crown Court and magistrates' courts may defer passing sentence on (since the Criminal Justice Act 1982 called "dealing with") an offender for up to six months so that, in determining how to deal with him, the court may have regard to the offender's conduct after conviction (including the making of any reparation for the offence) or to any change in his circumstances (Powers of Criminal Courts Act 1973, s. 1) (as amended by the Criminal Law Act 1977, s. 64(5)). By virtue of the Act of 1973, s. 1(8), (8A) (added by the Criminal Justice Act 1982, s. 63), a magistrates' court dealing with an offender after a period of deferment now has the power to commit him to the Crown Court (under the Magistrates'

Courts Act 1980, ss. 37, 38) in the same way as it would have had if it had dealt with him originally without any deferment. The 1982 amendments also enable the courts to impose a custodial sentence on the occasion of dealing with an offender after a deferment, thus reversing the decision in *R.* v. *Gilby* (1975) 61 Cr.App.R. 112, C.A.

Delivery of pleadings. The term "delivery" is now used of pleadings only in the county courts, where the High Court term ("service") is being more commonly used.

Delivery order. The Sale of Goods Act 1893, s. 62(1), has been repealed and replaced by the Sale of Goods Act 1979, s. 61(1), which applies the terms of the Factors Acts in the same way as the Act of 1893.

Delivery, Writ of. The occasions on which a writ of delivery may be used have been affected by the abolition of detinue (*q.v.*) (Torts (Interference with Goods) Act 1977, s. 2(1)), but the forms of writ and the procedure for their issue remain substantially the same. For restrictions on the forms of judgments which may be entered where goods are detained see the Torts (Interference with Goods) Act 1977, s. 3. See CONVERSION; DETINUE.

Demand. The Limitation Act 1939 has been repealed and replaced by the Limitation Act 1980, subject to amendments made by intervening Limitation Acts and the Limitation Amendment Act 1980.

Demand note. The matters which must be contained in a demand note are prescribed in the General Rate Act 1967, s. 5.

Denizen. The British Nationality Act 1948, has been repealed and replaced by the British Nationality Act 1981, which made significant amendments to this part of the law.

Dental Estimates Board. See the National Health Service Act 1977, s. 37.

Dentist. The Dentists Act 1957, s. 24, was repealed by the Dentists Act 1983, s. 33(3), Sched. 3, Part I. The Act of 1983 contained further general provisions dealing with the constitution and regulation of the profession (Part II, ss. 3–16) and control of fitness to practice (Part III, ss. 17–22), together with restrictions on practice (Part IV, ss. 23–25) and control over dental auxiliaries (Part V, ss. 26–34). The Act of 1983 was then repealed and replaced by the Dentists Act 1984, the relevant provisions being ss. 2(4), (5), 28–31, 33, Sched. 1, para. 8(2) and Sched. 3.

Deponent. The practice of using the first person in the text of affidavits is prescribed by R.S.C. Ord. 41, r. 1(4), and the C.C.R. 1981, Ord. 20, r. 10 (applying the Supreme Court provisions).

Deportation. The Immigration Act 1971 provisions (s. 6, Sched. 3) have been modified by the Criminal Justice Act 1982, s. 64, Sched. 10.

Deposit. The Sale of Goods Act 1893, s. 5, has been repealed and replaced by the Sale of Goods Act 1979, s. 5 without change of effect.

The Protection of Depositors Act 1963, has been repealed by the Banking Act 1979, s. 51(2), Sched. 7.

Part I (ss. 1–20) of the Banking Act 1979, provides a system of control over deposit-taking under the general supervision of the Bank of England, which is empowered to licence institutions which are engaged in deposit-taking activities (ss. 3–10). The term "deposit" is extensively defined (s. 1(4)–(6)). Contravention of the restrictions on deposit-taking (which prohibit deposit-taking by an unlicensed person) constitutes an offence for which the maximum penalty on summary conviction is a fine (*q.v.*) not exceeding £2,000 and on conviction on indictment imprisonment not exceeding two years or a fine or both (s. 1(7)). The main exceptions from the prohibition on deposit-taking are the Bank of England, recognised banks (determined in accordance with criteria set out in Sched. 3), licensed institutions and certain other persons (listed in Sched. 1 and ranging from the central bank of each of the member states of the European Communities (other than the Bank of England), the Post Office, municipal banks, building and friendly societies, members of the Stock Exchange in the course of business as stockbrokers or stockjobbers, to credit unions (*q.v.*) and local authorities). Under the scheme the Bank of England has extensive powers to grant licences (including conditional licenses) (s. 10), to obtain information and to require the production of documents (s. 16), conduct investigations (s. 17), and to present winding-up petitions (s. 18). Information secured to the Bank is normally classed as confidential (ss. 18, 20).

Advertisement inviting the making of deposits may be restricted by regulations made by the Treasury after consulting the Bank of England (s. 34); the Bank has power to issue specific prohibitions and other directives to licensed institutions in connection with misleading advertisements issued or proposed to be issued by the institutions (s. 35).

Deposit of wills. The procedure for the deposit in and withdrawal of wills from the Principal Registry of the Family Division is laid down in the Wills (Deposit for Safe Custody) Regulations 1978 (S.I.1978 No. 1724), made under the Judicature Act 1925, s. 172, which provided for the deposit of the wills of living persons; this section has been repealed and replaced by the Supreme Court Act 1981, s. 126, without significant change of effect.

Further (prospective) provision has been made for the deposit of wills (Administration of Justice Act 1982, s. 24).

Deposit Protection Board. This is a body corporate which is charged with duties relating to deposit-taking (Banking Act 1979, s. 21), its constitution, administration and organisation being statutorily prescribed (Act of 1979, Sched. 5). The Board has power (ss. 27–33) to levy contributions to the Deposit Protection Fund (established by s. 22) maintained at the Bank of England (s. 22(2)). Contributions may be repaid in certain circumstances (ss. 32, 33). Payments are to be made out of the Fund in certain cases of insolvency affecting licensed deposit-taking institutions or licensed banks (ss. 28–31). See also DEPOSIT.

Deposition. The Magistrates' Courts Act 1952, s. 41, has been repealed and replaced by the Magistrates' Courts Act 1980, s. 105, without change of effect. The Magistrates' Courts Rules 1968, rr. 4 and 29, have been revoked and replaced by the Magistrates' Courts Rules 1981, rr. 7 and 33, without change of effect. The Criminal Justice Act 1967, s. 2, has been repealed and replaced by the Magistrates' Court Act 1980, s. 102, without change of effect.

Deprivation of citizenship. The British Nationality Act 1948 provisions have been repealed and replaced by the British Nationality Act 1981, s. 40. Although the words of the new provisions are similar to those of the 1948 Act, it is highly likely that intervening case law has changed the result from what was intended in the 1948 enactment (see *e.g. Zamir* v. *Secretary of State for the Home Department* [1980] A.C. 930, H.L.).

Deputy. The Administration of Justice Act 1973, s. 2(7), has been repealed and replaced by the Justices of the Peace Act 1979, s. 15 (which refers to the appointee as an "acting stipendiary magistrate").

A new text for the Courts Act 1971, s. 24, has been substituted (Supreme Court Act 1981, s. 146), which provides for the appointment of deputy circuit judges and assistant recorders.

Deputy steward. The Copyhold Act 1894, s. 94, has been repealed without replacement or savings by the Statute Law (Repeals) Act 1969, s. 1, Sched., Part III.

Derelict, Dereliction. The maximum penalty on summary conviction for failing to report a danger to navigation (*i.e.* the offence under the Merchant Shipping Act (Safety and Load Line Conventions) Act 1932, s. 24) has been increased to £500 (Merchant Shipping Act 1979, s. 43, Sched. 6, Part III). See also FINE.

The Railway and Canal Traffic Act 1888, s. 45, has been repealed by the Transport Act 1968, ss. 112(7), 165(c), Sched. 18, Part III, and its place has been taken by the Act of 1968, s. 112, which makes general provision for the extinguishing of statutory rights and obligations in respect of canals which are not comprised in the undertaking of the Waterways Board (set up under the Act of 1968).

Descent. This concept also figures in nationality law: *e.g.* one may be a British citizen by descent (British Nationality Act 1981, s. 2) or a citizen of the British Dependent Territories by descent (s. 16).

Description. The Sale of Goods Act 1893, ss. 13, 30 (as amended), have been repealed and replaced by the Sale of Goods Act 1979, ss. 13, 30, without change of effect.

Desertion. The Merchant Shipping Act 1894, ss. 221 *et seq.*, have been repealed by the Merchant Shipping Act 1970, s. 100(3), Sched. 5, The provision relating to the offence of being absent recklessly or deliberately without reasonable cause at the time of sailing (Merchant Shipping Act 1970, s. 31), which replaced the desertion provision of the Act of 1894, has been repealed by the Merchant Shipping Act 1974, s. 19(3), without replacement, leaving the matter to be dealt with under the various codes of practice now operative in the merchant shipping service.

Detention. The Criminal Justice Act 1961, s. 4, has been repealed by the Criminal Justice Act 1982, s. 78, Sched. 16. Its place has been taken by the Prison Act 1952, s. 43 (as substituted by the Act of 1982, s. 11), which gives detention centres into the care of the Prison Department.

Dentinue. The common law tort of detinue was abolished by the Torts (Interference with Goods) Act 1977, s. 1(1), and the tort of conversion was extended to cover much of the area of law formerly covered by the law of detinue (s. 1(2)). The Sale of Goods Act 1893, s. 52, has been repealed and replaced by the Sale of Goods Act 1979, s. 52, without change of effect. The Limitation Act 1939, s. 3, has been repealed and replaced by the Limitation Act 1980, ss. 2, 3 (replacing earlier provisions but incorporating the amendment made by the Limitation Amendment Act 1980, Sched. 1, para. 5, in connection with the abolition of detinue).

Devastavit. The Limitation Act 1939, s. 19, has been repealed and replaced by the Limitation Act 1980, s. 21, without significant change of effect.

Development. The Town and Country Planning General Development Order 1973 has been revoked and replaced by the Town and Country Planning General Development Order 1977 (S.I.1977 No. 289), which is in broadly similar terms.

The Town and Country Planning (Determination of Appeals by Appointed Persons) (Prescribed Classes) Regulations 1972 (S.I.1972 No. 1652), have been revoked and replaced by the Town and Country Planning (Determination of Appeals by Appointed Persons) (Prescribed Classes) Regulations 1981 (S.I.1981 No. 804). The Town and Country Planning (Determination by Appointed Persons) (Inquiries Procedure) Rules 1968, have been revoked and replaced by the Town and Country Planning (Determination by Appointed Persons) (Inquiries Procedure) Rules 1974 (S.I.1974 No. 420). See also STRUCTURE PLAN.

The issue of an established use certificate renders immune from enforcement proceedings the use specified in the certificate (Act of 1971, s. 94(1)). The certificate is conclusive of the matters contained in it for the purposes of any appeal to the Secretary of State against any enforcement notice served in respect of the land (s. 94(7); *Broxbourne Borough Council* v. *Secretary of State for the Environment* [1980] Q.B. 1, D.C.). The Town and Country Planning General Regulations 1969 (S.I.1969 No. 286), have been revoked and replaced by the Town and Country Planning General Regulations 1974 (S.I.1974 No. 596), which have in their turn been revoked and replaced by the Town and Country Planning General Regulations 1976 (S.I.1976 No. 1419).

The General Development Order 1977 has been amended by S.I.1977 No. 1781; 1980 No. 1946; 1981 Nos. 235, 246, 1569 and 1983 No. 1615.

Planning permission, once given, enures for the benefit of the land and all persons interested in it, so that a valid permission which is still capable of implementation is not capable of lapse by abandonment by the conduct of an owner or occupier of the land (*Pioneer Aggregates (U.K.) Ltd.* v. *Secretary of State for the Environment* [1984] 3 W.L.R. 32, H.L.).

The meaning of "development" in town and country planning law is modified when mineral workings are involved (see the Town and Country Planning Act 1971, s. 22(3A) (added by the Town and Country Planning (Minerals) Act 1981, s. 1)).

Development Commissioners. For the establishment of a corporate body called the Development Commissioners in place of (or, rather, in continuation of) the Development Commissioners see the Miscellaneous Financial Provisions Act 1983, s. 1, Sched. 1.

Development corporations. The maximum number of members of a development corporation has been increased from seven to eleven (New Towns (Amendment) Act 1976, s. 15).

Development land. The Community Land Act 1975 has been repealed without replacement by the Local Government, Planning and Land Act 1980, s. 194, Sched. 34, Part XI.

Devolution. The devolution of governmental powers to elected assemblies to Scotland and Wales has been the subject of elaborate statutory provisions, the Scotland Act 1978 and the Wales Act 1978; both were repealed before they even came into operation (S.I.1979 Nos. 928 (Scotland) and 933 Wales)).

Dies non or **Dies non juridicus.** When the time for taking some procedural step falls on a *dies non* the step may be taken on the next day when the court offices are open for business (R.S.C. Ord. 3, r. 4; *Pritam Kaur* v. *S. Russell & Sons* [1973] Q.B. 336, C.A.).

Diocese or **Diocess.** For the constant scrutiny of diocesan boundaries and related matters, the Dioceses Commission has been established (Dioceses Commission Measure 1978, ss. 1–8).

Diplomatic privilege. For analogous provisions affording immunities for states see the State Immunity Act 1978.

Directions, Summons for. For the amendment of the procedural rules in relation to orders for directions in personal injury actions see the Rules of the Supreme Court (Amendment No. 2) 1980 (S.I.1980 No. 1010).

Director. On the first registration of a company the names of the directors must be notified to the Registrar of Companies (Companies Act 1976, s. 21), and subsequent changes in their membership must also be notified (s. 22). The provisions of the Companies Act 1967, have been amended, making the requirements in connection with the giving of notices about directors' dealings with their companies' securities more stringent (Companies Act 1976, ss. 24–27). Further regulation of the activities of directors was effected by the Companies Act 1980 ss. 46–47, and "insider dealing" with shares prohibited by ss. 63–67 of that Act.

Director of Public Prosecutions. The various statutory provisions mentioned have been repealed and replaced by the Prosecution of Offences Act 1979, which re-enacts the principal provisions relating to the functions of the Director of Public Prosecutions. The Regulations of 1946 have been revoked and replaced by the Prosecution of Offences Regulations 1978 (S.I.1978 No. 1357, as amended by S.I.1978 No. 1846), in substantially the same terms.

Recent restrictions on the prosecution of offences requiring the consent of the Director include the following: the Bail Act 1976, s. 9(5); the Companies Act 1976, s. 25(4); the Criminal Law Act 1977, ss. 4(1), (3), 53(2); the Energy Act 1976, ss. 6, 7 (see Sched. 6, para. 6)); the Lotteries and Amusements Act 1976, s. 2(3); the Protection of Children Act 1978, s. 1(3); the Banking Act 1979, s. 39; the Merchant Shipping Act 1979, s. 44; the Companies Act 1980, s. 72(2); and the Child Abduction Act 1984. s. 5.

Directors' report. Further detailed provision has been made for these reports (Companies Act 1981, ss. 13–16).

Disability. The grounds on which a marriage is void or voidable are now contained in the Matrimonial Causes Act 1973, ss. 11, 12, respectively.

The Limitation Act 1939, has been repealed and replaced by the Limitation Act 1980, subject to amendments first contained in the Limitation Amendment Act 1980.

Disability. The Disabled Persons (Employment) Act 1944, s. 2, has been repealed by the Education and Training Act 1973 (s. 14, Sched. 4), which makes general provision for the supply of vocational training courses by education authorities. The Wages Councils Act 1959, s. 13, has been repealed and replaced by the Wages Councils Act 1979, s. 16, without change of effect.

Mechanically propelled vehicles registered in the name of disabled persons are exempt from vehicles excise duty (the restriction in the Finance Act 1976, s. 13, having been repealed by the Finance Act 1978, ss. 8, 9).

The relief from rates formerly enjoyed under the General Rate Act 1967, s. 45, has been abolished (Rating (Disabled Persons) Act 1978, s. 9, Sched. 2), and replaced by a statutory scheme of rebates (Act of 1978, ss. 1–3).

Disapply. Apparently, to exclude the operation of, to over-ride. See the Local Government Act 1972, Sched. 14, para. 25; the Limitation Act 1939, s. 2D (added by the Limitation Act 1975, s. 1, and now repealed and replaced by the Limitation Act 1980, s. 33); the Merchant Shipping (Foreign Deserters) (Disapplication) Order 1979 (S.I.1979 No. 120), which terminates certain arrangements concerning deserting seamen; the Companies Act 1980, s. 18; and the

Mental Health Act 1983, s. 113.

Discharge. By virtue of the Insolvency Act 1976, a debtor who has been adjudged bankrupt may be automatically discharged in certain cases (s. 7), and in prescribed circumstances the official receiver of a bankrupt may apply to the court for the discharge of the bankrupt (s. 8).

The Criminal Justice Act 1948, s. 7, and the Criminal Justice Act 1967, s. 52, have been repealed and replaced by the Powers of Criminal Courts Act 1973, s. 7, without change of effect.

Disclaim, Disclaimer. For the curious effect of a disclaimer under the Companies Act 1948, s. 323, of a lease which had been assigned to a company, see *Warnford Investments Ltd.* v. *Duckworth* [1979] Ch. 127 (the disclaimer relieved the company of liability for the rent but left the original tenant liable and without recourse to the company to which the term had been assigned).

Discontinuance. The C.C.R. 1936, Ord. 18 and Ord. 23, r. 2, have been revoked and replaced by the C.C.R. 1981, Ord. 18 (without change of effect) and Ord. 21, r. 2 (which has been modified so as to apply to matters as well as actions).

Discovery. The decision in *Davidson* v. *Lloyd Aircraft Services Ltd.* [1974] 1 W.L.R. 1042, was overruled in *McIvor* v. *Southern Health and Social Services Board* [1978] 1 W.L.R. 757, H.L., where it was held that the discovery to be made under the Act of 1970 should not be restricted to the medical advisers alone. In *Church of Scientology* v. *Department of Health and Social Security* [1979] 1 W.L.R. 723 (not under the Act of 1970), the Court of Appeal reserved the right to restrict discovery of medical reports in special cases. For fresh provision for the disclosure of experts' reports in personal injury cases see the Rules of the Supreme Court (Amendment No. 2) 1980 (S.I.1980 No. 629).

In any event the Act of 1970, ss. 31, 32, have been repealed and replaced by the Supreme Court Act 1981, ss. 33–35. The 1981 provisions contain amendments which authorise the imposition of restrictions on disclosure of medical reports in personal injury cases. (Equivalent provisions apply in the county courts (County Courts Act 1984, ss. 52–54, replacing the Supreme Court Act 1981, ss. 33–35, applied to county courts by s. 149(3)); the procedural rules of the Supreme Court are followed in county courts (C.C.R. 1981, Ord. 13, r. 7)).

The rule in *Mexborough* v. *Whitwood Urban District Council* [1897] 2 Q.B. 111, has been abolished (except in criminal proceedings) since the rule of law whereby in any legal proceedings a person cannot be compelled to answer any question or produce any document or thing if to do so would tend to expose him to a forfeiture has been abrogated (Civil Evidence Act 1968, s. 16(1)(*a*)).

The principle expounded in *Distillers Co.* (*Biochemicals*) *Ltd.* v. *Times Newspapers Ltd.* [1975] Q.B. 613, has been confirmed in *Medway* v. *Doublelock Ltd.* [1978] 1 W.L.R. 710 and *B.* v. *B.* (*Matrimonial Proceedings: Discovery*) [1979] Fam. 181.

Even if innocent and not under any personal liability, a person who is connected with some wrong-doing or becomes so linked with the tortious acts of others as to facilitate their wrong-doing comes under a personal duty of assist the person who suffers from the wrongful act or omission by providing him with full information about (including the identity of) the wrongdoer (*Norwich Pharmacal Ltd.* v. *Commissioners of Customs and Excise* [1974] A.C. 133, H.L., applying *Orr* v. *Diaper* (1877) 4 Ch. D. 92).

For a further erosion of the quasi-privilege of non-disclosure (as a result of the Supreme Court Act 1981, s. 72) see CONFIDENTIAL COMMUNICATIONS.

The C.C.R. 1936, Ord. 14, has been revoked and replaced by the C.C.R. 1981, Ord. 14, which is in broadly similar terms but embodies amendments to assimilate the procedure to that already in operation under R.S.C. Ord. 24.

Discretionary trust. The provisions relating to capital transfer tax have been repealed and consolidated in the Capital Transfer Tax Act 1984.

Discrimination. See RACIAL RELATIONS and SEX DISCRIMINATION.

Dismissal of action. Any judgment, order or verdict which has been obtained in the absence of a party when the case is called on for trial may be set aside on such terms as the court thinks just; an application for such a setting aside must be made within seven days of the trial (R.S.C. Ord. 35, r. 2).

Disposal of uncollected goods. The Disposal of Uncollected Goods Act 1952, has been repealed (Torts (Interference with Goods) Act 1977, s. 15(1)), and fresh provision has been made for the disposal of goods remaining in the hands of a bailee (Act of 1977, s. 12) and for the authorisation of sales by order of the court (s. 13) (see also Sched. 1, Part I, for the power to impose an obligation to collect goods, and Sched. 1, Part II, for provisions relating to the giving of notice of intention to sell goods).

Disqualified. For the disqualification for driving of a person found guilty of certain road traffic offences, and under related provisions, see the Road Traffic Act 1972, ss. 93–100 (as amended by the Road Traffic Act 1974) and the Transport Act 1981, s. 19. See also TOTTING-UP PROCEDURE.

Dissection. The Anatomy Act 1832 has been (prospectively) repealed and replaced by the Anatomy Act 1984; the expression "executor" in the Act of 1832 has been replaced by the expression "person lawfully in possession of the body" (Act of 1984, s. 4(2), (3)).

Dissenters. The Congregational churches in England have, for the most part, joined with the Presbyterian Church of England to form the United Reformed Church (see the United Reformed Church Acts 1972 (c. xviii) and 1981 (c. xxiv)). Some of the Congregational churches have remained outside this new group, being commonly known as Independent Congregational Churches.

The Trustee Appointment Act 1850, and the Trustees Appointment Act 1890, have been repealed by the Charities Act 1960, s. 48, Sched. 7, Part I. It is provided that if the provisions of the 1850 and 1890 (and certain other) Acts relating to the appointment of trustees applied in relation to any land at the commencement of the 1960 Act, they should have effect as if contained in the conveyance or other instrument declaring the trusts on which the land is held (Act of 1960, s. 35(6)). Most dissenting congregations are now organised as religious charitable institutions (see CHARITY) and are registered with the Charity Commissioners (*q.v.*).

The Marriage and Registration Act 1856, s. 17 (the Act ran only to 26 sections), has been repealed and replaced by the Marriage Act 1949, s. 48(1), (2); marriages in dissenting chapels and churches are normally conducted under a licence issued (under the Act of 1949, ss. 41–44) for the particular building where the ceremony is conducted.

Dissolution. The Mental Health Act 1959, s. 103(1)(*b*), has been repealed and replaced by the Mental Health Act 1983, s. 96(1)(*g*), without change of effect.

Distance. The Interpretation Act 1889, s. 34, has been repealed and replaced by the Interpretation Act 1978, s. 8; the new provision applies to all Acts passed and subordinate legislation made after the passing of the 1978 Act, and to all Acts of Parliament passed after 1889 (s. 22(1), Sched. 2, para. 3).

Distress. The tithe annuities substituted under the Tithe Acts 1936 and 1951, for tithe rentcharge were abolished in 1977 after a double payment in October 1977 (Finance Act 1977, s. 56).

The amount of wearing apparel and bedding exempt from execution has been increased from £20 in value to £100, and the tools of trade which are exempt increased to the value of £150 (Protection from Execution (Prescribed Value) Order 1980 (S.I.1980 No. 26)).

The Limitation Act 1939, s. 17, has been repealed and replaced by the Limitation Act 1980, s. 19, without change of effect. The County Courts Act 1959, ss. 124, 137, 152, have been repealed and replaced by the County Courts Act 1984, ss. 89, 102, 116, without change of effect. See also the Distress for Rent Rules 1984 (S.I.1984 No. 1917).

Distress signals. The regulations now in force are the Merchant Shipping (Signals of Distress) Rules 1977 (S.I.1977 No. 1010 (amended by 1983 No. 708)), and the Collision Regulations and Distress Signals Order 1977 (S.I.1977 No. 982 as heavily amended), giving effect to the International Regulations for Preventing Collisions at Sea 1972 (Cmnd. 5471). See also the Safety (Collision Regulations and Distress Signals) Regulations 1979 (S.I.1979 No. 1659, amended by S.I.1983 Nos. 708 and 769).

Distribution. The statutory legacy in favour of a surviving spouse allocated under the Intestates' Estates Act 1952 (as amended), was increased from £15,000 to

£25,000 where the estate was survived by issue, and from £40,000 to £55,000 in the event of there being no surviving issue (but certain other close relatives) (Family Provision (Intestate Succession) Order 1977 (S.I.1977 No. 415)). These sums were again increased (to £85,000 and £40,000, respectively) in 1981 (S.I.1981 No. 255). The rate of interest payable on statutory legacies was increased from four per cent. to seven per cent. (Intestate Succession (Interest and Capitalisation) Order 1977 (S.I.1977 No. 1491)) and then reduced to six per cent. (Intestate Succession (Interest and Capitalisation) Order 1983 (S.I.1983 No. 1374)).

The Matrimonial Proceedings and Property Act 1970, s. 40, has been repealed and replaced by the Matrimonial Causes Act 1973, s. 18(2), (3), without any significant change of effect.

District auditor. Fresh provision for local government audit was made by the Local Government Finance Act 1982, Part III (ss. 11–36), under which an independent Audit Commission was established. It is no longer possible for a private "approved auditor" to conduct audits of local authorities. The Local Government Act 1972, ss. 154–167, have been repealed and replaced by the 1982 provisions.

District council. A miscellany of widely differing additional powers has been conferred on district councils by the Local Government (Miscellaneous Provisions) Act 1976, Part I (ss. 1–44). A scheme for the grant by district councils of hackney carriage licences and private hire vehicle licences is set out in the same Act (Part II, ss. 45–80)).

District health authority. See the Health Services Act 1980, ss. 1, 2, which gave the minister power to establish these bodies, thus displacing area health authorities (*q.v.*).

District registries. The district registries established under the Act of 1925 (now repealed and replaced by the Supreme Court Act 1981) are detailed in the Civil Courts Order 1983 (S.I.1983 No. 713, already amended several times).

The Judicature Act 1925, ss. 84, 108, have been repealed and replaced by the Supreme Court Act 1981, ss. 99 and 104, without change of effect. The R.S.C. Ord. 32, r. 26 and Ord. 63, rr. 13, 14, have been revoked without replacement by the Rules of the Supreme Court (Amendment No. 2) 1982 (S.I.1982 No. 1111) in connection with revisions consequent upon the Oliver Report (Cmnd. 8205).

Distringas. The Administration of Justice (Miscellaneous Provisions) Act 1938, s. 11, was repealed by the Courts Act 1971, s. 56(4), Sched. 11, Part IV. The current equivalent may be found in the Supreme Court Act 1981, ss. 46, 79 (replacing the Courts Act 1971, s. 6(1)).

Distringas, Notice in lieu of. The eight day period allowed for response to the warning notice (under R.S.C. Ord. 50, r. 12) has been increased to fourteen days (Rules of the Supreme Court (Amendment) 1980 (S.I.1980 No. 629)).

Disturbance. The scheme for disturbance under the Agricultural Holdings Act 1949, s. 34 has been modified slightly (Agricultural Holdings Act 1984, s. 10(1), Sched. 3) in connection with the revision of the scheme for statutory succession to agricultural holdings.

The Housing Act 1957, ss. 32, 63(1) and 100, were repealed by the Land Compensation Act 1973, s. 86, Sched. 3, in connection with the general provisions for compensation contained in that Act.

Ditch. The Highways (Miscellaneous Provisions) Act 1961, s. 6, has been repealed and replaced by the Highways Act 1980, s. 101, without change of effect.

Diversion of highways. The Highways Act 1959, ss. 108–115, Sched. 12, have been repealed and replaced by the Highways Act 1980, ss. 116–123, Sched. 12, without change of effect.

Dividend. The temporary power conferred on the Treasury by the Counter-Inflation Act 1973, s. 10, was made permanent by the Price Commission Act 1977, s. 14, but that provision, together with the Dividends Act 1978 (which was to the same effect), has been repealed by the Competition Act 1980, s. 33(4), Sched. 2.

Dividend stripping. By the Finance Act 1984, s. 44(1), (4), a trustee savings bank is deemed to be a body corporate within the scope of the Income and Corporation Taxes Act 1970, s. 281.

Divisional Courts. The Judicature Act 1925, s. 63 (together with the amendments effected by the Administration of Justice

Act 1970, s. 6), has been repealed and replaced by the Supreme Court Act 1981, s. 66, without change of effect. The Judicature Act 1925, s. 31(1)(*f*), has been repealed and replaced by the Supreme Court Act 1981, s. 18 (subject to slight amendments).

Most appeals from county courts since 1934 have been routed to the Court of Appeal (by virtue of the Administration of Justice (Appeals) Act 1934, s. 2, Sched.). Appeals still lie to the Divisional Court in cases where the appeal would have been to the Divisional Court before the Act of 1934 and the proceedings were not listed in the Schedule to the Act (see, *e.g.* the Pilotage Act 1913, s. 28(4) (now replaced by the 1983 Act of the same name) and R.S.C. Ord. 74, r. 2; and the Land Registration Act 1925, and R.S.C. Ord. 93, r. 10(1)). The appeal route prescribed by the Act of 1934, s. 2(1); and the County Courts Act 1934, s. 105, was confirmed by the County Courts Act 1959, s. 101, which has now been repealed and replaced by the County Courts Act 1984, s. 77, without significant change of effect.

The R.S.C. Ord. 56, r. 4A, now extends to care (as will as affiliation) proceedings and appeals on case stated under the Domestic Proceedings and Magistrates' Court Act 1978 go to a divisional court of the Family Division (R.S.C. Ord. 90, r. 16).

Divisions of the High Court. The Judicature Act 1925, ss. 1–5, and the Administration of Justice Act 1970, s. 1, have been repealed and replaced by the Supreme Court Act 1981, ss. 4–7, without change of effect. The Act of 1981, s. 63(1), (3), Sched. 1, provide for the distribution of business between the divisions.

Divorce. The consideration given to "exceptional hardship" and "exceptional depravity" in the Matrimonial Causes Act 1973, s. 3, in *C.* v. *C.* (*Divorce—Exceptional Hardship*) [1980] Fam. 23, C.A., and earlier cases has become merely historical since the three-year period has been reduced to one year, without benefit of exceptions (Act of 1973, s. 3 (as substituted by the Matrimonial and Family Proceedings Act 1984, s. 1)).

The period between the decree nisi and the decree absolute has been reduced to six weeks by the Matrimonial Causes (Decree Absolute) General Order 1972 (as amended by the Matrimonial Causes (Decree Absolute) General Order 1973).

The principles on which maintenance is to be assessed have been revised (see the Matrimonial Causes Act 1973, ss. 25, 25A, 27(3), 33A (as inserted by the Act of 1984, ss. 3, 4)).

Divorce county courts. The Matrimonial Causes Act 1967 s. 1, has been (prospectively) repealed and replaced by the Matrimonial and Family Proceedings Act 1984, s. 33. In due course the Courts Act 1971, s. 45, will also be repealed and replaced by the Act of 1984, ss. 38, 39.

Dock defence. Dock briefs are obsolete on account of the extension of legal aid (*q.v.*) to criminal proceedings.

Dock warrant. The Sale of Goods Act 1893, s. 62, has been repealed and replaced by the Sale of Goods Act 1979, s. 61, without change of effect.

Dock workers. See also the Dock Work Regulation Act 1976, reconstituting the National Dock Labour Board and making general provision for the industry.

Docking and nicking of horses. The maximum fine which may be imposed for the offences under the Docking and Nicking of Horses Act 1949, s. 1, was raised to £200 by the Criminal Law Act 1977, s. 31, Sched. 6. For the general revision of the levels of fines which may be imposed on summary conviction see also FINE.

Dockyard. The General Rate Act 1967, s. 35, has been repealed and replaced by the Local Government Act 1974, s. 19, Sched. 3, para. 8, without substantial change of effect.

Document. The Sale of Goods Act 1893, ss. 25, 47, have been repealed and replaced by the Sale of Goods Act 1979, ss. 25, 47, without change of effect.

Dog. The maximum fine upon conviction was increased from £25 to £50 by the Criminal Law Act 1977, s. 31. For the general revision of the levels of fines which may be imposed on summary conviction see also FINE.

Guard dogs are required to be kept under the control of a handler (Guard Dogs Act 1975, s. 1) and must not be left loose to roam around premises unless a proper warning sign is displayed at each entrance to the premises (s. 1(3)). The keeping of guard dog kennels is prohibited except on licence obtained from the local authority (ss. 2, 3). Appeals against a refusal to grant such a licence lie to the magistrates' court (s. 4). Contravention of the provisions restricting the use of guard dogs is an offence and on summary conviction a fine (*q.v.*) not exceeding £1,000 may be imposed (s. 5).

Domestic court. A specially constituted magistrates' court comprised of magistrates who are members of the domestic court panel (see the Magistrates' Courts Act 1980, ss. 67, 68 (replacing the Magistrates' Courts Act 1952, ss. 56A, 56B, which were inserted by the Domestic Proceedings and Magistrates' Courts Act 1978, s. 80)).

Domestic proceedings. The Magistrates' Courts Act 1952, ss. 56–62, have been repealed and replaced by the Magistrates' Courts Act 1980, ss. 67–74, without change of effect. The Domestic Proceedings and Magistrates' Courts Act 1978, s. 79, contains an elaborate definition, and the persons entitled to attend the proceedings were listed (1978, s. 81) and severe restriction on newspaper reports were prescribed (s. 82).

Domestic workers. The Department of Health and Social Security no longer publishes leaflet N.I. 11.

Dominion. See also the Malta Republic Act 1975 (clarifying the operation of law in Malta, a republic within the Commonwealth); the Seychelles Act 1976 (establishing the Seychelles as a fully responsible republic within the Commonwealth); the Trinidad and Tobago Act 1976 (establishing Trinidad and Tobago as a republic within the Commonwealth); the Solomon Islands (establishing the Solomon Islands as an independent dominion within the Commonwealth); the Tuvalu Act 1978 (providing for the attainment of independence within the Commonwealth by Tuvalu); the Kiribati Act 1979 (providing for the attainment of fully responsible status within the Commonwealth by the Gilbert Islands); the Southern Rhodesia Act 1979 and the Zimbabwe Act 1979 (providing for that country's transition to fully independent status as a republic); and the Papua, New Guinea, Western Samoa and Nauru (Miscellaneous Provisions) Act 1980 (which provides for the independence of Papua New Guinea and the Commonwealth membership of Western Samoa and Nauru). See also CANADA.

Donatio inter vivos. The Finance Act 1975, s. 19, and the Finance Act 1976, ss. 73–129, have been repealed and replaced by the Capital Transfer Tax Act 1984, which consolidated the provisions relating to the tax.

Door. The Towns Improvement Clauses Act 1847, ss. 71, 72, were repealed and replaced by the Highways Act 1959, s. 132, without change of effect, and this has in turn been repealed and replaced by the Highways Act 1980, s. 153, without change of effect.

Dormant funds. The Supreme Court Funds Rules 1927, r. 97, has been revoked and replaced by the Supreme Court Funds Rules 1975 (S.I.1975 No. 1803), r. 56. Since all funds paid into district registries were transmitted to London (1975 Rules, r. 59), the former r. 96, was revoked without replacement. Later amendments (S.I.1981 No. 1581) have revoked the 1975 Rules, rr. 59, 60, so that transmission to London is no longer required.

The code of procedure provided by the County Court Funds Rules 1965, ss. 36–39, has been extended by the addition of rr. 39A and 39B (County Court Funds (Amendment) Rules 1982 (S.I.1982 No. 786)).

Double taxation. The Finance Act 1894, s. 20, was repealed by the Finance Act 1975, s. 59(5), Sched. 13, in connection with the replacement of estate duty by capital transfer tax. See now the Capital Transfer Tax Act 1984, ss. 158, 159.

Draft, Draught. The Solicitors' Remuneration Order 1883, has been revoked and replaced by the Solicitors' Remuneration Order 1972 (S.I.1972 No. 1139); there is no longer any specific provision relating to the ownership of drafts of documents. On general principles they are the property of the client (subject to a lien for payment of the solicitor's professional charges).

Drain; drainage. The maximum fine on conviction of an offence under the Public Health Act 1936, s. 110, appears to have been increased to £50 by the Criminal Law Act 1977, s. 31, Sched. 6; see also FINE.

The Public Health Act 1936, ss. 14, 16, 28, 35, were repealed by the Water Act 1973, s. 40, Sched. 9; the Act of 1973, ss. 22 *et seq.*, made general provision for water supply and related operations.

The Public Health Act 1961, ss. 17, 18, have been repealed and replaced by a new text of s. 17 (of the same Act) (Local

Government (Miscellaneous Provisions) Act 1980, s. 27), without affecting the citation.

Drawback. The Customs and Excise Act 1952, ss. 266–273 (as variously amended), have been repealed and replaced by the Customs and Excise Management Act 1979, ss. 132–137, without change of effect.

Dredger. The Pilotage Act 1913, s. 12, has been repealed and replaced by the Pilotage Act 1983, s. 32(1), without change of effect.

Driving licence. See also the Road Traffic (Drivers' Ages and Hours of Work) Act 1976, which provides for the ages at the various types of driving licence may be issued (s. 1), and introduces further Community rules about drivers' hours to English law. By the Road Traffic (Driving Licences) Act 1983, the law was extended so as to enable persons with driving licences from other places to drive in the United Kingdom without further test.

The regulations now in force relating to "ordinary" driving licences are the Motor Vehicle (Driving Licences) Regulations 1981, (S.I.1981 No. 952, as heavily amended). The rules relating to licences for heavy goods vehicle drivers have been consolidated in the Heavy Goods Vehicles' Drivers' Licences) Regulations 1977 (S.I.1977 No. 1309, as variously amended).

Drug. The Food and Drugs Act 1955, s. 135(1), has been repealed and replaced by the Food Act 1984, s. 132(1), without change of effect.

Drug addict. The Matrimonial Proceedings (Magistrates' Courts) Act 1960, has been repealed and replaced by the Domestic Proceedings and Magistrates' Courts Act 1978, which contains a new code for applications in magistrates' courts for financial provision. The new Act (s. 1(*c*)) provides (*inter alia*) for an order to be made where the respondent has behaved in such a way that the applicant cannot reasonably be expected to live with the respondent.

The doctrine of *R.* v. *Lipman* [1970] 1 Q.B. 152, received confirmation in *R.* v. *Majewski* [1977] A.C. 443, H.L.

Drunkenness. The fine for an offence under the Merchant Shipping Act 1894, s. 287, was increased to £50 (Merchant Shipping Act 1979, s. 43, Sched. 6, Part I). For the general revision of the levels of fines which may be imposed on summary conviction see also FINE.

The powers of arrest of persons suspected of driving or attempting to drive when under the influence of drugs or alcohol have been revised (Road Traffic Act 1972, ss. 6–12 (as substituted by the Transport Act 1981, s. 25, Sched. 8)).

Duces tecum, Subpoena. In the Supreme Court the procedure for the issue of a subpoena *duces tecum* is laid down in R.S.C. Ord. 38, rr. 14–19, and the forms of writ are prescribed (App.A, Nos. 28, 29, 30).

An analogous procedure is used in the Chancery Division to compel the production of papers before a master sitting in chambers (R.S.C. Ord. 32, r. 15).

The Courts Act 1971, s. 4(8), has been repealed and replaced by the Supreme Court Act 1981, s. 45(4), without change of effect.

Dum casta vixerit. The modern practice makes it highly unlikely that a clause of this kind would be inserted in any orders made under the Matrimonial Causes Act 1973, Part II (ss. 21–49), which relate to the financial arrangements between the parties to a marriage and the children of the family.

Durham, County Palatine of. See also COUNTY PALATINE.

Duress. For a full report of *Abbott* v. *The Queen* see [1977] A.C. 755, P.C.

In the law of marriage, albeit the secular law, duress is a matter which makes a marriage voidable since a party under duress can claim that he did not validly consent to the marriage (Matrimonial Causes Act 1973, s. 12(*c*)).

Dwelling-house. The Rent Act 1968, s. 1, has been repealed and replaced by the Rent Act 1977, s. 1, without change of effect (see also the Act of 1977, ss. 6, 26).

See also the Housing Defects Act 1984, which treats of defective dwellings disposed of by public sector authorities.

E

Easement. Being both an incorporated hereditament and incapable of being held in gross, an easement cannot be the subject of a tenancy agreement (*Land Reclamation Co. Ltd.* v. *Basildon District Council* [1979] 1 W.L.R. 767, C.A.).

The easement of a way of necessity was considered in *Nickerson* v. *Barraclough* [1981] Ch. 426, C.A., where the earlier authorities were reviewed.

For the restriction of the operation of the Law of Property Act 1925, s. 198, by the Law of Property Act 1969, s. 24, see LAND CHARGE.

Easter. By the Easter Act 1928, provision was made for fixing the date of Easter so that Easter Day would fall on the first Sunday after the second Saturday in April (s. 1(1)). The commencement of the Act was made subject to affirmative resolutions of both House of Parliament, prior regard being had to any opinion officially expressed by an church or other christian body (s. 2(2)). The Act has yet to be brought into operation, thus being the most ancient case of delayed commencement.

Easter term. The Judicature Act 1925, ss. 52, 53, have been repealed and replaced by the Supreme Court Act 1981, s. 71, without major change of effect, leaving vacations to be regulated under the R.S.C.

Education. The duty to implement a comprehensive education policy has been abolished (Education Act 1979, s. 1, repealing the Education Act 1973, ss. 1–3).

Further significant amendments to the system of education are contained in the Education Acts 1980 and 1981 (which makes arrangements for the provision of special schools for children who are disabled in some way).

Eggs. The Diseases of Animals Act 1950, s. 49(1)(*b*), has been repealed (without replacement) by the Animal Health Act 1981, s. 96(2), Sched. 6.

The fines which may be imposed under the Game Act 1831 (including the penalty under s. 24) are now all limited to level one on the standard scale (see FINE).

The Protection of Birds Act 1954, ss. 1, 6(1), and the Protection of Birds Act 1967, ss. 1, 2, 4, have been repealed and replaced by the Wildlife and Countryside Act 1981, ss. 1–8, without significant change of effect.

Egyptian. The fine under the Highways Act 1835, s. 72, was increased to £10; for the general revision of the levels of fines which may be imposed on summary conviction (by the Criminal Justice Act 1982) see FINE.

For further amendments of the law relating to caravan sites see the Local Government, Planning and Land Act 1980, ss. 173–178.

Ejectment. The limit under the County Courts Act 1959, s. 48, was increased to £1,000 by the Administration of Justice Act 1973, s. 6, Sched. 2; the 1959 provision has now been repealed and replaced by the County Courts Act 1984, s. 21(1), without significant change of effect. The expression "county court limit" is now used to define the jurisdiction, being contained in the Act of 1984, s. 147(1), and subject to revision by statutory instrument.

Election. See also the European Assembly Election Regulations 1984 (S.I. 1984 No. 137).

Election agent. The Representation of the People Act 1949, ss. 55(1), (2), 59 and 171(1), and the Act of 1969, s. 11, have been repealed and replaced by the Representation of the People Act 1983, ss. 67(1), (2), 71, 202(1) and ss. 67–68, without change of effect.

Election expenses. The amount which may be paid out for election expenses was increased by the Representation of the People Act, 1978, s. 1, and a general power to vary the permitted amount was conferred on the Secretary of State (Act of 1978, s. 2); the power was exercised by the making of S.I. 1980 No. 375, S.I. 1981 No. 191 and S.I. 1982 No. 363.

The expenses allowed in parliamentary elections were again increased in 1978, and power was given to the Secretary of State to allow further increases subject to parliamentary approval (Representation of the People Act 1978). The Representation of the People Act 1974, was repealed by the

Act of 1978, s. 3(2).

In the course of consolidation the Representation of the People Act 1949, ss. 60(1), (2), 61, 62, 63, 64, have been repealed and replaced by the Representation of the People Act 1983, ss. 72(1), (2), 73, 74, 75, respectively, without change of effect. The modifications made by the Act of 1969, ss. 8, 9(4), and Sched. 2, para. 16, have been repealed without replacement, their effect being incorporated into the new provisions.

Election petitions. The Representation of the People Act 1949, ss. 107–110, 112–114, 115 and 119–137 (which deal with the procedure on election petitions), have been repealed and replaced by the Representation of the People Act 1983, ss. 120–124, 127–129, 130 and 136–157, without change of effect.

Elector; Electoral franchise. By the Representation of the People Act 1980, amendments were made to the 1949 provisions relating to the registration of electors who have a service qualification and to the corrections which may be made in registers of electors (for the commencement of these provisions see S.I. 1980 No. 1030). The Act of 1949, s. 1(1), has now been repealed and replaced by the Representation of the People Act 1983, s. 1(1), without change of effect. The modifications contained in the Representation of the People (Armed Forces) Act 1976, s. 206, Sched. 9, have been repealed, since they have been incorporated into the 1983 provisions (ss. 1–3).

Electoral register. The compilation and public display, etc., of the electoral register is now governed by the Representation of the People Act 1983, s. 13.

Elegit. The power to impose a charging order on the land of a judgment debtor is now contained in the Charging Orders Act 1979, which empowers the High Court and county courts to make such orders. The county court is usually the proper tribunal for all cases involving sums less than £5,000 (Act of 1979, s. 1(2)). The procedure for obtaining such an order is laid down in R.S.C. Ord. 50, s. 1, and the C.C.R. 1981, Ord. 31 (replacing the C.C.R. 1976, Ord. 25, r. 6A). The order has to be registered in the register of land charges (Land Charges Act 1972, s. 6) or entered as a caution against the title to registered land (Land Registration Act 1925, s. 59) before it will bind purchasers of the land it affects. The Administration of Justice Act 1956, s. 35, and the County Courts Act 1959, s. 141, were repealed by the Charging Orders Act 1979, s. 7(2). See also CHARGING ORDER.

The issue of writs of elegit having been discontinued by the Administration of Justice Act 1956, the writ itself has been abolished (Supreme Court Act 1981, s. 141).

Employer. In employment law this term is often used in the statutory sense, where its meaning is as follows: (a) where the reference is to an employer in relation to an employee, the person by whom the employee is (or, in a case where employment has ceased, was) employed, and (b) in any other case, means a person regarded in that person's capacity as one for whom one or more workers work, or have worked or normally work or seek to work (Trade Union and Labour Relations Act 1974, s. 30(1)). The term also includes various health authorities even though the workers concerned may not perform their work under a contract of service (Act of 1974, s. 30(2)). See also WORKER.

The position of an employers' association has been assimilated (in the repeal of the Trade Union and Labour Relations Act 1974, s. 14, by the Employment Act 1982, s. 15) to that of a trade union (*q.v.*) in relation to liability in tort, etc.

Employment Appeal Tribunal. The Employment Protection Act 1975, ss. 87, 88, Sched. 6, have been repealed and replaced by the Employment Protection (Consolidation) Act 1978, ss. 135, 136, Sched. 11, without change of effect.

The Tribunal is composed of such judges of the High Court and of the Court of Appeal as may be nominated by the Lord Chancellor (subject to the judge's consent to the nomination) and lay members appointed from time to time on the recommendation of the Secretary of State jointly with the Lord Chancellor (Act of 1978, s. 135(2)). The lay members are required to be persons who appear to the Lord Chancellor and the Secretary of State to have special knowledge or experience of industrial relations either as employers' representatives or as workers representatives (within the meaning given to the terms "employer" (*q.v.*) and "worker" (*q.v.*) by the Trade

Union and Labour Relations Act 1974, s. 30(2)) (Act of 1978, s. 135(2)).

The Tribunal has no original jurisdiction, being concerned solely with appellate proceedings. There are two classes of appeals: first, those relating to questions of law and, secondly, those relating to questions of fact. In the first group come cases concerning any decision of, or arising under any proceedings before, an industrial tribunal or by virtue of the Equal Pay Act 1970, the Sex Discrimination Act 1975, the Employment Protection Act 1975, the Race Relations Act 1976 or the Employment Protection (Consolidation) Act 1978. In the second group come cases concerning any proceedings before, or arising from any decision of, the Certification Officer (*q.v.*) under the Trade Union Act 1913, ss. 3–5, or the Trade Union (Amalgamations, etc.) Act 1964, s. 4. The Tribunal also determines questions either of law or of fact arising in proceedings before, or arising from any decision of, the Certification Officer under the Trade Union and Labour Relations Act 1974, s. 8 or the Employment Protection Act 1975, s. 8 (but see *General and Municipal Workers Union* v. *Certification Officer* [1977] I.C.R. 183).

Appeal lies from the Tribunal to the Court of Appeal on any question of law, provided the Tribunal or the Court of Appeal grants leave for the appeal (Act of 1978, s. 136(4)).

Employment Service Agency. The Agency and it employees were granted the status of Crown servants and were to be treated as a government department for the purposes of civil proceedings arising out of their functions (Employment and Training Act 1973, s. 1(7)–(8). See also LABOUR EXCHANGE. The Agency has, however, now been abolished (Employment and Training Act 1981, s. 9).

En ventre sa mère. A child en ventre sa mère cannot be a "child of the family" for the purposes of the Matrimonial Causes Act 1973, Part II (which deals with the financial arrangements between the parties to a marriage and the children of the family) (*A.* v. *A.* (*Family: unborn child*) [1974] Fam. 6).

Enactment. It is also provided that where an Act repeals and re-enacts a previous enactment (with or without modification), unless the contrary intention appears, any reference in any other enactment to the repealed enactment is to be construed as a reference to the re-enacted provision, and in so far as anything done under the repealed enactment or which has effect as if so made or done could have been made or done under the re-enacted provision, it has effect as if made or done under that provision (Interpretation Act 1978, s. 17(2), replacing the Interpretation Act 1889, s. 38(1)).

Endemic disease. The Public Health Act 1936, ss. 143(1)–(7), (10), 147–170, have been repealed by the Public Health (Control of Diseases) Act 1984, s. 78, Sched. 3. The use of the expression "endemic disease" in the Act of 1984 is not apparent.

Endowment or **Indowment.** The endowments subject to the National Health Service Act 1946, s. 7, were allocated to a fund called the Hospital Endowments Fund (s. 7(4)). This fund was wound up by virtue of the National Health Service Reorganisation Act 1973, s. 23, the assets being distributed among regional health authorities (Act of 1973, s. 23(2)). Further provisions for the administration of these funds are now contained in the National Health Service Act 1977, ss. 90–96).

Enemy Property. All but ss. 15, 18 and part of s. 4 of the Enemy Property Act 1953, have been repealed (Statute Law (Repeals) Act 1976, s. 1(1), Sched. 1, Part XX).

Energy, Secretary of State for. Earlier provisions and fresh powers have been combined in a general Act relating to the nation's resources and use of energy (Energy Act 1976). See also the Energy Conservation Act 1981.

Enforcement notice. The registration of an enforcement notice as a local land charge is now effected under the terms of the Local Land Charges Act 1975, s. 1.

The Town and Country Planning Act 1971, ss. 87–88, have been replaced by a revised (and expanded) text (Act of 1971, ss. 87, 87A, 88, 88A, 88B, inserted by the Town and Country Planning (Amendment) Act 1981, s. 1, Sched.), giving better control over listed buildings. See also the Act of 1971, ss. 92A, 96, 97, 97A, 100, 104.

The text of the stop notice provision (Town and Country Planning Act 1971, s. 90) has been revised to eliminate difficulties caused by the original formulation (Town and Country Planning (Amendment) Act 1977, s. 1, substituting a new s. 90 into the Act of 1971).

England. The Wales and Berwick Act 1746, s. 3, has been repealed and replaced by the Interpretation Act 1978, s. 25, Sched. 3. By s. 5 of and Sched. 1 to the Act of 1978, the term "England" means, subject to any alteration of boundaries under the Local Government Act 1972, Part IV, the area consisting of the counties established by s. 1, of that Act, together with Greater London and the Isles of Scilly.

Enlargement. A scheme for the enlargement of certain residential tenancies is contained in the Leasehold Reform Acts 1967 and 1979; see LEASEHOLDS.

Somewhat comparable provisions (though with more far-reaching social effects) for what was effectively the enlargement of tenancies of public-sector dwellings into freeholds, were introduced by the Housing Act 1980, Part I (ss. 1–50), and have now been significantly extended by amendment (by the Housing and Building Control Act 1984, Part I (ss. 1–38)).

Enrol; enrolment; Enrolment Office. The Enrolment of Deeds (Change of Name) Regulations 1949, 1951 and 1974, have been revoked and replaced by the Enrolment of Deeds (Change of Name) Regulations 1983 (S.I. 1983 No. 680) (set out in the notes to R.S.C. Ord. 63, r. 10).

The Crown Debts Act 1801, s. 6, has been (prospectively repealed by the Civil Jurisdiction and Judgments Act 1982, s. 54, Sched. 14.

Enter. The requirement that a defendant should enter an appearance has been abolished and replaced by the requirement that he should send to the court office an acknowledgement of service (R.S.C. (Writ and Appearance) 1979 (S.I. 1979 No. 1716)).

The office of Chancery Division Registrar has been abolished in the course of reforms following on the Oliver Report (Cmnd. 8205) (see the Rules of the Supreme Court (Amendment No. 2) 1982 (S.I. 1982 No. 1111)). The revised procedures for entering judgments in the Chancery Division are contained in R.S.C. Ord. 42, r. 6, and explained in *Practice Direction* [1982] 1 W.L.R. 1189 (which deals with the general organisation of Chancery Chambers).

Enticement. The Law Reform (Miscellaneous Provisions) Act 1970, s. 5, has been supplemented by the Administration of Justice Act 1982, s. 2, which provides for the abolition of actions for the loss of services of certain persons.

Entire animals. For increases in the levels of fines and a certain level of standardisation see FINE.

Episcopalia or **Onera Episcopalia.** The Ecclesiastical Commissioners Act 1860, s. 2, has been repealed by the Statute Law Revisions Act 1964, s. 1, Sched.

Equal pay. See the Equal Pay Act 1970 (set out, as amended, in the Sex Discrimination Act 1975, s. 8, Sched. 1, Part II); and SEX DISCRIMINATION.

Equalisation of water charges. See the Water Charge Equalisation Act 1977, which has been repealed without replacement by the Water Act 1983, ss. 8, 11(3), Sched. 5, Part I.

Equitable claims and defences at common law. The Judicature Act 1925, ss. 36 *et seq.*, have been repealed and replaced by the Supreme Court Act 1981, s. 49, without change of effect.

Equitable execution. For the procedures for the appointment of receivers see R.S.C. Ord. 30 (general provisions) and Ord. 51 (special provisions for receivers appointed by way of equitable execution). The power to appoint receivers contained in the Administration of Justice Act 1956, s. 36, has been repealed by the Supreme Court Act 1981, s. 152(4), Sched. 7.

The Judicature Act 1925, s. 45, has been repealed and replaced by the Supreme Court Act 1981, s. 37. The 1981 provision contains additional express powers to issue an injunction (*q.v.*) based on the "Mareva" case, being more liberally drafted.

Equitable mortgage. The Judicature Act 1925, s. 56, has been repealed and replaced by the Supreme Court Act 1981, s. 61(1), (3), and Sched. 1, para. 1(*b*), without significant change of effect.

Equity. The Judicature Act 1925, s. 36, has been repealed and replaced by the Supreme Court Act 1981, s. 49, without change of effect.

Equity of redemption. The Limitation Act 1939, s. 18, has been repealed and replaced by the Limitation Act 1980, s. 20, without change of effect.

Escape. The penalties under the Prison

Act 1952, s. 39, and the Criminal Justice Act 1961, s. 22(1), are subject to the general regime for fines which has been introduced by the Criminal Justice Act 1982, ss. 35–48; see FINE. The Mental Health Act 1959, s. 129, has been repealed and replaced by the Mental Health Act 1983, s. 128, without change of effect.

Essence of the contract. The Sale of Goods Act 1893, s. 10(1), has been repealed and replaced by the Sale of Goods Act 1979, s. 10(1), without change of effect.

Established use certificate. See DEVELOPMENT.

Estate. Rentcharges (*i.e.* any annual or other periodic sum charged on or issuing out of land, except rent reserved by way of a lease or tenancy, or any sum payable by way of interest), may, generally speaking, no longer be created (Rentcharges Act 1977, s. 2(1)). Such rentcharges as already exist are being extinguished over a period of 60 years (s. 3). Tithe redemption annuities have been brought to an end (Finance Act 1977, s. 56).

Estate agent. Extensive new provision has been made for the regulation of the work of estate agents (Estate Agents Act 1979). By virtue of the Estate Agents Act (Commencement No. 1) Order 1981 (S.I. 1981 No. 1519), ss. 1–15, 18, 20, 21, 23–24, 36, Scheds. 1 and 2, came into operation on 21 May 1981.

Estoppel. The rule that an estoppel is not enough to found proceedings has been illustrated by describing it as "a shield, not a sword" (*Combe* v. *Combe* [1951] 2 K.B. 215, C.A., following *Central London Property Trust Ltd.* v. *High Trees House Ltd.* [1947] K.B. 130). It has been held that it is proper for the plaintiff to plead an estoppel in reply to a defence (*Powell* v. *Henderson Hait* [1977] 4 W.W.R. 757).

Estreat. The Criminal Justice Act 1948, s. 14, and the Criminal Justice Act 1967, s. 47, have been repealed and replaced by the Powers of Criminal Courts Act 1973, s. 31, without substantial change of effect. The Magistrates' Court Act 1952, s. 96, has been repealed and replaced by the Magistrates' Courts Act 1980, s. 120, without change of effect. The nature of estreat proceedings has been considered and determined to be civil (*R.* v. *Marlow Justices, ex p. O'Sullivan* [1984] Q.B. 381, D.C.).

European Court. Detailed provision for references to the European court is made by R.S.C. Ord. 114, and the C.C.R. 1981, Ord. 19, r. 11. In both cases the proceedings are stayed from the time when the reference is made until the decision of the European court has been transmitted back to the court from which the reference was made.

European Monetary Agreement. The European Monetary Agreement Act 1959, and the related amendments in the National Loans Act 1968, have been repealed without direct replacement by the European Monetary Fund Act 1979, s. 6(1), Sched., Part II.

Eviction. There are extensive and complex provisions governing the eviction of tenants of residential property (*e.g.* the Rent Act 1977), and criminal sanctions have been attached to a number of practices relating to the eviction or harrassment of residential occupiers by methods which do not conform with the prescribed rules (Protection from Eviction Act 1977; see also the Criminal Law Act 1977, ss. 6–13, which deal with offences relating to entering and remaining on property, and the Housing (Homeless Persons) Act 1977, which provides (*inter alia*) for people who have been evicted and are in need of accommodation.

Evidence. Further provisions designed to enable the High Court to assist in obtaining evidence required for use in proceedings in other jurisdictions and related matters are contained in the Evidence (Proceedings in Other Jurisdictions) Act 1975; the related procedural requirements (in civil cases) are set out in R.S.C. Ord. 70.

For the effect of the Criminal Evidence Act 1979, see CHARACTER.

Ex parte. For a curious example of an "opposed *ex parte*" application see *Pickwick International Inc.* (*G.B.*) *Ltd.* v. *Multiple Sound Distributors Ltd.* [1972] 1 W.L.R. 1213.

Ex turpi causa non oritur actio. The courts also have a restricted power to modify the forfeiture rule under the Forfeiture Act 1982; see FORFEITURE.

Examination. On the application of the official receiver the public examination of a bankrupt may be dispensed with by order of the court if the court thinks fit to make such an order having regard to all the circumstances of the case (Insolvency Act

1976, s. 6).

In appropriate cases an examination before examining justices may be converted into summary trial and vice versa (see the Magistrates' Courts Act 1980, s. 25).

Examining surgeon. The Factories Act 1961, s. 151, has been repealed by the Employment Medical Advisory Service Act 1972, s. 9(2), Sched. 3. The Act of 1972 uses the term "employment medical adviser" instead of "examining surgeon." See EMPLOYMENT MEDICAL ADVISORY SERVICE.

Except; Exception. The Magistrates' Courts Act 1952, s. 81, has been repealed and replaced by the Magistrates' Courts Act 1980, s. 101, without change of effect.

Exceptions clauses. *Suisse Atlantique Society d'Armèmènt Maritime S.A.* v. *N.V. Rotterdamsche Kolen Centrale* was reported at [1967] 1 A.C. 361.

Extensive new provision has been made for the restriction of the use of exceptions clauses in "consumer contracts" (Unfair Contract Terms Act 1977). See UNFAIR CONTRACT TERMS. See also EXEMPTION CLAUSES.

Exchange control. All restrictions except those in relation to Southern Rhodesia were relaxed on October 24, 1979 (S.I. 1979 No. 1339, 1660), and those relating to Southern Rhodesia were terminated on 13 December 1979 (S.I. 1979 No. 1662). See also the Exchange Control (Authorised Dealers and Depositaries) (Revocation) Order 1984 (S.I. 1984 No. 1459) for the closing stages of de-regulation.

Exchange, Deed of. In connection with the modification of other powers to dispose of land (now contained in the Housing Act 1959, ss. 104–104C (as extended by the Housing Act 1980, s. 90 and the Housing and Building Control Act 1984, s. 23, Sched. 6), the Housing Act 1957, s. 105(1), (2) and (5), were repealed by the Housing Act 1980, s. 91, thus emasculating the minister's powers originally conferred by the section.

Exchange equalisation funds. The remaining provisions relating to exchange equalisation have been repealed and consolidated in the Exchange Equalisation Account Act 1979.

Exchequer. Fresh provision has been made for the functions of the Audit Department (see the National Audit Act 1983).

Exchequer Chamber. The Judicature Act 1925, s. 26, has been repealed and replaced by the Supreme Court Act 1981, s. 15 (which relates to the general jurisdiction of the Court of Appeal and replaces both ss. 26 and 27 of the Act of 1925). Section 15(2)(*b*), however, states "there shall be exercisable by the Court of Appeal all such jurisdiction (whether civil or criminal) as was exercisable by it immediately before the commencement of this Act", thus defining the jurisdiction in terms of the repealed 1925 provision.

Exchequer Division. The Judicature Act 1925, s. 4, has been repealed and replaced by the Supreme Court Act 1981, s. 5 (which deals with the establishment of Divisions of the High Court. All references to the Exchequer Division have disappeared.

Excise. There have been extensive consolidating measures in this field. The powers and functions of the Commissioners of Customs and Excise (*q.v.*) are now contained in the Customs and Excise Management Act 1979. The principal provisions imposing duties are the Alcoholic Liquor Duties Act 1979, the Hydrocarbon Oil Duties Act 1979, the Matches and Mechanical Lighters Duties Act 1979 and the Tobacco Duties Act 1979. Reliefs from duties are dealt with in the Customs and Excise Duties (General Reliefs) Act 1979. Power to regulate the rate of charge to duty is given by the Excise Duties (Surcharges and Rebates) Act 1979. The vast majority of the Customs and Excise Act 1952, was repealed when it was replaced by the legislation of 1979.

Exclusion clause. Since clauses which restrict liability are less strictly construed than those which exclude liability, such a clause may more readily survive in the event of the complete failure of performance by the party who relies on it (*Ailsa Craig Fishing Co. Ltd.* v. *Malvern Fishing Co. Ltd.* [1983] 1 W.L.R. 964, H.L.).

Exclusion orders. The Prevention of Terrorism (Temporary Provisions) Act 1976, has been repealed and replaced by the Prevention of Terrorism (Temporary Provisions) Act 1984, of which ss. 3–8 relate to exclusion orders. The Act of 1984 is due to lapse on 21 March 1989 (s. 17(3)) but also requires annual renewal in the meantime.

If the court by or before which a person is

convicted of an offence committed on licensed premises is satisfied that the offender resorted to violence or offered to do so, it may make an exclusion order in respect of him, prohibiting him from entering those premises or any other precified premises unless he has the express permission of the licensee or of the licensee's servant or agent (Licensed Premises (Exclusion of Certain Persons) Act 1980, s. 1(2)). Such an order must be of at least three months' duration, but may not last more than two years (s. 1(3)). Failure to comply with the order is an offence carrying a penalty (on summary conviction) of a fine (*q.v.*) not exceeding £200 or two months' imprisonment or both (s. 2(1)).

Execution. The making of a charging order (*q.v.*) now constitutes a completed act of execution for the purposes of the Companies Act 1948, s. 325, and the Bankruptcy Act 1914, s. 40 (Charging Orders Act 1979, s. 4), without the need for any further act on the part of the chargee.

Execution of wills. By the Administration of Justice Act 1982, s. 17, a new text has been substituted into the Wills Act 1837, s. 9. The essential difference is that the new provisions authorise the witnesses to sign (or acknowledge their signatures) separately if they wish, provided they do so in the presence of the testator. The requirement of signature "'at the end or foot [of the will]" has been replaced by a provision which requires an intention on the part of the testator "by his signature . . . to give effect to the will."

Executive councils. The National Health Service Act 1946, s. 31, and the Health Services and Public Health Act 1968, s. 16, Sched. 1, have been repealed by the National Health Service Reorganisation Act 1973, s. 57(2), Sched. 5. Executive councils have been replaced by family practitioner committees (*q.v.*).

Executor. The Judicature Act 1925, s. 160(1), has been repealed and replaced by the Supreme Court Act 1981, s. 114(1); the new s. 114 incorporates an amendment so that it is no longer essential for two persons to act, the court having a discretion to appoint a sole individual in certain cases. The Administration of Estates Act 1925, s. 23 (and associated amending Acts), also has been affected by the new s. 114.

The British Nationality Act 1948, Sched. 4, Part II, has been repealed by the British Nationality Act 1981, s. 52(8), Sched. 9, but without affecting the amendment already effected to the Status of Aliens Act 1914, s. 17.

The Judicature Act 1925, s. 165, has been repealed and replaced by the Supreme Court Act 1981, s. 118, with slight modifications but otherwise without substantial change of effect.

For the effect of the introduction of the Administration of Estates Act 1925, s. 21A (by the Limitation Amendment Act 1980, s. 19), see DEBTOR-EXECUTOR.

The Legacy Duty Act 1796, the Finance Act 1894, and the Law of Property Act 1925, s. 16, have been repealed by the Finance Act 1975, s. 59(5), Sched. 13, in connection with the introduction of capital transfer tax (*q.v.*). Executors are liable for the capital transfer tax in respect of the estate which comes into their hands so far as the tax is attributable to the value of the property which was not immediately before the death comprised in a settlement or was so comprised and consists of land in the United Kingdom which devolves upon or vests in the personal representatives of the deceased (Capital Transfer Tax 1984, s. 200(1), (3), replacing the Finance Act 1975, s. 25(5)). See also the Act of 1984, ss. 21 *et seq.*

The rate of interest payable on any unpaid statutory legacy is now varied from time to time by order made by the Lord Chancellor (Administration of Estates Act 1925, s. 46; Administration of Justice Act 1977, s 28; see S.I. 1977 No. 1491 and S.I. 1983 No. 1374).

Executory interest. The restrictions on accumulations (Law of Property Act 1925, s. 164) which apply to executory interests have been amended by the Perpetuities and Accumulations Act 1964 (s. 13); see ACCUMULATION.

Exemplary damages. A claim for exemplary damages must be specifically pleaded in proceedings in the Supreme Court (R.S.C. Ord. 18, r. 8(3)), but need not be so pleaded in proceedings in the county court (*Drane* v. *Evangelou* [1978] 1 W.L.R. 455, C.A.).

The Law Reform (Miscellaneous Provisions) Act 1934, s. 1(2), has been amended by the Administration of Justice Act 1982, s. 2(4), so as to exclude from claims not only exemplary damages but also any damages for loss of income in respect of any period after the [deceased's] death (Act of 1934, s. 1(2)(*a*)(ii)). A live plaintiff may, however, still claim for loss of earnings in the "lost years" (*Pickett* v. *British Rail Engineering Ltd.* [1980] A.C. 136, H.L.).

Exempt private companies. The Companies Act 1948, s. 127, has been repealed by the Companies Act 1976 s. 42(2), Sched. 3. The preparation of company accounts is provided for by the Act of 1976, ss. 1–20. See BOOKS OF ACCOUNT.

Exemption clause. Such clauses must be expressly incorporated in the relationship between the parties from the outset, being incapable of being introduced unilaterally at a later stage (*Thornton* v. *Shoe Lane Parking Ltd.* [1971] 2 Q.B. 163, C.A.). The requirement that the party relying on the exemption must be performing his part of the contract has been re-affirmed (*Levison* v. *Patent Steam Carpet Cleaning Co. Ltd.* [1978] Q.B. 69, C.A.). See also *Photo Production Ltd.* v. *Securicor Transport Ltd.* [1978] A.C. 283, H.L. Further restrictions have been imposed by the Unfair Contract Terms Act 1977 (see especially s. 13, and UNFAIR CONTRACT TERMS.

Expatriation. The British Nationality Act 1948, s. 19, has been repealed and replaced by the British Nationality Act 1981, s. 12; citizenship may be resumed (s. 13) after expatriation, but only once (s. 13(2)).

Expectation of life. The rule in *Oliver* v. *Ashman* [1962] 2 Q.B. 210, C.A., was overruled by the House of Lords in *Pickett* v. *British Rail Engineering Ltd.* [1980] A.C. 136, where it was ruled that the loss of wages which would have been earned during the "lost years" should be taken into account as a separate head of damage. Such an award, it was held, might survive for the benefit of the estate of a person who has died as a result of the wrong which he has suffered (*Gammell* v. *Wilson* [1982] A.C. 270). The rule has been amended so that the income for the "lost years" cannot now be claimed by the estate (Law Reform (Miscellaneous Provisions) Act 1934, s. 1(2)(*a*)(ii) (as substituted by the Administration of Justice Act 1982, s. 4(2)).

The conventional sum awarded for the loss of expectation of life appeared to increase to £750 (*McCann* v. *Sheppard* [1973] 1 W.L.R. 290), and then to £1,250 (*Gammell* v. *Wilson* (above)).

The provisions of the Administration of Justice Act 1982, s. 1, made many of these matters into mere history (although those rules are preserved for cases deriving from before 1983). The right to damages for loss of expectation of life has been abolished (Act of 1982, s. 1(1)), although this abolition does not extend to damages in respect of loss of income (s. 1(2)). If the injured person's expectation of life has been reduced by his injuries, however, the court is entitled to take account of the suffering caused or likely to be caused him by his awareness of that reduction (s. 1(1)(*b*)). See also BEREAVEMENT and EXEMPLARY DAMAGES.

Expert; expert evidence. In personal injuries proceedings in the High Court the parties' expert medical reports are required to be included in the documents supplied to the court office when the case is set down for trial (*Practice Direction* [1979] 1 W.L.R. 290).

Since in all classes of proceedings the reports of experts (other than medical advisers) will normally be ordered to be exchanged between the parties, this should normally be done without recourse to any order of the court (*Ollett* v. *Bristol Aerojet Ltd.* [1979] 1 W.L.R. 1197).

The general provisions of R.S.C. Ord. 38, rr. 37–39, 41–44, are applied to county court proceedings by the C.C.R. 1981, Ord. 21, r. 28; see also the C.C.R. 1981, Ord. 21, r. 26 (which relates to the use of statements of opinion).

Fresh provision has been made for disclosure of the contents of experts' reports (Rules of the Supreme Court (Amendment No. 2) 1980 (S.I. 1980 No. 1010)).

Export guarantees. The Export Guarantees Act 1975, has been repealed and replaced by the Export Guarantees and Overseas Investment Act 1978 (which also incorporates the amendments to the 1975 Act). The functions of the Export Credits Guarantee Department and of the Export Guarantees Advisory Council are continued by s. 12 of the Act of 1978.

Exposure, Indecent. The Criminal Justice Act 1925, s. 42 (which contained repeals of part of the Vagrancy Act 1824, s. 4), has been repealed by the Statute Law Revisions Act 1950, s. 1(1), Sched. 1.

Exposing person with contagious disease. The Public Health Act 1936, s. 148, has been repealed and replaced by the Public Health (Control of Diseases) Act 1984, s. 17, which relates to notifiable diseases (listed in s. 10, as cholera, plague, relapsing fever, smallpox and typhus).

Exposing unfit food for sale. The Food and Drugs Act 1955, s. 8, has been repealed and replaced by the Food Act 1984, s. 8, without change of effect.

Express carriage. The Road Traffic Act 1960, ss. 117 and 118, and the Transport Act 1968, s. 145(1), have been repealed and replaced by the Transport Act 1980, s. 69, Sched. 9, Part I. By s. 3 of the 1980 Act an express carriage is defined by reference to the normal minimum distance between picking-up and setting-down points (normally they must be at least 30 miles apart).

Extinguishment of highway. The Highways Act 1959, ss. 108, 109, 114, 115 and 116, have been repealed and replaced by the Highways Act 1980, ss. 116, 117, 122, 123 and 130, without change of effect. The Civil Aviation Act 1949, s. 23, has been repealed and replaced by the Civil Aviation Act 1982, s. 48, without change of effect.

The extinguishment of a highway may result, albeit by accident, from the designation of a way as a "footpath" when a revised definitive map is drawn up under the National Parks and Access to the Countryside Act 1949 (*Suffolk County Council* v. *Mason* [1979] A.C. 705, H.L.).

Extinguishment of tithe rentcharge. The extinguishment of these annuities was provided for in the Finance Act 1977, s. 56, which first required on October 1, 1977, the payment of twice what would ordinarily have been due on that date under the Tithe Acts 1936 and 1951, and then abolished the annuities. See also TITHES.

Extortion. The County Courts Act 1959, s. 31, was repealed by the Supreme Court Act 1981, ss. 149(2), 152(4), Sched. 7, without replacement.

Extradition. The list of extradition crimes (set out in the Extradition Act 1870, Sched. 1) has been further amended by the Protection of Aircraft Act 1971, s. 5 (now repealed and replaced by the Aviation Security Act 1982); the Internationally Protected Persons Act 1978, s. 3(1); the Suppression of Terrorism Act 1978, s. 3(1) (which adds to the list all offences in the Explosive Substances Act 1883; all indictable offences under the Firearms Act 1968; and any attempt to commit any crime included in the list including crimes added after the passing of the Act of 1978); the Protection of Children Act 1978, s. 1(6)); the Taking of Hostages Act 1982, s. 3; the Nuclear Material (Offences) Act 1983, ss. 2, 5(1) and the Child Abduction Act 1984, s. 11.

Extraordinary traffic. The Highways Act 1959, s. 62, has been repealed and replaced by the Highways Act 1980, s. 59, without change of effect.

Extra-parochial. The Extra-Parochial Places Act 1857, has been repealed by the Statute Law (Repeals) Act 1974, s. 1, Sched., Part X, without replacement. The Pastoral Measure 1968, s. 16, has been repealed and replaced by the Pastoral Measure 1983, s. 17, without change of effect.

F

Fabrics, Inflammable. Related provisions are contained in the Consumer Safety Act 1978, which enables the Secretary of State to make safety regulations in respect of goods (s. 1), creating offences for contravention of those regulations (s. 2), as well as imposing civil liability in certain circumstances (s. 6).

Under the Fabrics (Misdescription) Act 1913, s. 1, there have been issued the Fabrics (Misdescription) Regulations 1980 (S.I. 1980 No. 726); these prescribe the qualifying standards which must be attained before textile fabrics may be described as resistant to ignition from smouldering cigarettes or lighted matches.

Fair trading. The powers of the Director General of Fair Trading have been extended in connection with the abolition of price controls and the encouragement of competition in industry (Competition Act 1980, ss. 9, 10, 21–41).

Fair wages resolution. The House of Commons has approved Fair Wages Resolutions from time to time since 1891, the latest having been promulgated in 1946. The Resolution instructs government departments which enter into any contract with a private contractor for the supply of goods or services to insert into the contract a number of terms. There are two significant provisions which are normally incorporated. First, there is an obligation on the contractor to provide his workers with terms and conditions which are not less favourable than those established for the trade or industry in the district where the work is to be carried out by machinery of negotiation or arbitration, alternatively, in the absence of such terms, terms no less favourable than the general conditions observed by other similar employers in the trade or industry. Secondly, the contractor is required to recognise the freedom of his workers to belong to a trade union.

Reports of non-compliance are required to be made to the department concerned, which may then take up the matter with the defaulting contractor. In the event of the contractor contesting the complaint the matter is referred to the Central Arbitration Committee, which is restricted to advising on whether the contractor is complying with the terms of the contract. Persistent failure of a contractor to observe the terms of the Resolution usually leads to withdrawal of its business by the government department involved.

Fairs. The Public Health Act 1875, s. 167, was repealed by the Food and Drugs Act 1938, s. 101, Sched. 4.

Falkland Islands. By virtue of the British Nationality Act 1981, s. 50(1), Sched. 6, these islands were classified (in nationality law) as nothing greater than British Dependent Territories. By the British Nationality (Falkland Islands) Act 1983, the status of citizenship was conferred on persons with connections with the Falkland Islands. Under the British Settlements Act 1945, the Falkland Islands and Dependencies (Interim Administration) Order 1982 (S.I. 1982 No. 824), has been issued.

False answer. See FALSE STATUTORY DECLARATION, ETC.

False character. Parts of the Servants' Characters Act 1792, ss. 1, 4, have been repealed without replacement by the Forgery and Counterfeiting Act 1981, s. 30, Sched., Part I, since written false characters will now normally come within the general law relating to forgery. The same course has been taken in respect of the provisions in the Seamen's and Soldier's False Characters Act 1906, ss. 1(1), 2.

False lights and signals. Consequent upon the abolition of the distinction between felonies and misdemeanours (see FELONY), the offence the Malicious Damage Act 1861, s. 47, has been reclassified as an indictable offence. The penalty for the offence of failing to comply with a notice to extinguish or screen any false light was (prospectively) increased to a fine (*q.v.*) not exceeding £1,000 (Merchant Shipping Act 1979, s. 43, Sched. 6, Part VI, para. 10).

False news. The Race Relations Act 1965, has been repealed (Race Relations Act 1976, s. 79(5), Sched. 5), but the text of the Public Order Act 1936, s. 5 (as substituted by the Act of 1965, s. 7), remains in force; this provides that any person who in a public place or at any public meeting (a) uses threatening, abusive or insulting words or behaviour or (b) distributes or displays any writing, sign or visible representation which is threatening, abusive or insulting, with intent to provoke a breach of the peace is likely to be occasioned is guilty of an offence.

The common law offence of conspiracy to spread false news has been abolished (Criminal Law Act 1977, s. 5; see CONSPIRACY).

False pretence. The offence of obtaining a pecuniary advantage by a deception (Theft Act 1968, s. 16) has been revised: three new offences have been created by the Theft Act 1978, ss. 1–3 (obtaining services by a deception, evasion of liability by a deception, and making off without payment), and the scope of the Act of 1968, s. 16, has been altered (s. 16(2)(*a*) has been repealed by the Act of 1978, s. 5(5)). See also DECEPTION.

The rules set out in *R.* v. *Page* (1971) 55 Cr.App.R. 184, were reviewed and affirmed (especially in the light of the expansion of the banks' cheque card system) in *R.* v. *Charles* [1977] A.C. 177, H.L.

False statutory declaration. If any person knowingly and wilfully makes (otherwise than on oath) a statement which is false in any material particular and the statement is made in statutory declaration, or in any account, report, etc., which he is authorised or required to make by any general Act for the time being in force, or in any oral declaration or oral answer which he is required to make by, under or in pursuance of any general public Act, he is guilty of an offence (Perjury Act 1911, s. 5). See also PERJURY.

Falsification. The scope and operation of the Companies Act 1948, s. 334, have been increased (by the Companies Act 1981, s. 92) so that they resemble the investigative powers of Department of Trade Inspectors (acting under the Companies Act 1948, ss. 164–165). The Act of 1948, s. 438, has been repealed by the Companies Act 1980, ss. 82(*f*), 88, Sched. 4.

Family arrangement. The Finance Act 1975, s. 47, and the Finance Act 1976, s. 21, have been repealed and replaced by the Capital Transfer Tax Act 1984, ss. 17, 93, 143, 145, without change of effect.

Family Division. The Administration of Justice Act 1970, s. 1, Sched. 1 provisions for the constitution of the Family Division have been repealed and replaced by the Supreme Court Act 1981, s. 61(1), (3), Sched. 1, para. 3, without change of effect.

Family planning. The National Health Service Reorganisation Act 1973, s. 4, has been repealed and replaced by the National Health Service Act 1977, s. 5(1)(*b*); see CONTRACEPTIVES.

Family Practitioner Committee. Originally constituted under the National Health Service Reorganisation Act 1973, ss. 5(5), (6), 6, to replace executive councils (*q.v.*). The membership of these bodies was prescribed by Sched. 1, Part II of that Act. These Committees now operate under the National Health Act 1977, s. 19, their constitution being provided for in Sched. 5, Part II, of that Act; their duties are laid down in s. 10 (as substituted by the Health and Social Security Act 1984, s. 5), by the new provisions FPCs were made independent of district health authorities (*q.v.*). See also Health and Social Security Act 1984, s. 28, Sched. 3.

Family provision. The jurisdiction of county courts to determine cases under the Act of 1975 was increased to estates not exceeding £15,000 in value (County Courts Jurisdiction (Inheritance—Provision for Family and Dependants) Order 1978 (S.I. 1978 No. 176)). The level has again been increased, thus bringing cases up to £30,000 into the county courts (County Courts Jurisdiction (Inheritance—Provision for Family and Dependants) Order 1981 (S.I. 1981 No. 1636)).

The 1975 provisions relating to the jurisdiction of county courts have now been repealed and replaced by the County Courts Act 1984, s. 25. By virtue of the Act of 1984, s. 24(2)(*g*), a memorandum of agreement signed by the parties or their respective solicitors or agents may be used to confer an extended jurisdiction on the county court named in the memorandum.

The Finance Act 1976, s. 122, has been repealed and its terms have been incorporated into the Capital Transfer Tax Act 1984, ss. 17, 43, 144, 146, 236, without significant change of effect.

The Matrimonial and Family Proceedings Act 1984, s. 25, makes (prospective) provision of the application of the 1975 Act to former spouses.

Fare. For the further revision of fines (*e.g.*, under the Tramways Act 1870, ss. 45, 51, 52) see FINE. The Road Traffic Act 1960, s. 135(4), has been repealed and replaced (in modified form) by the Public Service Vehicles Act 1981, s. 33.

Farriers. Detailed alterations to the scheme of registration and control of farriers have been introduced by the Farriers (Registration) (Amendment) Act 1977.

Fast day. The R.S.C. Ord. 64, r. 7, and the C.C.R. 1981, Ord. 2, r. 2, no longer make specific provision in respect of fast days, but both sets of rules allow for various *dies non* to be directed by order.

Fee. The Administration of Estates Act 1925, s. 46, has been amended by S.I. 1977 No. 415 (which revoked S.I. 1972 No. 916, and increased the amounts of the statutory legacy in favour of a surviving spouse). The section has been further amended to allow for the periodical revision of the rate of interest allowed on any unpaid statutory legacy (Administration of Justice Act 1977, s. 28; see also S.I. 1977 No. 1491 and S.I. 1981 No. 255 (increasing the relevant sums to £25,000 and £40,000 when issue survive, and £55,000 and £85,000 in other cases)). See also DISTRIBUTION.

Fee-farm rent. In so far as a fee-farm rent is a rentcharge it is subject to the provisions for extinguishment of rentcharges (*q.v.*) to be effected by the Rentcharges Act 1977, s. 3.

Feeble-minded persons. The definition provisions of the Mental Health Act 1983, s. 1(2) (replacing the Act of 1959, s. 4(2)), deal with the terms "mental impairment," "severe mental impairment" and "mental disorder," and appear to include such persons. The Education Act 1981, provides for the establishment of special arrangements for the education of children with "special educational needs," at the same time imposing a general obligation to educate such children in ordinary schools as far as possible (s. 2(2)).

Fees. The Supreme Court Fees Order 1970, has been revoked and replaced by the Supreme Court Fees Order 1980 (S.I. 1980 No. 821); the County Court Fees Order 1971, was revoked and replaced by the County Court Fees Order 1978 (S.I. 1978 No. 1243), which has in turn been revoked and replaced by the County Court Fees Order 1982 (S.I. 1982 No. 1706).

Fence. For some of the limitations of the Railways Clauses Consolidation Act 1845, s. 68, see *Short* v. *British Railways Board* [1974] 1 W.L.R. 781. The Highways Act 1959, ss. 85, 86, have been repealed and replaced by the Highways Act 1980, ss. 80, 81, without change of effect.

Ferry. The ministerial control over local authorities' acquisitions of ferries (under the National Parks and Access to the Countryside Act 1949, s. 53) has been abolished (Local Government, Planning and Land Act 1980, s. 1(7), (8), Sched. 7, para. 1). By the Highways Act 1980, s. 24(4) (replacing the Highways Act 1959, s. 26(3)), the minister and local authorities each have power to provide and maintain new road-ferries.

Fiat. The Criminal Justice Act 1925, s. 34, has been repealed and replaced by the Prosecution of Offences Act 1979, s. 7; this provides that any document purporting to be the consent of a Law Officer of the Crown for or to the institution of any criminal proceedings in any particular form is admissible as prima facie evidence without further proof.

For a list of proceeding which required the fiat or the consent of the Attorney-General for their commencement or continuation see ATTORNEY-GENERAL.

Fiduciary note issue. By the Fiduciary Note Issue (Extension of Period) Order 1980 (S.I. 1980 No. 192), the period during which the fiduciary note issue may exceed the (former) statutory maximum of £1,575 million was extended from March 14, 1980, for a period of two years. The renewal in 1982 was effected for a further two year period (by S.I. 1982 No. 198, which also revoked the Order of 1980) from March 14, 1982.

The Currency and Bank Notes Act 1954, s. 2 has now been repealed and replaced by the Currency Act 1983, s. 2, by which the statutory restriction has been fixed at £13,500 million (subject to temporary excesses not exceeding 25 per cent. of the statutory £13,500 million: see the Act of 1983, s. 2(2), (3)).

Field gardens. The Acquisition of Land (Authorisation Procedure) Act 1946, s. 1, Sched. 1, Part III, para. 11, has been repealed and replaced by the Acquisition of Land Act 1981, s. 19, Sched. 3, para. 6, without significant change of effect.

Fieri facias. The rate of interest on a judgment is no longer fixed at four per cent. By the Administration of Justice Act 1970 s. 44, power was given for the rate of interest on a judgment (under the Judgment Debts Act 1838, s. 17) to be varied from time to time; the rate is currently 12 per cent. (S.I. 1982 No. 1427).

For the ordinary forms of the writ see R.S.C., App. A, Forms 53, 54, 56 (see also Forms 62, 63). The scope of the writ was amended by the Supreme Court Act 1981, s. 138.

The County Courts Act 1959, s. 127, has been repealed and replaced by the County Courts Act 1984, s. 102, without change of effect.

Fieri facias de bonis ecclesiasticis. For

the form of writs see R.S.C., App. A, Forms 58 (fieri facias) and 59 (sequestration).

File. Virtually all fees for filing documents in court in the course of proceedings have been abolished (*e.g.*, the Supreme Court Fees Order 1970, Fee 61, has been revoked without replacement by the Supreme Court Fees Order 1975 (now also revoked)). The use of stamps to indicate the payment of fees is now also not the usual practice, payment of fees normally being evidenced by a till-receipt being printed on the document in respect of which the fee is payable.

Finance Acts. The collection of taxes under the authority of a resolution of the Committee of Ways and Means is authorised by the Provisional Collection of Taxes Act 1968, which consolidates the provisions of the Provisional Collection of Taxes Act 1913 (as amended). The Act of 1913 was passed as a result of the decision in the case *Bowles* v. *Bank of England* [1913] 1 Ch. 57, where it was ruled that the previous legislative practice did not permit the (lawful) collection of tax between the expiration of the Finance Act of the previous year and the passing of the Finance Act for the current year of assessment.

Financial year. The Interpretation Act 1889, s. 22, has been repealed and replaced by the Interpretation Act 1978, s. 5, Sched. 1, without change of effect.

Fine. The maximum fine which may be imposed on summary conviction of an offence which is triable either way (*i.e.* in the absence of any special provision authorising a larger fine) was increased to £1,000 by the Criminal Law Act 1977, s. 28; this "prescribed sum," however, may be altered by the Secretary of State (Act of 1977, s. 61). The Magistrates' Courts Act 1952, s. 27(3), was amended so that the maximum alternative penalty was no longer £100 but (a) for an offence triable either way, £1,000 (or the "prescribed sum" ordered under the Act of 1977, s. 61) and (b) for a summary offence, £200, but subject to the restriction that the fine must not be so high that the offender's failure to pay it would subject him to a longer term of imprisonment or detention than that to which he would be liable on conviction of the offence (Criminal Law Act 1977, s. 32(2)). Further provision was made for the enforcement of fines imposed on young offenders (Act of 1977 s. 36).

Some measure of rationalisation has been introduced into the levels of fines which may be imposed on summary conviction (Criminal Justice Act 1982, ss. 37–48). The "standard scale" consists of five levels (1–5, in increasingly large amounts), and the amounts for these levels may be varied by Order (Magistrates' Courts Act 1980, s. 143, Sched. 6A (as amended and inserted by the Act of 1982, s. 48, Sched. 5)). The original levels (£25, £50, £200, £500 and £1,000) have already been doubled (Criminal Penalties etc. (Increase) Order 1984 (S.I. 1984 No. 447)) for offences committed after April 1984. There are complex provisions (Criminal Justice Act 1982, ss. 38 *et seq.*) for adjustments of various fines under more specialised legislation. The same Act (of 1982) provided for the abolition of enhanced penalties on second and subsequent convictions (ss. 35, 36).

In connection with matters relating to real property, the Limitation Act 1939 has been repealed and replaced by the Limitation Act 1980 (which also incorporates amendments derived from the Limitation Acts 1963 and 1975 and the Limitation Amendment Act 1980).

Finger prints. The Magistrates' Courts Act 1952, s. 40, has been repealed and replaced by the Magistrates' Courts Act 1980, s. 49, without change of effect.

Fire certificate. This certificate is issued by the local fire authority and is required in respect of premises which come within the scope of the Fire Precautions Act 1971 (see s. 1). The premises for which a certificate is required are those designated by orders (s. 1), certain premises being exempt (s. 2); the fire authority may require certain premises to be regulated (s. 3) subject to appeal (s. 4). The issue of a certificate is regulated by the Act (s. 5), as are the matters specified in it (s. 6). Contravention of the requirements may amount to an offence (s. 7). See also FIRE PRECAUTIONS.

Fire, False alarm of. This offence now carries a maximum penalty of a fine of £1,000 or three months' imprisonment or both (Criminal Law Act 1977, s. 31, Sched. 6; Criminal Justice Act 1982, ss. 33 *et seq.*; see also FINE).

Fire precautions. The maximum fine which may be imposed for a contravention of the Public Health Act 1936, s. 60 (which requires a means of escape to be provided in certain high buildings), was increased from £5 to £500 (Criminal Law Act 1977, s. 31, Sched. 6) and has again been increased (see the Criminal Justice Act 1982, ss. 38 *et seq.*, and FINE). The Offices, Shops and Railway Premises Act 1963, ss. 32, 45, have been repealed (S.I. 1974 No. 1943); ss. 29, 37, 38, 42, 43, 46, have been repealed in part (S.I. 1984 No. 1943 and 1975 No. 1011). The operation of all the legislation has been affected by the introduction of safety regulations under the Health and Safety at Work, etc., Act 1974.

Firearms. The fees for registration of dealers have been altered (see S.I. 1980 No. 574, for the amendments).

The possession of a firearm which is honestly thought to be antique (Act of 1968, s. 58) but which is not actually within that classification is an offence since this is a matter of strict liability (*R.* v. *Howells* [1977] Q.B. 614, C.A.).

The scope of the 1968 Act has been widened so that it also applies to imitation firearms which are readily convertible into firearms which are subject to the Act of 1968, s. 1 (Firearms Act 1982, s. 1).

The Mental Health Act 1959, s. 117(1)(*d*), has been repealed and replaced by the Mental Health Act 1983, s. 131(1)(*d*), without change of effect.

Fireguards. The Consumer Protection Act 1961, was (prospectively) repealed by the Consumer Safety Act 1978, s. 10, Sched. 3. S.I. 1973 No. 2106 was amended by S.I. 1977 No. 167, and the effects of both Orders will be preserved by the Interpretation Act 1978, s. 17(2); see ENACTMENT.

Fire-hydrant. For the general revision of the levels of fines which may be imposed on summary conviction see FINE.

Fireworks. The Highways Act 1959, s. 117(1)(*d*), has been repealed and replaced by the Highways Act 1980, s. 131(1)(*d*), without change of effect.

Firm. The Moneylenders Act 1927, s. 2, was repealed by the Consumer Credit Act 1974, s. 192(3)(*b*), Sched. 5, without direct replacement. See CONSUMER CREDIT.

Fish. See also the Import of Live Fish (England and Wales) Act 1980, and the Diseases of Fish Act 1983 (the main subjects of which are the import of salmon, controls of infected water and information about fish farming).

The fishing industry is also regulated by the Fisheries Act 1981, which consolidated legislation relating to the sea fish industry.

Fishery. British fishery limits were extended to 200 miles (Fishing Limits Act 1976, s. 1), power being granted to the minister to make orders to allow foreign vessels of specified countries and of specified groups to come within those limits for specified purposes (s. 2).

Fines under the Theft Act 1968, Sched. 1, have been revised (see FINE).

See also the Fisheries Act 1981.

Flat. The Housing Finance Act 1972, ss. 90–91A, have been repealed and replaced by the Housing Act 1980, s. 136, Sched. 19, para. 16, which defines "flat" without change of effect.

Floating charge. Registration of a floating charge (under s. 95) amounts to the equivalent of registration of a land charge (under the Land Charges Act 1972), thus acting as notice to a purchaser (Act of 1972, ss. 3(7), 4).

Floods. The Coastal Flooding (Emergency Provisions) Act 1953, has been repealed by the Statute Law (Repeals) Act 1977, s. 1(1), Sched. 1, Part XIX. The Agriculture Act 1970, ss. 88–91, have been repealed and replaced by the Land Drainage Act 1976, ss. 32, 92, 101, and by s. 98 of that Act district councils are empowered to undertake general drainage works against flooding as if they were drainage authorities.

Folio. The provision relating to the cost of preparing copies of documents in the Supreme Court is now R.S.C. Ord. 62, App. 2, Item 4 (as substituted by S.I. 1979 No. 35); for county court cases see the C.C.R. 1981, App. A, Item 4.

Food. The Food and Drugs Act 1955, s. 135, has been repealed and replaced by the Food Act 1984, s. 131(1), without change of effect. The Public Health Act 1961, s. 39, has been repealed and replaced by the Public Health (Control of Diseases) Act 1984, s. 18, without significant change of effect.

Foot and mouth disease. The Diseases of Animals Act 1950, has been repealed and replaced by the Animal Health Act 1981. Section 31, and Sched. 3, para. 3, of the

1981 Act refer to foot and mouth disease and provide for optional slaughter of affected animals and compulsory compensation for any slaughter so ordered.

Football. The authority for the penalty of £10 (the Highways Act 1959, s. 140), has been repealed and replaced by the Highways Act 1980, s. 161, which continued the £10 penalty; fines have been the subject of general statutory revisions (see FINE).

Footpath; Footway. The designation of a footpath as such under the National Parks and Access to the Countryside Act 1949, may result in the extinguishment of a highway (*Suffolk County Council* v. *Mason* [1973] A.C. 705, H.L.).

The Highways Act 1959, ss. 295(1), 27–32, 46 and 53, 30, 67, 76, 118, 119, 110–113, 126, 69A, 44 and 59(4), have been repealed and replaced by the Highways Act 1980, ss. 329(1), 25–29, 43, and 50, 27, 66, 75, 133, 134, 118–121, 147, 70, 41 and 56(4), respectively.

The Countryside Act 1968, s. 27, has been modified by the Wildlife and Countryside Act 1981, s. 65, which extends the power to erect signs, etc., to all byways open to all traffic. The 1968 Act, s. 28, has been repealed and replaced by the Highways Act 1980, s. 146, without change of effect.

The Highways Act 1971, ss. 18, 40, have been repealed and replaced by the Highways Act 1980, ss. 35, 184, without change of effect.

The Local Government Act 1972, s. 187(2), has been repealed and replaced (in part) by the Highways Act 1980, s. 50; s. 188(7) of the Act of 1972 has been repealed and replaced by the Act of 1980, s. 35.

The preparation of plans and maps under the National Parks and Access to the Countryside Act 1949, ss. 27–35, has come to an end (Wildlife and Countryside Act 1981, s. 73, Sched. 17, Part II), and under new provisions (Act of 1981, ss. 53–58, 66) a continuous review is to be maintained over paths and footways.

Forcible detainer. The Forcible Entry Acts 1381, 1429 and 1623, have been repealed (Criminal Law Act 1977, s. 13(2)); all common law offences of forcible detainer have been abolished (s. 13(1)). The Act of 1977 created new offences relating to entering and remaining on property (ss. 6–11), also providing powers of entry for the purposes of the Act (s. 11).

Forcible entry. The Forcible Entry Acts 1381, 1429 and 1623, have been repealed (Criminal Law Act 1977, s. 13(2)). The common law offence of forcible entry has also been abolished (Act of 1977, s. 13(1)). The use of violence, or threats of violence, to secure entry to premises is now an offence in certain circumstances (s. 6), punishable on summary conviction by a fine not exceeding £2,000 (see FINE) or by a term of imprisonment not exceeding six months or both (s. 6(5)). There is a power of arrest attached to this offence (s. 6(6)). Provision has also been made for the punishment of adverse possession of residential premises (s. 7) and for trespassing with a weapon of offence (s. 8). Intrusion into the premises of foreign missions and like institutions has been made a criminal offence (s. 9), as has the obstruction of court officers who are executing process for possession against unauthorised occupiers (s. 10).

Foreclosure. The jurisdiction of the county court was increased to include actions up to £15,000 in value (County Courts Jurisdiction Order 1977 (S.I. 1977 No. 600)), and was then further increased to a limit of £30,000 (County Courts Jurisdiction Order 1981 (S.I. 1981 No. 1123)). The County Courts Act 1959, s. 52, has been repealed and replaced by the County Courts Act 1984, s. 23, without change of effect. The limit of jurisdiction may be further amended by order under the Act of 1984, s. 145.

The Judicature Act 1925, s. 56 (relating to the jurisdiction of the Chancery Division), has been repealed and replaced by the Supreme Court Act 1981, s. 61(1), (3), Sched. 1, para. 1(*b*), without change of effect.

Forecourt. The duty under the Occupiers' Liability Act 1957, has been modified in certain cases by the Occupiers' Liability Act 1984.

Foreign awards. The regulations specifying the countries which are parties to the Geneva Convention of 1927 (which comprises Sched. 2 to the Arbitration Act 1950) and which are New York Convention states, have been re-issued (Arbitration (Foreign Awards) Order 1984 (S.I. 1984 No. 1168)).

Foreign country. The British Nationality Act 1948, ss. 1(3), 32(1), have been repealed and replaced by the British Nationality Act 1981, s. 50(1), Sched. 3, without change of effect.

Foreign currency. Following the decision in *Miliangos* v. *George Frank (Textiles) Ltd.* [1976] A.C. 443, H.L., the use of foreign currency in litigation in the Supreme Court is now permitted when justified (see *Practice Directions* [1976] 1 W.L.R. 83 and [1977] 1 W.L.R. 197). Former restrictions on the use of foreign currency in judgments have been abolished (Administration of Justice Act 1977, s. 4). The payment into court of foreign currencies was at first regulated by the Supreme Court Funds Rules 1975 (S.I. 1975 No. 1803), r. 16, but the special provision has been revoked without replacement (S.I. 1981 No. 1589).

Foreign divorce, etc. The recognition of orders and decrees of courts outside England and Wales is regulated by the Recognition of Divorces and Judicial Separations Act 1971, which enabled the United Kingdom to give effect to the Hague Convention on the Recognition of Divorces and Legal Separations (1970) (Cmnd. 6248). Even if the foreign proceedings are recognised in the English courts, it has been held that no proceedings for financial provision (see MAINTENANCE) might be taken in respect of the marriage (or divorce) in question (see *Quazi* v. *Quazi* [1980] A.C. 744, H.L.). The statutory reversal of this ruling (recommended by the Law Commission) is contained in the Matrimonial and Family Proceedings Act 1984, s. 12; under s. 13 of that Act the leave of the court will be required before the institution of proceedings. Neither provision (nor any of the related provisions in Part III of the Act (ss. 12–25)) has been brought into operation.

Foreign judgments. Limitations on the extent to which English courts will recognise and allow the enforcement of foreign judgments have been imposed by the Protection of Trading Interests Act 1980. See also DAMAGES.

Substantial (prospective) amendment of the law is contained in the Civil Jurisdiction and Judgments Act 1982.

Foreign law. The Judicature Act 1925, s. 102, has been repealed and replaced by the Supreme Court Act 1981, s. 69(5), without change of effect. The County Courts Act 1959, s. 97, has been repealed and replaced by the County Courts Act 1984, s. 68, without change of effect.

Foreign seaman. The Merchant Shipping Act 1894, s. 238, has been repealed by the Merchant Shipping Act 1970, s. 100(3), Sched. 5. By s. 89 of the 1970 Act, deserters from foreign ships are dealt with under reciprocal arrangements (Orders under the 1894 Act being maintained in force under the 1970 Act, s. 89(1)).

Foreign sovereign. See the State Immunity Act 1978, which makes new provision with respect to proceedings by or against other states, reducing the areas in which immunity was formerly enjoyed.

Foreshore. The power to make by-laws under the Public Health Act 1936, s. 231, with respect to public bathing has been slightly modified (Local Government (Miscellaneous Provisions) Act 1976, s. 17) so as to extend the possible area of operation of the by-laws. For the Secretary of State's confirmation of by-laws see also the Act of 1976, s. 17(2).

The Limitation Act 1939, s. 31, has been repealed and replaced by the Limitation Act 1980, s. 15(6), (7), Sched. 1, para. 11, without change of effect.

Forestry. Further relief in respect of capital transfer tax in relation to woodlands was made by the Finance Act 1978, s. 65, which has now been repealed and replaced by the Capital Transfer Tax Act 1984, Part V, Chapter III (ss. 125–130), without significant change of effect. The reliefs originally contained in the Finance Act 1975, Sched. 9, and the Finance Act 1976, s. 75, have been likewise repealed and replaced by the Act of 1984 (Part V, Chapter III).

The powers of the Forestry Commissioners to make grants and loans have been restated (Forestry Act 1979, s. 1), and the references in earlier legislation in imperial measurements have been converted into metric measurements (s. 2).

Further small changes in the law were made by the Forestry Act 1981.

Forfeiture. The Customs and Excise Act 1952, ss. 275–280, have been repealed and replaced by the Customs and Excise Management Act 1979, ss. 139–144, without change of effect.

FORFEITURE

Powers of forfeiture under the Misuse of Drugs Act 1971, s. 27, are restricted in their scope and may be exercised only when offences under the Act are involved (*R.* v. *Cuthbertson* [1981] A.C. 470, H.L.).

By virtue of the Forfeiture Act 1982, it has become possible for the courts to exclude or modify the operation of the "forfeiture rule" (defined in s. 1(1)), so that a person who has unlawfully killed another may be re-enabled to take a benefit from the estate of the dead person. The Social Security Commissioner decides whether to apply the new powers in social security cases (s. 4). The new powers conferred by these provisions are excluded in all cases of murder (s. 5).

The County Courts Act 1959, s. 191, has been repealed and replaced by the County Courts Act 1984, s. 138, without change of effect. The scope of the provision was examined in *Di Palma* v. *Victoria Square Property Co. Ltd.* [1984] 2 W.L.R. 761 and *Jones* v. *Barnett* [1984] 3 W.L.R. 333; the outcome appears to be that the High Court's jurisdiction to grant relief from forfeiture in certain landlord and tenant cases is not excluded by the Act of 1984, s. 138.

Forgery. The mode of trial of forgery of a valuable security (Forgery Act 1913, s. 2(1)(*a*)) depended on the value of the subject-matter of the proceedings (Criminal Law Act 1977, s. 16, Sched. 2, para. 13, Sched. 3, para. 15, displacing the Magistrates' Courts Act 1952, s. 19 (repealed)). Offences under the Act of 1913, s. 4, were made triable either way (Criminal Law Act 1977, s. 16, Sched. 3, para. 15(*b*)), as were cases of demanding property on forged documents (Act of 1913, s. 7) provided the value of the property did not exceed £1,000 (Criminal Law Act 1977, s. 16, Sched. 3, para. 15(*c*)).

The Forgery Act 1913 has now been repealed and replaced by the Forgery and Counterfeiting Act 1981. Part I of the new Act (ss. 1–13) deals with forgery and kindred offences and includes the abolition of forgery at common law (s. 13). Counterfeiting and kindred offences are dealt with in Part II (ss. 14–28). Though expressed to be "fresh provision", in the main the Act repeats the substance of the previous provisions in modified terminology. The classification of cases triable either way remains for the principal forgery cases (Act of 1981, s. 6; Magistrates' Courts Act 1980, ss. 17 *et seq.*, replacing the Magistrates' Courts Act 1952, s. 19)).

The Forgery and Counterfeiting Act 1981 also made appropriate modifications to the Counterfeit Currency (Convention) Act 1935.

The Road Traffic Act 1960, s. 233, has been repealed and replaced by the Forgery and Counterfeiting Act 1981, s. 12, without significant change of effect. Section 234 of the 1960 Act has been repealed without direct replacement by the Transport Act 1980, s. 69, Sched. 9, Part II.

The Road Traffic Act 1967, s. 86, has been repealed and replaced by the Road Traffic Regulation Act 1984, ss. 115, 116, without change of effect.

Foster child. The provisions mentioned have nearly all been repealed and replaced by the Foster Children Act 1980 (a consolidating Act). The new Act provides for the position of children who have been privately fostered, imposing certain duties and powers on local authorities (ss. 3, 8–10), and requiring those who have the care of foster children to notify the local authority of the fostering arrangements (ss. 4–6). Further provisions include special arrangements for proceedings (ss. 11–14), and the prohibition of placing of advertisements for the fostering of children (s. 15). Children who are in the care of a local authority are excluded from the provisions of this Act, but are similarly provided for in the Child Care Act 1980. The Foster Children Act came into force on the day appointed for the commencement of the Child Care Act 1980 (Foster Children Act 1980, s. 24(2)), and therefore came into operation on 1 April 1981 (Child Care Act (Commencement) Order 1980 (S.I. 1980 No. 1935)).

Four corners. A doctrine by this name was propounded by Lord Thring, who said that "it is not fair to a legislative assembly that they should, as a general rule, have to look beyond the four corners of a Bill in order to comprehend its meaning." The principle of including in the texts of Bills before Parliament all the materials to make it comprehensible without reference to the legislation which is being amended has been widely adopted by parliamentary draftsmen, but has come under strong attack from users of legislation. For a general account see "The Preparation of Legislation" (Cmnd. 6053), Chap. 7.

Fowl pest. The Diseases of Animals Act 1950, has been repealed and replaced by the Animal Health Act 1981; s. 88(3) of the new Act includes "fowl pest, including Newcastle disease and fowl plague" in the diseases which may be controlled by treatment or slaughter under the general provisions of the Act.

Fox. The legislation which provides for the destruction of foxes in areas infected is now the Animal Health Act 1981, s. 19 (replacing the Rabies Act 1974, s. 1(1)).

Fraction of a day. The rule that an Act of Parliament becomes law as soon as the day on which it is passed commences has been recognised by statute (Interpretation Act 1978, s. 4(*b*)); when the commencement of an Act is delayed, the provisions come into operation at the beginning of the day on which they are brought into force (s. 4(*a*)).

Franked investment income. For the treatment of franked investment income in relation to corporation tax (*q.v.*) see the Finance Act 1972, ss. 88–90.

Fraud. The Theft Act 1968, s. 16, has been repealed in part and further offences related to obtaining by a deception have been added to the criminal law (see DECEPTION) by the Theft Act 1978. The Protection of Depositors Act 1963, has been repealed (Banking Act 1979, s. 51(2), Sched. 7), and replaced by provisions which establish the Deposit Protection Board (*q.v.*) and control businesses which involve the taking of any deposit (*q.v.*) (Banking Act 1979, ss. 1–33). Any person who by any statement, promise or forecast which he knows to be misleading, false or deceptive, or by any dishonest concealment of material facts, or by the reckless making (whether dishonestly or otherwise) of any statement, promise or forecast which is misleading, false or deceptive, induces or attempts to induce another person to make a deposit with him or any other person, or to enter into or offer to enter into any agreement for that purpose is liable on conviction on indictment to a term of imprisonment of up to seven years or to a fine or both (Banking Act 1979, s. 39(1)).

The Limitation Act 1939, s. 26, has been repealed and replaced by the Limitation Act 1980, s. 32, without change of effect. The Insurance Companies Act 1974, ss. 63, 69, have been repealed and replaced by the Insurance Companies Act 1982, ss. 73, 79, without change of effect.

Fraudulent mediums. For the revision of fines which may be made on offenders see FINE.

Freedom of a borough. A slight extension of the power to create freemen has been enacted (Local Government, Planning and Land Act 1980, s. 180).

Freeman. A slight extension of the power to create freemen has been enacted (Local Government, Planning and Land Act 1980, s. 180).

Frequenting. The offence under this part of the Vagrancy Act 1824, s. 4, has been abolished without replacement by the Criminal Attempts Act 1981, s. 8. Its place has been taken (in part) by the offence of interfering with vehicles (established by s. 9 of the Act of 1981). On summary conviction of this offence the punishment is a fine (*q.v.*) of up to £1,000 (originally £500) or three months' imprisonment or both. A constable may arrest without warrant any person who is or whom he reasonably suspects of committing this offence (s. 9(4)).

Friendly society. The levels of tax reliefs (Income and Corporation Taxes Act 1970, s. 332) are revised periodically, the latest amendments being made by the Finance Act 1980, s. 57(1) and the Finance Act 1984, s. 73(2). The Insurance Companies Act 1974, Part II (ss. 12–61), which provided for the exemption of friendly societies from the insurance companies legislation, has been repealed and replaced by the Insurance Companies Act 1982, Part II (ss. 15–71), without change of effect (s. 15(2) continuing the exemption).

Fringe benefits. The Finance (No. 2) Act 1975, s. 35, has been repealed by the Finance Act 1976, s. 132(5), Sched. 15, Part II. Further provisions relating to the taxation of fringe benefits were enacted in the Finance Act 1977, ss. 33–36, and the Finance Act 1978, s. 23.

See now the Finance Act 1976 ss. 60–72 (including ss. 64A (added by the Finance Act 1981, s. 69 and amended by the Finance Act 1982, s. 46) and 66A (added by the Finance Act 1983, s. 22)).

For recent consideration of the provisions

of the Act of 1943 see *B.P. Exploration Co. (Libya) Ltd.* v. *Hunt* (*No. 2*) [1979] 1 W.L.R. 783.

Fundamental breach. A term used in considering the effects of a breach of contract (*Suisse Atlantique Society d'Armement Maritime S.A.* v. *N.V. Rotterdamsche Kolen Centrale* [1967] 1 A.C. 361, H.L.) See EXCEPTIONS CLAUSES; EXEMPTION CLAUSE.

Further advance or charge. The Land Registration Act 1925, s. 106 (as originally enacted and variously amended), has been replaced by a revised text which, in effect, abolishes the obsolete procedure of registration of a mortgage caution in respect of registered land (Administration of Justice Act 1977, s. 26).

Future goods. The Sale of Goods Act 1893, s. 62, has been repealed and replaced by the Sale of Goods Act 1979, s. 61, without change of effect.

G

Game. The penalty for an offence under the Night Poaching Act 1828, s. 9, was amended so that on summary conviction the court has the power to impose a penalty of a term of imprisonment not exceeding six months or a fine not exceeding £500 or both (Criminal Law Act 1977, s. 65(4), Sched. 12). Offences under s. 1 of the Act of 1828 were made subject to a maximum fine of £200 and became triable only summarily (Act of 1977, ss. 15, 30, Sched. 1). Fines have been further revised by the Criminal Justice Act 1982, ss. 35 *et seq.* (see FINE).

Game licence. Penalties under the Night Poaching Act 1828, have been amended by the Criminal Law Act 1977, ss. 15, 30, Scheds. 1, 12; see GAME and FINE. Penalties under the Game Act 1831, are all on level one on the standard scale (see FINE).

Gamekeepers. See also the Betting, Gaming and Lotteries (Amendment) Act 1980. The limit of £1,000 imposed by the Gaming Act 1968, s. 20(3), may now be increased by order of the Secretary of State (Gaming (Amendment) Act 1980, s. 1).

The Finance (No. 2) Act 1975, s. 21, has been repealed and replaced by the Value Added Tax 1983, s. 13, without change of effect.

Garnishee. The classes of funds which may be made subject to garnishee proceedings have been widened, and accounts with the National Savings Bank have been brought within it (Supreme Court Act 1981, s. 139). In the Supreme Court the minimum debt enforceable by these proceedings is £50 (R.S.C. Ord. 49, r. 1(1)); in the county courts it is £25 (C.C.R. 1981, Ord. 30, r. 1(1)).

Gas. Where the annual supply of gas to any premises exceeds 25,000 therms there must be a special arrangement between the consumer and the Gas Corporation, or certain special rates of charge apply (Gas Act 1980, s. 1).

Gate. The Highways Act 1959, s. 133, has been repealed by the Local Government Act 1972, ss. 188(3), 272, Scheds. 21, 30. The Highways Act 1959, s. 125, has been repealed and replaced by the Highways Act 1980, s. 145, without change of effect. The Town and Country Planning (General Development) Order 1963, has been revoked and replaced by the Town and Country Planning (General Development) Order 1977 (S.I. 1977 No. 289), which has been subject to periodic amendments (see GENERAL DEVELOPMENT ORDER) without major change of effect.

Gauge of railways. The Railways Regulation (Gauge) Act 1846, has been repealed by the Statute Law Revision Act 1959, s. 22, Sched. 2.

General Dental Council. The constitution and duties of the General Dental Council has been amended (Dentists Act 1983, ss. 1, 2, respectively). See also DENTIST.

General Development Order. The Town and Country Planning (General Development Order 1963, has been revoked and replaced by the Town and Country Planning (General Development) Order 1977 (S.I. 1977 No. 289), which embodies the former provisions with various amendments made from time to time. (The 1977 Order has been amended by S.I. 1977 No. 1781 (which was revoked by S.I. 1977 No. 2085), S.I. 1980 No. 1496, 1981 Nos. 245, 246 and 1569, and S.I. 1983 No. 1615.)

General Medical Council. The Medical Act 1956, ss. 1–6, have been repealed by the Medical Act 1978, s. 31, Sched. 7. The General Medical Council was, however, continued in being on broadly the same lines, still being composed of appointed, nominated and elected members (Act of 1978, s. 21). The powers of control over registered medical practitioners continued by virtue of the Act of 1978, ss. 5–14. Subsidiary activities of the Council were also provided for (Act of 1978, ss. 15–29).

The entire corpus of the Medical Act 1956, the Medical Act 1969 and the Medical Act 1978, was repealed by the Medical Act 1983, s. 56(1), (2), Sched. 7, Part I. By the Act of 1983, s. 1, Sched. 1, the functions and authority of the G.M.C. were continued.

General Nursing Council. The Nurses Act 1957, was repealed by the Nurses, Midwives and Health Visitors Act 1979, s. 23(5), Sched. 8. By the Act of 1979 it is provided that various functions (which were formerly carried out by the General Nursing Council) are to be the responsibility of the Central Council for Nursing, Midwifery and Health Visiting (*q.v.*) (see s. 1).

General synod. See NATIONAL ASSEMBLY OF THE CHURCH OF ENGLAND.

Geneva Agreement. The Finance Act 1948, ss. 8, 9, have been repealed by the Import Duties Act 1958, s. 16, Sched. 7.

Gift. The Finance Act 1965, s. 22(4), which subjected gifts to capital gains tax, was repealed and replaced by the Capital Gains Tax Act 1979, s. 19(3), without change of effect. The Finance Act 1975, ss. 3–52, have been repealed and replaced by the Capital Transfer Tax Act 1984, ss. 1–17 (for the principal provisions relating to the charge), and ss. 18–29 (for the principal provisions relating to exemptions).

For a new presumption in favour of a testamentary gift (enacted by the Administration of Justice Act 1982, s. 22) to a spouse see WILL.

Gilbert Islands. See KIRIBATI.

Giro. The power of the Post Office to provide a "banking service of the kind commonly known as a giro system" has been extended, so that the Post Office's powers are now in more general terms, which permit the provision of "a banking service" (Post Office Act (Banking Services) 1976, s. 1(1), amending the Post Office Act 1969, s. 7(1)(*b*)). The services maintained under this provision come within the exceptions listed in the Banking Act 1979, s. 2, Sched. 1, so that the Post Office is not required to submit to the licensing and control provisions of the Act of 1979 (see DEPOSIT and DEPOSIT PROTECTION BOARD).

Glanders (or **Farcy**). The Diseases of Animals Act 1950, has been repealed and replaced by the Animal Health Act 1981. Order already made under the 1950 Act are preserved in operation by the Act of 1981, s. 95(1). "Disease" is defined in s. 88, and the statute repeats the 1950 provision authorising the issue of instruments which extend the statutory definition of "disease" by adding new ones to the list (s. 88(2)).

Glebe. Glebe land formerly invested in the incumbent of any benefice has vested in the Diocesan Boards of Finance without the need for any conveyance or other assurance (Endowments and Glebe Measure 1976, s. 15). Glebe land held by each diocese is held for the benefit of the diocesan stipends fund under a scheme prepared by the diocese and submitted to the Church Commissioners (s. 19). General powers of control and dealing with glebe land have been conferred on the appropriate authorities (see ss. 16–18, 20–28).

Gold clause. A comparable device was the subject of *Multiservice Ltd.* v. *Marden* [1979] Ch. 84, where the sums to be repaid in respect of a mortgage were linked to the value of the Swiss franc.

Gold coins. The provisions relating to the fineness of the Queen's Maundy money have been revised (Coinage Act 1971, s. 1 (substituted by the Currency Act 1983, s. 1)). The quantities of coins which are legal tender have been re-stated: cupro-nickel or silver coins of more than 20p in value, legal tender for payment of any amount not exceeding £10; cupro-nickel or silver coins of not more than 10p in value, legal tender for payment of any amount not exceeding £5; bronze coins, legal tender for payment of any amount not exceeding 20p (Coinage Act 1971, s. 2(1A)) (as substituted by the Currency Act 1983, s. 1(3)(*a*)).

Gold francs. Formerly commonly used in limitation clauses in international contracts for the carriage of goods or people, this unit of currency is being replaced by special drawing rights (see, *e.g.*, the Merchant Shipping Act 1981, ss. 1–3, the Merchant Shipping (Sterling Equivalents) (Various Enactments) Order 1984 (S.I. 1984 No. 1548), and the Carriage by Air (Sterling Equivalents) Order 1984 (S.I. 1984 No. 1582) (which relates to compensation payable under the Warsaw Convention and the Hague Protocol)).

Goldfish. The Public Health Act 1936, s. 154, has been repealed and replaced by the Public Health (Control of Diseases) Act 1984, s. 55, without change of effect.

Good Friday. The C.C.R. 1936, Ord. 1, r. 2, has been revoked and replaced by the C.C.R. 1981, Ord. 2, r. 2, without change of effect. The Rules of 1936, Ord. 48, r. 10, has been revoked and replaced by the Rules of 1981, Ord. 1, r. 9(4), which refers to "days when the court office is closed" rather than to specific days. The period to be computed has been reduced from seven days to three days in the 1981 revision (this change not having been made in the R.S.C.).

Goods. The Sale of Goods Act 1893, s. 62, has been repealed and replaced by the Sale of Goods Act 1979, s. 61, without change of effect. The amount which is exempt from execution has been increased from £20 to £100 or £150 according to the nature of the items involved (see DISTRESS and S.I. 1980 No. 26).

Government Chemist. The Food and Drugs Act 1955, s. 112, has been repealed and replaced by the Food Act 1984, s. 99, without change of effect.

Governor. The Interpretation Act 1889, ss. 18, 42, have been repealed by the Interpretation Act 1978, s. 25(1), Sched. 3. In relation to any British possession, "governor" includes the officer for the time being administering the government of the possession (Act of 1978, s. 5, Sched. 1).

Governor-General. By virtue of the Interpretation Act 1978, s. 5, Sched. 1, this term includes the person who for the time being has the powers of the Governor-General.

Specialised duties related to the constitution of Canada and the implementation of the Canada Act 1982 have been imposed on the Governor-General of Canada (Canada Act 1982, ss. 38(1), 41, 48, 58–59).

Grain, poisoned. The Protection of Birds Act 1954, s. 10(1), has been repealed and replaced by the Wildlife and Countryside Act 1981, s. 16, without significant change of effect.

Gramophone. The Independent Broadcasting Act 1973, s. 4(6)(*b*), has been repealed and replaced by the Broadcasting Act 1981, s. 4(7), without significant change of effect.

Greater hardship. The Rent Act 1968, s. 10, Sched. 3, Part I, Case 8, and Part III, para. 1, have been repealed and replaced by the Rent Act 1977, s. 98, Sched. 15, Part II, Case 9, and Part II, para. 1, without substantial change of effect; there are certain restrictions based on the date of the landlord's acquisition of the property (see Case 9, conditions (i)–(iv)).

Green belt. Development plans are being replaced by structure plans (*q.v.*) drawn up under the Town and Country Planning Act 1971, ss. 6–10 (as variously amended).

Greenwich Hospital. Admissions to this institution are also authorised by the Reserve Forces Act 1980, s. 55.

Greenwich time. The Statutes (Definition of Time) Act 1880, s. 1, has been repealed and replaced by the Interpretation Act 1978, s. 9, which provides that (subject to the provisions of the Summer Time Act 1972, s. 3) unless otherwise specifically stated, whenever an expression of time appears in any Act the time referred to is Greenwich mean time.

Gretna Green marriage. The Marriage (Scotland) Act 1939, s. 5, has been repealed by the Marriage (Scotland) Act 1977, s. 28(2), Sched. 3. Notice of intention to marry is still required (Act of 1977, ss. 3 *et seq.*), and special provision has been made for the registration (and, therefore, recognition) of irregular marriages (s. 21).

Grogging. The Customs and Excise Act 1952, s. 109, has been repealed and replaced by the Alcoholic Liquor Duties Act 1979, s. 34, without change of effect.

Gross weight. The maximum permitted weights of containers for certain goods are prescribed (see, *e.g.*, the Weights and Measures Act 1963, Sched. 4, Part XI (as substituted by the Weights and Measures Act 1979, s. 20, Sched. 5, para. 20)).

Guarantee payment. In employment law there are two classes of payment called by this name. There are occasions when a collective agreement (*q.v.*) contains provisions designed to ensure that workers receive some of their normal wages in the first days or weeks of any lay-off. There is also a system of statutory guarantee payments (Employment Protection (Consolidation) Act 1978, ss. 12 *et seq.*). The right to a guarantee payment arises where an employee is not provided with his normal work by reason of a diminution in the requirements of the employer's business for work of the kind the employee is employed to do or by reason of any other occurrence which affects the normal working of the employer's business (s. 12(1)). The right does not arise when the employer's failure to provide work is a consequence of a trade dispute (s. 13(1)), nor if the employer has offered to make suitable alternative work available and the employee has refused to take that work, nor if the employee fails to comply with any reasonable requirement of his employer to ensure that his services are available (s. 13(2)). The amount of a statutory guarantee payment is calculated in accordance with special provisions (ss. 14–16 (modified by the Employment Act 1980, s. 14)). Disputes about payments are within the jurisdiction of an industrial tribunal (s. 17). When a collective agreement provides for guarantee payments or any wages order is in force, the statutory scheme may be excluded by ministerial order (s. 18). In any event, a worker is not entitled to a guarantee payment unless he has been continuously employed for a period of four weeks ending with the last complete week before the day in respect of which the payment is claimed (see generally s. 14(3)).

Guaranteed minimum pension. A component of the contracting-out arrangements related to the government pension scheme; see the Social Security Pensions Act 1975, s. 35 (as amended by the Social Security (Miscellaneous Provisions) Act 1977, ss. 3, 22(7), and the Social Security Act 1979, s. 21(4), Sched. 3, para. 18). See also OCCUPATIONAL PENSIONS BOARD.

Guardian. Further changes in the law relating to guardianship were made by the Domestic Proceedings and Magistrates' Courts Act 1978, which assimilated the domestic jurisdiction of magistrates to that already enjoyed by county courts (with certain exceptions). The Magistrates' Courts (Guardianship of Minors) Rules 1974 (S.I. 1974 No. 706), have been amended by S.I. 1979 No. 953 and S.I. 1980 No. 1585, the main reason for alterations being the introduction of the revised domestic jurisdiction under the Domestic Proceedings and Magistrates' Courts Act 1978.

The Chancery Division no longer regularly exercises the High Court's general jurisdiction over minors, the Family Division having been invested with this function (Supreme Court Act 1981, s. 61(1), (3), Sched. 1, para. 3, replacing the Judicature Act 1925, s. 56, as amended by the Administration of Justice Act 1970, s. 1, Sched. 1, para. 3).

The Mental Health Act 1959, ss. 33–35, have been repealed and replaced by the Mental Health Act 1983, ss. 7–10, without significant change of effect. The C.C.R. 1936, Ord, 6, r. 4, and Ord. 46, have been revoked and replaced by the C.C.R. 1981, Ord. 3, r. 4, and Ord. 47 (which contains miscellaneous provisions relating to domestic proceedings under various statutes), without substantial change of effect.

A new class of guardian *ad litem* was introduced by the Guardians *ad litem* and Reporting Officers (Panels) Regulations 1983 (S.I. 1983 No. 1908), which were made in conjunction with the Children Act 1975, s. 103(1)(*a*). The net result of the new provisions is that in contested adoption proceedings there may now be many separate "parties" before the court with the right to make independent representations.

Guest. The duty of care imposed by the Occupiers' Liability Act 1957 has been modified by the Occupiers' Liability Act 1984.

Gunbarrels. The Gun Barrel Proof Acts 1868 and 1950 (31 and 32 Vict. c. cxii and 14 Geo. VI, c. iii) have been amended by the Gun Barrel Proof Act 1978, in connection with the alteration of the law to enable the United Kingdom to accede to the Convention for the Reciprocal Recognition of Proof Marks of Small Arms made at Brussels in 1969, and both the earlier Acts have been applied to Scotland and Northern Ireland (Act of 1978, s. 6).

H

Habeas corpus. The County Courts Act 1959, s. 86, has been repealed and replaced by the County Courts Act 1984, s. 57, without change of effect.

Habitual drunkard. In addition to the "black list" provisions, there is now power for criminal courts to make an order prohibiting certain people from entering specified licensed premises for specified periods from three months up to two years (see EXCLUSION ORDER).

The procedure for obtaining a matrimonial order in reliance upon habitual drunkenness no longer obtains, the Act of 1960 having been repealed and the domestic jurisdiction of magistrates having been revised by the Domestic Proceedings and Magistrates' Courts Act 1978.

Hackney carriages. A new code for the regulation of hackney carriages has been enacted (Local Government (Miscellaneous Provisions) Act 1976, Part II (ss. 45–80)) and this may be adopted by a district council, subject to giving notice of intention to pass a resolution to implement the provisions of the 1976 Act (s. 45(2), (3)). The new provisions also govern the use of private hire vehicles. Further provision has been made for London by the London Cab Act 1973, which increased the penalties for contraventions of the 1968 Act (s. 1), and empowered the Secretary of State to make rules prohibiting the display of various signs on private hire-cars (s. 2).

The Public Health Act 1936, ss. 159–160, have been repealed and replaced by the Public Health (Control of Diseases) Act 1984, ss. 33–34, without change of effect.

Half-timer. In connection with the restrictions on the employment of persons under school-leaving age see the Education (Work Experience) Act 1973.

Hallamshire. The Criminal Justice Administration Act 1962, s. 3, has been repealed by the Local Government Act 1972, s. 272, Sched. 30, without being replaced.

Handling stolen goods. The offence under the Theft Act 1968, s. 22, may be tried either way (Magistrates' Courts Act 1980, ss. 17 *et seq.*, replacing the Criminal Law Act 1977, s. 16(1), Sched. 2, para. 20(*a*)), and on summary conviction of the offence the maximum penalty is a period of imprisonment not exceeding six months or a fine (*q.v.*) not exceeding £2,000 or both (Act of 1980, ss. 32, 33, replacing the Act of 1977, ss. 28, 29).

Harassment. The Rent Act 1965, s. 30 (as amended by the Criminal Justice Act 1972, s. 30), has been repealed and replaced by the Protection from Eviction Act 1977, s. 1, under which the penalty on conviction was (at enactment) a fine (*q.v.*) not exceeding £400 or a term of imprisonment not exceeding six months or both, and on conviction on indictment a fine or imprisonment for a term not exceeding two years or both (s. 1(4)). The Rent Act 1968, s. 107, has been repealed and replaced by the Protection from Eviction Act 1977, s. 6 (imposing restrictions on the institution of proceedings under the Act) without change of effect.

Harbouring. The provisions relating to deserting seamen (Merchant Shipping Act 1894, ss. 236, 238) have been repealed (Merchant Shipping Act 1970, s. 100(3), Sched. 5); such matters are now to be the subject of codes of practice regulating the relationship between employers and seamen (see the Merchant Shipping Act 1970, ss. 27 *et seq.*).

See also ABUSING CHILDREN.

Hawker. Power to control the sale of food by hawkers has been granted to local authorities (Local Government (Miscellaneous Provisions) Act 1982, ss. 18, 19), but without defining "hawker."

Hawks. The Protection of Birds Act 1954, has been repealed and replaced by the Wildlife and Countryside Act 1981, Part I (ss. 1–8), subject to minor modifications. S.I. 1962 No. 2592, has been revoked and replaced by the Wild Birds (Revocation of Orders) Order 1982 (S.I. 1982 No. 1218). Under the Act of 1981, ss. 7, 22, Sched. 14, all hawks (the *Accipitridae*) kept in captivity must be ringed and registered.

He. The Interpretation Act 1889, s. 1, has been repealed and replaced by the Interpretation Act 1978, s. 6(*a*), without change of effect. The Act of 1978 breaks new ground by providing that words importing the feminine gender are to include the masculine (s. 6(*b*)), but the eminently suitable occasion for the introduction of this form of pronoun was not taken in the drafting of the Nurses, Midwives and Health Visitors Act 1979 (see especially s. 11).

Hearsay evidence. The admission of hearsay and expert evidence in matrimonial causes is now regulated by the Matrimonial Causes Rules 1977 (S.I. 1977 No. 344), r. 43.

Heating. The Consumer Protection Act 1961 has been (prospectively) repealed by the Consumer Safety Act 1978, s. 19(1), Sched. 3, but any orders made under the Act of 1961 will remain in force notwithstanding the repeal of the earlier Act.

Herrings. The Sea Fish Industry Act 1970, has been repealed (except for ss. 14, 42 and 62) by the Fisheries Act 1981, s. 46, Sched. 5, Part I.

High bailiffs. The County Courts Act 1959, s. 207, has been repealed and replaced by the County Courts Act 1984, s. 148(2), Sched. 3, para. 7, without change of effect.

High Court of Justice. The Judicature Act 1925, has been repealed and replaced (in somewhat amended form) by the Supreme Court Act 1981. The three Divisions of the High Court remain unchanged (Act of 1981, s. 61(1), (3), Sched. 1, para. 1). The Courts Act 1971, s. 2, has been repealed and replaced by the Act of 1981, s. 71, without change of effect.

The number of judges of the High Court is now regulated under the Act of 1981, s. 4(1), which allows for 80 puisnes; this number may be increased by Order in Council (s. 4(4)).

Deputy High Court judges are now allowed under the Act of 1981 s. 9(4). Deputy circuit judges (and assistant recorders) are now appointed under the Courts Act 1971, s. 24 (of which a new text was substituted by the Supreme Court Act 1981, s. 146).

Highway. The Highways Act 1959, the Highways (Miscellaneous Provisions) Act 1961, the Highways (Amendment) Act 1965, the Local Government Act 1966, ss. 27–34 and the Highways Act 1971, have been repealed and replaced by the Highways Act 1980, which is a general consolidating Act. For revision of the levels of penalty in certain cases see FINE.

Highway authorities. The Highways Act 1959, s. 1, has been repealed and replaced by the Highways Act 1980, s. 1, without change of effect. The Highways (Miscellaneous Provisions) Act 1961, s. 1, has been repealed and replaced by the Act of 1980, s. 58, also without change of effect. The London Government Act 1963, ss. 16–18 and the Transport (London) Act 1969, s. 29, have been repealed by the Highways Act 1980, s. 343(3), Sched. 25.

Highway Code. The Road Traffic Act 1972, s. 37, has been modified by the introduction of a new text into the Act by the Transport Act 1982, s. 60; the change relates to the method and scope of revisions of the Code. The former s. 37(5) has been re-enacted in the new s. 37(7).

Hijacking. The Hijacking Act 1971, ss. 1, 2, 3 and 5, have been repealed and replaced by the Aviation Security Act 1982, ss. 1 (and 3, 6, and 8), 6, 9, 8, respectively. The Protection of Aircraft Act 1973, has been repealed and replaced by the Act of 1982.

Hire-purchase. The Supply of Goods (Implied Terms) Act 1973, s. 13, has been repealed by the Unfair Contract Terms Act 1977, s. 31(4), Sched. 4. By s. 6(1) of the Act of 1977 it is provided that liability for breach of the obligations arising from the seller's implied undertakings as to title, etc., (which are the result of the Supply of Goods (Implied Terms) Act 1973, s. 8) cannot be excluded or restricted by reference to any contract term. The same prohibition of exclusion or restriction of liability for a seller's undertakings under the Act of 1973, ss. 9–11, is effected by the Act of 1977, s. 6(2), though this liability may be excluded as against any person not dealing as a consumer provided the exclusion is reasonable (s. 6(3)). See also UNFAIR CONTRACT TERMS.

The Sale of Goods Act 1893 (as amended), has been repealed and replaced by the Sale of Goods Act 1979, without change of effect.

Hire-purchase dealings fall outside the scope of the provisions of the Supply of Goods and Services Act 1982 (Act of 1982, s. 1(2)(*b*)).

Historic Buildings. The Housing Act 1974, s. 113, was repealed by the Housing Rebates and Subsidies Act 1975, s. 17(5),

Sched. 6, Part IV. The Listed Buildings Regulations 1968, were revoked and replaced by S.I. 1972 No. 1362, which has in turn been revoked and replaced by the Town and Country Planning (Listed Buildings and Buildings of Conservation Areas) Regulations (S.I. 1977 No. 228).

The Finance Act 1975, s. 34, and the Finance Act 1976, s. 84, have been repealed and replaced by the Capital Transfer Act 1984, s. 35, Sched. 5. See also the Act of 1984, s. 27, Sched. 4, for provisions relating to funds for the maintenance of historic buildings.

The Finance Act 1976, s. 55, was repealed and replaced by the Capital Gains Tax Act 1979, s. 82 (amended by the Finance Act 1982, s. 85). By virtue of the Finance Act 1984, s. 68, Sched. 23, the specific relief in cases of certain disposals relating to maintenance funds for historic buildings was brought to an end with effect from April 1984.

In view of these extensive taxation provisions it is curious that the Historic Buildings Council for England has been abolished (National Heritage Act 1983, s. 39), though admittedly replaced by the Historic Buildings and Monuments Commission for England (Act of 1983, s. 32, Sched. 3).

Historic Churches Preservation Trust. See also the Finance Act 1975, s. 29, Sched. 6 and the Capital Gains Tax Act 1979, s. 146 (which provided for an exception for gifts to bodies listed in the Act of 1975, Sched. 6—which includes the Historic Churches Preservation Trust). The capital transfer tax provisions of the Finance Act 1975, Sched. 6, para. 12, have been repealed and replaced by the Capital Transfer Tax Act 1984, s. 25(1), Sched. 3.

Hoarding. The Highways Act 1959, ss. 147–148, have been repealed and replaced by the Highways Act 1980, ss. 172–173, without change of effect.

Holding company. The Protection of Depositors Act 1963, has been repealed by the Banking Act 1979, s. 51(2), Sched. 7; the Companies Act 1948, s. 127 and the Companies Act 1967, s. 47(1), have been repealed by the Companies Act 1976, s. 42(2), Sched. 3.

For the usual statutory definitions both of "holding company" and of "subsidiary company" see the Companies Act 1948, s. 154.

For the purposes of corporation tax, holding companies may be used in order to secure the advantages offered by the group relief provisions of the Income and Corporation Taxes Act 1970, ss. 258–264.

Holding over. The jurisdiction of the county court has been increased: where the new annual value for rating of the premises concerned does not exceed £1,000 the county court is the normal tribunal; if the value exceeds £1,000 the defendant or his landlord may apply for the proceedings to be transferred to the High Court (see the County Courts Act 1959, s. 49 and the Administration of Justice Act 1973, s. 6, Sched. 2, for the original provisions, now repealed and incorporated into the County Courts Act 1984, s. 40).

Home work. Additional powers to stop work so as to prevent the spread of disease have been granted to local authorities (Public Health (Control of Disease) Act 1984, s. 20).

Homicide. The offence under the Infant Life (Preservation) Act 1929, s. 1, is specifically preserved in the legislation relating to abortion (see the Abortion Act 1967, s. 5, and ABORTION).

Honour. The form of address for a circuit judge in court is now prescribed by *Practice Direction* [1982] 1 W.L.R. 101, which revokes and replaces the earlier Directions without change of effect.

Hops. The Hop Trade Act 1800, has been repealed by the Statute Law (Repeals) Act 1973, s. 1(1), Sched. 1, Part VIII: the Hop Trade Act 1814, has been repealed by the Hops Certification Regulations 1979 (S.I. 1979 No. 1095), as have the remaining portions of the Hop (Prevention of Frauds) Act 1866.

Horse. The Diseases of Animals Act 1950, s. 37, has been repealed and replaced by the Animal Health Act 1981, ss. 40 (horses) and 41 (ponies), and the Ponies Act 1969 has been repealed by the Act of 1981, s. 96, Sched. 6. The Highways Act 1959, ss. 70, 295(1), have been repealed and replaced by the Highways Act 1980, ss. 71, 329(1), without change of effect.

Horse breeding. For the revision of the levels of fines which may be imposed on summary conviction see FINE.

Horseflesh. The Food and Drugs Act

1955, s. 24, has been repealed and replaced by the Food Act 1984, s. 29, without change of effect.

Horserace Betting Levy Board. The system of collection of the levy has been revised (Horserace Betting Levy Act 1981).

Hosepipe. The maximum penalty on conviction for contravention of a prohibition or restriction on the use of hosepipes (Water Act 1945, s. 16(3)) was increased to £200 (Criminal Law Act 1977, s. 31, Sched. 6); for the general revision of the levels of fines which may be imposed on summary conviction see also FINE.

Hospitals. The National Health Service Act 1946, s. 6, and the National Health Service Reorganisation Act 1973, ss. 21, 22, 28, have been repealed by the National Health Service Act 1977, s. 129, Sched. 16, and replaced by the Act of 1977, ss. 88, 90, 91, 94, respectively, without substantial change of effect.

The suggestion about incorporation under the Companies Act 1948 has been overtaken by recent amendments to company law: the Companies Act 1948, s. 14, was repealed by the Charities Act 1960, ss. 38(1), (3), 48(2), Sched. 7, Part VII; the Act of 1948, s. 15, has been repealed by the Companies Act 1980, s. 88(2), Sched. 4; and the Act of 1948, ss. 17–19, have been repealed by the Companies Act 1981, s. 119(5), Sched. 4.

House. The Rent Act 1968, s. 1, has been repealed and replaced by the Rent Act 1977, s. 1(1), without change of effect.

House of Commons. The remuneration paid to Members of Parliament, the allowances they may claim and the other financial arrangements made for them are constantly under revision, normally needing no more than a resolution of the House for their authorisation.

Housing. See also the Housing (Homeless Persons) Act 1977, which created a scheme intended to deal with the difficulties facing people who are either already homeless or are about to become so. Not only does this Act impose duties on housing authorities, but it also creates a right of action for breach of statutory duty in favour of any person who qualifies for re-housing under the terms of the legislation (see *Thornton* v. *Kirklees Metropolitan Borough Council* [1979] Q.B. 626, C.A.). The Home Purchase Assistance and Housing Corporation Guarantees Act 1978, makes further provision in connection with the law governing advances by building societies and with housing association law. The Housing Act 1980 introduced a scheme for the disposal of local authority housing to tenants on favourable terms, but the original scheme has been massively modified by the Housing and Building Control Act 1984, Part I (ss. 1–38).

Housing societies. The Housing Finance Act 1972, ss. 81–88, have been repealed and replaced by the Rent Act 1977, ss. 86–91, 94(1), 95(1), 96(1)–(3), 97, 141, without substantial change of effect.

Hovercraft. The Road Traffic Regulation Act 1967, s. 101, has been repealed and replaced by the Road Traffic Regulation Act 1984, s. 139, without change of effect.

Human rights. The Rome Convention for the Protection of Human Rights and Fundamental Freedoms has been considered on a number of occasions by the courts, but until now it has been clearly held that the Convention does not have the force of law in the United Kingdom (see, *e.g. Malone* v. *Metropolitan Police Commissioner* [1979] Ch. 344).

Human tissue. Certain parts of the Human Tissue Act 1961 have been (prospectively) repealed by the Anatomy Act 1984. See also ANATOMY and CREMATION.

Husband and wife. The duty to maintain the other spouse and children has been repeated in the Supplementary Benefit Act 1976, s. 17 (which omitted to repeal the National Assistance Act 1948, ss. 42, 43); the new provision includes the putative child of a man and a woman's illegitimate children (s. 17(2)).

Hydrogen cyanide. See CYANIDE FUMIGATION.

Hypnotism. For the general revision of the levels of fines on summary conviction see FINE.

I

Ice. The maximum penalty on summary conviction under the Merchant Shipping (Safety and Load Line Conventions) Act 1932, s. 30(2) (which relates to avoidance of danger from ice) was (prospectively) increased to £1,000 (Merchant Shipping Act 1979, s. 43, Sched. 6, Part V). See also FINE.

Ice-cream. The Food and Drugs Act 1955, ss. 16, 135(1), have been repealed and replaced by the Food Act 1984, ss. 16, 132(1), without change of effect.

Identification; Identity. The courts have been subjected to considerable scrutiny on the question of identification of defendants in criminal proceedings. Guidance for the police in the conduct of identity parades is now laid down in Home Office Circular 109/1978, which follows recommendations by the Devlin Committee.

The Road Traffic Regulation Act 1967, ss. 85, 89, 90, have been repealed and replaced by the Road Traffic Regulation Act 1984, ss. 112–114, without change of effect.

Idiocy; Idiot; Ideot. The Mental Health Act 1959 (as amended, most recently by the Mental Health Amendment Act 1982) has been (with minor exceptions) repealed and replaced by the Mental Health Act 1983 (which is a consolidating Act).

Illegal practices. The Representation of the People Act 1949, ss. 91–98, have been repealed and replaced by the Representation of the People Act 1983, ss. 106–112, without change of effect.

Illicit. The Licensing Act 1953 (as variously amended) was repealed and replaced by the Licensing Act 1964, without affecting the example in the text.

Immigration. The right of abode provisions have been revised in consequence of the amendment of nationality law by the British Nationality Act 1981, (see, *e.g.* the Immigration Act 1971, s. 2 (as substituted by the British Nationality Act 1981, s. 39) and the other amendments made to the 1971 Act by the Act of 1981, s. 39, Sched. 4).

Immunity. Foreign sovereigns and states are immune from legal process in the United Kingdom subject to a number of exceptions; detailed provision on this matter has been made by the State Immunity Act 1978.

Imperial preference. The Finance Act 1919, s. 8, has been repealed by the Finance Act 1978, s. 80, Sched. 13, Part I; the Import Duties Act 1932, has been repealed by the Import Duties Act 1958, s. 16(4), Sched. 7; and the Import Duties Act 1958, s. 2, has been repealed by the European Communities Act 1972, Scheds. 3, 4, and by the Customs Duties (Repeals) (Appointed Day) Order 1977 (S.I. 1977 No. 2028). Since the entry of the United Kingdom into the European Communities, the various provisions relating to imperial preference are required to be brought to an end.

Importuning. Penalties under the Street Offences Act 1959 have been restricted by the Criminal Justice Act 1982, s. 71. For the general revision of the levels of fines which may be imposed on summary conviction see FINE.

Impossibility. For a consideration of the Law Reform (Frustrated Contracts) Act 1943, and its application to a complex factual situation see *B.P. Exploration Co.* (*Libya*) *Ltd.* v. *Hunt* (*No. 2*) [1977] 1 W.L.R. 783.

A person may now be guilty of attempting to commit an offence even if the facts of the case are such that the commission of the offence is impossible (Criminal Attempts Act 1981, s. 1(2)).

Imprisonment. The Magistrates' Courts Act 1952, ss. 71, and 74(6) (as amended), have been repealed and replaced by the Magistrates' Courts Act 1960, ss. 88, 93(6), without change of effect. See also the Powers of Criminal Courts Act 1973, s. 31. The restrictions in respect of unpaid fines which have for long applied to imprisonment for non-payment of fines imposed by magistrates' courts now also apply to Crown Court fines (Criminal Justice Act 1982, s. 69).

The terms of release on licence (under the Criminal Justice Act 1967, ss. 59–64, Sched. 2) have been modified (Criminal Justice Act 1982, ss. 32, 33; see also the

Eligibility for Release on Licence Order 1983 (S.I. 1983 No. 1958)); time spent in custody before sentence now counts towards any period of imprisonment ordered by the court (Act of 1982, s. 34).

See also SENTENCE.

Improvement area. The Housing Act 1974, s. 50, has (effectively) been repealed by the Housing Act 1980, ss. 109, 152, Sched. 13, para. 2, Sched. 26. The Act of 1974, ss. 52–55, and Sched. 5, have been repealed by the Act of 1980, ss. 109, 152, Sched. 26.

Improvement lines. The Highways Act 1959, s. 72, has been repealed and replaced by the Highways Act 1980, s. 73, without change of effect.

Improvements, Tenants'. Where a lease (whenever made) contains any covenant, condition or agreement against making improvements without the licence or consent of the landlord, that term is deemed to include a proviso that the consent will not be unreasonably withheld (Landlord and Tenant Act 1927, s. 19(2)). This proviso is displaced in the case of secure tenants, protected tenants and statutory tenants: in these cases there is an implied term that the tenant will not make any improvement without the written consent of the landlord (Housing Act 1980, s. 81(2)), and any consent unreasonably withheld is treated as given (s. 81(3)). In this context the term means "any addition to, or alteration in, a dwelling-house, and includes (a) any addition to, or alteration in, landlord's fixtures and fittings and any addition or alteration connected with the provision of any services to a dwelling-house; (b) the erection of any wireless or television ariel; and (c) the carrying out of external decoration" (s. 81(5)).

In camera. When a county court hears an appeal on a matter which could have been heard *in camera* or an appeal is taken from a county court on a matter which could have been heard in that manner, the appeal proceedings may also be heard *in camera* (Domestic and Appellate Proceedings (Restriction of Publicity) Act 1968, s. 1).

Whilst not strictly a hearing *in camera,* the determination of committal proceedings before a magistrates' court may be likened to proceedings *in camera* since there are severe restrictions on the matters which may be reported unless the defendant (or one or more of several defendants) requires the restrictions to be lifted and the court makes an order accordingly (Magistrates' Courts Act 1980, s. 8). When there is more than one person accused in committal proceedings, the restrictions on publicity may be lifted only if the court is satisfied that it is in the interests of justice to remove the restrictions (Act of 1980, s. 8(2A) (added by the Criminal Justice (Administration) Act 1981, s. 1)).

In custodia legis. The County Courts Act 1959, s. 137, has been repealed and replaced by the County Courts Act 1984, s. 102, without change of effect.

In jure non remota causa sed proxima spectatur. The rule in *Hadley* v. *Baxendale* (1854) 9 Exch. 341, has been modified in its operation by the decision of the House of Lords in *Czarnikow Ltd.* v. *Koufos (The Heron II)* [1969] 1 A.C. 350.

In person. The Magistrates' Courts Act 1952, s. 99, has been repealed and replaced by the Magistrates' Courts Act 1980, s. 122, without change of effect.

The restriction which prevented a party in person applying for the committal of a person for contempt has been removed (see, *e.g. Bevan* v. *Hastings Jones* [1978] 1 W.L.R. 294, applying the relaxation in the Chancery Division as well as in the Queen's Bench Division). It is unlikely that the (technical) restriction in cases of motions for mandamus would now be enforced.

Incest. As a result of *R.* v. *Whitehouse* [1977] Q.B. 868, C.A., the Criminal Law Act 1977, s. 54, was passed, making it an offence for a man to incite to have sexual intercourse with him a girl under the age of 16 whom he knows to be his granddaughter, daughter or sister. On summary conviction the punishment may be either a fine not exceeding £2,000 (see FINE) or six months' imprisonment or both, and on conviction on indictment the penalty is imprisonment not exceeding two years (s. 54(4)).

Incitement to disaffection. For the general revision of the levels of fines see FINE.

Income tax. The main personal allowances against income tax are frequently revised (normally annually), as are the levels of tax and the bands of liable income on which the tax due is levied; see, for example, the Finance Act 1984, ss. 21 (for the allowances) and 17 (for the bands and rates), and the Income Tax (Indexation) Order 1984 (S.I. 1984 No. 344) (made under the Finance Act 1980, s. 24(9) (for the revision of upper rates and threshholds for investment income surcharge).

For the effect of the "Miras" scheme (under the Finance Act 1982) see BUILDING SOCIETY.

Indecency. The procedure for a matrimonial order consequent upon conviction under the Act of 1960 no longer obtains, the jurisdiction of magistrates having been revised by the Domestic Proceedings and Magistrates' Courts Act 1978. For the general revision of the levels of fines which may be imposed on summary conviction see FINE.

Indecent advertisements. For the general revision of the levels of fines see FINE.

Indemnity; Indemnification. It is an offence to agree with any person to indemnify that person against any liability which the other may incur as a surety to secure the surrender to custody of a person accused or convicted of or under arrest for any offence, both parties to the agreement being liable for the offence (Bail Act 1976, s. 9(1)). It is irrelevant when the agreement is made, and the fact that neither party actually becomes a surety is likewise discounted (s. 9(2)). Offenders may be committed to the Crown Court for sentence in serious cases (s. 9(3)). On summary conviction the penalty is a term of imprisonment not exceeding three months or a fine not exceeding £400 or both (for the general revision of the levels of fines in 1982 see FINE); and on conviction on indictment (or if sentenced by the Crown Court as mentioned above), a term of imprisonment not exceeding one year or a fine or both (s. 9(4)). Proceedings may be commenced only with the consent of the Director of Public Prosecutions (s. 9(5)).

Indemnity. Indemnity by way of contribution under the Law Reform (Married Women and Tortfeasors) Act 1935, s. 6, has been replaced by a modified system set out in the Civil Liability (Contribution) Act 1978; see CONTRIBUTION.

The scheme for providing indemnity upon rectification of the Land Register has been amended so as to make it clear (i) that the High Court has an unrestricted power to order rectification, and (ii) that some fault on the part of the proprietor is required before rectification will be permitted (Administration of Justice Act 1977, s. 24, amending the Land Registration Act 1925, s. 82(3)).

Independent contractor. In the case of social security the distinction between an "employed earner" and a "self-employed earner" may be said to rest on the distinction between an employee and an independent contractor (or a contract of service and a contract for services). See *B.S.M. (1257) Ltd.* v. *Secretary of State for Social Services* [1978] I.C.R. 894 (discussed at 42 M.L.R. (1979) 462).

India. The Government of India Act 1935, has been repealed by the Statute Law (Repeals) Act 1976, s. 1(1), Sched. 1, Part VII, with the exception of ss. 1, 311(4) and (5).

Indictment. Bills of indictment may no longer be preferred before grand juries under the provisions of the Administration of Justice (Miscellaneous Provisions) Act 1933, Sched. 1, since those provisions have been repealed by the Criminal Law Act 1967, s. 10, Sched. 3, Part III.

The usual definition of "indictable offence" is an offence which, if committed by an adult, is triable on indictment, whether it is exclusively so triable or triable either way (Criminal Law Act 1977, s. 64(1)(*a*)).

The Indictments (Procedure) (Amendment) Rules 1984 (S.I. 1984 No. 284) have made fresh provisions for lodging indictments and for the extension of time limits on written application to a judge.

Indorsement of claim. Claims for possession of land are subject to special requirements intended to make clear whether the land in question relates to a tenancy protected under the Rent Act 1977, s. 4; see *Practice Direction* [1977] 1 W.L.R. 577, and R.S.C. Ord. 6, r. 2(1)(*c*)(ii).

Indorsement of service. The requirement of an indorsement of service was abolished by the Rules of the Supreme Court (Amendment No. 2) 1979 (S.I. 1979 No. 402), rr. 2–14.

Industrial and Provident Societies. The amounts of the deposits which an industrial and provident society may take without becoming a banking business have been increased (Industrial and Provident Societies Act 1978, s. 1). Further increases in the relevant sum may be made by statutory instrument (see s. 2); the power has already been exercised (see, *e.g.* S.I. 1981 Nos. 394, 395).

Industrial assurance. The Friendly and Provident Societies Act 1968, s. 20(1)(*b*), Sched. 2, have been repealed by the Friendly Societies Act 1974, s. 116(4), Sched. 11.

Industrial development. The Co-operative Development Agency and Industrial Development Act 1984 has repealed and replaced a number of like-named Acts by way of consolidation. S.I. 1972 No. 903 was revoked and replaced by S.I. 1972 No. 996; then in turn there were revoked and replaced that Order and S.I. 1974 No. 1283, S.I. 1974 No. 2028, and S.I. 1976 No. 565; the last in this string of instruments is the Town and Country Planning (Industrial Development Certificates: Exemption) Order 1979 (S.I. 1979 No. 839), which provided for a general exemption on specified projects up to 50,000 square feet in area.

Industrial Development Advisory Board. The Industry Act 1972, ss. 7–9, have been repealed and replaced by the Industrial Development Act 1982, ss. 7, 8, 10, without substantial change of effect.

Industrial disease. The Factories Act 1961, ss. 81, 83, 84, have been repealed by the Factories Act (Repeals and Modifications) Regulations 1974 (S.I. 1974 No. 1941), made under the Health and Safety at Work, etc., Act 1974. Section 85 of the Act of 1961 has been repealed by the Employment Medical Advisory Service Act 1972, s. 9, Sched. 3.

Industrial Estates Corporation. The legislation relating to this body has been repealed and replaced by the English Industrial Estates Corporation Act 1981.

Industrial tribunals. The former appeal procedure under R.S.C. Ord. 94, r. 9A (now revoked), has been replaced by an appeal (under the Employment Protection (Consolidation) Act 1978, ss. 135, 136) to the Employment Appeal Tribunal (*q.v.*). Industrial tribunals also are the appropriate forum for the determination of the various claims in employment now regulated by the Employment Protection (Consolidation) Act 1978 (replacing some of the provisions of the Employment Protection Act 1975), and the actual procedural rules are contained in the Industrial Tribunals (Rules of Procedure) Regulations 1980 (S.I. 1980 No. 884), which replaced earlier similar regulations.

Infamous conduct. The Medical Act 1956, s. 33, was repealed by the Medical Act 1978, s. 31, Sched. 7, By s. 7 of the Act of 1978 the power to deal with "serious professional misconduct" was continued on comparable terms, and included cases involving provisionally registered persons (s. 7(8)). The Act of 1978, s. 31, has now been repealed and replaced by the Medical Act 1983, s. 36 (the former s. 7(8) appearing in s. 36(8)), without significant change of effect.

Infant. The Sale of Goods Act 1893, s. 2, has been repealed and replaced by the Sale of Goods Act 1979, s. 3, without change of effect.

The general superintendence and protective jurisdiction of the Court of Chancery is now exercised by the Family Division (*q.v.*) of the High Court instead of the Chancery Division (Supreme Court Act 1981, s. 61(1), (3), Sched. 1, para. 3, replacing the Administration of Justice 1970, s. 1, Sched. 1, para. 3 (which effectively replaced the Judicature Act 1925, s. 56(1)). The Chancery Division still deals with cases involving any application for the appointment of an administrator of a minor's estate alone.

The Judicature Act 1925, ss. 165, 44, 56, have been repealed and replaced by the Supreme Court Act 1981, ss. 118, 49, 83, respectively. The Act of 1981, s. 118, contains a modification of the earlier provision so that property does not vest (in a minor) until a grant of probate is made (thus enabling the court to control such cases under the general provisions of the Non-contentious Probate Rules 1954).

The C.C.R. 1936, Ord. 46, rr. 1, 9, have been revoked and replaced by the C.C.R. 1981, Ord. 47, rr. 1, 7, without change of effect.

Infectious diseases. The Public Health Act 1936, ss. 143, 151, 152, 154, 155 and 156, have been repealed and replaced by the Public Health (Control of Diseases) Act 1984, ss. 13 (and 15 and 76, in part), 22, 24, 55 and 25–26, respectively, without change of effect. The Public Health Act 1961, ss. 38–42, have been repealed and replaced by the Act of 1984, ss. 35, 18, 23, 20 and 55(2), respectively, without change of effect. The Health Services and Public Health Act 1968, ss. 47, 53, 54, have been repealed and replaced by the Act of 1984, ss. 10, 35, 36, without change of effect.

Inferior court. The Courts Act 1971, s. 10(5), has been repealed and replaced by the Supreme Court Act 1981, s. 29(3), without change of effect.

The Inferior Courts Judgments Extension Act 1882 has been (prospectively) repealed by the Civil Jurisdiction and Judgments Act 1982, ss. 53, 54, Sched. 13, Part II and Sched. 14. The 1982 Act provides for a new system of international recognition and enforcement of judgments and orders.

Information. For the requirements governing informations before justices see the Magistrates' Courts Act 1980, ss. 1(1), (3), 9–16, 18, 24, 27 and the Magistrates' Courts Rules 1981, rr. 4, 12 *et seq.* See also *Shah* v. *Director of Public Prosecutions* [1984] 1 W.L.R. 886, H.L., where the detailed format of informations was discussed. The hearing of two informations may be conducted at the same time if the defendant has consented to such a course; this may also be done in the absence of the defendant when the interests of justice do not require separate hearings (*In re Clayton* [1983] 2 A.C. 473, H.L.).

Initials. Registration of Business Names Act 1916, s. 22, has been repealed by the Companies Act 1981, s. 119, Sched. 4, without replacement.

Injunction. In employment law the grant of an injunction is restricted by statute. First, whether by an order for specific performance or an injunction restraining a breach or threatened breach of a contract of employment, no court may compel any employee to do any work or to attend at any place for the doing of any work (Trade Union and Labour Relations Act 1974, s. 16). Further, where an application is made for the grant of an injunction in the absence of the party against whom the injunction is sought to be granted (or any representative of his), and that party claims (or the court is of the opinion that he would be likely to claim) that he acted in contemplation or furtherance of a trade dispute (*q.v.*), the court may not grant the injunction unless satisfied that all reasonable steps have been taken to bring notice of the application to the attention of the absent party and that he has had an opportunity of being heard on the application (Act of 1974, s. 17(1)). Where such an application is made for an interim injunction pending the trial of an action, and the party against whom the order is sought claims that he acted in contemplation or furtherance of a trade dispute, in exercising its discretion whether to grant an injunction, the court must have regard to the likelihood of that party's success in establishing a defence under ss. 13 or 15 of the Act of 1974 (which provide defences to actions in tort where the acts done were in contemplation or furtherance of a trade dispute and authorise the conduct of peaceful picketing (Trade Union and Labour Relations Act 1974, s. 17(2) (added by the Employment Protection Act 1975, s. 125, Sched. 16, Part III, para. 6) and repealed in part by the Employment Act 1982, s. 21, Sched. 4)).

The High Court's power to grant an injunction (originally under the Judicature Act 1925, s. 45, but now under the Supreme Court Act 1981, s. 37) was extended in 1975 to cases where an action for a debt due and owing was brought against a defendant who was not within the jurisdiction but who had assets in this country; in such cases an *ex parte* or interim injunction could be granted preventing the removal of the assets (whether goods or money) from the jurisdiction pending the trial of the action (*Mareva Compania Naviera S.A.* v. *International Bulk Carriers Ltd.* [1975] 2 Lloyd's Rep. 609, C.A.). The application for such an order could not (originally) stand alone but had to be ancillary to some ordinary cause of action (*Siskina* v. *Distos Compania Naviera S.A.* [1979] A.C. 210, H.L.). See also *Third Chandris Shipping Corporation* v. *Unimarine S.A.* [1979] Q.B. 645, C.A.

The statutory provisions were consolidated in the Supreme Court Act 1981, s. 37, which recognised the extension effected by the Mareva case, and extended the powers of the courts by removing the need for any "overseas" element. The difficulties which might be caused to third parties have been discussed, and have to be taken into account in all cases before any injunction is granted (*Z Ltd.* v. *A–Z and AA–LL* [1982] Q.B. 558, C.A.).

The requirement of attachment to a "main" cause of action first disappeared in *Chief Constable of Kent* v. *V.* [1983] Q.B. 34, C.A., when the police obtained an order against a suspected criminal where no other (civil) proceedings were pending or intended.

Stemming from what was called an "opposed *ex parte* injunction" (*Pickwick International (G.B.) Ltd.* v. *Multiple Sound Distributors Ltd.* [1972] 1 W.L.R. 1213), there has been a stream of cases relating to a specialised form of mandatory injunction. These orders are commonly called "Piller orders" after the main case, *Anton Piller K.G.* v. *Manufacturing Processes Ltd.* [1976] Ch. 55, C.A.); they are specialised mandatory injunctions which require the party against whom they are made to allow entry and a search of premises for materials, plans and other things which the defendant might otherwise remove or destroy. Following *Rank Film Distributors Ltd.* v. *Video Information Centre* [1982] A.C. 380, H.L., statutory recognition of the form of order (the Supreme Court Act 1981, s. 72) reversed the ruling of the House of Lords.

Innuendo. For the requirement specifically to plead certain details of an innuendo in a defamation action see R.S.C. Ord. 82, r. 2.

Inquiry. The procedure for examining account and conducting inquiries was revised at the time when the organisation of the Chancery Division was revised after the Oliver Report (Cmnd. 8205) (see S.I. 1982 No. 1111, amending R.S.C. Ord. 43).

Insanity. The Divorce Reform Act 1969, s. 1, has been repealed and replaced by the Matrimonial Causes Act 1973, s. 1, without change of effect.

The Sale of Goods Act 1893, s. 2, has been repealed and replaced by the Sale of Goods Act 1979, s. 3, without change of effect; both statutes use the term "mental incapacity or drunkenness."

Insider dealing. A transaction in shares, etc., by a person who possesses unpublished price-sensitive information; such deals are restricted or prohibited by the Companies Act 1980, Part V (ss. 68–73),

Insolvency Services Account. Formed by the amalgamation of the former Bankruptcy Estates Account and Companies Liquidation Account, this is an account maintained at the Bank of England by the Secretary of State for the handling of funds received in respect of proceedings under the Bankruptcy Act 1914 (see BANKRUPT; BANKRUPTCY; BANKRUPTCY COURTS), or under the Companies Act 1948, in connection with the winding up (*q.v.*) of companies in England and Wales (Insolvency Act 1976, s. 3). Funds in excess of those required for day-to-day payments in respect of bankrupts' or companies' estates are transferred to the Insolvency Services Investment Account (*q.v.*) (Act of 1976, s. 3(4)).

Inspection. The C.C.R. 1936, Ord. 13 provision has been revoked and replaced by the C.C.R. 1981, Ord. 13, r. 7, without significant change of effect. The Rules of 1936, Ord. 14, has been revoked and replaced by C.C.R. 1981, Ord. 14 (see especially rr. 3–6).

Further provisions for the inspection of company files and accounts, etc., are contained in the Companies Act 1981, ss. 86 *et seq.*

Instalment. The Sale of Goods Act 1893, s. 31, has been repealed and replaced by the Sale of Goods Act 1979, s. 31, without change of effect. The County Courts Act 1959, s. 99, has been repealed and replaced by the County Courts Act 1984, s. 66, without change of effect.

Instrument. The Forgery Act 1913, s. 7, has been repealed by the Forgery and Counterfeiting Act 1981, s. 30, Sched., Part I. The telegram service has been discontinued.

Insurance. The form of policy set out in the Marine Insurance Act 1906, Sched., is now obsolescent if not altogether obsolete; members of Lloyd's now normally underwrite risks on the basis of various standard forms of policy settled in the years 1981–1982.

Insurance broker. The "industry" of insurance broking has been provided for in the Insurance Brokers (Registration) Act 1977, which establishes a number of methods of registration, including the Insurance Brokers Registration Council and a register of insurance brokers (ss. 1, 2). For relevant cases see *Birn* v. *Insurance Brokers' Registration Council*; *Pickles* v. *Insurance Brokers' Registration Council* [1984] 1 W.L.R. 784.

Interest. The question of interest on

damages for personal injuries was generally considered by the House of Lords in *Lim Poh Choo* v. *Camden and Islington Area Health Authority* [1980] A.C. 174. It has been held that in actions for damages for personal injuries the interest rate on the non-economic loss items in the claim should be allowed at 2 per cent. (*Wright* v. *British Railways Board* [1983] 2 A.C. 773, H.L.).

The principles on which awards of interest will be made are now regulated by the Supreme Court Act 1981, s. 35A (inserted by the Administration of Justice Act 1982, s. 15, Sched. 1; the terms of the Law Reform (Miscellaneous Provisions) Act 1934, s. 3 and the Administration of Justice Act 1969, s. 22, no longer apply (Act of 1982, s. 15(5)).

A judgment debt in the High Court bears interest at the prescribed rate (Judgments Act 1838, s. 17; Administration of Justice Act 1970, s. 44; the rate is revised from time to time and the changes are recorded in the *Supreme Court Practice* (1985), note 42/1/12 (being currently 12 per cent. per annum (see S.I. 1982 No. 1427)).

It may be argued that the High Court provisions should also be applied to the county courts by way of ancillary relief (see *K.* v. *K.* (*Divorce Costs*) (*Interest*) [1977] Fam. 39, C.A.).

Interest on overdue income tax is likewise varied from time to time (see, *e.g.* the Income Tax (Interest on Unpaid Tax and Repayment Supplement) Order 1979 (S.I. 1979 No. 1687)).

Interest may not be awarded at common law by an arbitrator unless there is a specific power granted in the instrument of submission; the statutory power (in the Supreme Court Act 1981) is restricted in its terms (*President of India* v. *La Pintada Navigacion S.A.* [1984] 3 W.L.R. 10, H.L.).

For interest on lump sum payments in matrimonial proceedings see the Matrimonial Causes Act 1973, s. 23(6) (prospectively added by the Administration of Justice Act 1982, s. 16).

For interest on money paid into court see PAYMENT INTO COURT.

Interlocutory. The time limit for appeals to the Court of Appeal has been standardised to four weeks in all cases (except appeals from decisions of the Social Security Commissioners, when the limit is six weeks) (R.S.C. Ord. 59, rr. 4, 21).

In certain cases the conduct and status of an appeal to the Court of Appeal may be affected by the question whether it is an interlocutory or a final appeal (Supreme Court Act 1981, s. 60(1)). The decision of the Court of Appeal whether a judgment is final or interlocutory for purposes connected with appeals to that court is not capable of further appeal (Act of 1981, s. 60(2)).

International Bank for Reconstruction and Development. The Bretton Woods Agreement Act 1945 was repealed by the Overseas Development and Co-operation Act 1980, s. 18, Sched. 2, Part I. The Act of 1980, ss. 4, 5, preserve the power to conduct dealings with the International Bank.

International development. The International Development Association Acts 1960 and 1964 have been repealed. See now the Overseas Development and Co-operation Act 1980, s. 9(2)(*c*).

International Finance. The International Finance Corporation Act 1955 has been repealed. See now the Overseas Development and Co-operation Act 1980, s. 9(2)(*b*).

International Monetary Fund. The legislation relating to this Fund has all been repealed and replaced by the International Monetary Fund Act 1979. See also the International Monetary Agreements Act 1983.

Interpleader. The County Courts Act 1959, ss. 68, 74 and 136, have been repealed and replaced by the County Courts Act 1984, ss. 44, 38 and 101, without change of effect.

Interpretation Act 1889. This Act has been repealed and replaced by the Interpretation Act 1978, which consolidates the previous legislation (including the Statutes (Definition of Time) Act 1880, s. 1, the Interpretation Measure 1925, s. 1, the Synodical Government Measure 1969, s. 2(2), and the Summer Time Act 1972, s. 1), as well as enacting several recommendations made by the Law Commissions (Cmnd. 7235). The Act of 1978 has made words of gender mutually interchangeable since not only do words importing masculine gender include the feminine (s. 6(*a*)), but words importing feminine gender also include the masculine (s. 6(*b*)). The Act applies to the interpretation of statutes, Measures of the General Synod of the Church of

England (and its predecessor) and to subordinate legislation (of all kinds: see s. 23) made under statutory authority; the use of the provisions of the 1978 Act in the interpretation of other documents (such as contracts and treaties) is an unreliable undertaking (see *Athanassiadis* v. *Government of Greece* [1971] A.C. 282, H.L.).

Interpretation section; Interpretation clause. The Interpretation Act 1889, has been repealed and replaced by the Interpretation Act 1978, with certain amendments suggested by the Law Commissions, but otherwise without substantial change of effect.

Interrogatories. The C.C.R. 1936, Ord. 14, has been revoked and replaced by the C.C.R. 1981, Ord. 14 (see especially rr. 11, 12). The new provisions apply the High Court provisions to county courts with appropriate modifications.

Intervene; Intervener. The procedural step of entering an appearance has been abolished (S.I. 1979 No. 1716) and replaced by the requirement that the defendant deliver to the court office an acknowledgment of service (and notice of intention to defend, if that be also appropriate) (see R.S.C. Ord. 12, r. 1). The procedure of "intervening" is still available to an occupier who has not been made defendant to an action for the recovery of land (see R.S.C. Ord. 113, r. 5).

Intervention by the Queen's Proctor in matrimonial causes is unusual; for an example see *Ali Ebrahim* v. *Ali Ebrahim* (*Queen's Proctor intervening*) [1983] 1 W.L.R. 1336.

Intoxicating liquors. The Customs and Excise Act 1952, Part IV (ss. 93–172), has been repealed and replaced by the Alcoholic Liquor Duties Act 1979, without substantial change of effect.

The provisions of the Licensing Act 1964, s. 174, have been supplemented by the Licensed Premises (Exclusion of Certain Persons) Act 1980, which authorises the making of an exclusion order (*q.v.*) in respect of any person who is convicted of any offence committed on licensed premises and who in the course of committing the offence uses or offers to use violence; failing to comply with an exclusion order constitutes an offence.

The up-grading of on-licences, and the provisions relating to permitted hours and special hours certificates have been amended (Licensing (Amendment) Act 1980).

Non-holders of justices' licences have been allowed to make up to four applications a year for an occasional permission type of licence (Licensing (Occasional Permissions) Act 1983).

Invalid carriage. The Road Traffic Regulation Act 1967, Sched. 5, has been repealed and replaced by the Road Traffic Regulation Act 1984, Sched. 6 (see Part I, Item 2).

Invalidity benefit. The non-contributory invalidity pension (under the original version of the Social Security Act 1975, s. 36) has been replaced by severe disablement allowance (Act of 1975, s. 36—as substituted by the Health and Social Security Act 1984, s. 11).

Investment. The Protection of Depositors Act 1963, has been repealed by the Banking Act 1979, s. 51(2), Sched. 7, in connection with the establishment of the Deposit Protection scheme under the Act of 1979, ss. 21 *et seq.* (see DEPOSIT PROTECTION BOARD).

The County Courts Act 1959, s. 52(3), has been repealed without replacement by the County Courts Act 1984, s. 148(3), Sched. 4. Section 168 of the 1959 Act has *not* been repealed in the 1984 consolidation.

Invitee. See also the Occupiers' Liability Act 1984.

Irish and Scottish judgments. The bulk of the Crown Debts Act 1801 (preamble and ss. 1–8), has been (prospectively) repealed without direct replacement (Civil Judgments and Jurisdiction Act 1982, s. 54, Sched. 14), as have the Judgments Extension Act 1868 and the Inferior Courts Judgments Extension Act 1882.

Iron and steel. The Iron and Steel Act 1975 has been repealed (see the Iron and Steel Act 1982, s. 38, Scheds. 6, 7).

Issue. The scope of the word "issue" in the law of wills has been modified in the text of the Wills Act 1837, s. 33 (as substituted by the Administration of Justice Act 1982, s. 19), but only in respect of people who die after 1982.

J

J.A., justice of appeal (*q.v.*).

Jactitation. The Administration of Justice Act 1970, s. 1, Sched. 1, have been repealed and replaced by the Supreme Court Act 1981, s. 61(1), (3), Sched. 1, para. 3, without change of effect.

Jewellers. The Merchant Shipping Act 1894, s. 502, has been (prospectively) repealed by the Merchant Shipping Act 1979, ss. 47(2), 50(4), Sched. 7, Part I; the limitation of liability of the owner of a British ship will be governed by the Act of 1979, ss. 18, 19, Sched. 4, when the repeal of the 1894 provision is brought into effect.

The Jewellery and Silverware Development Council Order 1948 (S.I. 1948 No. 2801) was revoked without replacement by the Jewellery and Silverware Development Council (Dissolution) Order 1953 (S.I. 1953 No. 287).

Jews. The Oaths Act 1909, s. 2, has been repealed and replaced by the Oaths Act 1978, s. 1(1), without change of effect.

Jobber. A jobber (in the statute called a "stockjobber") is specifically excepted from the licensing provisions which regulate the taking of deposits (Banking Act 1979, ss. 1, 2, Sched. 1, para. 9); see DEPOSIT.

Jockey Club. In *Nagle* v. *Fielden* [1966] 2 Q.B. 633, C.A., it was stated that membership of this body should be open to women as well as men; see now the Sex Discrimination Act 1975, s. 1.

The Diseases of Animals Act 1950, s. 40, has been repealed and replaced by the Animal Health Act 1981, ss. 47, 48, without change of effect.

Joint. The position of those who are jointly liable in respect of any damage (but not, therefore, joint contractors) has been altered by the Civil Liability (Contribution) Act 1978; see CONTRIBUTION.

Joint tenancy. The inclusion of a prayer in a divorce petition for the disposal of jointly held matrimonial property is not enough to constitute a severance of the joint tenancy involved (*Harris* v. *Goddard* [1983] 1 W.L.R. 1203, C.A.).

Joint tortfeasors. Further alterations to the law have been enacted in the Civil Liability (Contribution) Act 1978; see CONTRIBUTION.

Journals of Parliament. The Forgery Act 1913, s. 3(3)(*g*), has been repealed and replaced by the Forgery and Counterfeiting Act 1981; the general provisions of the 1981 Act cover the former specific provisions without significant change of effect.

Joy-riding. One of the punishments available on conviction of an offence under the Theft Act 1968, s. 12 (whether on summary conviction or on indictment) is disqualification for driving for such period as the court thinks fit (Road Traffic Act 1972, s. 93(2), Sched. 4, Part III, para. 2).

Judge. The Judicature Act 1925, ss. 9, 12, have been repealed and replaced by the Supreme Court Act 1981, ss. 10, 11, without significant change of effect, although a judge of the High Court no longer has (under the statute, as least) to complete a year's service before being eligible for appointment to the Court of Appeal.

Judge in Lunacy. The Mental Health Act 1959, s. 100, has been repealed and replaced by the Mental Health Act 1983, s. 93, without change of effect.

Judge's note. The County Courts Act 1959, s. 112, has been repealed and replaced by the County Courts Act 1984, s. 80, without change of effect.

Judge's order. In the Chancery Division an order made in the course of chambers work by a judge (rather than by a master) may be identified by his name appearing on the order (*Practice Direction* [1974] 1 W.L.R. 321). See also R.S.C. Ord. 42, r. 1(3), which requires orders (other than consent orders under Ord. 42, r. 5A) to be marked with the name of the judge, referee or master by whom they are made.

Judges' Rules. The Judges' Rules have been re-issued by the Home Secretary with the agreement of the Lord Chief Justice; the associated Administrative Directions have been brought up to date to take account of appropriate Home Office Circulars which bear on matters arising under the rules, changes in the law and in practice since 1964 (see Home Office Circular 89/1979).

For a devastating criticism of the ineffectiveness of the Rules and their application by the courts see 100 L.Q.R. (1984) 46, 49.

These rules will in due course be replaced by codes of practice under the Police and Criminal Evidence Act 1984, ss. 64 *et seq.*

Judgment. The rate of interest on a judgment debt is varied from time to time; see INTEREST. For the possible application of the same rule to county court judgments see *K.* v. *K.* (*Divorce Costs*) (*Interest*) [1977] Fam. 39, C.A.

The Judicature Act 1925, s. 225, has been repealed and replaced by the Supreme Court Act 1981, s. 151(1), without change of effect. The Judgments Extension Act 1868 has been (prospectively) repealed by the Civil Jurisdiction and Judgments Act 1982, s. 54, Sched. 14.

Judicature Act. The Judicature Act 1925, has been repealed by the Supreme Court Act 1981, s. 152(4), Sched. 7; the Act of 1981 is both an amending and a consolidating statute.

Judicial Committee of the Privy Council. See also the Judicial Committee (General Appellate Jurisdiction) Rules Order 1982 (S.I. 1982 No. 1676), which revokes and replaces (with amendments) earlier provisions of a like kind.

Judicial pensions. The main corpus of legislation in respect of judicial pensions has been repealed and replaced by the Judicial Pensions Act 1981, without change of effect.

Judicial review. This name is given to the procedure for applications to the High Court for any order of certiorari (*q.v.*), mandamus (*q.v.*) or prohibition (*q.v.*), as well as for an order under the Supreme Court Act 1981, s. 30 (which replaces the provisions of the Administration of Justice Act 1938, s. 9), restraining any person from acting in any office in which he is not entitled to act. The procedure is laid down by R.S.C. Ord. 53 (as entirely substituted by S.I. 1977 No. 1955 and later amended), and follows the earlier requirements in several ways. The new procedure, however, enables the applicant to include a claim for damages in his application for a review, and the court which hears the application may make such an award if it is satisfied that the applicant could have been awarded damages if the claim had been made in an action begun by the applicant at the time he made the application for judicial review (R.S.C. Ord. 53, r. 7).

It has been held that when an application may be made for judicial review it should be made in preference to other procedures (such as proceedings for a declaration) (*O'Reilly* v. *Mackman* [1983] 2 A.C. 237, H.L.); this is, however, by no means a firm rule (see *e.g. Wandsworth London Borough Council* v. *Winder* [1984] 3 W.L.R. 563, C.A.).

Since it may amount to an abuse of the appeal procedures, leave to make an application for judicial review may well be refused when (for example) the normal channels of appeal have been deliberately ignored (*R.* v. *Battle Justices, ex p. Shepherd* (1983) 5 Cr. App. Rep. (S.) 124, D.C.).

Judicial separation. The Administration of Justice Act 1970, s. 1, Sched. 1, have been repealed and replaced by the Supreme Court Act 1981, s. 61, Sched. 1, para. 3, without change of effect. The Matrimonial Proceedings (Magistrates' Courts) Act 1960, has been repealed and replaced by a substantially revised code of remedies and procedures (Domestic Proceedings and Magistrates' Courts Act 1978).

Judicial trustee. The procedures to be observed by a judicial trustee have been consolidated into the Judicial Trustee Rules 1983 (S.I. 1983 No. 370).

Jurat. The Oaths Act 1888, s. 4, has been repealed and replaced by the Oaths Act 1978, s. 6(2), without change of effect.

Jury. The right to jury trial where a term of imprisonment for a term exceeding three months may be imposed has been abolished and replaced by a right to trial by jury in cases which are triable only on indictment (Criminal Law Act 1977, s. 14(*a*)) or those which are triable either way (s. 14(*c*)). The Act of 1977 listed the cases which changed their status so as to become triable only by magistrates (ss. 15, 30, Sched. 1), those which are triable only on indictment (s. 16, Sched.2), and provided a list of cases triable either way (Sched. 3); the last group corresponded in some measure with the group of offences which formerly carried a right to jury trial by virtue of the Magistrates' Courts Act 1952, s. 25 (repealed). The 1977 provisions about classification of offences by mode of trial have been repealed and replaced by the Magistrates' Courts Act 1980, ss. 17 *et seq.*, Sched. 1, without change of effect.

A juror may be discharged (Juries Act 1974, s. 16) otherwise than in open court provided there is good cause for the usual course not being followed (*R.* v. *Richardson* [1979] 1 W.L.R. 1316, C.A.).

The use of juries in personal injury proceedings is obsolete following on *Ward* v. *James* [1966] 1 Q.B. 273, C.A. In civil cases the court's discretion to order a jury is required to be exercised in the interests of all the parties, so that a party's belief that the judge is biased against him will not normally suffice to found an application for jury trial (*Williams* v. *Beesley* [1973] 1 W.L.R. 1295, H.L.). The option to order jury trial in civil cases has been preserved by the Supreme Court Act 1981, s. 69.

The amount of any allowance paid to jurors in connection with their attendance is now determined administratively instead of under a statutorily prescribed scheme (Administration of Justice Act 1977, s. 2, Sched. 2).

Originally it was held that the disclosure of what happens in a jury-room was not automatically a contempt of court but was in any event undesirable (*Attorney-General* v. *New Statesman* [1981] Q.B. 1, D.C.). By the Contempt of Court Act 1981, s. 8, however, such a course of conduct was made punishable as contempt.

New disqualifications from jury service were introduced by the Juries (Disqualification) Act 1984, which prevents certain ex-prisoners from serving as jurors.

The County Courts Act 1959, s. 96, has been repealed and replaced by the County Courts Act 1984, s. 67, without change of effect.

Further amendments have been made to the provisions relating to coroners' juries (Coroners' Juries Act 1983).

Jus disponendi. The reservation of the right to pass property in goods subject to some condition (such as payment for them) has been judicially considered in *Aluminium Industrie Vaassen B.V.* v. *Romalpa Aluminium* [1976] 1 W.L.R. 676, C.A. See also *Re Bond Worth* [1980] Ch. 228, and *Borden (U.K.) Ltd.* v. *Scottish Timber Products* [1981] Ch. 25, C.A. It might be said that where the contract between the parties reserves the title to the seller until payment is made and the goods remain identifiable, the property does not pass; where the goods will inevitably become incapable of identification and this is known to the parties (as in the *Borden* case) before payment is either made or expected to be made, the property in the goods passes regardless of reservations expressed in the contractual arrangements. See also the Sale of Goods Act 1979, ss. 17–19.

Jus tertii. In an action for wrongful interference with goods, the prohibition on the pleading of *jus tertii* has been abolished (Torts (Interference with Goods) Act 1977, s. 8(1)); see THIRD PARTY.

Justice. The Judicature Act 1925, s. 2(4), has been repealed and replaced by the Supreme Court Act 1981, s. 4(2), without change of effect.

Justices of Appeal. The Judicature Act 1925, s. 6(3), has been repealed and replaced by the Supreme Court Act 1981, s. 2(3), without change of effect.

Justices of the peace. The Justices of the Peace Act 1949, and associated legislation, in so far as related to the qualifications and appointment of justices have been repealed and replaced by the Justices of the Peace Act 1979, without change of effect.

The jurisdiction conferred by the Merchant Shipping Act 1894, s. 164, has been abolished on account of the repeal of the provision by the Merchant Shipping Act 1970, s. 100(3), Sched. 5 (for the payment of wages and associated matters, see ss. 9-18 of the Act of 1970).

Juvenile offender. Borstal institutions (*q.v.*) having been abolished, juvenile offenders are now subject to a range of orders and sentences including attendance centre (*q.v.*), youth custody (*q.v.*), fines, discharges (absolute or conditional), and probation (see PROBATION OF OFFENDERS).

K

Kidnapping. The law relating to this offence was reviewed in *R.* v. *D.* [1984] 3 W.L.R. 186, H.L. See also the Child Abduction Act 1984.

Kiribati. With effect from July 12, 1979, the Gilbert Islands have become a republic within the Commonwealth and taken this name (Kiribati Act 1979); the constitution is provided for by the Kiribati Independence Order 1979 (S.I. 1979 No. 719), and a final appeal to the Judicial Committee of the Privy Council is prescribed by the Kiribati Appeals to Judicial Committee Order 1979 (S.I. 1979 No. 720).

L

Label. The Food and Drugs Act 1955, ss. 6, 7, have been repealed and replaced by the Food Act 1984, ss. 5–7, without change of effect.

Labour exchange. The Employment and Training Act 1948, has been repealed and replaced by the Employment and Training Act 1973, s. 14(2), Sched. 4. The Act of 1973 dealt with the provision of employment exchanges under the aegis of the Manpower Services Commission, the Employment Service Agency and the Training Services Agency (ss. 1–4); the Employment Service Agency (*q.v.*) and the Training Services Agency (*q.v.*) have both since been abolished.

Laches. The Limitation Act 1939 (as amended by the Limitation Amendment Act 1980), has been repealed and replaced by the Limitation Act 1980.

Laden in bulk. For modifications and partial repeals of the Merchant Shipping (Safety Conventions) Act 1949, s. 24, see the Merchant Shipping (Safety Conventions) Act 1967, s. 1(5), and the Merchant Shipping Act 1979, ss. 43, 47(2), 50(4), Sched. 6, Parts V, VI, para. 14, and Sched. 7, Part II.

Lambeth degrees. The Medical Act 1956, s. 31, Sched. 3, have been repealed and replaced by the Medical Act 1983, ss. 4(1) (which, like the 1956 provision, omits even to mention Lambeth degrees) and 49(1), without change of effect.

Land. The Interpretation Act 1889, s. 3, has been repealed and replaced by the Interpretation Act 1978, ss. 22, 23, Sched. 2, para. 5(a), which preserve the 1889 definition for Acts passed before the 1978 Act. By s. 5, Sched. 1, of the new Act it is provided that "land" includes buildings and other structures, land covered with water, and any estate, interest, easement, servitude or right in or over land; this definition applies to Acts of Parliament and all subordinate legislation passed or made after 1978.

Land Authority for Wales. For the general repeal of the Community Land Act 1975, see the Local Government, Planning and Land Act 1980, ss. 101, 194, Scheds. 17, 34. Fresh provision was made for the Authority (retained in being despite the general repeal of the 1975 Act), see the Act of 1980, ss. 102–111, Scheds. 18–22.

Land charge. The statutory period of title required to be shown was reduced to 15 years in 1969 (Law of Property Act 1969, s 23); as a result it may be impossible to ascertain the names of all the persons who have registered charges against any given portion of land, so leaving even a purchaser who has conducted the usual searches ignorant of the charges which have been registered. In such cases it is provided that the charge is not to affect the purchaser (in these circumstances the Law of Property Act 1925, s. 198, relating to constructive notice, is excluded) and compensation is made available from the Chief Land Registrar to remedy any loss caused by any undisclosed land charges (Act of 1969, s. 25).

The Matrimonial Homes Act 1967, s. 2,

Sched., have been repealed and replaced by the Matrimonial Homes Act 1983, s. 2, without change of effect. The procedures in the case of registered land are regulated by the Land Registration (Matrimonial Homes) Rules 1983 (S.I. 1983 No. 40). The Finance Act 1975, Sched. 12, para. 18(3), has been repealed and replaced by the Capital Transfer Tax Act 1984, s. 277, Sched. 9, the appropriate part of the Land Charges Act 1972 having been amended by the Capital Transfer Tax Act 1984, s. 276, Sched. 8, para. 3.

Land drainage. The legislation comprised in the Land Drainage Act 1930, and other Acts through to the Land Drainage (Amendment) Act 1976, has been repealed and replaced by the consolidated provisions contained in the Land Drainage Act 1976. The Water Act 1973, s. 19, has been repealed and replaced by the Land Drainage Act 1976, ss. 1, 6, 62. See also the Local Government, Planning and Land Act 1980, ss. 181, 182, which modify the rating provisions in respect of land drainage.

Landlord and tenant. The Judicature Act 1925, s. 46, has been repealed and replaced by the Supreme Court Act 1981, s. 38. Other charges in the law (*e.g.* the Housing Act 1980, the Housing and Building Control Act 1984) have been noted under appropriate headings.

Lands Clauses Acts. With insignificant exceptions, the Acquisition of Land (Authorisation Procedure) Act 1946, has been repealed and replaced by Acquisition of Land Act 1981, without significant change of effect.

Lands Tribunal. The procedure before the Lands Tribunal is regulated by the Lands Tribunal Rules 1975 (S.I. 1975 No. 299). As a result of amendments made in 1977 (see S.I. 1977 No. 1920) some cases may be determined without a hearing being necessary.

Lapse. The former version of the Wills Act 1837, s. 33, has been repealed and replaced by a new text (Administration of Justice Act 1982, s. 19), which applies to deaths after 1982: subject to a contrary intention appearing, the new provision ensures a "generation gap jump" of the gift, avoiding the risk of the gift falling to benefit creditors or a trustee in bankruptcy. The Family Law Reform Act 1969, s. 16, has been repealed (Administration of Justice Act 1982, s. 75(1), Sched. 9, Part I), since its effect (to extend the lapse provisions to cases involving illegitimate children) is provided for in the new version of s. 22.

Lascar. The Merchant Shipping Act 1894, s. 125, has been repealed by the Merchant Shipping Act 1970, s. 110(3), Sched. 5. Agreements for the employment of seamen are now controlled by regulations made under the Merchant Shipping Act 1970, s. 2.

Laundry. The Public Health Act 1936, s. 152, has been repealed and replaced by the Public Health (Control of Diseases) Act 1984, s. 24, without change of effect.

Lavatories. The Public Health Act 1936, s. 89, has been repealed and replaced by the Local Government (Miscellaneous Provisions) Act 1976, s. 81, Sched. 2. By s. 20 of the Act of 1976 a local authority (other than a county council or the Greater London Council) has power to require "sanitary appliances" to be provided and maintained at places of entertainment, subject to appeal to the county court (s. 21).

Lay-off. See GUARANTEE PAYMENT.

Lead works. The Factories Act 1961, s. 74, has been repealed by the Control of Lead at Work Regulations 1980 (S.I. 1980 No. 1248), which provide for precautions and safety measures against lead contamination at work.

Leader of the Opposition. The salaries of the Leaders of the Opposition (both the House of Lords and the House of Commons contain such an appointment) are increased from time to time (see, *e.g.* S.I. 1979 No. 905).

Leap-frog case. This is the common designation of an appeal made from the High Court or a Divisional Court direct to the House of Lords on the certificate of the trial judge or judges (Administration of Justice Act 1969, ss. 12–15; *Practice Direction* [1970] 1 W.L.R. 97).

Lease. The Judicature Act 1925, s. 56, has been repealed and replaced by the Supreme Court Act 1981, s. 61(1), (3), Sched. 1, para. 1, without change of effect.

Leaseholds. The Rent Act 1968, Scheds. 15, 17 (which contained amendments and repeals), have been repealed by the Rent Act 1977, s. 156, Sched. 25. The statutory scheme for purchase of leaseholds has been amended by the Leasehold Reform Act 1979, which restricts the price which may be demanded of the tenant-purchaser, and nullifies the effect of the decision of the House of Lords in *Jones* v. *Wrotham Park Settled Estates* [1980] A.C. 74.

Leave to defend. For the abolition of appearances and the introduction of acknowledgements of service see APPEARANCE.

Legacy. Payment into court is now effected under R.S.C. Ord. 92, r. 2, in conjunction with the Supreme Court Funds Rules 1975 (S.I. 1975 No. 1803), r. 18(iii).

The former R.S.C. Ord. 44, r. 19, has been revoked and replaced (see the Rules of the Supreme Court (Amendment No. 2) 1982, (S.I. 1982 No. 1111)) by Ord. 44, r. 9 (under which the judgment debt interest rate is applied in respect of debts which do not carry their own interest rates).

Legal aid. The financial limits which are applied to applicants both for legal advice and assistance and for legal aid are constantly under review, the amounts involved normally being revised at least annually.

Legal advice and assistance (the "Green Form Scheme") is given under the authority of the Legal Advice and Assistance Regulations 1980 (S.I. 1980 No. 477 as amended), which revoked and replaced earlier regulations, taking into account amendments in the law made by the Legal Aid Act 1979 and other legislation. The Act of 1979 authorised legal representation before a court or tribunal under the Green Form Scheme (s. 1, adding a new s. 2A to the Legal Aid Act 1974), and simplified the procedure for the amendment of the financial limits involved in the various schemes (ss. 2–4) as well as amending the provisions (Act of 1974, s. 9) relating to the charge on property recovered for the recipient of legal aid (Act of 1979, s. 5).

The responsibility for the administration of the criminal legal aid scheme (Act of 1974, Part II (ss. 28–40)) has been transferred from the Home Secretary to the Lord Chancellor (Transfer of Function (Legal Aid in Criminal Proceedings) Regulations 1980 (S.I.1980 No. 705)), thus combining in the Lord Chancellor the responsibility for all types of financial assistance in legal proceedings.

The charge which is conferred on the Law Society by the Legal Aid Act 1974, s. 9, has been held to be capable (subject to the consent of the Law Society) of being transferred to other property than that which is preserved or recovered in the proceedings for which legal aid was granted (*Hanlon* v. *Law Society* [1981] A.C. 124, H.L.).

For additional amendments to the system of criminal legal aid see the Legal Aid Act 1982. "Through" orders, allowing legal aid on one certificate to deal with proceedings both in a set of magistrates' courts proceedings and subsequent Crown Court proceedings are now possible.

Legal custody. A person who is in custody in pursuance of the sentence of a court or of any authority acting under the Service Acts comes within the exceptions to the right to bail in criminal proceedings (Bail Act 1976, s. 4, Sched. 1, Part I, para. 4 imprisonable offences), Part II, para. 4 (non-imprisonable offences)).

Prisoners are deemed to be in the legal custody of the governor of the prison (Prison Act 1952, s. 13(1)), and this extends to cover all the times when they are outside the prison in the custody or under the control of an officer of the prison (s. (2)).

Legal executive. By the County Courts (Rights of Audience) Direction 1978 (made under the County Courts Act 1959, s. 89A (now repealed and replaced by the County Courts Act 1984, s. 61, without change of effect)), Fellows of the Institute of Legal Executives have been authorised to appear in open court in the county court on an unopposed application for an adjournment as well as on an application for judgment by consent of the parties.

Leprosy. The Public Health (Leprosy) Regulations 1966, have been revoked and replaced by the Public Health (Infectious Diseases) Regulations 1968 (S.I. 1968 No. 1366, as variously amended).

Letter patent or **Letters overt.** The Patents Act 1949, has been affected by the Patents Act 1977; see PATENTS.

Level crossings. Fresh provision for safety arrangements are contained in the (short) Level Crossings Act 1983.

Lex loci contractus. The Supply of Goods (Implied Terms) Act 1973, ss. 5, 6, have been repealed and replaced by the

Sale of Goods Act 1979, s. 56, Sched. 1, para. 13, and s. 56, Sched. 13, paras. 11, 13, respectively. The Act of 1973, s. 13, was repealed by the Unfair Contract Terms Act 1977, s. 31(4), Sched. 4; the provision equivalent to s. 13 is now the Act of 1977, s. 27.

Liabilities adjustment. The Liabilities (War-time Adjustment) Acts 1941 and 1944 were (eventually) repealed by the Statute Law (Repeals) Act 1971, s. 1, Sched., Part V.

Libel. The Criminal Justice Act 1967, s. 5, has been repealed and replaced by the Magistrates' Courts Act 1980, s. 8(9), without change of effect.

Liberty. The Liberties Act 1850 has been repealed by the Local Authorities (Miscellaneous Provisions) (No. 4) Order 1974 (S.I. 1974 No. 1351), made under the Local Government Act 1972, ss. 254, 266.

Originally a liberty was the possession by a subject of a part of the royal prerogative, normally shown by the holding of courts independently of the king's courts; by association with the area where the privilege was exercised the title "liberty" came to mean that area, an alternative name being "soke" (as in Soke of Peterborough).

Libraries. The capital transfer tax exceptions in the Finance Act 1975, Sched. 6, para. 12, have been repealed and replaced by the Capital Transfer Tax Act 1984, s. 25(1), Sched. 3, without change of effect.

Licence. By virtue of the Limitation Act 1980, Sched. 1, para. 8(4) (replacing the Limitation Act 1939, s. 10(4), which was added by the Limitation Amendment Act 1980, s. 4), it is provided that (for the purpose of determining whether a person occupying land is in adverse possession of it) it is not to be assumed by implication of law that his occupation is by permission of the person entitled to the land merely because his occupation is not inconsistent with the present or future enjoyment of the land by the person entitled to it; this provision is not to be taken as prejudicing a finding to the effect that a person's occupation of any land is by implied permission of the person entitled to the land in any case where the facts of the case justify such a finding.

Licence to assign. The Race Relations Act 1965, s. 5, has been repealed and replaced by the Race Relations Act 1976, s. 24, without change of effect.

Licensee. The Occupiers' Liability Act 1957, has been supplemented by the Occupiers' Liability Act 1984.

Licensing Acts. Persons who are not justices' off-licence holders may apply for occasional–permission–type licences for the sale of intoxicating liquor by their organisations under the Occasional Permissions Act 1983, an upper limit of four occasions per year being fixed by the statute (Licensing (Occasional Permissions) Act 1983).

Lien. The Sale of Goods Act 1893, ss. 38, 39, 41–48, have been repealed and replaced by the Sale of Goods Act 1979, ss. 38, 39, 41–48, without change of effect.

Where a solicitor discharges himself, the client or any new solicitor is entitled to have the papers in the cause from the discharged solicitor on an undertaking to hold them without prejudice to the discharged solicitor's lien and to return them after the hearing (*Robins* v. *Goldingham* (1872) L.R. 13 Eq. 440); see also *Gamlen Chemical Co.* (*U.K.*) v. *Rochem* [1980] 1 W.L.R. 614, C.A.

The Merchant Shipping Act 1894, s. 167, has been repealed and replaced by the Merchant Shipping Act 1970, s. 18, without substantial change of effect from 1 January 1973 (see S.I. 1972 No. 1977).

The Disposal of Uncollected Goods Act 1952, has been repealed and replaced by the Torts (Interference with Goods) Act 1977, ss. 12, 13, Sched. 1; the 1977 provisions are wider in their terms and apply to all classes of bailees, the scheme being simpler than the one contained in the Act of 1952.

The Judicature Act 1925, s. 56(1), has been repealed and replaced by the Supreme Court Act 1981, s. 61(1), (3), Sched. 1, para. 1, without change of effect; the term "lien," however, no longer appears.

Life. Note also the Cestui que Vie Act 1666, under which there is a prima facie presumption of death after seven years' absence. See also LIVES, LEASES FOR.

Life, Expectation of. Damages may no longer be awarded under this head (Administration of Justice Act 1982, s. 1(1)). See EXPECTATION OF LIFE.

Life peeress. A barony by writ descends to heirs generally, so that a woman may be a peeress in her own right, but "the privilege of acting as an hereditary counsellor to the Crown was considered to be confined to the male sex, no woman having been summoned to sit in the House of Lords" (see 1 Anson, 227). Although the Sex Disqualification (Removal) Act 1919, removed the disqualification of women for the exercise of public office, it was held that the Act merely removed a disability and did not create a right, so that (by a majority of 22 votes to 4) the Viscountess Rhondda's petition for the issue of a writ was rejected (*Viscountess Rhondda's Claim* [1922] A.C. 339). When life peerages were introduced by the Life Peerages Act 1958, it was expressly provided that the title and dignity might be conferred on a woman (s. 1(3)). The peerage is conferred by letters patent (s. 1.(1)), it entitles the appointee to rank as a baron under the style appointed by the letters patent and to receive a writ of summons to attend the House of Lords and to sit and vote in that House, provided she is not otherwise disqualified by law (s. 1(4)).

Light. *Price* v. *Hildich* [1930] 1 Ch. 500, was not considered in *Allen* v. *Greenwood* [1980] Ch. 119, C.A., in which it was held that a right to the high degree of light needed for a greenhouse might be acquired under the Prescription Act 1832, s. 3.

Lights on vehicles. Detailed requirements are set out in the Road Vehicles Lighting Regulations 1984 (S.I. 1984 No. 812).

Limitation of actions. Further amendments in this branch of the law were made by the Limitation Amendment Act 1980, of which the following list records the main items. Certain loans have been made the subject of special provision (Limitation Act 1939, s. 1(2AA) (added by the Act of 1980, s. 1)); new rules were introduced to deal with cases involving theft (Act of 1939, s. 3A (added by the Act of 1980, s. 2), and the accrual of a right of action in respect of certain tenancies (Act of 1939, s. 9 (amended by the Act of 1980, s. 3)). A licence (*q.v.*) may no longer be implied by law so as to defeat a claim to title on the ground of adverse possession, only a licence justified by the facts of the case (Act of 1939, s. 10(4) (added by the Act of 1980, s. 4)). New rules also apply to cases concerning relief for trustees retaining trust property as beneficiaries (Act of 1939, s. 19(1A) (added by the Act of 1980, s. 5)), as well as to the effect of acknowledgment or part payment on the accrual of a right of action (Act of 1980, s. 6, amending various provisions of the Act of 1939). Amended provisions now govern the postponement of the limitation period in cases of fraud, concealment or mistake (Act of 1939, s. 26 (as substituted by the Act of 1980, s. 7)), and cases of new claims in pending actions (with appropriate provision for the making of rules of court) (Act of 1939, s. 28 (as substituted by the Act of 1980, s. 8)). Admiralty actions are also dealt with (Act of 1980, s. 9) and additional provisions deal with the case of a debtor who becomes the personal representative of his creditor (Administration of Estates Act 1925, s. 21A (added by the Act of 1980, s. 10)). The provisions of the 1980 Act are applied to the Crown in the same way as the 1939 provisions (Act of 1980, s. 11).

The bulk of the 1939 to 1980 statutory corpus was later repealed and consolidated into the Limitation Act 1980, as follows: the Act of 1939, ss. 16, 2(1), 22, 23, 19, 30(1) with 32, 2A 2D and 4, have been replaced by the Act of 1980, ss. 17 with 25(3), 2 with 5 and 7 and 9(1), 28, 29, 21, 37–38, 11, 33, 2–9 with 11 and 24 and 36, Sched. 1, paras. 10, 11, respectively.

In due course the effect of foreign law on limitation will be observed in this country too (Foreign Limitation Periods Act 1984).

The Magistrates' Courts Act 1952, s. 104, has been repealed and replaced by the Magistrates' Courts Act 1980, s. 127, without change of effect.

Limitation of liability. The Merchant Shipping Act 1894, s. 502, has been repealed and replaced by the Merchant Shipping Act 1979, s. 18, without substantial change of effect. The Act of 1894, s. 503, has been (prospectively) repealed and replaced by the Act of 1979, s. 17, Sched. 4, Part I, introducing the rules contained in the Convention on Limitation of Liability for Maritime Claims to English law together with ancillary provisions (Sched. 4, Part II). See also the Act of 1979, s. 35(1), which provided for immediate modifications to the Act of 1894, s. 503, before its repeal takes effect.

Limited owner. The Finance Act 1894, has been repealed in connection with the abolition of estate duty and its replacement by capital transfer tax (*q.v.*); the provisions making a limited owner's charge registrable under the Land Charges Act 1972, s. 2(1), Class C(ii), now apply to the case of a tenant for life who has paid capital transfer tax in respect of the estate (Capital Transfer Tax Act 1984, s. 276, Sched. 8, para. 3, replacing the amendment originally made by the Finance Act 1975, s. 52, Sched. 12, para. 18).

Liquidated demand. The procedure for entering an appearance has been abolished (see S.I. 1979 No. 1716) and replaced by service of an acknowledgment of service and notice of intention to defend. The procedure under R.S.C. Ord. 6, r. 2(1), has been amended accordingly.

Litre. S.I. 1963 No. 1354 was revoked and replaced by the Units of Measurement Regulations 1976 (S.I. 1976 No. 1674), which have in their turn been revoked and replaced by the Units of Measurement Regulations 1980 (S.I. 1980 No. 1070).

Litter. The Litter Acts 1958 to 1971, together with the Public Health Act 1961, s. 4 and the Control of Pollution Act 1974, s. 24, have been repealed and replaced by the Litter Act 1983, without change of effect. The Highways Act 1959, s. 156, has been repealed and replaced by the Highways Act 1980, s. 185, without change of effect.

Liturgy. Alternative rites to those contained in the Book of Common Prayer were promulgated under the Prayer book (Alternative Services) Measure 1965, and modified forms of these now appear in the Alternative Service Book issued for use from November 1980.

Lloyd's. The Insurance Companies Act 1974, ss. 12(4), 73, have been repealed and replaced by the Insurance Companies Act 1982, ss. 15(4), 83, without change of effect. Under the Act of 1982, there have been issued the Insurance (Lloyd's) Regulations 1983 (S.I. 1983 No. 224), which revoked and replaced the earlier subordinate legislation about Lloyd's.

The Lloyd's Act 1871, ss. 11, 12, 18–27 and 29, have been repealed by the Lloyd's Act 1982 (c.xiv).

Lloyd's Register. The Merchant Shipping Act 1894, s. 443, was repealed by the Merchant Shipping (Safety and Load Line Conventions) Act 1927, s. 67, Sched. 4, Part II.

Loan. The limitation period for certain loans of money has been amended (Limitation Act 1980, s. 6 (replacing the Limitation Act 1939, s. 1(2AA) (added by the Limitation Amendment Act 1980, s. 1)); see also LIMITATION OF ACTIONS.

Loan society. For a new form of institution see CREDIT UNION.

Local and personal Acts. The Interpretation Act 1889, s. 9, has been repealed and replaced by the Interpretation Act 1978, ss. 3, 21(1), without change of effect. The revival of the use of personal Acts (in the marriage field) has been remarkable—there being one such Act in 1980 and two in 1982.

Local government. Further amendments to the system of local government finance were made by the Local Government Finance Act 1982. The franchise provisions were repealed and replaced by the Representation of the People Act 1983, ss. 1–13, 31–59, without significant change of effect.

Local land charges. The Local Land Charges Act 1975, came into operation on August 1, 1977 (Local Land Charges Act 1975 (Commencement) Order 1977 (S.I. 1977 No. 984). Computerisation of local land charges registers has been provided for (Local Government (Miscellaneous Provisions) Act 1982, s. 34), subject to making registers available for inspection "in visible form".

Local loans. Under the Finance Act 1982, s. 154(2), the limit of lending by the Public Works Loan Commissioners to local authorities was increased (with effect from 24 February 1984) to £12,000 million (Local Loans (Increase of Limit) Order 1984 (S.I. 1984 No. 194)).

Local valuation courts. For the purposes of the law of contempt (*q.v.*), it was held that a local valuation court was not a court of law but a body with administrative functions (*Attorney-General* v. *B.B.C.* [1981] A.C. 303, H.L.), and the passing of the Contempt of Court Act 1981, seems not to have affected the ruling (see the Act of 1981, s. 19, for the appropriate definition).

Location of Offices Bureau. The Bureau has been dissolved and its assets were to be distributed by the Secretary of State for the Environment (Location of Offices Bureau (Revocation) Order 1980 (S.I. 1980 No. 560)).

Lock-out. There is special provision in connection with dismissal of employees in connection with a lock-out, strike or other industrial action (Employment Protection (Consolidation) Act 1978, s. 62), but no definition of the term. Further complex provisions in the Employment Act 1982, s. 9, do not assist in defining the term.

Locus standi. For a consideration of the issues involved when determining whether a party has *locus standi* see *R.* v. *I.R.C., ex p. National Federation of Self-Employed and Small Businesses Ltd.* [1982] A.C. 617, H.L.

Lodger. The Housing Act 1957, s. 90, as originally enacted, has been replaced by a new text introduced by the Housing Act 1980, s. 146(1), which extends the scope of controls in respect of overcrowding.

Loitering. That portion of the Vagrancy Act 1824, s. 4, which related to this offence has been repealed by the Criminal Attempts Act 1981. The 1981 Act, s. 9, introduced a new, summary offence of interfering with vehicles, the essence of which (s. 9(2)) is interference intending that there shall be committed the theft of the vehicle in question (or any associated trailer of any part of it), the theft of anything in or on the vehicle or trailer, or an offence of taking and driving away (under the Theft Act 1968, s. 12). The maximum penalty (s. 9(3)) is three months' imprisonment or a fine not exceeding £500 (now £1,000; see FINE) or both. Arrest without warrant by a constable is authorised against a person who is or whom the constable reasonably suspects of committing an offence (s. 9(4)).

The penalties under the Street Offences Act 1959, s. 1, have been modified (see FINE), principally by the abolition of enhanced penalties (Criminal Justice Act 1982, s. 35) and the abolition of imprisonment for the offence.

Lord-lieutenant. The general provisions relating to the powers and duties of the lords-lieutenant in relation to the reserve forces have been repealed and replaced by the Reserve Forces Act 1980, ss. 130–138, without significant change of effect.

Lord Lyon King of Arms. See also the Lyon King of Arms Act 1867.

Lord President of the Council. The salary of the Lord President of the Council is increased from time to time (see, *e.g.* S.I. 1979 No. 905).

Lord Privy Seal. The salary of the Lord Privy Seal is increased from time to time (see, *e.g.* S.I. 1979 No. 905).

Lords of Appeal in Ordinary. The Judicature Act 1925, s. 6(2), has been repealed and replaced by the Supreme Court Act 1981, s. 2(2), without change of effect. The Act of 1981, s. 2(4), contains power to increase the number of judges in the Court of Appeal, which has now been increased from the original 18 to 23 (Maximum Number of Judges Order 1983 (S.I. 1983 No. 1705)).

Lorry area. The Highways Act 1971, s. 30, has been repealed and replaced by the Highways Act 1980, s. 115, without change of effect.

Loss leaders. The Resale Prices Act 1964, s. 2(1), has been repealed and replaced by the Resale Prices Act 1976, s. 11(1), without change of effect.

Lost property. The London Hackney Carriage Act 1853, s. 11 (as variously amended), has been repealed by the Statute Law (Repeals) Act 1976, s. 1(1), Sched. 1, Part XVII. See also the Local Government (Miscellaneous Provisions) Act 1982, s. 41.

Lottery. See also the Betting, Gaming and Lotteries (Amendment) Act 1980.

Luminising. The Factories Act 1961, s. 76, has been repealed by the Factories Act 1961, etc., (Repeals and Modifications) Regulations 1974 (S.I. 1974 No. 1941).

Lump, The. S.I. 1975 No. 1960 has been amended by the Income Tax (Sub-Contractors in the Construction Industry) Regulations 1980 (S.I. 1980 No. 1135), which bring Class 4 National Insurance contributions within the advance collection arrangements formerly restricted to income tax payments.

M

Maintenance. The distribution of assets, etc., on divorce or decree of nullity commences from the assumption that a "one third part to the wife" is the proper division before the statutory requirements are observed (*Wachtel* v. *Wachtel* [1973] Fam. 72, C.A.). The constant flux of opinions is usefully noted by Deech, 98 L.Q.R. (1982) 621.

The Matrimonial and Family Proceedings Act 1984, has revised the basis on which financial provision is to be ordered in divorce or nullity proceedings (Matrimonial Causes Act 1973, ss. 25, 25A (as substituted and inserted by the Matrimonial and Family Proceedings Act 1984, s. 3)). Associated and similar modifications are made by the Act of 1984, ss. 4–8.

The Administration of Justice Act 1970, s. 1, Sched. 1, have been repealed and replaced by the Supreme Court Act 1981, s. 61(1), (3), Sched. 1, para. 3, without change of effect.

Man, Isle of. The Interpretation Act 1889, s. 18(1), has been repealed and replaced by the Interpretation Act 1978, s. 5, Sched. 1, without change of effect.

See also the Isle of Man Act 1979, which deals with the inter-relation of taxes of the Isle of Man and of the United Kingdom, giving effect to an agreement signed on 15 October 1979. The Act of 1958 has been repealed (Act of 1979, s. 14(5), Sched. 2).

Manager. The appointment of a manager for a company is conducted under the provisions of the Companies Act 1948, ss. 366–376.

Mandamus. The procedure for an application for an order of mandamus has been revised (see S.I. 1977 No. 1955), and it is now possible for a claim for damages to be added to the claim for the order (R.S.C. Ord. 53, r. 7). See JUDICIAL REVIEW.

The meaning of the Tribunals and Inquiries Act 1971, s. 14, is that, even when pre-1958 legislation provides that "any order or determination shall not be called into question in any court, or any provision in such an Act which by similar words excludes any of the powers of the High Court," that will not be effective (*inter alia*) to prejudice the powers of the High Court to make orders of mandamus.

The statutory basis of orders of mandamus is now the Supreme Court Act 1981, s. 31(1); the Judicature Act 1925, s. 45(1), has been repealed and replaced by the Act of 1981, s. 37, without significant change of effect. The Courts Act 1971, s. 10(5), has been repealed and replaced by the Act of 1981, s. 29(4), without change of effect.

Manifest. The Revenue Act 1884, s. 3, was repealed and replaced by the Customs and Excise Act 1952, s. 54, which has, in its turn, been repealed and replaced by the Customs and Excise Management Act 1979, s. 66. In its final form the provision has been redrafted without using the term, using the words "document relating to the cargo" in its place.

Manslaughter. A new description of the offence of causing death by reckless driving has been enacted (Road Traffic Act 1972, s. 1 (as substituted by the Criminal Law Act 1977, s. 50(1)).

Margarine. The Food and Drugs Act 1955, ss. 4, 7, 123, have been repealed and replaced by the Food Act 1984, ss. 4, 7, 118, without change of effect.

Marine boards. The Merchant Shipping Act 1894, ss. 244, 245, have been repealed by the Merchant Shipping Act 1970, s. 100(3), Sched. 5 (see S.I. 1972 No. 1977, for commencement provisions for the Act of 1970).

Market, Open. The Coal Industry Nationalisation Act 1946, s. 14, has been repealed by the Statute Law (Repeals) Act 1973, s. 1(1), Sched. 1, Part X.

For the purposes of assessing the development land tax (*q.v.*) due under the Act of 1976, the market value of an interest in land is defined as the price which might reasonably be expected in the open market (no regard being had to the effect on prices of flooding the market) (Development Land Tax Act 1976, s. 7(1)).

Market overt. The Sale of Goods Act 1893, s. 22(1), has been repealed and replaced by the Sale of Goods Act 1979 s. 22(1), without change of effect.

Markets and fairs. The right to hold a market and the restrictions involved have occasioned a burst of litigation (see *Gloucestershire County Council* v. *Farrow* [1984] 1 W.L.R. 262, *and Sevenoaks District Council* v. *Patullo & Vinson Ltd.* [1984] Ch. 211, C.A., where the authorities are reviewed). The Food and Drugs Act 1955, Part III, has been repealed and replaced by the Food Act 1984, Part III (ss. 50–61), without change of effect. The power to authorise the holding of temporary markets has been conferred on local authorities (Local Government (Miscellaneous Provisions) Act 1982, s. 37).

Marlebridge, Statute of. The statute 52 Hen. 3, c. 2, has been repealed by the Statute Law Revision Act 1948, s. 1, Sched. 1. Chapter 23 of the statute is still in force and deals with waste by fermors.

Marriage. The Marriage Act 1983, provides special procedures for the marriage (on the authority of a superintendent registrar's certificate issued under the Marriage Act 1949, Part III) of house-bound people at the place where they usually reside.

In relation to declarations about marital status, the Administration of Justice Act 1970, s. 1, Sched. 1, have been repealed and replaced by the Supreme Court Act 1981, s. 61(1), (3), Sched. 1, para. 3(*a*), without change of effect.

Married women's property. The Administration of Justice Act 1970, s. 1, Sched. 1, have been repealed and replaced by the Supreme Court Act 1981, s. 61(1), (3), Sched. 1, para. 3, without change of effect.

Masculine. The Interpretation Act 1889, has been repealed and replaced by the Interpretation Act 1978 (see s. 6). By s. 6(*b*), words importing the feminine gender include the masculine, but the obviously suitable opportunity of using this form of pronoun was not utilised in the drafting of the Nurses, Midwives and Health Visitors Act 1979.

Master and servant. In connection with an employer's duty to provide safe methods of work, competent co-employees and safe equipment, see also the Employers' Liability (Compulsory Insurance) Act 1969, which requires employers to have insurance in respect of liability for bodily injury or disease sustained by their employees and arising out of and in the course of their employment (s. 1). The Act provides for penalties on summary conviction of failing to comply with the requirements, directors, managers, secretaries and other officers of corporations (if they are at fault) being liable as well as the employer (s. 5).

The Contracts of Employment Act 1972 (as variously amended), has been repealed and replaced by the Employment Protection (Consolidation) Act 1978, ss. 1–11, without substantial change of effect.

The majority of the provisions of the Act of 1978 apply to Crown employment (Employment Protection (Consolidation) Act 1978, s. 138), as well as to House of Commons staff (s. 139), thus negativing the generally contrary proposition in *Wood* v. *Leeds Area Health Authority* (*Training*) [1974] I.C.R. 535.

The Law Reform (Married Women and Tortfeasors) Act 1935, s. 6, has been repealed and replaced by the Civil Liability (Contribution) Act 1978 without substantial change of effect in the context in which the 1935 Act is mentioned; see CONTRIBUTION. Guarantee payments (*q.v.*) are now made under the Employment Protection (Consolidation) Act 1978, ss. 12–18, and the rights of pregnant women have been consolidated in the same Act, ss. 33–48. The written statement of reasons for dismissal is now dealt with by the Act of 1978, s. 53, and itemised pay statements are the subject of s. 8 of that Act.

Master of the Rolls. The Judicature Act 1925, s. 6(2), has been repealed and replaced by the Supreme Court Act 1981, s. 2(2)(*e*), without change of effect.

Masters of the Supreme Court. R.S.C. Ord. 89, r. 1, has been revoked, being replaced (but only in the Family Division) by the Matrimonial Causes Rules 1977, rr. 104–106.

The masters of the Chancery Division now exercise their powers in accordance with R.S.C. Ord. 32, r. 14, and *Practice Directions* [1975] 1 W.L.R. 129, [1975] 1 W.L.R. 405, [1976] 1 W.L.R. 637 and [1977] 1 W.L.R. 1019.

The Judicature Act 1925, ss. 45, 51, have been repealed and replaced by the Supreme Court Act 1981, ss. 37, 42 (respectively), without change of effect. The County Courts Act 1959 (as variously amended), has been repealed and replaced by the County Courts Act 1984, without change of effect. The terms of the Courts Act 1971, s. 26, have been repealed and incorporated into the Supreme Court Act 1981, s. 89, Sched. 2.

Maternity benefit. For the associated (lump-sum) payments under the maternity grant scheme see the Social Security Act 1980, s. 5.

Maternity pay. A statutory scheme for maternity pay and the right of a woman who has been absent from her job on account of pregnancy or confinement to return to her employment are contained in the Employment Protection (Consolidation) Act 1978, Part III (ss. 33–49), repeating the terms of earlier legislation. Failure to permit a woman to return to her job after confinement when she wishes to exercise her right to do so constitutes an unfair dismissal (*q.v.*) (Act of 1978, s. 56). Dismissal on the ground of a woman's pregnancy also constitutes an unfair dismissal, unless at the termination date the woman's pregnancy will have made her incapable of adequately doing her job or at that date she will no longer be able to do her work without contravening statutory duties or restrictions related to pregnancy (Act of 1978, s. 60).

The Employment Act 1980, ss. 11–13, modified the scheme, containing (*inter alia*) an exclusion of the right to return to work (Employment Protection (Consolidation) Act 1978, s. 56A, added by the Act of 1980, s. 12) and time off work for ante-natal care (Act of 1978, s. 3A, added by the Act of 1980, s. 13).

Matrimonial causes. The Judicature Act 1925, s. 225, has been repealed and replaced by the Supreme Court Act 1981, s. 151(1), generally, but "matrimonial causes" no longer appears, although it does appear in the Act of 1981, Sched. 1, para. 3(*a*), which allocates "all matrimonial causes and matters (whether at first instance or on appeal)" to the Family Division. The Administration of Justice Act 1970, s. 1, Sched. 1, have been repealed and replaced by the 1981 Act, s. 61(1), (3), Sched. 1, para. 3, without change of effect.

The Matrimonial Causes Act 1967, s. 1, and the Courts Act 1971, s. 45(3), have been (prospectively) repealed and replaced by the Matrimonial and Family Proceedings Act 1984, s. 33. That Act adopts the 1925 definition, without change of effect, with the exception of the restitution of conjugal rights (see s. 32).

Matrimonial home. The Matrimonial Homes and Property Act 1981, extended the concept (propounded in the 1967 Act) of "matrimonial right of occupation" to include beneficial estates and interests but also made changes to debar a claim against a spouse who had an estate or interest which was not "beneficial" (*e.g.* where property was held in a spouse's name as trustee or nominee). The various Acts from 1967 to 1981 have be repealed and consolidated into the Matrimonial Homes Act 1983, without change of effect. The Land Registration (Matrimonial Homes) Regulations 1967, have been revoked and replaced by the Land Registration (Matrimonial Homes) Regulations 1983 (S.I. 1983 No. 40), without significant change of effect.

Matrimonial proceedings in magistrates' courts. The Matrimonial Proceedings (Magistrates' Courts) Act 1960, has been repealed and replaced by the Domestic Proceedings and Magistrates' Courts Act 1978. The new Act (from 1 April 1981) provides a code for financial provision which is closely modelled on the general provisions for divorce (*q.v.*) and judicial separation (*q.v.*), with three main exceptions: (1) a magistrates' court cannot sever the legal union of the parties; (2) the ground of living separate and apart (whether by consent (the two-year case) or not (the five-year case)) figures in the 1978 Act in a modified form (see s. 7); and (3) mere adultery is no ground for an order. Orders may be made on a consent basis (s. 6), and interim orders may also be made (s. 19).

The courts have the power to refuse to make an order and to refer the matter to the High Court if the case is more suitable for that tribunal (s. 29).

Major changes in the system include (1) the power to award a lump sum (not exceeding £500) (s. 2(3)); and (2) the modification of the periodicity provisions: the earlier scheme allowed only weekly payments, but the 1978 scheme allows orders to be made for "such payments, and for such term, as may be specified in the order" (s. 2(1)(*a*)), leaving the periodicity to be determined by the court.

Maundy Thursday. The provision relating to the fineness of the Maundy money have been revised (Coinage Act 1971, s. 1, Sched. 1, as substituted and amended by the Currency Act 1983).

Mayor's and City of London Court. The special status of this court in its capacity as a county court was preserved by the County Courts Act 1984, s. 1(3), when the County Courts Act 1959 was repealed and replaced.

Measure of damages. For a more recent statement of the measure of damages in contract see *C. Czarniskow Ltd.* v. *Koufos* (*The Heron II*) [1969] 1 A.C. 350, H.L. The grant of exemplary damages is restricted to the cases set out in *Rookes* v. *Barnard* [1964] A.C. 1129, H.L.; such damages must be specifically pleaded (R.S.C. Ord. 18, r. 8(3)) unless the case is proceeding in the county court (*Drane* v. *Evangelou* [1978] 1 W.L.R. 455).

The rules governing damages on a breach of contract for the sale of land have been reviewed (see *Malhotra* v. *Choudhury* [1980] Ch. 52, C.A., excluding *Bain* v. *Fothergill* (1874) L.R. 7 H.L. 158), so that it is no longer an absolute rule that the plaintiff may recover only his "out-of-pocket expenses."

Damages for personal injuries have been reviewed with special reference to cases of extreme severity (see *Lim Poh Choo* v. *Camden and Islington Area Health Authority* [1980] A.C. 174, H.L., and *Pickett* v. *British Rail Engineering Ltd.* [1980] A.C. 136 H.L.).

Medical inspection. The National Health Service Reorganisation Act 1973, s. 3, has been repealed and replaced by the National Health Service Act 1977, s. 5(1) without change of effect.

The authority for medical inspection in nullity cases is now the Matrimonial Causes Rules 1977 (S.I. 1977 No. 344), rr. 30, 31, under which the 1963 Practice Direction is kept in operation.

Medical officer of health. The Public Health Act 1936, s.3, has been repealed and replaced by the Public Health (Control of Diseases) Act 1984, s. 3, without change of effect. The Food and Drugs Act 1955, s. 86, has been repealed and replaced by the Food Act 1984, s. 73, without change of effect.

Medical practitioner. The bulk of the Medical Acts 1956 to 1978 has been repealed and replaced by the Medical Act 1983; the Act of 1956, ss. 27, has been replaced by the Act of 1983, s. 46; the privilege once conferred by the Act of 1956, s. 30, has disappeared.

Meeting. The Companies Act 1948, s. 130, has been repealed by the Companies Act 1980, s. 88, Sched. 4. The penalties for not holding the proper annual meetings (Act of 1948, s. 131) were modified by the Companies Act 1980, s. 80, Sched. 2.

Mental deficiency. The Mental Health Act 1959 (as amended by various Acts, including the Mental Health Amendment Act 1982), has been repealed and replaced by the Mental Health Act 1983 (which consolidates the amendments).

Mental health. The Mental Health Act 1959 (as amended by various Acts, including the Mental Health Amendment Act 1982), has been repealed and replaced by the Mental Health Act 1983 (which consolidates the amendments). The procedural requirements have been restated in the Mental Health Review Tribunal Rules 1983 (S.I. 1983 No. 942).

Power was taken to abolish the appointment of Deputy Master of the Court of Protection (Supreme Court Act 1981, s. 89(6) (as amended by the Administration of Justice Act 1982, s. 60)), and this has been done (see COURT OF PROTECTION).

Merchant shipping. Further provisions governing merchant shipping are the Merchant Shipping Act 1971, the Merchant Shipping (Safety Conventions) Act 1977 and the Merchant Shipping Act 1979. By the Merchant Shipping Act 1981, arrangements are made for the conversion of gold francs into special drawing rights in certain provisions limiting the liability of shipowners and certain other persons. The like-named Act of 1982 provides for the implementation of the Geneva Convention (1974) on a Code of Conduct for Liner Conferences and associated matters (*e.g.* the exclusion of the Restrictive Trade Practices Act 1976, s. 11). The 1983 Act is concerned with the measurement of small ships and their registration, and the 1984 Act with improvement and prohibition notices and the ascertainment of limitation tonnage.

Merchantable. The Sale of Goods Act 1893, s. 14(2), has been repealed and replaced by the Sale of Goods Act 1979, s. 14(2), without change of effect. Terms comparable to those contained in the Sale of Goods Act have been applied (unless there is an effective exclusion clause) to contracts for the transfer of property in goods and contracts for the hire of goods (Supply of Goods and Services Act 1982, ss. 4, 9).

Merton, Statute of. The final portions of this statute (cc. 1 (damages on writ of dower), 2 (widow's bequest of corn on her land), 4 (commons) and 9 (special bastardy)), were repealed by the Statute Law Revision Act 1950, the Statute Law Revision Act 1948, the Statute Law Revisions Act 1953, and the Act of 1948, respectively.

Mesne process. The writ *ne exeat regno* (*q.v.*) may now (by analogy) issue only if the requirements of the Debtors Act 1869, s. 6, are satisfied (see *Felton* v. *Callis* [1969] 1 Q.B. 200).

Mesne profits. The rule in *Elliot* v. *Boynton* has been modified by *Canas Property Co. Ltd.* v. *K.L. Television Services Ltd.* [1970] 2 Q.B. 433, C.A.

The authority for joiner of a claim for arrears of rent and mesne profits with a claim for possession is R.S.C. Ord. 15, r. 1(1); by Ord. 13, r. 5, a plaintiff is authorised to enter judgment in default of acknowledgment of service in such proceedings, and by Ord. 19, r. 6, the same course is authorised on the defendant's failure to serve a defence.

Methyl alcohol. The Customs and Excise Act 1952, ss. 115, 121, have been repealed and replaced by the Alcoholic Liquor Duties Act 1979, ss. 35, 80, without change of effect.

Methylated spirits. The Customs and Excise Act 1952, ss. 116–121, 172, and the Hydrocarbon Oil (Customs and Excise) Act 1971, have been repealed and replaced by the Alcoholic Liquor Duties Act 1979, ss. 75–80, and the Hydrocarbon Oil Duties Act 1979, respectively, without substantial change of effect.

Metre. S.I. 1963 No. 1354 was revoked and replaced by the Units of Measurement Regulations 1976 (S.I. 1976 No. 1674), which have in their turn been revoked and replaced by the Units of Measurement Regulations 1980 (S.I. 1980 No. 1070).

Metric system. S.I. 1970 No. 1709 has been amended by the Units of Measurement (No. 2) Regulations 1980 (S.I. 1980 No. 1742). S.I. 1971 No. 827 has been revoked and replaced by the Measuring Intruments (EEC Requirements) (Amendment) Regulations 1978 (S.I. 1978 No. 1962).

Metrological Co-ordinating Unit. This is a body corporate which has been established by the Weights and Measures Act 1979, ss. 6–14, with a general responsibility to conduct research and to give advice on weights and measures matters (s. 7) as well as to supervise the functions of inspectors (s. 8). The functions of the Unit (listed in s. 7) may be transferred to the Secretary of State or other bodies (s. 11(1)) and the Unit may be abolished by him (s. 11(1)(*c*)). The tenure of members of the Unit, proceedings and other related matters are dealt with in Sched. 3 to the Act of 1979; ss. 6, 7, 14 and Sched. 3 were made subject to delayed commencement provisions (see s. 24(3)).

Metropolitan stipendiary magistrate. The principal provisions relating to the appointment of these magistrates have been repealed and consolidated in the Justices of the Peace Act 1979, ss. 31–34.

Midwife. The Midwives Act 1951, has been repealed and replaced by the Nurses, Midwives and Health Visitors Act 1979. The structure of the profession has been amended by the abolition of the Central Midwives Board and its replacement by the Central Council for Nursing, Midwifery and Health Visiting (*e.g.*) with two standing committees, of which one must be the Midwifery Committee (s. 41). The Medical Act 1956, ss. 10–11, have been repealed and replaced by the Medical Act 1983, ss. 4(1)–(2), 6, in more general terms.

Militia. See also the Reserve Forces Act 1980, which consolidates extensive portions of the enactments relating to the reserve and auxiliary forces of the Crown.

Minerals. The Town and Country Planning General Development Order 1963, has been revoked and replaced by the Town and Country Planning General Development Order 1977, without substantial change of effect (see DEVELOPMENT).

The Town and Country Planning (Minerals) Act 1981, modified the effect of the general provisions of the Town and Country Planning Act 1971 in order to provide a more effective and more detailed control over mineral workings, whilst retaining the principal machinery of the 1971 planning system.

Minibus. The word "minibus" is not defined in the Minibus Act 1977, which excludes from the category of public services vehicles (*q.v.*) any vehicle which is adapted to carry more than 7 but not more than 16 passengers and is used for hire or reward, provided (a) there is a permit issued in respect of the vehicle under the provisions of the Act; (b) the vehicle is not being used for the carriage of the public at large nor with a view to profit (whether directly or indirectly); and (c) the vehicle is being used by the permit holder and in accordance with any conditions subject to which it is granted (Act of 1977, s. 1(1)).

Minister. The salary of a minister (*i.e.* a member of the Government) is revised from time to time (see, *e.g.* S.I. 1979 No. 905).

Ministry. The salaries under the Ministerial and other Salaries Act 1975, are revised from time to time (see, *e.g.* S.I. 1979 No. 905).

Mint. The Mint moved to Llantrisant, Pontyclun, Mid Glamorgan in November 1975, though a shop and exhibition are still maintained at Tower Hill and a London Office at 7 Grosvenor Gardens, SW1W 0BH.

Minutes. For the abolition of the Chancery registrars see CHANCERY.

Miras. An acronym for mortgage interest relief at source (introduced by the Finance Act 1982, ss. 26, 27); see BUILDING SOCIETY.

Misrepresentation. By the Unfair Contract Terms Act 1977, s. 8, a new test has been substituted into the Misrepresentation Act 1967, s. 3, so that liability for misrepresentations may be excluded only if the exclusion clause satisfies the requirement of reasonableness (set out in the Act of 1977, s. 11, Sched. 2). See also UNFAIR CONTRACT TERMS.

Mistake. The decision in *Gaillie* v. *Lee* [1969] 2 Ch. 17, was affirmed in *Saunders* v. *Anglia Building Society* [1971] A.C. 1004, H.L., where it was held that the plea *non est factum* would not be available if the document signed was of the kind the signatory thought it was (even though its actual effect differed from what was expected or intended); the plea would have sufficed to render void only a document of a wholly different nature from that which the signatory thought himself to be executing.

Mitigation. A plaintiff is required to mitigate the loss he sustains as a result of the defendant's wrongdoing (*British Westinghouse Co.* v. *Underground Railway* [1912] A.C. 673, H.L.); if the steps he reasonably takes cause further loss the defendant can be charged for that extra damage (*Wilson* v. *United Counties Bank* [1920] A.C. 102, H.L.). Pre-breach arrangements which reduce the plaintiff's loss (*e.g.* arranging and paying for a pension (see *Parry* v. *Cleaver* [1970] A.C. 1, H.L.)) will not accrue to the defendant's advantage, though mitigation (properly so called) reduces his eventual liability.

Mobile homes. The Mobile Homes Act 1975 (as variously modified), has been repealed and replaced by the Mobile Homes Act 1983; see CAMPING.

Mobility allowance. This was provided for by the Social Security Act 1975, s. 37A (added by the Social Security Pensions Act 1975, s. 22(1)).

Mock auction. By virtue of being a conspiracy to defraud, the common law offence of holding a mock auction is exempt from the general abolition of the common law offence of conspiracy (*q.v.*) (Criminal Law Act 1977, s. 5(2)).

Molestation. This word is also applied ("non-molestation order") to the personal protection orders which are available to a party to a marriage or to a child of the family (Matrimonial Proceedings and Magistrates' Courts Act 1978, ss. 16–18), and to matrimonial injuctions in the county court (Domestic Violence and Matrimonial Proceedings Act 1976, s. 1).

The offence under the Conspiracy and Protection of Property Act 1875, s. 7, is no longer triable on indictment (Criminal Law Act 1977, s. 65(5), Sched. 13).

Money of account. Since claims may now be made and judgments may be entered in the money of account (see *Miliangos* v. *George Frank* (*Textiles*) *Ltd.* [1976] A.C. 443, H.L., and *Practice Direction* [1976] 1 W.L.R. 83), the provisions which required sterling to be used instead of the money of account have been repealed (Administration of Justice Act 1977, s. 4).

Moneylender. Even the formerly prohibited rate of interest of 48 per cent. per annum (see the (repealed) Moneylenders Act 1927, s. 10) has been accepted as not "extortionate" under the Consumer Credit Act 1974, s. 138 (*A. Ketley* v. *Scott* [1981] I.C.R. 241).

The various monetary limits under the Consumer Credit Act 1974 are revised from time to time; see, *e.g.* the Consumer Credit (Increase of Monetary Amounts) Order 1983 (S.I. 1983 No. 1571) and the Consumer Credit (Increase of Monetary Limits) Order 1983 (S.I. 1983 No. 1878).

Monomachy. See *Ashford* v. *Thornton* (1819) 1 Barn. & Ald. 405 and the Appeal of

Murder, etc., Act 1819 (repealed).

Month. The Interpretation Act 1889, s. 3, has been repealed and replaced by the Interpretation Act 1978, ss. 5, 22, 23, Sched. 1, Sched. 2, para. 5, without change of effect. The former R.S.C. Ord. 64, r. 1, was replaced in 1965 by the current Ord. 3, r. 1 (whose effect is noted).

Mora. See also LACHES and LIMITATION OF ACTIONS.

Mora debitoris non debit esse creditori damnosa. The Sale of Goods Act 1893, s. 20, has been repealed and replaced by the Sale of Goods Act 1979, s. 20, without change of effect.

Moravians. The Oaths Act 1888, has been repealed by the Oaths Act 1978; s. 5 of the 1978 Act confers a general right to affirm instead of taking an oath.

Mortgage. The Rent Act 1968, Part VIII, has been repealed and replaced by the Rent Act 1977, Part X (ss. 129–136), without change of effect.

See also OPTION MORTGAGE.

Motion. Applications for injunctions are made under R.S.C. Ord. 29, r. 1, and applications for the appointment of a receiver are made under R.S.C. Ord. 30, r. 1.

Motor car. Thc agc limits for driving various classes of vehicle are laid down in the Road Traffic Act 1972, s. 96 (as substituted by the Road Traffic (Drivers' Ages and Hours of Work) Act 1976, s. 1); s. 4 of the Act of 1972 has been repealed (Act of 1976, s. 1(5), Sched. 3, Part I).

The offence under the Road Traffic Act 1972, s. 29, has been supplemented by a new offence of interference with a vehicle (see LOITERING).

Virtually all front seat passengers and the drivers of motor cars are now required to wear seat belts (Road Traffic Act 1972, s. 33A (added by the Transport Act 1981, s. 27(11)); Motor Vehicles (Wearing of Seat Belts) Regulations 1982 (S.I. 1982 No. 1203); Motor Vehicles (Wearing of Seat Belts by Children) Regulations 1982 (S.I. 1982 No. 1342)).

Motor cycle. For further provision in respect of head gear see the Road Traffic Act 1972, s. 33AA (added by the Transport Act 1982, s. 57(1)).

Motor Insurers' Bureau. The Bureau's agreements with the Ministry of Transport are revised from time to time; the latest edition is dated November 22, 1972, and deals with compensation for victims of uninsured drivers and victims of untraced drivers.

Motor vehicle. The Civic Amenities Act 1967, ss. 19–22, and associated statutes, have been repealed and replaced by the Refuse Disposal (Amenity) Act 1978, without substantial change of effect.

Motor vehicle tests are now conducted under the general provisions of the Motor Vehicles (Tests) Regulations 1976 (S.I. 1976 No. 1977) (as variously amended).

Motorways. The Highways Act 1959, s. 11, has been repealed and replaced by the Highways Act 1980, s. 16, without change of effect (see generally ss. 16–20). The Motorway Traffic Regulations 1959, have been revoked and replaced by the Motorway Traffic (England and Wales) Regulations 1982 (S.I. 1982 No. 1163), which re-enacts the 1959 provisions (as amended in 1971) with minor modifications which include a definition of "hard shoulder" and certain restrictions on the use of the third and fourth lanes.

Multiple occupation. The Housing Act 1961, s. 20, has been repealed by the Housing Act 1980, ss. 145, 152, Sched. 23, para. 1 and Sched. 26. See also OVERCROWDING.

Multiplicity. The Judicature Act 1925, s. 43, has been repealed and replaced by the Supreme Court Act 1981, s. 49, without change of effect. The Act of 1925, s. 201, was repealed by the Courts Act 1971, s. 56(4), Sched. 11, Part IV; the Act of 1925, ss. 202, 203, have been repealed and their effect has been integrated into the new constitution of the Supreme Court in the Act of 1981.

Multiplier; Multiplicand. Both used in the law of damages with reference to the amount of damages to be awarded for personal injuries or death, the multiplier is the number of years' purchase (which ought to be but is only rarely on an actuarial basis), and the multiplicand is the yearly income (*i.e.* the dependency) which is to be compensated for. Multipliers above 18 are rare, as are multipliers of 15 or more for a person who was over 35 at the time of his death. The multiplier will be increased in cases where the deceased might have been expected to work on after normal retirement age (*e.g.* in the case of self-employed authors and editors). See *Kemp and Kemp*.

Munitions of war. The Patents Act 1949, s. 18, has been repealed and replaced by the Patents Act 1977, ss. 23, 24, which are substantially the same in their effects although the administration is different.

Murder. The principle in *D.P.P.* v. *Smith* [1961] A.C. 290, has been modified by the Criminal Justice Act 1967, s. 8, which provides that a court or jury, in determining whether a person has committed an offence, (a) is not bound in law to infer that he intended or foresaw a result of his actions by reason only of its being a natural and probable consequence of those actions, but (b) is to decide whether he did intend or foresee that result by reference to all the evidence, drawing such inferences from the evidence as may appear proper in the circumstances.

Murder cases are always excluded from the new powers of the court to set aside the general forfeiture (*q.v.*) rule (Forfeiture Act 1982, s. 5).

Museum. The Finance Act 1975, Sched. 6, para. 12, has been repealed and replaced by the Capital Transfer Tax Act 1984, s. 25, Sched. 3, without change of effect.

Music and dancing licences. The general provisions noted have been repealed and replaced by the Local Government (Miscellaneous Provisions) Act 1982, s. 42, Sched. 7, Part I: see DANCING-HOUSE.

Mutiny Act. The continuation in force of the Army Act 1955, is now effected by annual Orders in Council (laid in draft before each House of Parliament for approval) under the Armed Forces Act 1981, s. 1.

Myxomatosis. The penalty on summary conviction under the Pests Act 1954, s. 12, was increased to £200 by the Criminal Law Act 1977, s. 31, Sched. 6. For the general revision of fines which may be imposed on summary convictions see FINE.

N

Name. The Enrolment of Deeds (Change of Name) Regulations 1949 (as variously amended), have been revoked and replaced by the Enrolment of Deeds (Change of Name) Regulations 1983 (S.I. 1983 No. 680). The text may be found in the notes to R.S.C. Ord. 63, r. 10, where the appropriate procedures are recorded.

The Registration of Business Names Act 1916, has been repealed without replacement by the Companies Act 1981, s. 119, Sched. 4. The same Act requires the disclosure of the names of persons who conduct business under any names other than their own, also imposing a very limited form of civil disability in court proceedings (ss. 28–30).

National assistance. The majority of the earlier Acts establishing and regulating the national assistance system have been repealed and replaced by the Supplementary Benefits Act 1976, without substantial change of effect; the modern term is supplementary benefit (*q.v.*).

National Audit Office. Set up by the National Audit Act 1983, ss. 3, 4, this is the administrative support section for the Comptroller and Auditor-General (*q.v.*).

National Dock Labour Board. First constituted under the provisions of the Dock Workers (Regulation of Employment) Act 1946, this is a corporate body, the reconstruction of which is provided for in the Dock Work Regulation Act 1976.

National Film Finance Corporation. The functions of this institution were slightly varied (Films Act 1980), and the general corpus of legislation (the Cinematographic Film Production (Special Loans) Acts 1949 to 1980) has been repealed and replaced by the (consolidating) National Film Finance Corporation Act 1981. The Act contains power to wind up the Corporation (s. 9(1)).

National Freight Corporation. The Transport Act 1968, ss. 1–8, were repealed by the Transport Act 1980, s. 69, Sched. 9, Part III, in view of the transfer of the undertaking of the National Freight Corporation to a successor organisation on the abolition of the NFC (Transport Act 1980, Part II (ss. 45–51)).

National Gallery. The Finance Act 1975, Sched. 6, para. 12, has been repealed and replaced by the Capital Transfer Tax Act 1984, s. 25, Sched. 3, without change of effect.

National Health Service. Further general provisions are contained in the National Health Service Act 1977, which repeals and consolidates substantial portions of the earlier legislation. See also the National Health Service Act 1980.

National Heritage Memorial Fund. Established to take the place of the abolished National Land Fund (*q.v.*), this Fund is vested in the Trustees of the National Heritage Memorial Fund, a corporate body (National Heritage Act 1980, s. 1(2)), whose duty is to provide financial assistance in the acquisition, maintenance and preservation of land, buildings and objects of outstanding historic and other interest. Grants and loans may be made from the Fund (s. 3), gifts may be accepted (s. 5), and any funds not immediately required may be invested (s. 6).

National insurance. The Tribunals and Inquiries Act 1958, has been repealed and replaced by the Tribunals and Inquiries Act 1971, without substantial change of effect. The National Insurance Commissioners are now styled Social Security Commissioners (Social Security Act 1980, s. 12).

See also SOCIAL SECURITY.

National Land Fund. The Finance Act 1946, s. 49, has been repealed by the Finance Act 1975, s. 59(5), Sched. 13, Part I, in connection with the replacement of estate duty (*q.v.*) by capital transfer tax (*q.v.*). The total abolition of the Fund is provided for in the National Heritage Act 1980, s. 15: see NATIONAL HERITAGE MEMORIAL FUND.

National parks. Additional provision are contained in the Wildlife and Countryside Act 1981, ss. 47–52; ss. 2 and 4 of the 1949 Act and s. 3 of the 1968 Act have been repealed (Act of 1981, s. 47(3)) and the status and procedures of the Countryside Commission have been modified (Act of 1981, s. 47(1), Sched. 13).

National Savings Bank. The National Savings Bank Act 1971, has been amended to enable the National Savings Bank to conduct a range of banking services formerly not available (Finance Act 1982, s. 151, Sched. 20).

National service. The National Service Act 1948, Part I (ss. 1–34), s. 61, Scheds. 1–4, have been repealed by the Statute Law (Repeals) Act 1977, s. 1(1), Sched., Part I, and the related legislation has been similarly dealt with.

National Steel Corporation. See also the Iron and Steel Act 1975, and the Iron and Steel (Amendment) Act 1976, which provide for the British Steel Corporation. See also IRON AND STEEL.

National Trust. The Finance Act 1975, Sched. 6, para. 12, has been repealed and replaced by the Capital Transfer Tax Act 1984, s. 25, Sched. 3, without change of effect. For the repeal of the Community Land Act 1975 see the Local Government, Planning and Land Act 1980, ss. 101, 194, Scheds. 17, 34, Part XI.

The National Trust enjoys a special status under a number of statutes; see, *e.g.* the Acquisition of Land Act 1981, s. 18.

Nationality. See the British Nationality Act 1981 for the general modification of nationality law. Appropriate entries appear under separate headings elsewhere in this work.

Natural justice. A leading case in this part of the law is *Ridge* v. *Baldwin* [1964] A.C. 40, H.L., where the earlier authorities are reviewed and the general principles are set out afresh.

Naturalisation. The British Nationality Act 1948, s. 10, Sched. 2, have been repealed and replaced by the British Nationality Act 1981, ss. 6, 18, Sched. 1, where the complex provisions for naturalisation as a British citizen are set out in extenso; there are two main groups: those who become British citizens (s. 8) and those who become British dependent territories citizens (s. 18).

Nature conservation. For further provisions relating to the Nature Conservancy Council see the Wildlife and Countryside Act 1981, s. 38. For general provisions about conservation see the Act of 1981, Part IV (ss. 28–52), Scheds. 11–13.

Naval reserves. The general provisions relating to the Royal Naval Reserve and the Royal Fleet Reserve have been consolidated in the Reserve Forces Act 1980, Part III (ss. 45–61).

Navigable; Navigation. The Highways Act 1971, ss. 10–13, have been repealed and replaced by the Highways Act 1980, ss. 106–110, without change of effect.

Ne exeat regno. For the modern practice see *Felton* v. *Callis* [1969] 1 Q.B. 200.

Necessaries. The Sale of Goods Act 1893, s. 2, has been repealed and replaced by the Sale of Goods Act 1979, s. 3, without change of effect.

A wife's agency of necessity has been abolished (Matrimonial Proceedings and Property Act 1970, s. 41).

Negative. The Magistrates' Courts Act 1952, s. 81, has been repealed and replaced by the Magistrates' Courts Act 1980, s. 101, without change of effect.

Negligence. Since the classical exposition of the law relating to liability in negligence in *Donoghue* v. *Stevenson* [1932] A.C. 562, H.L., the scope of this tort has been increased substantially. The wide range now encompassed by this single legal field of liability is well illustrated by noting the major decisions of recent years: *Hedley Byrne & Co.* v. *Heller & Partners* [1964] A.C. 465, H.L. (there is a duty to ensure the accuracy of a banker's reference); *Rondel* v. *Worsley* [1969] 1 A.C. 191, H.L. (a barrister's duty of care does not extend to make him liable for the conduct of the case in the court itself); *Dorset Yacht Co.* v. *Home Office* [1970] A.C. 1004, H.L. (the governor is under a duty to restrain the inmates of a borstal institution); *Herrington* v. *British Railways Board* [1972] A.C. 877, H.L. (there is a duty to take steps for the safety of children known to be likely to trespass); *Sutcliff* v. *Thackrah* [1974] A.C. 727, H.L. (an architect is under a duty to ensure the accuracy of building contract certificates); *Arenson* v. *Arenson* [1977] A.C. 405, H.L. (a valuer may be liable since in carrying out a valuation he is not acting in an arbitral or quasi-arbitral capacity); *Anns* v. *Merton London Borough Council* [1978] A.C. 728, H.L. (confirming *Dutton* v. *Bognor Regis Urban District Council* [1972] 1 Q.B. 373, C.A.) (there is a duty on a local authority inspector to ensure the proper laying of house foundations); *Midland Bank Trust Co. Ltd.* v. *Hett, Stubbs & Kemp* [1979] Ch. 384 (a solicitor ought to register a client's option to purchase a legal estate in land); *Ross* v. *Caunters* [1980] Ch. 297 (a solicitor owes a duty of care towards beneficiaries under the wills he draws up); *Saif Ali* v. *Sydney Mitchell & Co.* [1980] A.C. 198, H.L. (liability may be imposed on a barrister for negligence in the preparation of a case before its actual presentation in court).

Nemo dat qui non habet; Nemo dat quod non habet. The Sale of Goods Act 1893, s. 21(1), has been repealed and replaced by the Sale of Goods Act 1979, s. 21(1), without change of effect.

Nemo ex suo delicto meliorem suam conditionem facere potest. This maxim holds good despite the revision of the terms of the Limitation Act 1939, s. 26 (substituted by the Limitation Amendment Act 1980, s. 7, and now repealed and replaced by the Limitation Act 1980, s. 32).

New penny. For the amendment allowing the "new penny" to be designated (merely) "penny" see PENNY.

New streets. The Highways Act 1959, ss. 157–172, have been repealed and replaced by the Highways Act 1980, Part X (ss. 186–202), without change of effect.

New towns. The borrowing limits imposed on the development corporations and the Commission for New Towns are revised from time to time (see, *e.g.* the New Towns Act 1980). The New Towns Act 1965 and associated legislation have been repealed and replaced by the New Towns Act 1981 (see s. 81(b), Sched. 13).

New Towns Staff Commission. Established by the New Towns (Amendment) Act 1976, s. 14, this body is charged with functions relating to transfer schemes for the staff of new town corporations (see NEW TOWNS).

New trial. The £20 limit noted derived from the County Courts Act 1959, s. 109; amendments made by the Supreme Court Act 1981, s. 149(1), Sched. 3, paras. 14, 15 (replacing the Act of 1959, s. 108 and omitting s. 109) resulted from a change in the provisions for appeals from county courts. The current provision is the County Courts Act 1984, s. 177. Under the earlier provision (whose effect is preserved by the Interpretation Act 1978, s. 17(2)(*b*)), the County Courts Appeals Order 1981 (S.I. 1981 No. 1749) restricted the bulk of appeals to those where the amount in issue exceeded one half (£2,500) of the county court limit (£5,000). The Judicature Act 1925, s. 30(1), has been repealed and replaced by the Supreme Court Act 1981,

s. 17, without change of effect.

Newspapers. Further restrictions on what judicial proceeding might be reported were imposed by the Sexual Offences (Amendment) Act 1976, ss. 4–6. The Criminal Justice Act 1967, s. 3 (as amended), has been repealed and replaced by the Magistrates' Courts Act 1980, s. 8, without change of effect.

Immunity from the requirement to disclose sources of information in contempt cases, and restrictions on publication of matters exempted from disclosure in court have been provided for in the Contempt of Court Act 1981, ss. 10, 11.

Next friend. The practice of the Family Division is now regulated by the Matrimonial Causes Rules 1977 (S.I. 1977 No. 344), rr. 112, 113.

The ability of a woman to act as a next friend is a matter of deduction from the general terms of R.S.C. Ord. 80, r. 3; the same position obtains in the county court, and this is particularly so since the express provision formerly made (C.C.R 1936, Ord. 48, r. 23) has been revoked (see generally the C.C.R. 1981) without specific replacement.

Next presentation. Prospective modifications of the system of patronage and appointments were made by the Pastoral (Amendment) Measure 1982, ss. 50 *et seq.* (adding, *inter alia*, ss. 69A and 73A to the 1968 provisions). By instrument under the hands of the Archbishops (*not* a statutory instrument) the 1982 Measure was brought into operation on 1 November 1983, whereupon the consolidating Pastoral Measure 1983 came into operation (see the Measure of 1983, s. 94(4)) immediately, completely repealing the 1982 Measure (1983, s. 93, Sched. 9). The current provisions are now in the Measure of 1983, Part IV (see especially ss. 69–73).

Night. The Customs and Excise Act 1952, s. 307(1), has been repealed and replaced by the Customs and Excise Management Act 1979, s. 1(1), without change of effect.

Night restriction order. A form of supervision order (*q.v.*), the restrictions on which make it virtually impossible to make or enforce (Children and Young Persons Act 1969, s. 12(3C)(*b*), (3D)–(3N), added by the Criminal Justice Act 1982, s. 20(11)).

Nihils or **Nichils.** Appointments of auditors under the Sheriffs Act 1887, s. 22, are now made by the Lord Chancellor instead of by the Treasury (Transfer of Functions (Treasury and Lord Chancellor) Order 1976 (S.I. 1976 No. 229)).

No case to answer. The *Practice Direction* [1962] 1 W.L.R. 227, has been supplemented by observations of the Court of appeal in *R.* v. *Galbraith* [1981] 1 W.L.R. 1039; it was ruled that (1) if there is no evidence that the alleged crime was committed by the defendant, the submission must succeed; (2) if the evidence is such that a properly directed jury could not properly convict, the submission must succeed; (3) if the prosecution evidence is such that its strength or weakness depends on the view taken of the witness, etc., and on one possible view of the facts there is evidence on which a jury could properly bring in a guilty verdict, the trial should continue.

Noise. A local authority is entitled to take proceedings in the High Court for an injunction (Control of Pollution Act 1974, s. 58(8)) instead of prosecuting (s. 58(4)), and is, in any event, under a positive duty to serve a notice (under s. 58(1)) (*Hammersmith London Borough Council* v. *Magnum Automated Forecourts* [1978] 1 W.L.R. 50, C.A.).

Nomination. The Representation of the People Act 1969, s. 12, Sched. 1, have been repealed and replaced by the Representation of the People Act 1983, s. 23, Sched. 1, r. 6, without change of effect.

Non impedit clausula derogatoria quo minus ab eadem potestate res dissolvantur a qua constituuntur. The Interpretation Act 1889, s. 10, has been repealed and replaced by the Interpretation Act 1978, s. 1, without change of effect.

Nonfeasance. The Highways (Miscellaneous Provisions) Act 1961, s. 1(2)–(3), has been repealed and replaced by the Highways Act 1980, s. 58(1)–(2), without change of effect; s. 1(1) of the 1961 Act was not replaced in the consolidation of 1980.

Nonsuit. The law on this topic was reviewed in *Clack* v. *Arthur's Engineering Ltd.* [1959] 2 Q.B. 211, C.A., where the modern procedure and practice are explained. The C.C.R. 1936, Ord. 23, r. 3, has been revoked and replaced by C.C.R. 1981, Ord. 21, r. 2; the new rule applies not only to actions (as did the 1936 provision) but also to matters (*i.e.*, originating applications, petitions and appeals).

Notice. It is provided that every Act is a public Act and will be judicially noticed as such unless the contrary is expressly provided by the Act (Interpretation Act 1978, s. 3, replacing the Interpretation Act 1889, s. 9); this rule applies to all Acts passed after 1850 (Act of 1978, ss. 22, 23, Sched. 2, para. 2).

Notice of dishonour. Notice of dishonour under the Bills of Exchange Act 1882, s. 49, is given when the drawers receive it, and if necessary, the law will take notice of parts of a day where what is involved is a sequence of events on the same day (see *Eaglehill Ltd.* v. *S. Needham Builders Ltd.* [1973] A.C. 992, H.L.).

Notice of judgment. In actions in the Chancery Division for (a) the administration of the estate of a deceased person, or (b) the execution of a trust, or (c) the sale of any property, and where the court gives a judgment which affects the rights and interests of non-parties, the court has power to direct that notice of the judgment be given to the absent persons (R.S.C. Ord. 44, r. 3(1)). A person served (or deemed to be served) with such a notice is bound by the judgment as if he had been a party to the action (*ibid.*).

Notice of trial. The *Practice Direction* [1974] 1 W.L.R. 1272, has been revoked and replaced by the *Practice Direction* [1979] 1 W.L.R. 1040. Under the new provisions, subject to complying with R.S.C. Ord. 3, r. 6 (which requires service of a notice of intention to proceed where there has been a year's delay), the plaintiff need not have leave of the court or the consent of the defendant before setting down an action for trial after expiry of the period fixed by any order under R.S.C. Ord. 34, r. 2(1). The 1979 arrangements have been applied in the Chancery Division (*Practice Direction* [1981] 1 W.L.R. 322).

Notice of writ of summons, etc. The procedure for serving proceedings out of the jurisdiction has been modified (there no longer being any Royal commands in writs, etc., to inhibit serving them in foreign jurisdictions), and R.S.C. Ord. 11, r. 3, has been revoked without replacement (Rules of the Supreme Court (Amendment No. 4) 1980 (S.I. 1980 No. 2000)). Under Ord. 11, r. 1(1), in certain cases leave is required before proceedings may be issued for service out of the jurisdiction (the cases being listed in r. 1(*a*)–(*p*)).

Notice to proceed. R.S.C. Ord. 3, r. 6, has been held to apply to proceedings in respect of taxation of costs (*Pamplin* v. *Frazer* [1984] 1 W.L.R. 1385).

Notice to quit. The Agricultural Holdings Act 1948, ss. 23, 24, have been repealed and replaced by the Agricultural Holdings (Notices to Quit) Act 1977, ss. 1, 2, without significant change of effect.

The Rent Act 1957, s. 15, and the Housing Act 1974, s. 123, have been repealed and replaced by the Protection from Eviction Act 1977, s. 5, without significant change of effect. See also the Rent Act 1977, s. 3(3) (which re-enacts the terms of the Rent Act 1968, s. 12(4)).

The Rent Restriction Acts have been repealed and replaced by later legislation; see now the Rent Act 1977 and the Protection from Eviction Act 1977, for the principal provisions.

Noting. The Bills of Exchange Act 1882, s. 57(2), has been repealed to allow the claim for liquidated damages to be made in a foreign currency in a proper case when a bill is dishonoured abroad (Administration of Justice Act 1977, ss. 4, 32, Sched. 5, Part I). See also FOREIGN CURRENCY.

Novelty. The Patents Act 1977, s. 2, which contains elaborate provisions amplifying the requirements of s. 1(1) of that Act, which restricts patentability to inventions which (a) are new, (b) involve an inventive step, (c) are capable of industrial application, and (d) are not excluded on various grounds (such as being works of any kind of art or the presentation of information).

The term has also been used to describe certain consumer goods and articles (Expanding Novelties (Safety) Order 1983 (S.I. 1983 No. 1791)).

Nuisance. Bomb hoaxes have been moved from the law of public nuisance into the criminal law (Criminal Law Act 1977, s. 51); see BOMB HOAX.

Nullity of marriage. Decrees nisi of nullity may now be made absolute after the expiration of six weeks from the date of the decree (Matrimonial Causes Act 1973, ss. 1(5), 15; Matrimonial Causes (Decree

Absolute) General Orders 1972 and 1973). The practice for the expedition of a decree absolute is set out in *Practice Direction* [1964] 1 W.L.R. 1473.

The authority for medical inspection in nullity cases is now the Matrimonial Causes Rules 1977 (S.I. 1977 No. 344), rr. 30, 31, under which the 1963 Practice Direction is kept in operation.

The Administration of Justice Act 1970, s. 1, Sched. 1, have been repealed and replaced by the Supreme Court Act 1981, s. 61(1), (3), Sched. 1, para. 3, without change of effect.

Nullum tempus aut locus occurit regi. The Limitation Act 1939, s. 30(1), refers to "the Customs Acts or the Acts relating to duties of excise," so that the substantial repeal of the Customs and Excise Act 1952 (see CUSTOMS) does not vitiate the general statement that there is no time limit under the 1939 Act (as variously amended and now repealed and replaced by the Limitation Act 1980, the original ss. 30, 32, now being ss. 37 and 39) in respect of matters covered by the legislation.

Numbering. The Rural District Councils (Urban Powers) Order 1949 (S.I. 1949 No. 2088), has lapsed with the abolition of those councils by the Local Government Act 1972.

Nurseries. The Children Act 1958, s. 3 (as amended), has been repealed and replaced by the Foster Children Act 1980, s. 5, without significant change of effect; s. 6 of the 1980 Act contains provisions requiring the termination of fostering to be notified to the local authority.

Nurses. The Nurses Act 1957, and related legislation have been prospectively repealed and replaced by the Nurses, Midwives and Health Visitors Act 1979, which contains a certain re-structuring of these three interrelated sections of the medical profession. The control over nurses' training institutions formerly authorised by the Tribunals and Inquiries Act 1958 (repealed and replaced by the Tribunals and Inquiries Act 1971, without significant change of effect), has disappeared with the 1979 legislation.

Nursing homes. Any homes registered under the Nursing Homes Act 1984, are exempt from the registration and inspections required for residential homes (*q.v.*) (Residential Homes Act 1980, s. 1(1)(*b*)).

The Registered Homes Act 1984, repeals and consolidates provisions (including the Nursing Homes Act 1975) relating to the conduct of such establishments. See also the Nursing Homes and Mental Nursing Homes Regulations 1984 (S.I. 1984 No. 1578).

O

Oath. The principal legislation (from the Oaths Act 1888, to the Administration of Justice Act 1977, s. 8 (which first made the alternative of an affirmation available as of right without reasons being required)) has been repealed and replaced by the Oaths Act 1978. The Unlawful Oaths Acts 1797 and 1812, have been repealed without replacement by the Statute Law (Repeals) Act 1981, s. 1(1), Sched. 1, Part I.

The Interpretation Act 1889, s. 3, has been repealed and replaced by the Interpretation Act 1978, s. 5, Sched. 1, without significant change of effect.

The law relating to the persons entitled to administer oaths, the administration of unlawful oaths, and the authorisation of oaths administered abroad remains unchanged.

A new form of oath for a jury has been introduced (*Practice Direction* [1984] 1 W.L.R. 1217), as follows: "I swear by Almighty God that I will faithfully try the defendant and give a true verdict according to the evidence."

Obligation. The Limitation Act 1939 (as variously amended), has been repealed and replaced by the Limitation Act 1980.

Obscenity. Amendments to the Obscene Publications Act 1959, have been enacted in order to restrict still further the use of obscene cinematographic material (Criminal Law Act 1977, s. 53).

Courts of quarter sessions have been

abolished and replaced by the Crown Court (Courts Act 1971, ss. 41 and 1 respectively (now repealed and replaced by the Supreme Court Act 1981)).

For the revision of the penalties which may be imposed on summary convictions see FINE.

Obstruction. The Motor Vehicles (Construction and Use) Regulations 1973 (heavily amended), have been revoked and replaced by the Motor Vehicles (Construction and Use) Regulations 1978 (already also heavily amended) without substantial relevant change of effect.

The Highways Act 1959, s. 121, has been repealed and replaced by the Highways Act 1980, s. 135, without change of effect. The Road Traffic Regulation Act 1967, s. 80, has been repealed and replaced by the Road Traffic Regulation Act 1984, s. 145, Sched. 12 (which, unusually, expressly claims to be a re-enactment of the 1967 provision), without change of effect. The Transport Act 1968, s. 131, has been repealed and replaced by the Road Traffic Regulation Act 1984, Sched. 12, without change of effect. The Fixed Penalty (Procedure) Regulations 1974 (S.I. 1974 No. 1474), have been revoked by the Fixed Penalty (Procedure) Regulations 1977 (S.I. 1977 No. 1111).

Under the Police Act 1964, s. 51(3), any behaviour which in fact makes it harder for a constable to do his duty, regardless of the good (or evil) intentions of the defendant, amounts to an offence (*Hills* v. *Ellis* [1983] Q.B. 680; *Lewis* v. *Cox* [1984] 1 W.L.R. 875, D.C.; *Willmott* v. *Atack* [1977] Q.B. 498, D.C.).

Obtaining credit. The offence of obtaining credit by deception is regulated by the Theft Act 1978, which makes provision for three classes of case: (1) obtaining services by a deception (s. 1); (2) evasion of liability by a deception (s. 2); and (3) making off without payment (s. 3). Each of these offences is punishable on conviction on indictment by a term of imprisonment not exceeding five years (two years in cases under s. 3), and on summary conviction by a fine (*q.v.*) not exceeding £2,000 or a term of imprisonment not exceeding six months or both (Act of 1978, s. 4). See also DECEPTION.

Occasional licence; Occasional permission. For these special forms of justices' licences see INTOXICATING LIQUORS.

Occupancy. In the law relating to the limitation of actions there is specific provision to prevent mere occupancy being converted into an implied licence merely by virtue of the fact that the occupation is not inconsistent with the present or future enjoyment of the land by the person entitled to the land (Limitation Act 1980, Sched. 1, para. 8(4), replacing the Limitation Act 1939, s. 10(4), added by the Limitation Amendment Act 1980, s. 4)); if the facts of a case justify it, however, such a licence may be implied (*ibid.*, proviso).

Occupational Pensions Board. Established by the Social Security Act 1973, ss. 66–68, the Board has various duties (under the Social Security Pensions Act 1975, ss. 53–57) in connection with arrangements for contracting out of certain parts of the government pension scheme (Act of 1975, ss. 26 *et seq.*).

Occupiers' liability. The common law also imposes a duty on occupiers to take such steps as common sense or common humanity would require to exclude trespassers, or to warn them of, or to reduce or avert a danger which may exist or arise on the premises, taking such steps as come within reasonable and practicable limits (*Herrington* v. *British Railways Board* [1972] A.C. 877, H.L.; *Pannett* v. *P. McGuiness & Co. Ltd.* [1972] 2 Q.B. 599, C.A.). See also the Occupiers' Liability Act 1984.

Offensive weapons. For the revision of the penalties which may be imposed on summary convictions see FINE. The enhanced penalties formerly available have been abolished by the same legislation.

Office development. The restrictions formerly imposed on office development have been brought to an end (Control of Office Development (Cessation) Order 1979 (S.I. 1979 No. 908)).

Officers of the Supreme Court. The Judicature Act 1925, ss. 105, 221–232 (this being a misprint, for the 1925 Act ran only to 227 sections), have been repealed and replaced by the Supreme Court Act 1981, Part IV (ss. 88–104), without significant change of effect.

Offices. The Offices, Shops and Railway Premises Act 1963, ss. 21, 25, 26, 32, 45, 50, have been repealed and replaced by the

Offices, Shops and Railway Premises Act 1963, (Repeals and Modifications) Regulations 1974 (S.I. 1974 No. 1943), in connection with the promulgation of new regulations under the Health and Safety at Work, etc., Act 1974. For the repeal of the Community Land Act 1975, see the Local Government, Planning and Land Act 1980, ss. 101, 194, Scheds. 17, 34.

Official log-book. The Merchant Shipping Act 1894, ss. 239, 240, have been repealed and replaced (without significant change of effect) by the Merchant Shipping Act 1970, s. 68, under which regulations may be made for the detailed control of log-books, the making of entries, etc.

Official referee. The Courts Act 1971, s. 25 and the Administration of Justice Act 1956, ss. 9, 10, have been repealed and replaced by the Supreme Court Act 1981, s. 68, without significant change of effect. The detailed administration of this specialised class of case is provided for by R.S.C. Ord. 36 (as substantially revised by the Rules of the Supreme Court (Amendment No. 2) 1982 (S.I. 1982 No. 1111)); cases may now be commenced as "Official Referees' business" (Ord. 36, r. 2), instead of having to be commenced in the general list and then transferred.

Official Solicitor. The current statutory basis for the activities of the Official Solicitor is the Supreme Court Act 1981, s. 90, replacing the Supreme Court of Judicature (Consolidation) Act 1925, s. 129.

Oil taxation. The principal provisions are contained in the Oil Taxation Acts 1975 and 1983, together with the Petroleum Revenue Tax Act 1980. See also the Oil and Gas (Enterprise) Act 1982. Detailed amendments to the taxation provision occur in successive annual Finance Acts.

Old age pensions. Further provisions are contained in the Social Security Pensions Act 1975, which also deals with the inter-relation of state and private pension schemes. See also SOCIAL SECURITY.

Omnia praesumuntur rite ac solemniter esse acta. Despite this presumption the Equal Opportunities Commission issued a directive to newspapers, etc., that advertisements for employment which use "ambiguous" words (*e.g.* foreman, manager) are assumed to be in contravention of the Sex Discrimination Act 1975.

Open court. The Magistrates' Courts Act 1952, s. 98(4), has been repealed and replaced by the Magistrates' Courts Act 1980, s. 121(4), without change of effect. The Criminal Justice Act 1967, s. 6, has been repealed and replaced by the Act of 1980, s. 4(2), without change of effect.

Open spaces. The New Towns Act 1965, ss. 7(2), 8(3), 21, have been repealed and replaced by the New Towns Act 1981, ss. 10(2), 11(3), 21, without change of effect. The Town and Country Planning Act 1968, s. 31, has been repealed and replaced by the Acquisition of Land Act 1981, s. 19, without change of effect.

Operator's licence. A licence of the kind required by the Transport Act 1968, ss. 60–70, for the operation of a goods vehicle for the carriage of goods for hire or reward or for or in connection with any trade or business (s. 60(1)). Additional controls were imposed on this type of operator's licence by the Transport Act 1982, s. 52, Sched. 4 (which added ss. 69A–69B to the Act of 1968).

In connection with hackney carriages and private hire vehicles, the term means a licence granted by the district council authorising the operation of private hire vehicles (Local Government (Miscellaneous Provisions) Act 1976, s. 80(1)).

Oppression. Oppressive behaviour by a government department or quasi-governmental institution is a ground for a claim for exemplary damages (*q.v.*) (*Rookes* v. *Barnard* [1964] A.C. 1129, H.L.).

Opticians. The National Health Service Act 1951, Sched., the National Health Service Act 1961, and the National Health Service Reorganisation Act 1973, Sched. 4, para. 59, have been repealed and replaced by the National Health Service Act 1977, s. 78, Sched. 12, para. 2, without substantial change of effect. Intricate amendments of the principal (1958) Act were made by the Health and Social Security Act 1984, ss. 1–4; the general effect is to remove the monopoly on the supply of glasses to adults and to expand the disciplinary powers of the General Optical Council.

Option. A solicitor's failure to register his client's option to purchase a legal estate in land may amount to negligence, making him liable to his client both in tort and in contract (*Midland Bank Trust Co. Ltd.* v.

Hett, Stubbs & Kemp [1979] Ch. 384).

A registered option to purchase land prevails over a mere prior right of pre-emption because the registered option constitutes an interest in land whereas the right of pre-emption is merely a matter of contract (*Pritchard* v. *Briggs* [1980] Ch. 338, C.A.).

Option mortgage. Established by the Housing Subsidies Act 1967, Part II (ss. 24–32), and amended by the Housing Act 1974, s. 119, Sched. 11, the option mortgage scheme was one whereby a borrower was entitled to an Exchequer subsidy to assist in the payments due to the mortgagee in respect of interest on a mortgage secured on residential premises being purchased for the occupation of the mortgagor. For those who paid income tax at the basic rate, the relief allowed against income tax in respect of payments of interest was more beneficial than claiming a subsidy under the scheme, which was introduced specifically for the benefit of those whose incomes were so low that they had no opportunity to claim such relief against income tax. Where a subsidy was granted in respect of a mortgage the actual interest payable by the mortgage was lower than under ordinary schemes but no relief against income tax was permitted. The scheme was discontinued by the Finance Act 1982, s. 27, in connection with the revision of the administrative scheme for giving relief against income tax.

Order. The Judicature Act 1925 has been repealed and replaced by the Supreme Court Act 1981.

Order and disposition. Exceptions to the general rule (Bankruptcy Act 1914, s. 38) have been provided for in relation to goods supplied on hire-purchase or under consumer hire or conditional sale or regulated agreements (Act of 1914, s. 38A (added by the Consumer Credit Act 1974, s. 192, Sched. 4, para. 6)).

Order of Council. The Medical Act 1956, ss. 49–51, have been repealed and replaced by the Medical Act 1983, ss. 50–52, without change of effect.

Order of discharge. Such orders may now result from the automatic discharge procedure as well as on the application of the official receiver of the bankrupt (Insolvency Act 1976, ss. 7, 8) (see BANKRUPTCY).

Ordnance, Board of. By the Ordnance Factories and Military Services Act 1984, the Secretary of State was invested with power to make schemes for (in effect) the de-nationalisation of the ordnance factories and their associated operations.

Ordnance Survey. The Interpretation Act 1889, s. 25, has been repealed and replaced by the Interpretation Act 1978, s. 5, Sched. 1, without change of effect.

The operation of the Ordnance Survey Act 1841, has been adjusted to take account of the reorganisation of local government (Local Government Act 1972, s. 191).

Originating summons. The procedure in the High Court is regulated in the main by R.S.C. Ords. 7, 28.

Ottawa Agreements. The Ottawa Agreements Act 1932 (with small exceptions), and the Finance Act 1937, s. 3, have been repealed by the Import Duties Act 1958, s. 16, Sched. 7, which have in their turn been (extensively) repealed by the European Communities Act 1972, s. 4, Scheds. 3, 4.

Overcrowding. By the Housing Act 1980, s. 146, a new version of the Housing Act 1957, s. 90, was substituted, which makes comparable provision for houses in multiple occupation (*q.v.*), but the age limit is twelve instead of ten years of age.

Overseas aid. The Overseas Aid Acts 1966 and 1968, have been repealed by the Overseas Development and Co-operation Act 1980, s. 18, Sched. 2, Part I. Part I (ss. 1–3) of the Act of 1980 contains general provisions which replace the earlier Acts.

Overseas Development, Ministry of. This ministry has again been dissolved and its functions have been transferred to the Secretary of State (Ministry of Overseas Development (Dissolution) Order 1979 (S.I. 1979 No. 1451)).

P

Package. Restrictions on the weight and form of wrappings for certain goods are prescribed by the Weights and Measures Act 1979, ss. 1–5 (see WEIGHTS AND MEASURES).

Panel. The Acquisition of Land (Assessment of Compensation) Act 1919, was repealed by the Land Compensation Act 1961, s. 40(3), Sched. 5.

Paper money. The Currency and Bank Notes Act 1914, has been repealed by the Currency and Bank Notes Act 1928, which has in its turn been in some measure repealed and replaced by the Currency and Bank Notes Act 1954.

Paper, Special. The *Practice Direction* [1958] 1 W.L.R. 1291, has been revoked and replaced by the *Practice Direction* [1981] 1 W.L.R 1296; the Special Paper List has disappeared as a result of the revision of the listing procedures.

Parish. The definition in the Local Government Act 1958, s. 66(1), has been repealed by the Statute Law (Repeals) Act 1978, s. 1(1), Sched. 1, Part VII. The Pastoral Measure 1968, s. 16, has been repealed and replaced by the Pastoral Measure 1983, s. 17, without change of effect.

Parish apprentices. The Children Act 1948, ss. 17, 20, have been repealed and replaced by the Child Care Act 1980, ss. 24, 27, without significant change of effect.

Parish register. The Parochial Registers Act 1812, was repealed and replaced by the Parochial Registers and Records Measure 1978, s. 26(2), Sched. 4; by that Measure a modern version of the provisions in respect of registers of baptisms and burials was enacted.

Park. S.I. 1974 No. 797 has been revoked and replaced by the Crown Roads (Royal Parks) (Application of Road Traffic Enactments) Order 1977 (S.I. 1977 No. 548)). For the application of the Road Traffic Acts to Crown roads see also the Road Traffic Regulation Act 1984, s. 131.

Parking. The Road Traffic Regulation Act 1967, s. 80 and the Transport Act 1968, s. 131, Sched. 18, have been repealed and replaced by the Road Traffic Regulation Act 1984, Sched. 12, without change of effect.

The Road Traffic Regulation Act 1984, Part IV (ss. 32–63), deals with off-street and unpaid parking places (ss. 32–44), parking on highways for payment (ss. 45–56), parish and community council arrangements (ss. 57–60), and contains various special provisions (ss. 61–63) which deal with Royal parks and stands and racks for bicyles.

Parking places. Fresh provision relating to the designation of such places has been made by the Local Government (Miscellaneous Provisions) Act 1976, ss. 63, 64.

The rules made under the Road Traffic Act 1972, s. 18, include the Road Vehicles Lighting (Standing Vehicles) (Exemption) (General) Regulations 1975 (S.I. 1975 No. 1494). See also PARKING.

Parochial church council. The Pastoral Measure 1968, Sched. 3, para. 12, has been repealed and replaced by the Pastoral Measure 1983, Sched. 3, paras. 12, 13, without change of effect.

Parole Board. The scheme for release of prisoners on parole has been modified by the Criminal Justice Act 1982, s. 33.

Part payment. A period of limitation in respect of a debt was modified so that it might be repeatedly extended by acknowledgments or part payments, but a right of action barred by the Limitation Act 1939, could not be revived by either of these methods (Limitation Act 1939, s. 23(5) (added by the Limitation Amendment Act 1980, s. 6(1)). The provisions of the Act of 1939, s. 25, were made subject to this new provision (Amendment Act of 1980, s. 6(3)). The earlier Acts have now been repealed and replaced by the Limitation Act 1980, s. 29, without change of effect.

Particulars. For amendments to the requirements as to further and better particulars see the Rules of the Supreme Court (Amendment No. 2) 1980 (S.I. 1980 No. 1010).

Parties. The Judicature Act 1925, s. 225, has been repealed and replaced by the Supreme Court Act 1981, s. 151(1), without change of effect.

Partition. The Judicature Act 1873, s. 25, was repealed and replaced by the Supreme Court of Judicature (Consolidation) Act 1925, s. 56(1), without significant change of effect. The 1925 provision has now itself been repealed and replaced by the Supreme Court Act 1981, s. 61(2), (3), Sched. 1, para. 1, also without change of effect.

Partitione facienda, De. The Judicature Act 1873, s. 25, was repealed and replaced by the Supreme Court of Judicature (Consolidation) Act 1925 s. 56(1), without significant change of effect. The 1925 provision has now itself been repealed and replaced by the Supreme Court Act 1981, s. 61(1), (3), Sched. 1, para. 1, also without change of effect.

Partnership. The Companies Act 1948, s. 429, and the Companies Act 1967, s. 119, have been repealed by the Banking Act 1979, s. 51(2), Sched. 7.

Pass. The Chancery Division procedure was amended when the administrative offices of the court were re-organised in 1982. The process of drafting an order now depends on the complexity of its terms, the parties being invited to assist in drawing up the order in appropriate cases (see *Practice Direction* [1982] 1 W.L.R. 1189, paras. 14, 15). The former R.S.C. Ord. 42, r. 7, has been revoked and replaced by Ord. 42, r. 6, to take account of these changes.

Passport. Offences under the Criminal Justice Act 1925, s. 36, are triable either summarily or on indictment (see the Magistrates' Courts Act 1980, s. 17, Sched. 1, para. 19 (replacing the Criminal Law Act 1977, s. 16, Sched. 3, para. 19)).

The Forgery and Counterfeiting Act 1981, s. 30, Sched. 1, repealed portions of the Act of 1925, s. 36, so as to restrict its operation to the making of false statements, etc., in connection with passport applications, or improperly obtaining such a document. The actual forgery of a passport comes within the general provisions of the Act of 1981 (see FORGERY), thus displacing the Act of 1920, s. 1; and the Act of 1981, s. 5(1), prohibits the possession of false instruments (*i.e.* documents) and specifically lists "passports and documents which may be used instead of passports" (s. 5(5)(*f*)). A "1981 forgery" is triable either way, and on conviction on indictment may be punished by imprisonment not exceeding two years (s. 6(4)).

Pastoral schemes. The Pastoral Measure 1968 has been repealed and replaced by the Pastoral Measure 1983, without major change of effect. The Sharing of Church Buildings Measure 1970, s. 1, has been repealed by the Pastoral Measure 1983, s. 93, Sched. 9, since its provisions have been incorporated into the principal parts of the 1983 Measure.

Patent agent. The Patents Act 1949, s. 88, has been repealed and replaced by the Patents Act 1977, s. 114, without significant change of effect.

Patents. Extensive new provision is made for patents by the Patents Act 1977, together with the Patents Rules 1978 (S.I. 1978 No. 216). The domestic law has been revised (Act of 1977, Part I (ss. 1–76)) so that, *inter alia*, the former "provisional protection" is replaced by a system of claiming priority from the date of any earlier application (s. 5); patent life has been extended from 16 to 20 years but extensions are no longer available (s. 25); the definition of infringement has been redrafted to include activities which previously were actionable only as procurring infringements by others (s. 60). Extensive transitional provisions exist to deal with the long period during which the new and old systems will both be operative (s. 127, Scheds. 1 and 2).

The system of European Patents has also been introduced into English law (Patents Act 1977, Part II (ss. 77–95), patents being granted by the European Patent Office under the Community Patent Convention (see ss. 86–88); courts of the United Kingdom will deal with infringements which occur within the jurisdiction, even though incapable of dealing with questions of validity (see s. 86).

Patents Appeal Tribunal. The Courts Act 1971, s. 46, provided for an appeal to the Court of Appeal from the Patents Appeal Tribunal in all cases on a point of law, or for alleged excess of jurisdiction with the leave of the Tribunal or of the Court of Appeal, in addition to the grounds of appeal permitted by the Patents Act 1949, s. 85. The conduct of such appeals is regulated by R.S.C. Ord. 59, r. 18.

The Patents Act 1977, has established a

Patents Court which is part of the Chancery Division (s. 96), and which deals with such proceedings relating to patents and other matters as may be prescribed by rules of court. The Act of 1977, s. 96, has now been repealed and replaced by the Supreme Court Act 1981, s. 6(1) (*a*), without change of effect. The new court took over the functions of the selected judge (see the Act of 1949, s. 84) who tried infringement actions and certain other matters and of the Patents Appeal Tribunal. Proceedings before the Tribunal were transferred to the new court unless the hearing had already been commenced (Act of 1977, s. 127, Sched. 4, para. 13).

Patient. The Mental Health Act 1959, ss. 101, 119, 138 and 147(1), have been repealed and replaced by the Mental Health Act 1983, ss. 94, 112, 142 and 145(1), without change of effect.

Pawnbroker. The Consumer Credit Act 1974 authorises the making of subordinate legislation in this area of the law; recent examples of appropriate instruments are the Consumer Credit (Conduct of Business) (Pawn Records) Regulation 1983 (S.I. 1983 No. 1565); the Consumer Credit (Pawn-Receipts) Regulations 1983 (S.I. 1983 No. 1566); and the Consumer Credit (Loss of Pawn-Receipt) Regulations 1983 (S.I. 1983 No. 1567).

Pay-as-you-earn. The provisions relating to this scheme (Income and Corporation Taxes Act 1970, ss. 204, 205; Finance (No. 2) Act 1975, s. 37) have been the subject of further detailed amending provisions (see, *e.g.* the Finance Act 1976, ss. 71, 132(5), Sched. 15, Part III).

Paymaster-General. The salary of the Paymaster-General is revised from time to time (see, *e.g.* S.I. 1979 No. 905). The Judicature Act 1925, s. 133, has been repealed and replaced by the Supreme Court Act 1981, s. 97, without change of effect.

Payment into court. In prescribed cases the fact of payment into court is required to be concealed from the judges when an appeal is taken to the Court of Appeal (R.S.C. Ord. 59, r. 12A).

The detailed procedure for effecting a payment into court is laid down by the Supreme Court Funds Rules 1975 (S.I. 1975 No. 1803), rr. 17–26, 57–58.

For interest on money paid into court see the Rules of the Supreme Court (Amendment No. 2) 1980 (S.I. 1980 No. 1010).

Payment out of court. The general provisions governing payment, transfer and delivery of funds out of court are contained in the Supreme Court Funds Rules 1975 (S.I. 1975 No. 1803), rr. 38–51.

Pedestrian crossing. The Road Traffic Regulation Act 1967, ss. 21–23, and associated enactments, have been repealed and replaced by the Road Traffic Regulation Act 1984, ss. 23–25, without change of effect.

Pedestrians. As a general rule, pedestrians are prohibited on motorways (Motorways Traffic (England and Wales) Regulations 1982 (S.I. 1982 No. 1163)).

Pedigree. The specific provisions formerly contained in the Forgery Act 1913, have been repealed without replacement by the Forgery and Counterfeiting Act 1981, s. 30, Sched., Part 1; see now FORGERY.

Penny. By the Decimal Currency Act 1967, s. 1(1), it is provided that a new penny, being one-hundredth part of a pound sterling, is to be one of the denominations of money in the United Kingdom. The composition of the coins is prescribed under the Coinage Act 1971 (see COIN). The original term was "new penny", but the official name has now been modified so as to allow the use of "penny" simply (Currency Act 1982, s. 1(1); by the Act of 1982, s. 1(2), the Decimal Currency Act 1967, s. 1(1), was repealed without replacement).

Pension. The provisions in respect of judicial pensions have been repealed and replaced by the Judicial Pension Act 1981, without change of effect.

Per quod servitium amisit. A preliminary abolition (by the Law Reform (Miscellaneous Provisions) Act 1970, s. 5) not appearing adequate, proceedings for loss of services, etc., have again been abolished (Administration of Justice Act 1982, s. 2).

Perishable goods. The Sale of Goods Act 1893, s. 48(3), has been repealed and replaced by the Sale of Goods Act 1979, s. 48(3), without change of effect. See also the International Carrriage of Perishable Foodstuffs Act 1976 (brought into operation on 1 October 1979 (S.I. 1975 No. 413)), under which the International Carriage of Perishable Foodstuffs Regulations 1979 (S.I. 1979 No. 415), have been made.

Perished goods. The Sale of Goods Act 1893, ss. 6, 7, have been repealed and replaced by the Sale of Goods Act 1979, ss. 6, 7, without change of effect.

Perjury. The law of perjury has been extended to cover a person making an unsworn statement in compliance with an order under the Evidence (Proceedings in Other Jurisdictions) Act 1975, s. 2 (Perjury Act 1911, s. 1A (added by the Act of 1975, s. 8(1), Sched. 2, para. 1)).

The Criminal Justice Act 1925, s. 28 (in part) and the Magistrates' Courts Act 1952, s. 19 (and amending Acts), were repealed by the Criminal Law Act 1977, s. 65(5), Sched. 13; offences under the Act of 1911, except those under ss. 1, 3, 4, were at the same time made triable either way (Act of 1977, s. 16, Sched. 2, para. 12, and Sched. 3, para. 14; the current equivalent provision is the Magistrates' Courts Act 1980, s. 17, Sched. 1, para. 14).

Perry. The Customs and Excise Act 1952, s. 307(c), has been repealed and replaced by the Alcoholic Liquor Duties Act 1979, s. 1(3), without significant change of effect.

Person. The Interpretation Act 1889, ss. 3, 19, have been repealed and replaced by the Interpretation Act 1978, ss. 5, 22, 23, Sched. 1, and Sched. 2, para. 4(5), without significant change of effect.

Persona designata. The original text of the Wills Act 1837, s. 33, has been repealed and replaced by a new version (Administration of Justice Act 1982, s. 9); for the effect of the new text see LAPSE.

Personal Acts of Parliament. Recent use of such Acts has been markedly matrimonial in subject-matter; all three are Marriage Enabling Acts (see 1980 c. *1* and 1982 cc. *1* and *2*).

Personal injuries scheme. Compensation for personal injuries is available from the Criminal Injuries Compensation Board; see CRIMINAL INJURIES COMPENSATION.

Personation. The Companies Act 1948, s. 48, has been repealed by the Theft Act 1968, s. 33(3), Sched. 3, Part 1. The behaviour formerly proscribed under the Act of 1948 appears to come within the new offences of obtaining property or a pecuniary advantage by a deception (Theft Act 1978, ss. 15, 16; see also the Theft Act 1978, ss. 1–3). The Representation of the People Act 1949, ss. 47, 146, and associated legislation, have been repealed and replaced by the Representation of the People Act 1983, ss. 60, 168, without change of effect.

Petitioning creditor. The minimum debt to support a bankruptcy petition was increased to £200 (Bankruptcy Act 1914, s. 4(1)(*a*); Insolvency Act 1976, s. 1, Sched. 1, Part I); a further increase has made the outstanding sum required not less than £750 (Insolvency Proceedings (Increase of Monetary Limits) Regulations 1984 (S.I. 1984 No. 1199)).

Petroleum. The Hydrocarbon Oil Duties Act 1971, has been repealed and replaced by the Hydrocarbon Oil Duties Act 1979, without change of effect.

The scheme for petroleum revenue tax has been amended by the Finance Act 1977, s. 54; the Finance Act 1978, s. 30; the Finance (No. 2) Act 1979, ss. 18–22; and the Petroleum Revenue Tax Act 1980. See also OIL TAXATION.

Petty sessional court. The Interpretation Act 1889, s. 13, has been repealed and replaced by the Interpretation Act 1978, s. 5, Sched. 1, where the definition of "magistrates' court" from the Magistrates' Courts Act 1952, s. 124 (now repealed), was adopted without change of effect. "Petty sessional courthouse" is no longer defined in the Interpretation Act. The Magistrates' Courts Act 1980, uses "petty sessional court-house" and "petty sessions area" in the same way as the repealed 1952 provision, but without containing any definition of its own.

Petty sessions. The Justices of the Peace Act 1949, s. 18 (as amended), has been repealed and replaced by the Justices of the Peace Act 1979, ss. 23, 24, without significant change of effect.

Photograph. Home Office Circular 9/1969 has been withdrawn and replaced by Circular 109/1978; see IDENTIFICATION; IDENTITY.

Physician. The Medical Act 1956, s. 27, has been repealed and replaced by the Medical Act 1983, s. 46, without change of effect.

Picketing. Now a highly controversial topic, yet ill-defined in the law. The Employment Act 1980, s. 16, substituted a new text into the Trade Union and Labour Relations Act 1974, s. 15, to restrict the scope of picketing, making secondary picketing subject to tort liability (see also the Act of 1980, s. 17). The Employment Act 1982, s. 15, further widened the risk of picketing resulting in liability since it removed the immunity formerly conferred by the Trade Union and Labour Relations Act 1974, s. 14. By the 1982 Act, s. 16, however, cash limits were placed on the damages which might be recovered; these are based on the membership size of the union in question, they may be varied by order (made by statutory instrument) of the Secretary of State (s. 16(4)), and do not apply to certain groups of proceedings (*e.g.* actions in respect of personal injury to any person in respect of negligence, nuisance or breach of statutory duty) (Act of 1982, s. 16(2)).

Picnics. The Highways Act 1971, ss. 26–29, have been repealed and replaced by the Highways Act 1980, ss. 112–114, without change of effect.

Pick-pocket or **Pick-purse.** The liability of a would-be pick-pocket whose activities are frustrated because there is nothing to steal or nothing worth stealing was reviewed in *Attorny-General's References (Nos. 1 and 2 of 1979)* [1980] Q.B. 180, C.A., where the earlier cases are collected. See also IMPOSSIBILITY.

Pilot. The Pilotage Act 1913, ss. 16, 23, have been repealed and replaced by the Pilotage Act 1983, ss. 12, 20, without change of effect.

Pilotage. The Pilotage Acts 1913 and 1936, have been repealed and replaced by the (consolidating) Pilotage Act 1983; the Act of 1913, s. 15, has been replaced by the Act of 1983, s. 35, without change of effect.

Pilotage Commission. This is a body corporate established by the Merchant Shipping Act 1979, ss. 1–5, with functions (s. 4) which include giving advice to the Secretary of State and pilotage, dock and harbour authorities on such matters as securing by means of pilotage the safety of navigation in ports of and waters off the coasts of the United Kingdom, ensuring that efficient pilotage services are available, together with suitable equipment, regulation of terms of service of pilots and their training and qualifications. The Commission is also concerned with a number of other matters which bear on its principal functions (ss. 6–12). The Act of 1979, ss. 1–5, have now been re-enacted in the Pilotage Act 1983, ss. 1–5, 8(5); ss. 6–12 of the 1979 Act have been distributed among a number of the 1983 provisions.

See also COMPULSORY PILOTAGE.

Piracy. This term is also commonly applied to breaches of copyright of films, cinema films and sound recordings (of whatever kind). For the new provisions for punishment of such activities see COPYRIGHT.

The proliferation of home computers and similar devices has encouraged the same kind of activity (also commonly called "piracy") in relation to computer programs; for the rejection of computer programs from the protection of copyright see COPYRIGHT.

Place of abode. The Magistrates' Courts Rules 1968, r. 82(1), has been revoked and replaced by the Magistrates' Courts Rules 1981, (S.I. 1981 No. 552), r. 99(1)(*b*), (*c*), without change of effect.

Planning inquiries. The Town and Country Planning Appeals (Determination by Appointed Persons) (Inquiries Procedure) Rules 1968, have been revoked and replaced by the Town and Country Planning Appeals (Determination by Appointed Persons) (Inquiries Procedure) (S.I. 1974 No. 420). The Town and Country Planning (Inquiries Procedure) Rules 1969, have been revoked and replaced by the Town and Country Planning (Inquiries Procedure) Rules 1974 (S.I. 1974 No. 419).

Plant. The Conservation of Wild Creatures and Wild Plants Act 1975, was repealed and replaced by the Wildlife and Countryside Act 1981 (see the Act of 1981, s. 13, Sched. 13).

The periods for which plant breeders rights may be exercised have been extended by the Plant Varieties Act 1983.

Plant and machinery. The decision of Fox J. was reversed in *Munby* v. *Furlong* [1977] Ch. 359, C.A., when it was determined that a lawyer's books qualified as "plant". The reasoning in *Yarmouth* v. *France* (1887) 19 Q.B.D. 647, has been followed in *Benson* v. *Yard Arm Club Ltd.* [1979] 1 W.L.R. 347, C.A., when a converted vessel used as a floating restaurant was excluded from the category of "plant" in assessing tax.

Pleasure boats. The Public Health Acts Amendment Act 1907, s. 94, has been amended by the Local Government (Miscellaneous Provisions) Act 1976, s. 18, so as to increase the control exercised over licensed pleasure boating, and the power (Public Health Act 1961, s. 76) to make by-laws relating to seaside pleasure boats has been amended by partial repeal for the same reason (Act of 1976, s. 81, Sched. 2).

Pleasure-grounds. The powers conferred on local authorities to make by-laws regulating certain pleasure-grounds have been amended (and repealed in part) with the especial purpose of enabling by-laws to be framed to take account of fire escape requirements (Local Government (Miscellaneous Provisions) Act 1976, s. 81, Sched. 2).

Plebiscite or **Plebiscitum.** In modern usage "plebiscite" is a common synonym for "referendum" (*q.v.*).

Plene administravit. Failure to put this plea forward at the proper time in an action may have disastrous consequences (see *Midland Bank Trust Co. Ltd.* v. *Green* [1979] 1 W.L.R. 460).

Plene administravit praeter. See *Midland Bank Trust Co. Ltd.* v. *Green* [1979] 1 W.L.R. 460.

Plimsoll mark. The penalties on conviction on indictment under the Merchant Shipping (Load Lines) Act 1967, ss. 2–4, were increased to a fine of unlimited amount, and the maximum fine on summary conviction from £400 to £1,000 (now £2,000: see FINE) (Merchant Shipping Act 1979, s. 43, Sched. 2, Part V).

Plumage. The Importation of Plumage (Prohibition) Act 1921, has been repealed by the Endangered Species (Import and Export) Act 1976 ss. 1, 3, 4, Sched. 3, paras. 19, 20, restrict the importation and exportation of plumage of all kinds, subject to exceptions set out in the Act. Later amendments include the substitution of a new version of the Act of 1976, Sched. 3, by the Endangered Species (Import and Export) Act 1976 (Modification) Order 1982 (S.I. 1982 No. 1230).

Plurality. The Pastoral Measure 1968, ss. 17, 88, have been repealed and replaced by the Pastoral Measure 1983, ss. 18, 85, without change of effect.

Poaching. For the revision of penalties which may be imposed on summary conviction (*e.g.*, under the Night Poaching Act 1828, the Game Act 1831 and the Poaching Prevention Act 1862), see FINE.

Poison. The Poisons Rules 1972 (S.I. 1972 No. 1939), have been revoked and replaced by the Poisons Rules 1978 (S.I. 1978 No. 1) (as now variously amended). See also the Poisons List Order 1978 (S.I. 1978 No. 2) (also amended).

Police. The Police Council for the United Kingdom has been replaced by the Police Negotiating Board (Police Negotiating Board Act 1980).

Police court. The Justices of the Peace Act 1949, s. 44(1), has been repealed by the Justices of the Peace Act 1979, s. 71(2), Sched. 2. "Magistrates' court" is now defined by the Magistrates' Courts Act 1980, s. 148(1) (replacing the Magistrates' Courts Act 1952, s. 124, and the Interpretation Act 1978, s. 5, Sched. 1), and the term "police court" is an anachronism.

Political fund. A union member may choose not to contribute to his union's political fund, thereupon losing his vote with respect to dealings with that fund (Trade Union Act 1913, ss. 3(1)(b), 5). Further provision has been made in the Trade Union Act 1984, ss. 12–17.

Poll. The Representation of the People Act 1949, s. 53, and the Representation of the People Act 1969, s. 53, have been repealed and replaced by the Representation of the People Act 1983, ss. 66, 38(2), without change of effect.

Polygamy. The right to grant matrimonial relief in respect of a polygamous marriage may be excluded in some cases on account of the operation of the Recognition of Divorces and Legal Separations Act 1971 (see *Quazi* v. *Quazi* [1980] A.C. 744, H.L.).

Poor law union. The Interpretation Act 1889, s. 16, has been repealed by the Interpretation Act 1978, s. 25(1), Sched. 3, without replacement.

Port. For customs and excise purposes a port is one specified by the Commissioners under the Customs and Excise Management Act 1979, s. 19 (Act of 1979, s. 1(1)). This definition is adopted by the Customs and Excise Duties (General Reliefs) Act 1979, s. 18(2), and the Hydrocarbon Oil Duties Act 1979, s. 27(3), for the purposes of those Acts.

Porter. The Customs and Excise Act 1952, s. 307(1), has been repealed and replaced by the Alcoholic Liquor Duties Act 1979, s. 1(3), without change of effect.

Portion. The Judicature Act 1925, s. 56, has been repealed and replaced by the Supreme Court Act 1981, s. 61(1), (3), Sched. 1, para. 1; although portions are no longer specifically mentioned in the list of court business allocated to the Chancery Divsion there is no doubt that the new provision makes no change in the law.

Possession. The Statutes of Forcible Entry 1381 to 1623, have been repealed and replaced by the Criminal Law Act 1977, ss. 1–5 (see FORCIBLE ENTRY).

The law of theft and presumptions based on possession of recently stolen property are now dealt with by the Theft Act 1968, s. 27(3), which enacts a statutory presumption against a person charged with handling stolen goods in certain circumstances.

The Limitation Act 1939, s. 10(4) (added by the Limitation Amendment Act 1980, s. 4), provided that a licence is not to be implied merely by operation of law so as to defeat a title based on adverse possession, but only if the facts justify finding such a licence. The Act of 1939, s. 10(4), has now been repealed and replaced by the Limitation Act 1980, Sched. 1, para. 8, without change of effect. See LIMITATION OF ACTIONS.

Possessory title. See also the Limitation Act 1939, s. 10(4) (added by the Limitation Amendment Act 1980, s. 4 and now consolidated into the Limitation Act 1980, Sched. 1, para. 8, without change of effect), which prevents a licence being implied in certain cases so as to defeat a title based on adverse possession, such a licence being required to be found as a matter of fact. See also LIMITATION OF ACTIONS.

Post Office. The telecommunications functions of the Post Office have been separated out into a private sector corporation (British Telecommunications Act 1981 and the Telecommunications Act 1984). The former monopoly on telecommunications (Post Office Act 1969, ss. 23–27) was originally transferred to British Telecommunications (Act of 1981, s. 12), but has now been abolished (Act of 1984, s. 2).

Post-mortem examination. For the (prospective) repeal of (parts of) the Human Tissue Act 1961 by the Anatomy Act 1984 see ANATOMY.

Posthumous child. The British Nationality Act 1948, s. 24, has been repealed and replaced by the British Nationality Act 1981, s. 48.

Poultry. The Diseases of Animals Act 1950, has been repealed and replaced by the Animal Health Act 1981. The scope of the 1967 Act has been extended (Animal Health and Welfare Act 1984, ss. 5–9).

Pound. For the reduction of "new penny" to "penny" see PENNY.

Pound-breach. The Highways Act 1959, s. 135, has been repealed and replaced by the Highways Act 1980, s. 155, without change of effect. For the revision of the penalties which may be imposed on summary conviction see FINE.

Power of attorney. The Powers of Attorney Act 1971, s. 2, has been repealed by the Supreme Court Act 1981, s. 152(4), Sched. 7; by virtue of s. 134 of the 1981 Act the separate file of powers filed before October 1971 is continued in being and may be examined.

Precept. Limitations on the issue of supplementary precepts were imposed by the Local Government Finance Act 1982, Part I (ss. 1–7), and similar provisions are contained in the Rates Act 1984.

Pre-emption. A solicitor's failure to register his client's right of pre-emption of a legal estate in land may amount to negligence, making him liable to his client both in tort and in contract (*Midland Bank Trust Co. Ltd.* v. *Hett, Stubbs & Kemp* [1979] Ch. 384).

Rights of pre-emption may also be conferred in respect of, for example, company shares (see the Companies Act 1980, ss. 17–18, which apply to both public and private companies).

Preferential payments. The sum allowed for preferential payments (Bankruptcy Act 1914, s. 33) was increased from £200 to £800 (Insolvency Act 1976, s. 1, Sched. 1, Part I).

Premium. The Rent Act 1968, ss. 85–92, have been repealed and replaced by the Rent Act 1977, ss. 119–126, without significant change of effect. Certain premiums are allowed to be taken in relation to long tenancies (Act of 1977, s. 127).

Prerogative of mercy. The Habeas Corpus Act 1679, s. 12, has been repealed by the Statute Law Revision Act 1948, s. 1,

Sched. 1.

Prerogative writs and orders. The procedure for the issue of these judicial instruments is contained in R.S.C. Ord. 53, (as substituted by S.I. 1977 No. 1955 and variously amended); see JUDICIAL REVIEW. The Administration of Justice (Miscellaneous Provisions) Act 1938, s. 7, has been repealed and replaced by the Supreme Court Act 1981, ss. 29, 30, which continue the Supreme Court's powers to issue orders in the nature of the abolished prerogative writs.

Presentee. The statute 1389, 13 Ric. 2, st. 1, c. 1 (Royal Presentations to Benefices), has been repealed by the Statute Law (Repeals) Act 1969, s. 1, Sched., Part II.

Preservatives in food. The Food and Drugs Act 1955, s. 4, has been repealed and replaced by the Food Act 1984, s. 4, without change of effect.

Press. It has been held that journalists have no privilege authorising them to conceal their sources of information and therefore may be required to divulge this information on discovery (*British Steel Corporation* v. *Granada Television* [1981] A.C. 1096, H.L.). The Contempt of Court Act 1981, s. 10, however, provides that no court may require any person to disclose the source of information contained in a publication for which he is responsible unless it (the court) is satisfied that disclosure is necessary in the interests of justice or national security or to prevent disorder or crime.

The intended "Charter on the Freedom of the Press" is no longer provided for by statute (Employment Act 1980, s. 19(*a*), repealing the Trade Union and Labour Relations Act 1974, s. 1A).

Presumption of gift. For a new presumption on this topic see WILL.

Presumption of life or death. The Administration of Justice Act 1970, s. 1, Sched. 1, has been repealed and replaced by the Supreme Court Act 1981, s. 61(1), (3), Sched. 1, para. 3, without change of effect.

Presumption of survivorship. The Finance Act 1958, s. 29 (as amended), was repealed and replaced by the Finance Act 1975, s. 22(9), in connection with the replacement of estate duty by capital transfer tax (*q.v.*) but otherwise without change of effect. The Act of 1975 has now itself been repealed and replaced by the Capital Transfer Tax Act 1984, ss. 4(2), 54(4); this modification of the ordinary rule helps to ensure the orderly succession of estates and the benefit of reliefs for rapidly succeeding deaths (see, *e.g.* the Act of 1984, s. 151, which deals with quick succession cases).

Previous conviction. The rule that a defendant in criminal proceedings looses his protection from being asked any question which tends to show that he is of bad character if he gives evidence against any other person charged with the same offence (*i.e.* the Criminal Evidence Act 1898, s. 1(f)(iii)), has been repealed and replaced so that the protection is withdrawn when the accused gives evidence against any other person charged in the same proceedings (Criminal Evidence Act 1898, s. 1(f)(iii), reversing the severe restriction imposed by the decision in *R.* v. *Hills* [1980] A.C. 26, H.L.).

The Magistrates' Courts Rules 1968, r. 56, has been revoked and replaced by the Magistrates' Courts Rules 1981 (S.I. 1981 No. 552), r. 68, without change of effect.

For the abolition of enhanced penalties on a second or subsequent conviction see FINE; for the amendment of appeals procedures when a probation order is made see PROBATION OF OFFENDERS.

Price control. Further provisions were enacted in the Price Commission Act 1977, and the Price Commission (Amendment) Act 1979, but the Price Commission has been abolished (Competition Act 1980).

Prices and Consumer Protection, Secretary of State for. The remaining functions of the Secretary of State for Prices and Consumer Protection have been transferred to the Secretary of State for Trade (Secretary of State for Trade Order 1979 (S.I. 1975 No. 578)). The Price Commission has been abolished (Competition Act 1980, s. 1, Sched. 1), and the associated statutory provisions have been repealed (Act of 1980, s. 33(4), Sched. 2).

Prime Minister. The salary of the Prime Minister is revised from time to time (see, *e.g.* S.I. 1979 No. 905). The Ministerial Salaries Consolidation Act 1965 and associated legislation were repealed and replaced by the Parliamentary and other Pensions Act 1972; the latter Act and the pension scheme established under it are subject to constant amendment, the latest being the

Parliamentary Pensions etc. Act 1984.

Priority notice. The period of protection afforded (under the Land Registration Act 1925, s. 11(5), (6)(*a*)) by an official search was increased in 1978 from 15 to 20 days (Land Registration (Official Searches) Rules 1978 (S.I. 1978 No. 1600)), and has been again extended (when the 1978 Rules were revoked and replaced) to 30 days (Land Registration (Official Searches) Rules 1981 (S.I. 1981 No. 1135)).

Priority neighbourhood. The Housing Act 1974, ss. 52–55, have been repealed by the Housing Act 1980, ss. 109, 152, Sched. 26.

Prisage. The Customs and Excise Act 1952 has been repealed and replaced (in this context) by the Alcoholic Liquor Duties Act 1979.

Private chattels scheme. The War Damage Act 1943 has been repealed without replacement by the Statute Law (Repeals) Act 1981, s. 1(1), Sched., Part XI.

Private company. The Companies Act 1948, s. 28, has been repealed by the Companies Act 1980, s. 88, Sched. 4. As a result of the revision of the classification of companies (Act of 1980, ss. 1–2), a private company can be categorised only as a company which is not a public company (s. 1(1)). The Act of 1948, ss. 48, 109, 130, were repealed by the Act of 1980, s. 130, in connection with the new public/private classification and organisation.

Private street. The Highways Act 1959, ss. 213, 37, 173–188, have been repealed and replaced by the Highways Act 1980, ss. 203, 34, 203–218, without change of effect. The Public Health Act 1961, ss. 43, 47, have been repealed and replaced by the Highways Act 1980, ss. 67, 230(7) and 338, respectively, without change of effect.

Prize court. The Judicature Act 1925, ss. 23, 56(3), have been repealed and replaced by the Supreme Court Act 1981, s. 27 and s. 61(1), (3), Sched. 1, para. 2(*c*), without change of effect. See also the Act of 1981, s. 62(2), which deals with the Admiralty Court (as part of the Queen's Bench Division) and allocates to it the High Court Admiralty jurisdiction and its jurisdiction as a prize court.

Prize fight. Indictable misdemeanours have vanished from English law; prize fighting is now dealt with as an assault (*q.v.*) of the kind appropriate to the conduct in question.

Probate. The jurisdiction of county courts was increased in 1977 so that they might deal with cases concerning estates up to £15,000 in value (County Courts Act 1959, s. 62, Administration of Justice Act 1977, s. 15(3)). A further increase to a limit of £30,000 was made in 1981 (County Courts Jurisdiction Order 1981 (S.I. 1981 No. 1123). The County Courts Act 1959, s. 62, has been repealed and replaced by the County Courts Act 1984, s. 32, without change of effect, the £30,000 limit being retained for the time being.

The Finance Act 1975 provisions in respect of capital transfer tax have been repealed and replaced by the Capital Transfer Tax Act 1984, without change of effect.

The Judicature Act 1925, s. 107, 108, have been repealed and replaced by the Supreme Court Act 1981, s. 104, without change of effect. The Administration of Justice Act 1970, s. 1, Sched. 1, has been repealed and replaced by the Act of 1981, s. 61(1), (3), Sched. 1, para. 3(*b*)(iv), without change of effect; contentious probate business was allocated to the Chancery Division by the Act of 1981, Sched. 1, para. 3(1)(*h*).

The Courts Act 1971, s. 26, has been repealed and replaced by the Supreme Court Act 1981, s. 89(1), without change of effect.

Probate. Divorce and Admiralty Division. The Administration of Justice Act 1970, s. 1, Sched. 1, has been repealed and replaced by the Supreme Court Act 1981, s. 61(1), (3), Sched. 1, without change of effect.

Probation of offenders. The distinction between probation hostels and probation homes has been abolished (Criminal Law Act 1977, s. 65(4), Sched. 12, Powers of Criminal Courts Act 1973, paras. 6–9).

The minimum period for a probation order has been reduced to six months (Probation Orders (Variation of Statutory Limits) Order 1978 (S.I. 1978 No. 474)).

The effect of the legislation which resulted in the decision in *R.* v. *Tucker* [1974] 1 W.L.R. 615, has been reversed by the Criminal Justice Act 1982, s. 66 (which amended the provisions in the Criminal Appeal Act 1968, s. 50, the Magistrates' Courts Act 1980, s. 108 and the Powers of Criminal Courts Act 1973, s. 11, Sched. 1).

Procedure. The Judicature Act 1925, has been repealed and generally replaced by the Supreme Court Act 1981, subject to various modifications. The associated "rule book" is the Rules of the Supreme Court (Revision) 1965 (S.I. 1965 No. 1776); the intervening years have seen massive amendments, which are all incorporated into the (now) triennial publication, *The Supreme Court Practice 1985.*

Procession. The Public Health Act 1961, s. 44, has been repealed and replaced by the Highways Act 1980, s. 287, without change of effect.

Procuration of women. The offence of conspiring to procure has been abolished and replaced by a statutory offence of consipiracy (*q.v.*) (Criminal Law Act 1977, s. 5(11)).

Profits tax. The Profits Tax Act 1949, has been repealed by the Finance Act 1958, s. 40(5), Sched. 9, Part II. The modern equivalent is corporation tax (*q.v.*).

Prohibition. A new code of procedure (R.S.C. Ord. 53) for an application for such an order was introduced by the Rules of the Supreme Court (Amendment No. 3) 1977 (S.I. 1977 No. 1955). The Administration of Justice (Miscellaneous Provisions) Act 1938, s. 7, has been repealed and replaced by the Supreme Court Act 1981, ss. 29, 30, which continue the Supreme Court's powers to issue orders in the nature of the abolished prerogative writs. The Courts Act 1971, s. 10(5), has been repealed and replaced by the Supreme Court Act 1981, s. 29(5), without change of effect.

No special provision is now made for applications (under the County Courts Act 1984, ss. 29, 30, replacing the County Courts Act 1959, ss. 116, 117) in respect of prohibition to a county court.

Proof. The Customs and Excise Act 1952, s. 172, has been repealed and replaced by the Alcoholic Liquor Duties Act 1979, ss. 2, 4(1), without change of effect.

Prospectus. The Companies Act 1948, s. 42, has been repealed by the Companies Act 1980, s. 88, Sched. 4; the Act of 1948, s. 41, has been modified by the Act of 1980, s. 80, Sched. 2; certain additional requirements (which also modify the Act of 1948, s. 45) are set out in the Act of 1980, ss. 15–16.

Prostitute. By express exception, the common law offence of conspiracy to corrupt public morals has escaped the general abolition of common law conspiracy (*q.v.*) (Criminal Law Act 1977, s. 5(3)(*a*)).

Protected shorthold. See SHORTHOLD.

Protected transactions. The Bankruptcy Act 1914, s. 40(2) (as substituted by the Charging Orders Act 1979, s. 4), provides that the making of a charging order (*q.v.*) under the Act of 1979, s. 1, is sufficient to amount to a completed act of execution for the purposes of the Act of 1914, thus reversing the effect of *Re Overseas Aviation Engineering* (*G.B.*) *Ltd.* [1963] Ch. 24.

Protection order. This term (or its equivalent, "personal protection order") is sometimes used to refer to orders made under the Matrimonial Proceedings and Magistrates' Courts Act 1978, ss. 16–18, as well as to matrimonial injunctions in the county court under the Domestic Violence and Matrimonial Proceedings Act 1976, s. 1.

The Summary Jurisdiction (Married Women) Act 1895, has been repealed and replaced by the Matrimonial Proceedings (Magistrates' Courts) Act 1960 (now itself repealed); see MATRIMONIAL PROCEEDINGS IN MAGISTRATES' COURTS.

Protective award. In certain cases involving dismissal for redundancy (see REDUNDANCY PAYMENTS), employers are required to enter into consultations with representatives of the appropriate trade union (Employment Protection Act 1975, s. 99), and to give notice to the Secretary of State (s. 100 (as amended by S.I. 1979 No. 958)). On non-compliance with the provisions relating to consultations, any appropriate trade union may present a complaint to an industrial tribunal (s. 101(1)); it is then incumbent on the employer to prove that there were special circumstances which rendered it impracticable for him to observe the s. 99 requirements, or that he took all such steps as were reasonably practicable in the circumstances (s. 101(2)). If the complaint is declared to be well-founded, the tribunal may make a protective award (s. 101(3)); this is an order that in respect of such descriptions of employee as may be specified (in the order), being employees who have been dismissed or whom it is proposed to dismiss and in respect of whose dismissal or proposed dismissal the employer has failed to observe the s. 99 requirements, the employer must pay remuneration for a specified period (s. 101(4)). The period for which the payments must continue is normally 30 days (s. 11(5) as amended by S.I. 1979 No. 958)). The amount of the remuneration to be paid is the subject of detailed provisions (s. 102). An employee may make a complaint to an industrial tribunal on his own account if his employer fails to pay him any amount due to him under a protective award (s. 103).

Protective trust. The Finance Act 1975, Sched. 5, para. 18, has been repealed and replaced by the Capital Transfer Tax Act 1984, s. 88, without change of effect.

Protest. The procedure for entering an appearance (*q.v.*) has been abolished (see S.I. 1979 No. 1716), but the new procedure (which involves sending to the court an acknowledgment of service and notice of intention to defend) contains special arrangements for those who wish to dispute the jurisdiction of the court in the proceedings (R.S.C. Ord. 12, rr. 7, 8 (as substituted by S.I. 1979 No. 1716)).

Proviso, Trial by. Applications by defendants for actions to be struck out for want of prosecution are now made under R.S.C. Ord. 18, r. 19.

Provocation. When considering a plea of provocation in a homicide case the jury is required to consider the effect of the alleged provocation on a person of the age, sex and characteristics of the accused, not merely their effect on a reasonable man (*R.* v. *Camplin* [1978] A.C. 708, H.L.).

Proxy. The Representation of the People Act 1949, ss. 12–15, 23–25, and the Representation of the People Act 1969, ss. 5, 6, and the Representation of the People (Armed Forces) Act 1976 have been repealed and replaced by the Representation of the People Act 1983, ss. 19–22, 32–34, without change of effect.

Psychopath. The Mental Health Act 1959, s. 4, has been repealed and replaced by the Mental Health Act 1983, s. 1(2), without change of effect.

Public accounts. The Public Accounts Commission has been established by the National Audit Act 1983, s. 2; this body has various duties in relation to the examination of public accounts, backing up the work of the National Audit Office (*q.v.*). See also COMPTROLLER; CONTROLLER.

Public analyst. The Food and Drugs Act 1955, s. 89, has been repealed and replaced by the Food Act 1984, s. 76, without change of effect.

Public body. The Race Relations Act 1968, s. 27(12), has been repealed and replaced by the Race Relations Act 1976, s. 75(5), which preserves the 1968 meaning of "public body" for pre-1976 rules. By s. 75 of the 1976 Act, the new law was applied to a number of carefully described persons; the equivalent to "public body" in the new Act is "statutory body" or "person holding a statutory office" (see s. 75(10)).

The Representation of the People Act 1949, s. 99, has been repealed and replaced by the Representation of the People Act 1983, s. 113, without change of effect.

Public document. For the position with regard to the production of documents by the Crown see PRIVILEGE.

Public health. The Control of Pollution Act 1974, contains extensive provisions which bear on the question of public health, as did the Rabies Act 1974; the Slaughterhouses Act 1974; the Biological Standards Act 1975; the Drought Act 1976; the Health Services Act 1976; the National Health Services (Vocational Training) Act 1976; the National Health Service Act 1977; the Medical Act 1978; the Refuse Disposal (Amenity) Act 1978; the Nurses, Midwives and Health Visitors Act 1979; the Public Health Laboratory Service Act 1979; the Vaccine Damage Payments Act 1979; several blocks of legislation have been consolidated into the Public Health (Control of Diseases) Act 1984. The impact of these Acts is considered under appropriate headings elsewhere in this work.

Public lending right. This right, conferred on authors by the Public Lending Right Act 1979, s. 1(1), carries with it an entitlement to receive payments from time to time in respect of such books as are lent out to the public by local library authorities (see LIBRARIES) in the United Kingdom (s. 1(2)). This is to be administered by the Registrar of Public Lending Right (s. 1(3), and Sched. (where the Registrar's duties and functions are detailed)). The Act provides for a central fund (s. 2) out of which payments are to be made, for the issue of a scheme (s. 3) for calculating how much is to be paid in respect of each publication and for the collection of appropriate information, as well as for the creation of a register which will record rights arising under the Act (s. 4). The Act is in force (S.I. 1980 No. 83) and the scheme has been both promulgated and amended (Public Lending Right Scheme 1982 (S.I. 1982 No. 719; the amendments are contained in S.I. 1983 Nos. 480 and 1688).

Public local inquiries. The Acquisition of Land (Authorisation Procedure) Act 1946, s. 5, has been repealed and replaced by the Acquisition of Land Act 1981, s. 5, without change of effect.

Public meeting. The penalty on summary conviction under the Public Meeting Act 1908, s. 1, was increased to a fine (*q.v.*) not exceeding £1,000 or six months' imprisonment or both (Criminal Law Act 1977, ss. 15, 30, Sched. 1, para. 3); the penalty on conviction on indictment remained the same. See also the Magistrates' Courts Act 1980, s. 17, Sched. 1, which replaced the 1977 provisions without change of effect.

The penalty on summary conviction under the Public Order Act 1936, s. 7, was increased to a fine (*q.v.*) not exceeding £500 or imprisonment not exceeding three months or both (Criminal Law Act 1977, s. 31, Sched. 6).

The Race Relations Act 1965, s. 6(1), has been repealed and replaced by the Public Order Act 1936, s. 5A (added by the Race Relations Act 1976, s. 70(2)), with certain amendments, but broadly similar to the 1965 legislation. The offence was made punishable on summary conviction by a fine (*q.v.*) not exceeding £400 or imprisonment not exceeding six months or both, and on conviction on indictment by a fine or imprisonment not exceeding two years or both (Act of 1936, s. 5A(5)). Prosecutions may be instituted only by or with the consent of the Attorney-General (s. 5A(5)).

The Highways Act 1959, s. 121, has been repealed and replaced by the Highways Act 1980, s. 137, without change of effect.

For the general revision of the penalties which might be imposed on summary convictions, see FINE.

Public mischief. The offence of conspiracy (*q.v.*) at common law has been abolished (Criminal Law Act 1977, s. 5(1)), and the matters comprised within the common law offence of conspiracy to effect a public mischief do not appear to come within the saving contained in the Act of 1977.

A conspiracy to indemnify a person of his bail is now the subject of the new statutory provisions relating to conspiracy and bail in criminal proceedings (see the Bail Act 1976, s. 9; and INDEMNITY; INDEMNIFICATION).

For the general revision of the penalties which might be imposed on summary convictions, see FINE.

Public morals. By express exception, the common law offence of conspiracy to corrupt public morals has escaped the general abolition of common law conspiracy (Criminal Law Act 1977, s. 5(3)(*a*)).

Public order. The Public Order Act 1936, has been widened in scope by the addition of s. 5A (by the Race Relations Act 1976, s. 70)), which deals with incitement to racial hatred (see PUBLIC MEETING).

Public service vehicle. The provisions governing the use of public service vehicles are excluded when the provisions of the Minibus Act 1977, are observed (see MINIBUS).

The Road Traffic Act 1960, Part III (ss. 117–163), and associated legislation, have been repealed and replaced by the Public Passenger Vehicles Act 1981, which is a consolidating Act.

Public sewer. The control of discharges into public sewers is also provided for by the Control of Pollution Act 1974, ss. 43–45.

Public Trustee. The fees chargeable by this officer are revised from time to time (see, *e.g.* the Public Trustee (Fees) Order 1977 (S.I. 1977 No. 508, as variously amended)).

The Public Trustee (Custodian Trustee) Rules 1984 (S.I. 1984 No. 109) enabled district health authorities to act as custodian trustees.

Public utility undertaking. The Trade Facilities Act 1924, s. 2, has been repealed by the Statute Law Revision Act 1963, s. 1, Sched. The War Damage (Public Utility Undertakings) Act 1949, Sched. 1, has been repealed without replacement by the Statute Law (Repeals) Act 1981, s. (1), Sched. 1, Part II.

Publication. For the purposes of patents applications under the Patents Act 1977, Part I (ss. 1–76), the rules formerly contained in the Patents Act 1949, s. 52, have been re-enacted (with no substantial alteration) in the Act of 1977, s. 6. Applications for patents must be published in the prescribed manner (Patents Act 1977, s. 16), as must the grant of a patent (s. 2).

Puffer. The Sale of Goods Act 1893, s. 58, has been repealed and replaced by the Sale of Goods Act 1979, s. 57, without change of effect.

Puis darrein continuance. R.S.C. Ord. 18, r. 9, permits any matter to be pleaded, whenever it arose, provided the pleading conforms to Ord. 18, r. 7(1) (which restricts pleadings to matters of fact), r. 10 (which prohibits departures (*q.v.*)), and r. 15(2) (which prohibits the introduction of a new cause of action by the statement of claim).

Puisne. The Judicature Act 1925, s. 2(4), has been repealed and replaced by the Supreme Court Act 1981, s. 4(2), without change of effect.

Punishment. For further information about punishment see also AMERCIAMENT OR AMERCIAMENT; AMERCE; COMMUNITY SERVICE ORDER; COMPENSATION ORDER; CONDITIONAL DISCHARGE; DEFERMENT OF SENTENCE; DISQUALIFIED; FINE; SUSPENDED SENTENCE; YOUTH CUSTODY.

Purchase notices. The Town and Country Planning General Regulations 1969 (S.I. 1969 No. 286), were revoked and replaced by the Town and Country Planning General Regulations 1974 (S.I. 1974 No. 596), which have in turn been revoked and replaced by the Town and Country Planning General Regulations 1976 (S.I. 1976 No. 1419). See also DEVELOPMENT.

Pyx. At the trial of the pyx, the Queen's Remembrancer has a discretion about whether the whole or only part of the verdict of the jury should be read out in his presence (see the Trial of the Pyx Order 1975 (S.I. 1975 No. 2192) (as amended by S.I. 1978 No. 185)).

Q

Quality or fitness. The Sale of Goods Act 1893, s. 14 (as amended), has been repealed and replaced by the Sale of Goods Act 1979, s. 14, without change of effect.

The same implied terms as in the Act of 1979 about quality or fitness have been applied to contracts for the transfer of property in goods and contracts for the hire of goods (Supply of Goods and Services Act 1982, ss. 4, 9).

Quarantine, Quarentine, Quarenteine. The Importation of Dogs and Cats Order 1928 (S.R. & O. 1928 No. 922 (as variously amended)), has been revoked and replaced by the Rabies (Importation of Dogs, Cats and other Mammals) Order 1974 (S.I. 1974 No. 2211 (as amended by S.I. 1977 No. 361)).

The Diseases of Animals Act 1950, has been repealed and replaced by the Animal Health Act 1981 (which also repealed and replaced the Rabies Act 1974), without change of effect; the general powers to regulate the movement of animals now appear in ss. 10, 24, Sched. 2, para. 2.

The provisions relating to port health authorities are now consolidated into the Public Health (Control of Diseases) Act 1984, ss. 1–4, 77, Scheds. 1, 2.

Quarries. The Mines and Quarries Act 1954, ss. 104, 106, 114, have been repealed by the Mines and Quarries Acts 1954 to 1971 (Modifications and Repeals) Regulations 1974, (S.I. 1974 No. 2013); the Act of 1954, ss. 116–122, 129, 138, 142, 144, 145, have been repealed by the Notification of Accidents and Dangerous Occurrences Regulations 1980 (S.I. 1980 No. 804); s. 146 was repealed by the Mines and Quarries Acts 1954 to 1971 (Modifications and Repeals) Regulations 1975 (S.I. 1975 No. 1102); and s. 167 was repealed by the Criminal Justice Act 1972, s. 64(2), Sched. 6, Part II. The provision of safety measures and regulation of working procedures is now dealt with by instruments issued (like the repealing instruments) under the Health and Safety at Work, etc., Act 1974.

Queen. The statutory provision conferring power to appoint judges (Judicature Act 1925, s. 11) has been repealed and replaced by the Supreme Court Act 1981, s. 10, without change of effect.

Queen's Bench Division. The Judicature Act 1925, s. 56(2), has been repealed and replaced by the Supreme Court Act 1981, s. 61(1), (3), Sched. 1, para. 2, without change of effect.

Queen's Coroner and Attorney. The Courts Act 1971, s. 26, has been repealed and replaced by the Supreme Court Act 1981, s. 89(1), without change of effect, and the Judicature Act 1925, s. 106(2), has been repealed and replaced by the Supreme Court Act 1981, s. 89(2), without change of effect.

Queen's Remembrancer. The Judicature Act 1925, s. 122 and the Courts Act 1971, s. 26(3), have been repealed and replaced by the Supreme Court Act 1981, s. 89(3)(*a*), (4), without change of effect.

Queen's warehouses. This term is defined in the Customs and Excise Management Act 1979, s. 1(1); see also ss. 38(4), 40.

Questions of fact. The Common Law Procedure Act 1852, s. 42, has been repealed. The modern equivalent is the trial of a question of fact under R.S.C. Ord. 33, r. 3; when this procedure is adopted the court may give directions as to the manner in which the question or issue is to be stated.

Questions of law. The use of the procedure under R.S.C. Ord. 33, r. 3 (or the county court equivalent), without a preliminary finding of the facts of the case has been deprecated as tending to increase the costs of litigation without justification (see *Tilling* v. *Whiteman* [1980] A.C. 1, H.L.).

Quit rent. The Law of Property Act 1925, s. 191, has been repealed by the Rentcharges Act 1977, s. 17(2), Sched. 1, in connection with the abolition of rentcharges (see RENT).

Quo warranto. Injunctions in the nature of quo warranto proceedings are now brought under the general provisions relating to applications for judicial review (*q.v.*); see R.S.C. Ord. 53, r. 1(1)(*b*). A claim for damages may be included in the claim for the order (R.S.C. Ord. 53, r. 7). The Administration of Justice (Miscellaneous Provisions) Act 1938, s. 7, has been repealed and replaced by the Supreme Court Act 1981, ss. 29, 30, which continue the Supreme Court's powers to issue orders in the nature of the abolished prerogative writs.

The decision in *Re a Solicitor* [1903] 2 K.B. 205, is unlikely to be followed in modern practice, especially after the decision in *Bevan* v. *Hastings Jones* [1978] 1 W.L.R. 294, where it was held that a litigant in person might move for an order of committal.

The Representation of the People Act 1949, s. 112, has been repealed and replaced by the Representation of the People Act 1983, s. 127, without change of effect.

Quota. The Militia Act 1882, s. 37, was repealed by the Territorial Army and Militia Act 1921, s. 4(1), Sched. 2, and the entire 1882 Act was repealed by the Reserve Forces Act 1980, s. 157(1)(*b*), Sched. 10, Part II. The Land Tax Act 1797, was repealed (with the exclusion of ss. 30, 31) by the Finance Act 1963, s. 73(8)(*b*), Sched. 14, Part VI.

R

Rabbits. The offence under the Night Poaching Act 1829, s. 1, is now triable only summarily (Criminal Law Act 1977, ss. 15, 30, Sched. 1); the maximum penalty was increased to £200 in 1977; for the general revision of the levels of fines conducted in 1982 see FINE.

Rabies. This is a notifiable disease within the Public Health (Infectious Diseases) Regulations 1968 (S.I. 1968 No. 1366, amended by S.I. 1976 No. 1226). The Rabies Act 1974, has been repealed and replaced by the Animal Health Act 1981, ss. 17 *et seq.*, without change of effect. Powers of search and arrest are conferred on inspectors and constables (Act of 1981, ss. 61–63).

Racial relations. The Race Relations Acts 1965 and 1968, have been repealed and replaced by the Race Relations Act 1976, without significant change of effect. The decision in *Dockers' Labour Club and Institute* v. *Race Relations Board* [1976] A.C. 285, H.L., has been reversed by the Act of 1976, ss. 20, 25, which prohibit discrimination in the provision of goods, facilities and services.

See also the Race Relations Code of Practice Order 1984 (S.I. 1984 No. 1081).

Rack-rent. The Highways Act 1959, s. 295, has been repealed and replaced by the Highways Act 1980, s. 329(1), without change of effect.

Rag dealer. The Public Health Act 1936, s. 52, has been repealed and replaced by the Public Health (Control of Diseases) Act 1984, s. 55, without change of effect.

Railway. The Transport Act 1968, ss. 1–8, have been substantially repealed and the National Freight Corporation (*q.v.*) has been abolished.

Rape. The decision in *D.P.P.* v. *Morgan* [1976] A.C. 182, H.L., caused substantial public controversy and led to the enactment of the Sexual Offences (Amendment) Act 1976. The mens rea of the offence of rape is defined in s. 1, which effectively adopts the decision of the House of Lords, confirming that the test to be applied is purely subjective. The Act of 1976 also imposes restrictions on the introduction of evidence of any previous sexual experience of the complainant with a person other than the defendant (ss. 2, 3), effectively abrogating the rule in *R.* v. *Bashir* [1969] 1 W.L.R. 1303. The anonymity of complainants and defendants in proceedings relating to "rape offences" (defined in s. 7(2)) is the subject of elaborately complex provisions in ss. 4–6, which attach criminal penalties to contravention of their terms. Guidance on the proper direction to be given about recklessness in rape cases was given in *R.* v. *Satnam*; *R.* v. *Kewal* (1984) 78 Cr.App.R. 149, C.A.

The Sexual Offences Act 1956, s. 44, provides that when it is necessary to prove any form of intercourse it is not necessary to prove the completion of intercourse by the emission of seed, intercourse being deemed complete upon proof of penetration only.

Rate. The Rating Act 1966, s. 9, the General Rate Act 1967, Sched. 9, and the Rate Rebate Act 1973, have been repealed and replaced by the Local Government Act 1974, ss. 11 *et seq.* which establish a new and more complex rate rebate system than was formerly operated. Local schemes may be drawn up (s. 12) provided they conform at least to the standards of the statutory scheme (s. 11). Special provisions govern the rating of hereditaments occupied by disabled people and the grant of rebates for institutions for the disabled (Rating (Disabled Persons) Act 1978, ss. 1–2).

Further amendments to the main rating "system" have been made by the Local Government, Planning and Land Act 1980, Part V (ss. 28–47) and Part VI (ss. 48–68); the latter group concern the introduction of a new system of rate support grant. Central government control of rating decisions of local authorities, commonly called "rate capping" have been increased (see the Local Government Finance Act 1982, Parts I and II (ss. 1–7, 8–10), and the Rates Act 1984).

See also VALUATION LIST.

Rate of exchange. *Di Fernando* v. *Smits* [1920] 3 K.B. 409, was based on the abrogated rule that judgments must be in sterling (see FOREIGN CURRENCY), and has been overruled by the House of Lords (*The Despina R* [1979] A.C. 685). The modern rules therefore appear to require the court to determine the currency of the contract and to award damages in that currency, any conversion to sterling for the purposes of enforcing the judgment being conducted at the commencement of the enforcement proceedings (see *Practice Direction* [1976] 1 W.L.R. 81, paras. 4, 5, 9, 11–13).

Rattening. This offence is no longer triable on indictment (Criminal Law Act 1977, s. 65(5), Sched. 13).

Reasonable time. The Sale of Goods Act 1893, ss. 11(2), 18(4), 29(4), 35, 37, 56, have been repealed and replaced by the Sale of Goods Act 1979, ss. 11(1), (5), 18(4), 29(5), 35, 37, 59, without change of effect.

Provisions comparable to those of the 1979 Act have been applied to contracts for the supply of services (Supply of Goods and Services Act 1982, s. 14).

Reasonableness test. Introduced by the Unfair Contract Terms Act 1977, s. 11, this test is also applied in certain cases of misrepresentation (*q.v.*); see UNFAIR CONTRACT TERMS.

The same reasonableness test is, in effect, applied to exclusion clauses in contracts for the transfer of property in goods or for the hire of goods (Supply of Goods and Services Act 1982, s. 11) or for the supply of services (Act of 1982, s. 16).

Receipt. The offence under the Forgery Act 1913, s. 4, was made triable either way in 1977 (Criminal Law Act 1977, s. 16, Sched. 3, para. 15).

The entire Forgery Act 1913, has been repealed by the Forgery and Counterfeiting Act 1981, s. 30, Sched., Part I. The general provisions of the Act of 1981 cover the offences for which specific provision was made under the Act of 1913.

Receiver. The Judicature Act 1925, s. 45, has been repealed and replaced by the Supreme Court Act 1981, s. 37, without change of effect.

Reckless cycling; reckless driving. See BICYCLES and DANGEROUS DRIVING.

Recognizance. The Magistrates' Courts Act 1952, s. 97 (which provided for the arrest of a person who failed to surrender to bail before a magistrates' court), was repealed and replaced by the Bail Act 1976, s. 7, with modifications to take account of the new scheme for bail in criminal proceedings (*q.v.*) introduced by the 1976 Act. No recognizance for his surrender to bail may now be taken from a person who has been granted bail (s. 3(2)); the duty to surrender to bail (s. 3(1)) and the offence of absconding (s. 6) have displaced recognizances by defendants.

The Courts Act 1971, s. 13(1), (5), has been repealed and replaced by the Supreme Court Act 1981, ss. 80, 81, subject to the amendments made in 1976.

Proceedings to recover the sum (if any) certified on a recognizance have been determined to be civil in nature (*R.* v. *Marlow Justices, ex p. O'Sullivan* [1984] Q.B. 381, D.C.).

Record. The procedure on setting down for trial an action begun by writ is contained in R.S.C. Ord. 34; the time for taking this step is prescribed by r. 2, and the sets of documents required to be deposited (one set for the use of the judge) are detailed in r. 3.

The former R.S.C. Ord. 36, r. 30, has been revoked without replacement.

Record and writ clerks. The Supreme Court of Judicature (Consolidation) Act 1925, s. 106, was repealed and (in effect) replaced by the Courts Act 1971, ss. 26, 27. The Act of 1971, s. 26, has now been repealed and replaced by the Supreme Court Act 1981, s. 96, without significant change of effect.

Recorder. The *Practice Direction* [1972] 1 W.L.R. 117, has been revoked and replaced (in due course) by the *Practice Direction* [1982] 1 W.L.R. 101, without change of effect.

A recorder of three years' standing is eligible for appointment as a circuit judge (see CROWN COURT) (Courts Act 1971, s. 16(3); Administration of Justice Act 1977, s. 12).

The Courts Act 1971 provisions cited have been variously repealed and replaced by the Supreme Court Act 1981, ss. 8–9, without significant change of effect.

Recovery. The jurisdiction of county courts has been increased so that they may now hear actions for the recovery of land where the net annual value for rating does not exceed the county court limit (currently £1,000) (County Courts Act 1984, s. 21, replacing the (repealed) County Courts Act 1959, s. 48, and the Administration of Justice Act 1973, s. 6, Sched. 2, Part I).

The Judicature Act 1925, s. 56(1), has been repealed and replaced by the Supreme Court Act 1981, s. 61(1), (3), Sched. 1, para. 1. The County Courts Act 1959, s. 52, has been repealed and replaced by the County Courts Act 1974, s. 23(*d*), without change of effect.

Rectification; Rectify. The jurisdiction of county courts was increased so that they might hear actions where rectification is sought provided the relief sought did not exceed £15,000 in value (County Courts Act 1959, s. 52(1)(*d*); County Courts Jurisdiction Order 1977 (S.I. 1977 No. 600)); the monetary limit was further increased to £30,000 in 1981 (County Courts Jurisdiction Order 1981 (S.I. 1981 No. 1123)).

The County Courts Act 1959, s. 52, has been repealed and replaced by the County Courts Act 1984, s. 23, without change of effect.

The rectification of wills is now permissible in the event of reliable extraneous evidence of the real intention being available; this permits the correction of clerical errors and discrepancies which show a patent failure to understand the instructions of the testator (Administration of Justice

Act 1982, s. 20). In the absence of leave of the court, any application for such a rectification must be made within six months of the first grant of any form of general representation to the estate of the deceased testator (s. 20(2)), and personal representatives are protected against liability if they have properly distributed assets before the application for rectification is commenced (s. 20(3)). It is possible to recover property distributed before a rectification (s. 20(3)). Ancillary provision has been made for the interpretation of wills and the general rules of evidence (Act of 1982, s. 21).

Rectory. The Ecclesiastical Commissioners Act 1840, s. 71, has been repealed by the Pastoral Measure 1968, s. 95, Sched. 9, and again by the Statute Law (Repeals) Act 1974, s. 1, Sched., Part VII.

Redeemable preference shares. The Companies Act 1949, s. 58, has been repealed and replaced by the Companies Act 1981, ss. 54–58, in modified form. Part II (ss. 36–62) of the 1981 Act allows wider exceptions to the (continued) ban on financial assistance from a company for the purchase of its own shares and allows the issue of redeemable equity shares as well as redeemable preference shares.

Reduction of contracts. When an insurance company has been proved to be unable to pay its debts, the court may (if it thinks fit) reduce the company's contracts on such terms and conditions as it thinks just instead of making a winding-up order (Insurance Companies Act 1982, s. 58, replacing the Insurance Companies Act 1974, s. 50); for an example, see *In re Capital Annuities Ltd.* [1979] 1 W.L.R. 170.

Redundancy payments. The Redundancy Payments Act 1965, ss. 1–26, have been repealed and replaced by the Employment Protection (Consolidation) Act 1978, Part VI (ss. 81–120), without significant change of effect. The 60- and 90-day periods mentioned in the Act of 1978, ss. 99–101, have been reduced to 30 days (Employment Protection (Handling of Redundancies) Variation Order 1979 (S.I. 1979 No. 958)). The Redundancy Rebates Act 1969, has been repealed by the Employment Protection (Consolidation) Act 1978, s. 159(3), Sched. 17. Rebates are dealt with in s. 104 of the 1978 Act together with the Redundancy Rebates Act 1977.

Failure to observe certain requirements of the Employment Protection (Consolidation) Act 1978, ss. 99–107, may result in the making of a protective award (*q.v.*). See also the Redundancy Rebates Regulations 1984 (S.I. 1984 No. 1066).

Redundant churches. Under the Act of 1969, the limit on grants for the period 1984–1989 has been set at £4,800,000 (Grants to Redundant Churches Fund Order 1984 (S.I. 1984 No. 203)).

The Pastoral Measure 1968 provisions have been repealed and replaced by the Pastoral Measure 1983, Part III (ss. 41–66), without change of effect.

Re-engagement. In employment law one of the remedies available in the event of an industrial tribunal finding a claim of unfair dismissal well-founded is an order for re-engagement; this requires the employer to take the employee back, but differs from re-instatement (*q.v.*) because the employee may be allocated to a different job from the one from which he was unfairly dismissed, provided the new job is comparable to the old one or is otherwise suitable (Employment Protection (Consolidation) Act 1978, s. 69(4)). The tribunal has a discretion about what award should be made in respect of lost benefits in the period between the unfair dismissal and the re-engagement. An order for re-engagement is secondary to an order for re-instatement and may be considered only after such an order has been rejected as unsuitable or impossible or if the employee states that he does not seek re-instatement (s. 69(5)). Failure to comply with an order for re-engagement leaves the employer open to a claim for compensation of unfair dismissal together with an additional compensatory award (ss. 71, 74, 75). See also UNFAIR DISMISSAL.

Re-exchange. The Bills of Exchange Act 1882, s. 57(2), has been repealed by the Administration of Justice Act 1977, ss. 4, 32, Sched. 5, Part I, in connection with the change in the law which permits the use of foreign currency (*q.v.*) in legal proceedings when that is justified.

Reform Acts. The Representation of the People Act 1949, has been repealed and replaced by the Representation of the People Act 1983, incorporating the various amendments made but otherwise without change of effect.

Referendum. This device was also provided for in the Scotland Act 1978, s. 85, and the Wales Act 1978, s. 80; both Acts, however, were repealed before even coming into operation (see DEVOLUTION).

Refresher. R.S.C. Ord. 62, App. 2, Part X, has been renumbered Part VII by the Rules of the Supreme Court (Amendment) 1979 (S.I. 1979 No. 35), r. 4(3).

Refreshment houses. The decision in *Ray* v. *Sempers* [1973] 1 W.L.R. 317, was reversed by the House of Lords (see *D.P.P.* v. *Ray* [1974] A.C. 370), but the behaviour in question is now dealt with by the Theft Act 1978, s. 3, which makes it an offence to make off without payment (see DECEPTION).

Additional powers of control of these establishments have been conferred on local authorities (Local Government (Miscellaneous Provisions) Act 1982, ss. 4–7).

Refuse disposal. The Civic Amenities Act 1967, ss. 18–23, and the related legislation, have been repealed and replaced by the Refuse Disposal (Amenities) Act 1978, without significant change of effect. The Public Health Act 1961, s. 34, and related legislation, remained unaffected.

Regional health authority. Part of the national health service (*q.v.*), regional health authorities may be established under the National Health Service Act 1977, ss. 8, 12, Sched. 5 (which repeats the terms of earlier legislation), with special power to delegate functions (s. 14) to other health authorities.

Register of directors and secretaries. The duty under the Companies Act 1948, s. 200, has been extended by the Companies Act 1981, s. 95, to include past directorships.

Registered Homes Tribunal. Consisting of a chairman (who must be a member of the legal panel appointed by the Lord Chancellor: Registered Homes Act 1984, s. 41(2)), and two other members (s. 41(1)) who are members of the experts panel appointed by the Lord President of the Council (s. 41(3)), the Tribunal deals with appeals relating to the registration of children's homes, residential care homes, nursing homes and mental nursing homes (Registered Homes Act 1984, Part III (ss. 39–44)). See also NURSING HOMES.

Registerd office. The Companies Act 1948, s. 107, has been repealed and replaced by the Companies Act 1976, s. 23; the difference between the provisions centres on the requirement of the 1976 Act that there be a registered office "at all times," whereas under the 1948 Act the registered office was essential from the commencement of business or from the fourteenth day after incorporation.

Registrar or **Registrary.** The Chancery registrars have been abolished; see CHANCERY. The County Courts Act 1959, s. 18, has been repealed and replaced by the County Courts Act 1984, s. 6, without change of effect.

Registration of births. The Merchant Shipping Act 1894, s. 245, has been repealed and replaced by the Merchant Shipping Act 1970, s. 72 (modified by the Merchant Shipping Act 1979, s. 30), under which (for example) the Merchant Shipping (Returns of Births and Deaths) Regulations 1972 (S.I. 1972 No. 1523), have been made (see also S.I. 1979 No. 1577).

The Forgery Act 1913, s. 3(2), has been repealed by the Forgery and Counterfeiting Act 1981, s. 30, Sched., Part I, the general provisions of the 1981 Act covering the ground of the former specific provision. See, however, the Act of 1981, s. 5(5)(*l*).

Registration of burials. The Burial Act 1853, s. 8, has been repealed by the Local Government Act 1972, s. 272, Sched. 30. The Burial Act 1900, has been repealed by the Statute Law (Repeals) Act 1978, s. 1(1), Sched. 1, Part XVII. Earlier provisions relating to registers and records have been consolidated into the Parochial Registers and Records Measure 1978 (see especially ss. 1, 3–6).

The Forgery Act 1913, s. 3(2), has been repealed by the Forgery and Counterfeiting Act 1981, s. 30, Sched., Part I, the general provisions of the 1981 Act covering the ground of the former specific provision. See, however, the Act of 1981, s. 5(5)(*l*).

Registration of deaths. The Merchant Shipping Act 1894, s. 245, has been repealed and replaced by the Merchant Shipping Act 1970, s. 72 (modified by the Merchant Shipping Act 1979, s. 30), under which (for example) the Merchant Shipping (Returns of Births and Deaths) Regulations 1972 (S.I. 1972 No. 1523), have been made (see also S.I. 1979 No. 1577).

The Forgery Act 1913, s. 3(2), has been repealed by the Forgery and Counterfeiting

Act 1981, s. 30, Sched., Part I, the general provisions of the 1981 Act covering the ground of the former specific provision. See, however, the Act of 1981, s. 5(5)(*l*).

Registration of electors. The Representation of the People Act 1949, s. 17, has been repealed and replaced by the Representation of the People Act 1983, s. 9, without change of effect.

Registration of marriages. The Parochial Registers Act 1812, has been repealed by the Parochial Registers and Records Measure 1978, s. 26(1), Sched. 3. Special provision is made in respect of marriage registers in the Measure of 1978 (s. 22). The Merchant Shipping Act 1894, ss. 240, 253, have been repealed and replaced by the Merchant Shipping Act 1970, ss. 68, 69, and the regulations made thereunder.

The Forgery Act 1913, s. 3(2), has been repealed by the Forgery and Counterfeiting Act 1981, s. 30, Sched., Part I, the general provisions of the 1981 Act covering the ground of the former specific provision. See, however, the Act of 1981, s. 5(5)(*l*).

Registration of title to land. For the further extension of the compulsory registration areas (Land Registration Act 1925, s. 120) see the Registration of Title Order 1975 (S.I. 1975 No. 150); the Registration of Title Order 1976 (S.I. 1976 No. 1782); and the Registration of Title Order 1977 (S.I. 1977 No. 828).

Power has been given for the register to be kept in non-documentary (*i.e.* computerised) form, a duty to provide a conversion into readable form being imposed (Land Registration Act 1925 ss. 1, 113A, as respectively substituted and added by the Administration of Justice Act 1982, s. 66). The rights of inspection of the register have been restated (Act of 1925, s. 113, as substituted by the Act of 1982, s. 67, Sched. 5).

For the extension of the priority period for searches see PRIORITY NOTICE.

Registry of ships. The Merchant Shipping Act 1894, s. 3(1), has been modified to exclude from registration those ships which do not exceed 13.7 metres in length (Merchant Shipping Act 1983, s. 4). See also TONNAGE.

Regulation. This term is also used in connection with European Communities law, where it means a legislative instrument of the Council; the EEC Treaty, Art. 189, provides that "A regulation shall have general application. It shall be binding in its entirety and directly applicable in all Member States." As a result, their terms become "law" in the Member States without further legislation being required, so that the effect of a regulation may be to pre-empt national legislative competence in certain cases.

Re-instatement. In employment law one of the remedies available in the event of an industrial tribunal finding a claim of unfair dismissal proved against an employer is re-instatement. This requires the employer to treat the employee as if he had never been dismissed, thus restoring all pension, pay, holiday and seniority rights, and arrears of pay must be made up to the employee (Employment Protection (Consolidation) Act 1978, s. 69(2)). Improvements in conditions of service which were introduced in the period between unfair dismissal and re-instatement must also be granted to the re-instated employee (s. 69(3)). It is only after the tribunal has decided that re-instatement is not the proper remedy that an order for re-engagement (*q.v.*) may be considered (s. 69(5)), unless the employee has indicated that he does not seek re-instatement (ss. 68(1), 69(5)). Failure to comply with the order leaves the employer open to a claim for compensation for unfair dismissal and a compensatory award (ss. 71, 74, 75). See also UNFAIR DISMISSAL.

Relator. For the procedural requirements for relator cases see R.S.C. Ord. 15, r. 11.

Relief. The Representation of the People Act 1949, s. 145 (as amended in 1969), has been repealed and replaced by the Representation of the People Act 1983, s. 167, without change of effect.

Remand. There are restrictions on the periods for which a defendant may be remanded (Magistrates' Courts Act 1980, ss. 10(3), 128, replacing the repealed Magistrates' Courts Act 1952, ss. 14(3), 105 (as modified by the Criminal Law Act 1977, s. 42)). Remand hearings may be transferred to any convenient court in certain cases (Act of 1980, s. 130, replacing the Criminal Law Act 1977, s. 41), though in practice this is only rarely done.

The Criminal Justice Act 1982, s. 59, Sched. 9, amended the Act of 1980 so as to allow a defendant remanded in custody to be further remanded in custody in his absence (provided he agrees), subject to a maximum (in effect) of four weeks between appearances in court.

Remand centres; remand homes. The Children and Young Persons Act 1969, ss. 35–45, have been repealed and replaced by the Child Care Act 1980, ss. 31–42; the Act of 1969, ss. 47–50, have been repealed and replaced by the Child Care Act 1980, ss. 43, 44, 72 (there being no need for a replacement of the former s. 49); the Act of 1969, s. 51, has been repealed and replaced by the Foster Children Act 1980, s. 3; the Act of 1969, ss. 53–59, have been repealed and replaced by the Foster Children Act 1980, ss. 1–11; and the Act of 1969, ss. 58, 59, have been repealed and replaced by the Child Care Act 1980, ss. 74, 75; all these alterations have been effected without significant change of effect.

Remedy. The revised text of the Coinage Act 1971, s. 1 (introduced by the Currency Act 1983, s. 1) and the amendments made to the Act of 1971, s. 3, neither affect nor discontinue the use of the term "remedy."

Remembrancer. The system of appointment as Senior Master also conferring the status and duties of Queen's Remembrancer has been continued by the Supreme Court Act 1981, s. 89(4).

Remit; Remission. When the House of Lords reverses or varies a decision of the Court of Appeal (or of the High Court or a Divisional Court in a "leap-frog" case (*q.v.*)) or orders any step to be taken by the court below, the order of the House is required to be made an order of the High Court under the procedure set out in R.S.C. Ord. 32, r. 10.

Remitted action. The jurisdiction of the county courts in many matters was increased to include cases involving up to £2,000 in value instead of only £750 (see the County Courts Jurisdiction Order 1977 (S.I. 1977 No. 600)); the limits of jurisdiction were again raised in 1981, the new general limit being £5,000 (County Courts Jurisdiction Order 1981 (S.I. 1981 No. 1123). The powers of the High Court to remit cases to the county court may now be exercised only when the value of the subject matter in issue is within the new county court limit. The use of the provisions is now more commonly called "transfer" (see the County Courts Act 1984, ss. 40–45, replacing the County Courts Act 1959, ss. 75A–75D, 68).

Removal. The County Courts Act 1959, has been repealed and replaced by the County Courts Act 1984, without significant change of effect; see REMITTED ACTION and TRANSFER.

Renewal of writs. Writs of execution may be renewed (R.S.C. Ord. 46, r. 8), but the issue of a new writ is the usual course except in cases where the priority of the writ is especially significant.

Rent. The creation of rentcharges whether at law or in equity is now prohibited (Rentcharges Act 1977, s. 2(1)) subject to exceptions (s. 2(3)). The extinguishment of existing rentcharges over a period of 60 years has been provided for (s. 3), together with procedures for apportionment (ss. 4–7) and redemption (ss. 8–10). In the Act of 1977, "rentcharge" means any annual or other periodic sum charged on or issuing out of land except (a) rent reserved by a lease of tenancy, and (b) any sum payable by way of interest (s. 1). The Act came into operation on 1 February 1978 (S.I. 1978 No. 15); purported creations of rentcharges since then are void (s. 2(2)) unless they come within special statutory exceptions. The Law of Property Act 1925, s. 191, has been repealed (s. 17(2), Sched. 2).

Rent restriction. The Rent Act 1968, together with a number of other statutes bearing on this topic, has been repealed and consolidated into the Rent Act 1977, and the Protection from Eviction Act 1977; the new statutes contain certain amendments to the law, most of which are of a purely technical nature. Significant omissions from the consolidating Acts are: Landlord and Tenant Act 1962; the Rent (Agriculture) Act 1976; the Housing (Homeless Persons) Act 1977; and the Criminal Law Act 1977, ss. 6–13.

The Matrimonial Homes Act 1967, s. 7, has been repealed and replaced by the Matrimonial Homes Act 1983, s. 7, Sched. 1, without significant change of effect.

Repeal. The Interpretation Act 1889, ss. 11, 38, have been repealed and replaced by the Interpretation Act 1978, ss. 15, 17(1) and 16(1), 17(2), without change of effect.

The increased use of delayed commencement provisions can have curious and tortuous results, especially where repeals are involved. The Pastoral Measure 1983 (1983 No. 1), Sched. 9, repealed the Church of England (Miscellaneous Provisions) Measure 1983 (1983 No. 2), s. 11; logically speaking this was an impossibility, since (when passed) there was nothing for the No. 1 Measure to repeal. The Pastoral Measure 1983 came into operation, however, immediately the Pastoral (Amendment) Measure 1982, was fully in force (see 1983, s. 94(4)); the 1982 Measure was brought fully into operation by instrument under the hands of the Archbishops (*not* a statutory instrument) on 31 July 1983, the commencement date being 1 November 1983—after the passing of the 1983 Measure No. 2 (on 9 May 1983). Therefore the Pastoral Measure 1983, though passed before another one in 1983, was able to repeal some of the other's provisions.

Replevin. Analogous rights and procedures have been established by statutes in connection with the abolition of detinue (Torts (Interference with Goods) Act 1977).

The County Courts Act 1959, ss. 104–106, have been repealed and replaced by the County Courts Act 1984, s. 144, Sched. 1, without change of effect. The £20 limit has remained unchanged in the 1984 re-enactment.

Report. References for inquiries and reports by referees and masters are conducted under R.S.C. Ord. 36; comparable facilities exist in county courts, where the registrar normally takes the matter (C.C.R. 1981 Ord. 19, rr. 7–10, replacing C.C.R. 1936, Ord. 19, r. 2).

Report, Law. The use of computerised databases has resulted in cautions being issued against the abuse of precedents which do not appear in the main series of reports (*Roberts Petroleum Ltd.* v. *Bernard Kenny Ltd.* [1983] 2 A.C. 192, H.L.).

Representation. For the effect of misrepresentation in contractual situations see MISREPRESENTATION; see also UNFAIR CONTRACT TERMS.

The Judicature Act 1925, ss. 36, *et seq.*, have been repealed and replaced by the Supreme Court Act 1981, s. 49, in modified form but without change of effect.

Representative. It has been emphasised that the R.S.C. Ord. 15, r. 12, procedure is appropriate only where the same common interests are involved, mere similarity between the interests of defendants not being adequate ground for a representative action (*Roche* v. *Sherrington* [1982] 1 W.L.R. 599).

Reputed ownership. Goods bailed under a hire-purchase agreement or a consumer hire agreement or agreed to be sold under a conditional sale agreement or subject to a regulated agreement under which a bill of sale is given by way of security may not be treated as the property of the bankrupt during the period between the service of a default notice under the Consumer Credit Act 1974, in respect of the goods and the date when the notice expires or is earlier complied with (Bankruptcy Act 1914, s. 38A (added by the Consumer Credit Act 1974, s. 192, Sched. 4, para. 6)).

Requisitioned houses. The Requisitioned Houses Act 1960 (as amended), has been repealed by the Statute Law (Repeals) Act 1978, s. 1(1), Sched., Part XII.

Requisitioning. The Requisitioned Houses and Housing (Amendment) Act 1955, has been repealed by the Statute Law (Repeals) Act 1978, s. 1(1), Sched., Part XII.

Res judicata. The inter-relation of the doctrine and the underlying rationale of the Foreign Judgments (Reciprocal Enforcement) Act 1933, was considered in the course of the judgments in *Black-Clawson International Ltd.* v. *Papierwerke Waldhof-Aschaffenburg* [1975] A.C. 591, H.L.

The common law rule that criminal proceedings do not constitute *res judicata* as regards civil proceedings arising out of the same facts must be read subject to the Civil Evidence Act 1968, s. 11, which provides for the use of convictions as evidence in civil proceedings.

The rules of estoppel *per rem judicatam* in criminal cases were considered in *D.P.P.* v. *Humphreys* [1977] A.C. 1, H.L., when it was determined that the doctrine of issue estoppel had no place in English criminal law.

See also the (prospective) provision made by the Civil Jurisdiction and Judgments Act 1982.

Res perit domino. The Sale of Goods Act 1893, ss. 7, 20, 32, 33, have been repealed and replaced by the Sale of Goods Act 1979, ss. 7, 20, 32, 33, without change of effect.

Resale. The Sale of Goods Act 1893, ss. 39, 48, have been repealed and replaced by the Sale of Goods Act 1979, ss. 39, 48, without change of effect. The outstanding provisions of the Resale Prices Act 1964, together with the Restrictive Trade Practices Act 1956, ss. 24–27, have been repealed and consolidated into the Resale Prices Act 1976.

Rescind; Rescission. The text of the Misrepresentation Act 1967, s. 3, has been amended so as to refer to the "reasonableness test" in the Unfair Contract Terms Act 1977, s. 11, Sched. 2 (Act of 1967, s. 3 (as substituted by the Act of 1977, s. 8)). See also UNFAIR CONTRACT TERMS.

Reserve. The Companies Act 1948, Sched. 8, has been renumbered as Sched. 8A, and a substitute Sched. 8 has been inserted (Companies Act 1981, s. 1(2), Sched. 1). The former provisions apply only to the companies not affected by the accounting rules of the 1981 Act (*i.e.* banking, insurances and shipping companies: see the Act of 1981, Sched. 2, para. 8); the new rules are stricter than the original 1948 provisions.

Reserve forces. The substantial majority of the legislation relating to the reserve forces of the Crown has been repealed and replaced by the Reserve Forces Act 1980, which consolidates provisions drawn from many statutes from the City of London Militia Act 1662, to the Criminal Law Act 1977.

Residence. In electoral law the concept of residence is sufficiently flexible for a person to have two residences and therefore to be registered as an elector in both places, although he may exercise his vote in only one of them (*Fox* v. *Stirk* [1970] 2 Q.B. 463, C.A.).

Habitual residence is used in matrimonial law to confer jurisdiction on the High court and on county courts in proceedings for decrees of divorce, judicial separation, nullity of marriage and of presumption of death (Domicile and Matrimonial Proceedings Act 1973, s. 5(2)(*b*), (3)(*b*), (4)(*b*)), but the meaning of "residence" is not defined.

Residential homes. Disabled persons' and old persons' homes and residential homes for mentally disordered persons must be registered and are subject to regulation and inspection by the Secretary of State (Residential Homes Act 1980, consolidating previous provisions to the same effect).

Respondeat ouster. Questions both of law and of fact are capable of being the subject of determination before trial in accordance with R.S.C. Ord. 33, r. 3. The practice of referring points of law for determination before the finding of any facts has been deprecated (*Tilling* v. *Whiteman* [1980] A.C. 1, H.L.) as tending to increase the costs of proceedings unnecessarily. Had this dictat been observed, the decision in *Donoghue* v. *Stevenson* [1932] A.C. 562, H.L., would probably never have been given, since it was a preliminary point of law which came before the House of Lords in that case, before a definitive finding of the facts.

Restrictive covenant. A new form of restrictive covenant relating to agreements affecting development land was introduced by the Housing Act 1974, s. 126; the provision is unusual in providing for a positive covenant which is binding on successors in title.

Restrictive trade practices. See also the Competition Act 1980, ss. 25–30, which make detailed amendments to the Act of 1976 in connection with the abolition of price controls and the encouragement of competition in industry.

The Restrictive Trade Practices Act 1976, proved to have been unsatisfactorily drafted and the like-named Act of 1977 was passed in order to ensure that agreements between banks and financial institutions for the provision of loan finance and credit facilities by way of consortium lending were excluded from the provisions of the 1976 Act. See also the Participation Agreements Act 1978.

Resumption. The Agricultural Holdings Act 1948, s. 33, has been repealed and replaced by the Agricultural Holdings (Notices to Quit) Act 1977, s. 10, without change of effect.

Retail. The Customs and Excise Act 1952, s. 148(4) (as amended), has been repealed and replaced by the Alcoholic Liquor Duties Act 1979, s. 4(4), without change of effect.

Returning officers. The Representation of the People Act 1949, s. 18, and the Local Government Act 1972, ss. 40, 41, have been repealed and replaced by the consolidated provisions contained in the Representation of the People Act 1983, ss. 24–30.

Revenue. The Judicature Act 1925, has

been repealed by the Supreme Court Act 1981, s. 152(4), Sched. 7.

Revised Statutes. The Revised Statutes are being replaced by a new work entitled "Statutes in Force" published by Her Majesty's Stationery Office under governmental authority.

Revivial; Revivor. The requirement of leave to issue a writ of execution is now contained in R.S.C. Ord. 46, r. 2(1).

Periods of limitation may now be repeatedly extended by acknowledgment or part payment, but a right of action, once barred by the Limitation Act 1939, cannot now be revived by acknowledgment or part payment (Limitation Act 1939, s. 23(5) (added by the Limitation Amendment Act 1980, s. 6)). The provisions has now been repealed and replaced by the Limitation Act 1980, s. 29, without change of effect.

Revocation. A new version of the text for the Wills Act 1837, s. 18, and an additional s. 18A, have been introduced (Administration of Justice Act 1982, s. 18); the modifications made take into account the new powers of the courts to rectify a will in certain circumstances (see RECTIFICATION; RECTIFY). The new s. 18A revises the effect of a will made before the dissolution or annulment of the marriage of the testator, avoiding any appointment of the (ex-) spouse as executor or trustee, gifts to the (ex-)spouse lapsing, and certain interests in remainder being accelerated. The Law of Property Act 1925, s. 177, has been repealed by the Act of 1982, s. 75(1), Sched. 9, Part I, since the new provisions of the Wills Act make it superfluous.

Reward. For the general revision of the penalties which may be imposed on summary conviction see FINE.

Rhodesia. The illegal regime in that country came to an end in 1979 (see the Zimbabwe Act 1979); see also ZIMBABWE.

Riding furiously. For the general revision of the penalties which may be imposed on summary conviction see FINE.

Right to buy. The Housing Act 1980, Part I (ss. 1–27), introduced a scheme enabling many public sector residential tenants (*i.e.* those whose landlords were local authorities (other than county councils), new town development corporations, the Development Board for Rural Wales, or certain housing associations) to claim the right to buy the freehold of their homes, or a long lease (s. 1). In such cases the price is determined by a statutory procedure (ss. 6, 11), subject to a discount based on the period of qualifying residence (s. 7). A right to a mortgage is integral to the scheme (ss. 9, 12, 14, 16). The scheme has been extended by the Housing and Building Control Act 1984, Part I, Chapter I (ss. 1–38).

Ringing the changes. The Coinage Offences Act 1936, s. 5(1), has been repealed and replaced by the Forgery and Counterfeiting Act 1981, s. 15, without change of effect.

Road haulage. A portion of the Transport Act 1968, Part V (*i.e.*, ss. 59–94), ss. 72–80, and parts of each of ss. 81–90, have been repealed by the Transport Act 1980, s. 69, Sched. 9, Part II.

Road humps. The use of road humps in actual practice is now authorised by the Highways Act 1980, ss. 90A–90F (inserted by the Transport Act 1981, s. 32, Sched. 10); the regulations made (the Highways (Road Humps) Regulations 1983 (S.I. 1983 No. 1087)) are so restricted in their terms as to occasion adverse public query on whether such devices can be lawfully installed to any useful effect.

Road, Rule of the. The Highway Code now current (issued in 1977), para. 39 (replacing the former para. 29), modifies the rule by adding a further exception: "except when road signs or markings indicate"; the former paras. 138–139 have been revoked and replaced by the new edition, para. 140, without significant change of effect.

Road service licence. The Road Traffic Act 1960, ss. 134–160, have been repealed by the Public Passenger Vehicles Act 1981, s. 88(5), Sched. 8; see now the Act of 1981, ss. 30–37.

Road Traffic. The Road Traffic Regulation Act 1967, has been repealed and replaced by the Road Traffic Regulation Act 1984, without change of effect. Other legislation is subject to constant amendment and replacement, the changes being noted under appropriate headings elsewhere in this work.

Road-ferry. The Highways Act 1959, ss. 295(1), 26, 107, 220, have been repealed and replaced by the Highways Act 1980, ss. 329(1), 24, 105, 238(1) and 244, without change of effect.

Rooker-Wise clause. The Finance Act 1977, s. 22(2), which provides that in the financial year 1979–80 and subsequent years specified tax reliefs (the basic personal reliefs allowed in respect of income tax) should be increased by no less than the percentage of increase in the retail price index for the previous calendar year, subject to limited powers conferred on the Treasury with the consent of the House of Commons.

Rota. The Judicature Act 1925, s. 67, has been repealed and replaced by the Supreme Court Act 1981, s. 142, without change of effect. Similar arrangements exist (see R.S.C. Ord. 36, r. 5(3)) for the distribution of business among the Official Referees (*q.v.*)

Roundabout. The current (1977) edition of the Highway Code, paras. 102–107 deal with the recommended procedure at roundabouts.

Royal assent. The rule in *Tomlinson* v. *Bullock* (1879) 4 Q.B.D. 230, received statutory recognition in the Interpretation Act 1889, s. 36, which has been repealed and replaced by the Interpretation Act 1978, s. 4, which contains an amendment designed to deal with the problems caused by complex commencement provisions.

Royal College of Physicians. The Medical Act 1956, s. 12, has been repealed and replaced by the Medical Act 1983, s. 4, under which the agreement might continue in operation.

Royal Courts of Justice. The Judicature Act 1925, s. 222, has been repealed without replacement by the Supreme Court Act 1981, s. 152(4), Sched. 7. The general provisions (Courts Act 1971, ss. 28–29) authorising the acquisition and management of buildings for the Supreme Court and county courts appear to be adequate to cover the omission.

Royal marine volunteers. The Naval Forces Act 1903, s. 2, has been repealed by the Royal Marines Act 1948, s. 1(6), without replacement. The Royal Marines Act 1948, s. 1(1), has been repealed and replaced by the Reserve Forces Act 1980, s. 3, without significant change of effect.

Royal marines. The relevant provisions of the Reserve Forces Act 1966, have been repealed and replaced by the Reserve Forces Act 1980, without significant change of effect.

Rule. The Judicature Act 1925, has been repealed and replaced by the Supreme Court Act 1981; ss. 84–85 of the Act of 1981 continue the powers to make rules in the Supreme Court.

Rules of court. The Interpretation Act 1889, s. 14, has been repealed and replaced by the Interpretation Act 1978, s. 5, Sched. 1, without change of effect.

Other common codes of procedure are the County Court Rules 1981 (S.I. 1981 No. 1687), made under the County Courts Act 1959, s. 102 (now repealed and replaced by the County Courts Act 1984, s. 75, without change of effect); and the Magistrates' Courts Rules 1981 (S.I. 1981 No. 552) and the Magistrates' Courts (Forms) Rules 1981 (S.I. 1981 No. 552), both made under the Magistrates' Courts Act 1980, s. 144. Procedure in the Crown court is governed by the Crown Court Rules 1982 (S.I. 1982 No.1109), made under the Supreme Court Act 1981, s. 86. All these sets of rules are frequently amended to take account of changing circumstance and developments in the law.

Running down case. Scales of fees which will normally be allowed on taxation of casts are promulgated from time to time by the Taxing Masters; for an example of the older levels see [1979] C.L.Y. 2134.

Rural dean. The current provisions are the Pastoral Measure 1983, s. 19 (which replace the Pastoral Measure 1968, s. 18, without change of effect), which deal with the establishment, variation and abolition of rural deaneries under pastoral schemes.

S

S.L.R. The Statutes Revised series has been replaced by a new publication entitled *Statutes in Force* (*q.v.*).

The sequence of Statute Law (Repeals)

Act has been continued with the Acts of 1977, 1978 and 1981.

Safe system of working. The common law duty on an employer is supplemented by the duty imposed by the Health and Safety at Work, etc., Act 1974, s. 2.

Safety at sea. See also the Merchant Shipping Act 1964 and the Merchant Shipping (Safety Conventions) Act 1971; the later Act was passed in order to enable effect to be given to the new International Convention for the Safety of Life at Sea signed in London in 1974 (replacing a like-named Convention signed there in 1960).

Sale. The Sale of Goods Act 1893 (as amended), has been repealed and replaced by the Sale of Goods Act 1979, without change of effect. Special provisions in the Act of 1979 preserve the law in force at various stages of amendment prior to 1979 (s. 1, Sched. 1). The Judicature Act 1925, s. 56(1), has been repealed and replaced by the Supreme Court Act 1981, s. 61(1), (3), Sched. 1, para. 1(*a*), without change of effect.

Sale of Goods Act. The Sale of Goods Act 1893 (as amended), has been repealed and replaced by the Sale of Goods Act 1979, without change of effect. Special provisions in the Act of 1979 preserve the law in force at various stages of amendment prior to 1979 (s. 1, Sched. 1).

Some of the 1979 provisions relating to implied terms or fitness, merchantability, etc., have been applied to contracts for the transfer of property in goods, contracts for the hire of goods and contracts for the supply of services (Supply of Goods and Services Act 1982).

Sale or return. The Sale of Goods Act 1893, s. 18, has been repealed and replaced by the Sale of Goods Act 1979, s. 18, without change of effect.

Salvage. The Administration of Justice Act 1956, ss. 1, 3, and the Administration of Justice Act 1970, s. 2, have been repealed and replaced by the Supreme Court Act 1981, ss. 20, 21, 6(1)(b); the County Courts Act 1959, ss. 55–61, have been repealed and replaced by the County Courts Act 1984, ss. 26–31; and the Civil Aviation Act 1949, s. 51, has been repealed and replaced by the Civil Aviation Act 1982, s. 82. All these Acts are consolidating provisions, so that there are only minor changes of effect.

Sample. The Customs and Excise Act 1952, s. 83, has been repealed by the Customs and Excise Management Act 1979, s. 177(3), Sched. 6, Part I; by s. 93 of the 1979 Act, warehousing regulations may be made controlling the deposit, keeping, security and treatment of goods in and their removal from warehouses, and the facilities afforded under the 1952 provisions are expected to continue.

The Sale of Goods Act 1893, s. 15, has been repealed and replaced by the Sale of Goods Act 1979, s. 15, without change of effect. The provisions of the Act of 1979 provided the model for fresh provision which has been made for implied terms in contracts for the transfer of property in goods and contracts for the hire of goods (Supply of Goods and Services Act 1982, ss. 5, 10).

The Food and Drugs Act 1955 has been repealed and replaced by the Food Act 1984 (see, *e.g.*, the Act of 1984, ss. 76–86).

Sanctions. The sanctions against Rhodesia have now been lifted; see ZIMBABWE. Sanctions were also envisaged against Iran; see the Iran (Temporary Powers) Act 1980.

Sand grouse. The Protection of Birds Acts 1954 to 1967, have been repealed and replaced by the Wildlife and Countryside Act 1981, ss. 1–8, Scheds. 1–4, without change of effect.

Sanderson order. An order requiring an unsuccessful defendant to pay a successful defendant's costs to him directly, and deriving its name from *Sanderson* v. *Blyth Theatre Co.* [1903] 2 K.B. 644, it is a simpler form of the order known as a Bullock order (*q.v.*).

Sanitary appliances. Local authorities (other than county councils and the Greater London Council) may serve a notice requiring the provision of sanitary appliances in certain circumstances (Local Government (Miscellaneous Provisions) Act 1976, s. 20); the term is stated to mean water closets, other closets, urinals and wash basins (s. 20(9)).

The control of sanitary appliances on vessels is authorised by the Control of Pollution Act 1974, s. 33.

Sanitary control of ships. The provisions of the Public Health Act 1936, s. 143, were supplemented by the Control of Pollution Act 1974, s. 33, which authorises the control of sanitary appliances on vessels. The 1936 provision has now been repealed and replaced by the Public Health (Control of Diseases) Act 1984, ss. 13, 15, 76, without significant change of effect.

Sanitary inspectors. The Sanitary Inspectors (Change of Designation) Act 1956, has been repealed by the Statute Law (Repeals) Act 1977, s. 1(1), Sched. 1, Part XI, without replacement.

Savings banks. The Trustee Savings Bank Act 1978, dealt with investments and borrowings by such institutions. The Trustee Savings Banks Acts 1969, 1976 and 1978, and a number of associated Acts, have now been repealed and replaced by the Trustee Savings Banks Act 1981, without significant change of effect.

The date for the Income and Corporation Taxes Act is 1970 (not 1870).

Scheduled territories. These have disappeared with the abolition of exchange controls, effected (principally) by the Exchange Control (Revocation) Directions 1979 (S.I. 1979 No. 1339); the Exchange Control (General Exemption) Order 1979 (S.I. 1979 No. 1660); and the Exchange Control (Revocation) (No. 2) Directions 1979 (S.I. 1979 No. 1662).

Scholarship. The exemption from taxation benefits only the student: see the Finance Act 1976, s. 62A (added by the Finance Act 1983, s. 20).

School. The comprehensive system of schooling was provided for by the Education Act 1976, ss. 1–3, but the duty to introduce that system was abolished by the repeal of the 1976 provisions (Education Act 1979, s. 1(1)).

School crossings. The Road Traffic Regulation Act 1967, ss. 24, 25, have been repealed and replaced by the Road Traffic Regulation Act 1984, ss. 26–28, without change of effect.

Scotland Act. See DEVOLUTION.

Scotland and Ireland. The execution throughout the United Kingdom of warrants of arrest and the like service of summonses in criminal proceedings (and citations) has been facilitated by the Criminal Law Act 1977, ss. 38, 39. The Judicature Act 1925, s. 49, has been repealed and replaced by the Supreme Court Act 1981, s. 36, without change of effect.

Scrip. The Companies Act 1948, s. 429, and the Companies Act 1967, s. 119, have been repealed by the Banking Act 1979, s. 51(2), Sched. 7.

Seal. The common law requirement that all contracts of a company should be under seal has been restricted so that in many cases ordinary contracts of trading companies are concluded by ordinary correspondence (see the Corporate Bodies' Contracts Act 1960).

The Forgery Act 1913, ss. 5, 18, have been repealed by the Forgery and Counterfeiting Act 1981, s. 30, Sched. 1, Part I; the general provisions of the 1981 Act cover the conduct formerly prohibited by the specific 1913 provisions (see FORGERY).

Search. The powers of search conferred by the Customs and Excise Act 1952, have been continued in the Customs and Excise Acts 1979, which have in large measure repealed and replaced the 1952 legislation.

A power to search individuals in order to ascertain whether they have any money with which to pay fines or penalties imposed has been enjoyed for some time by magistrates' courts (Magistrates' Courts Act 1980, s. 80 (replacing the Magistrates' Courts Act 1952, s. 68)), and has now been conferred on the Crown Court (Powers of Criminal Courts Act 1973, s. 34A (added by the Criminal Law Act 1977, s. 49)).

Search warrant. A warrant becomes spent with the first search made under it unless special provision to the contrary is contained in the warrant or the statutory provisions under which it is issued (*R.* v. *Adams* [1980] Q.B. 575; see also *Dickinson* v. *Brown* (1794) 1 Esp. 218).

Searches. The operation of the Law of Property Act 1925, s. 198, has been restricted by the Law of Property Act 1969, s. 24, in connection with the reduction (by the Act of 1969, s 23) of the statutory period of root of title: see LAND CHARGES. Searches in respect of local land charges are conducted under the Local Land Charges Act 1975; see LOCAL LAND CHARGES.

The Law of Property (Amendment) Act 1926, s. 4, was repealed and replaced by the Land Charges Act 1972, s. 11, by which protection periods of 15 and 30 days were prescribed for various purposes, the 30-day period being appropriate in the context.

Tithe redemption annuities have been abolished (Finance Act 1977, s. 56).

Seas, Beyond the. The Limitation Act 1939 has been repealed and replaced by the Limitation Act 1980 (which consolidated the amendments in the Acts of 1963, 1975 and the Limitation Amendment Act 1980).

Seat belt. Virtually all front seat passengers and the drivers of motor cars are now required to wear seat belts (Road Traffic Act 1972, s. 33A (added by the Transport Act 1981, s. 27(11)); Motor Vehicles (Wearing of Seat Belts) Regulations 1982 (S.I. 1982 No. 1203); Motor Vehicles (Wearing of Seat Belts by Children) Regulations 1982 (S.I. 1982 No. 1342)).

Seaworthiness. The Merchant Shipping Act 1894, ss. 463, 483, have been repealed by the Merchant Shipping Act 1970, s. 100(3), Sched. 5. The Act of 1894, s. 457, has been repealed and replaced by the Merchant Shipping Act 1979, s. 44; the new provision makes it an offence both for the master and for the owner to have a dangerously unsafe ship in a port in the United Kingdom or such a ship registered in the United Kingdom and which is in any other port.

Secret reserve. The Companies Act 1948, Sched. 8, has been renumbered as Sched. 8A, and a substitute Sched. 8 has been inserted (Companies Act 1981 s. 1(2), Sched. 1). The former provisions apply only to the companies not affected by the accounting rules of the 1981 Act (*i.e.*, banking, insurances and shipping companies: see the Act of 1981, Sched. 2, para. 8); the new rules are stricter than the original 1948 provisions.

Secretary. See also REGISTER OF DIRECTORS AND SECRETARIES.

Secretary of State. The Interpretation Act 1889, s. 12(3), has been repealed and replaced by the Intepretation Act 1978, s. 5, Sched. 1, without change of effect.

The salary of a Secretary of State is revised from time to time (see, *e.g.* S.I. 1979 No. 905).

Secure tenancy. A class of public sector residential tenancy, linked to the "right to buy" (*q.v.*) and conferring rights of succession (Housing Act 1980, ss. 30–31); the security of tenure provisions (s. 32) prevent the landlord terminating the tenancy otherwise than by court order. The general landlord and tenant provisions (Law of Property Act 1925, s. 146) for relief against forfeiture apply to certain cases where the tenancy is for a fixed term (Act of 1980, s. 32(3)).

The implied terms of a secure tenancy include limited provisions for sub-letting, accommodation of lodgers, and the making of tenants' improvements (Housing Act 1980, ss. 35–41; Housing and Building Control Act 1984, ss. 25–29). The grounds for regaining possession are set out in the Acts (1980, s. 34; 1984, s. 25).

Security. The law relating to bail in criminal proceedings has been amended so as to prohibit the taking of recognizance for surrender to custody from the person admitted to bail (Bail Act 1976, s. 3(2)), and to restrict the taking of any security from him or any other person (see ss. 3(3), 8).

Security for costs. In the Supreme Court it has been indicated that when the "resident abroad" ground is relied on, credit may be given if the respondent plaintiff is resident in the EEC (*Landi den Hartog BV* v. *Stopps* [1976] F.S.R. 497).

In county courts security for costs may be ordered to be given if it appears to the court, on the application of the defendant to an action or other proceedings, that the plaintiff is ordinarily resident outside England and Wales and that it is reasonable to order security (C.C.R. 1981 Ord. 13, r. 8).

Sedition. The Unlawful Oaths Acts 1797 and 1812, have been repealed without replacement by the Statute Law (Repeals) Act 1981, s. 1(1), Sched. 1, Part I.

Seduction. A preliminary abolition (by the Law Reform (Miscellaneous Provisions) Act 1970, s. 5) not appearing adequate, proceedings for loss of services, etc., have again been abolished (Administration of Justice Act 1982, s. 2).

Seeds. The Plant Varieties and Seeds Act 1983 extended the validity of the protected monopoly periods under the 1964 scheme (see PLANT).

Selected action. In county courts this was the name for a procedural device which enabled actions by a multiplicity of plaintiffs against the same defendant or by the same plaintiff against a multiplicity of defendants to be stayed pending the determination in a single action of some question common to all the actions (C.C.R. 1936 Ord. 17). The old procedure has been replaced by a modified form (C.C.R. 1981

Ord. 13, r. 9); the current term is consolidation of proceedings (see CONSOLIDATION OF ACTIONS for the Supreme Court equivalent).

Sentence. The power of a magistrates' court to vary the terms of a sentence or order (Criminal Justice Act 1972, s. 41) may now be exercised up to 28 days after the original decision (Magistrates' Courts Act 1980, s. 142, replacing the Criminal Law Act 1977, s. 65(4), Sched. 12 (now repealed), with slight modifications).

The scheme of suspended sentences (Powers of Criminal Courts Act 1973, ss. 22–27) has been supplemented by the scheme for partially suspended sentences. These provisions (see the Criminal Law Act 1977, s. 47, which provided for part of the sentence to be served forthwith, the remainder remaining in suspense from release until the outstanding period of imprisonment has run) were brought into operation on 29 March 1983 (Criminal Law Act 1977 (Commencement No. 1) Order 1982 (S.I. 1982 No. 243)). The scheme was almost immediately heavily amended by the Criminal Justice Act 1982, ss. 30, 31, which reduced the minimum periods of suspension and the proportions required to be observed, thus making the sentence more readily available to magistrates' courts. It is impossible partially to suspend the operation of a suspended sentence which is just coming into operation after some part of its principal suspension has run (*R.* v. *Bow* [1983] 5 Cr.App.R.(S.) 250, C.A.).

See also DEFERMENT OF SENTENCE.

Separatists. The Oaths Act 1888, has been repealed and replaced by the Oaths Act 1978; by s. 5 of the 1978 Act, any person who objects to being sworn is entitled to affirm without needing to show cause.

Service charge. The tenant of a flat (*q.v.*) who is obliged to pay service charges in excess of a prescribed sum may demand information about the calculation of the charge (Housing Finance Act 1972, s. 90); the tenants of local authorities and similar bodies are excluded from these provisions (s. 91). The recovery of such charges is restricted so as to enable tenants to avoid paying any charge which is unreasonable (s. 91A (added by the Housing Act 1974, s. 125)); the tenants of local authorities and similar bodies are excluded from these provisions as are those who hold under protected, statutory or furnished tenancies (s. 91A(8)).

Service of process. Personal service of a document in High Court proceedings no longer involves showing the original but is fully effective if a copy of the document is left with the person to be served (R.S.C. Ord. 65, r. 2 (as amended by S.I. 1979 No. 402)). The alternatives to personal service of originating process include service by post (R.S.C. Ord. 10, r. 1(2)); no special leave is required for using this procedure. Acceptance of service by a solicitor is now authorised by R.S.C. Ord. 10, r. 1(4). A defendant who acknowledges service of a writ which has not in fact been properly served is deemed to have been served (R.S.C. Ord. 10, r. 1(5)).

The Interpretation Act 1889, s. 26, has been repealed and replaced by the Interpretation Act 1978, s. 7, without change of effect.

Set-off. The modern law and practice is reviewed in *British Anzani* (*Felixstowe*) *Ltd.* v. *International Marine Management* (*U.K.*) *Ltd.* [1980] Q.B. 137.

Settled land. Although the creation of rentcharges (see RENT) is now prohibited, there is an exception in favour of the creation of rentcharges which have the effect of making the land on which the rent is charged into settled land by virtue of the Settled Land Act 1925, s. 1(1)(*v*) (Rentcharges Act 1977, s. 2(3)(*a*)).

Sewer. The Land Drainage Acts 1930 to 1961, together with appropriate parts of the Water Act 1973, and the Land Drainage (Amendment) Act 1976, have been repealed and replaced by the Land Drainage Act 1976, which consolidates the statutory provisions in the field.

Sex change. The decision in *Corbett* v. *Corbett* (*orse Ashley*) [1971] P. 110, was given statutory force in the Nullity of Marriage Act 1971, s. 1(*c*) (now repealed and replaced by the Matrimonial Causes Act 1973, s. 11(*c*), without change of effect).

Sexual offences. Restrictions on reports of "rape cases" (see RAPE) have been introduced together with statutory recognition of the common law rule (*D.P.P.* v. *Morgan* [1976] A.C. 182, H.L.) relating to mens rea (Sexual Offences (Amendment) Act 1976). Indecent photographing of children has been proscribed (Protection of Children Act 1978). The crime of incest (*q.v.*) has been extended (Criminal Law Act 1977, s. 54).

Matrimonial orders are no longer made on the ground simply of a conviction under the Sexual Offences Act 1956, ss. 1–29, the matimonial jurisdiction of magistrates having been revised by the Domestic Proceedings and Magistrates' Courts Act 1978.

Share pushing. The Protection of Depositors Act 1963, has been repealed and replaced by the Banking Act 1979, Part I (ss. 1–20); see DEPOSIT.

The issue of share capital and associated matters were modified by the Companies Act 1980, Part II (ss. 14–38); and the Companies Act 1981, Part III (ss. 36–62), concerning share capital, and Part IV (ss. 63–83), which relates to the disclosure of interests in shares.

Share options and share incentive schemes. See also the Finance Act 1984, ss. 38–41.

Ship. The Merchant Shipping Act 1894, s. 502, has been repealed and replaced by the Merchant Shipping Act 1979, s. 18, without substantial change of effect. The Act of 1894, s. 503, has been repealed and replaced by the Act of 1979, s. 17, Sched. 4, Part I, introducing the rules contained in the Convention of Limitation of Liability for Maritime Claims to English law together with ancillary provisions (Sched. 4, Part II); see also the Act of 1979, s. 35(1).

Sheep-scab. The Diseases of Animals Act 1950, ss. 42, 43, have been repealed and replaced by the Animal Health Act 1981, ss. 14, 56, without change of effect.

Shell fish. The Food and Drugs Act 1955, s. 25, has been repealed and replaced by the Food Act 1984, s. 30, without change of effect.

Shew cause. The Judicature Act 1925 has been repealed and (generally) replaced by the Supreme Court Act 1981.

Ship. The Administration of Justice Act 1956, ss. 1–3, have been replaced by the Supreme Court Act 1981, ss. 20–22, without significant change of effect. See also ADMIRALTY COURT.

Shooting. The Customs and Excise Act 1952, s. 72, has been repealed and replaced by the Customs and Excise Management Act 1979, s. 85(2), without change of effect.

The power to regulate shooting galleries has been amended so as to allow regulations to take account of the precautions required to deal with outbreaks of fire (Local Government (Miscellaneous Provisions) Act 1976, s. 22).

Shop. Claims to qualify under the special provisions relating to Jews (under the Shops Act 1950, s. 53), must now be supported by an official certificate of an appointee of the Board of Deputies of British Jews (S.I. 1979 No. 1294).

The right and duty of local authorities to enforce the Sunday trading restrictions against offending shops in their respective areas has been confirmed (*Stoke-on-Trent City Council* v. *B & Q (Retail) Ltd.* [1984] 2 W.L.R. 929, H.L.).

Shop-lifting. The Magistrates' Courts Act 1952, s. 19, has been repealed and replaced by the Criminal Law Act 1977, ss. 14–16, without substantial change of effect; the 1977 provisions have, in their turn, been repealed and replaced by the Magistrates' Courts Act 1980, s. 17, Sched. 1, without change of effect.

Shop steward. This official appears in employment law solely in his capacity as a trade union official; the status of such an official is defined as follows: "any person who is an officer of the union or a branch or section of the union or who (not being such an officer) is a person elected or appointed in accordance with the rules of the union to be a representative of its members or of some of them, including any person so elected or appointed who is an employee of the same employer as the members, or one or more of the members, whom he is to represent" (Trade Union and Labour Relations Act 1974, s. 30(1)). The authority of a trade union official, and therefore of a shop steward, to bind his union has its source in the written rule book of the union together with the custom and practice of the union (see generally *Hestons Transport* (*St. Helens*) *Ltd.* v. *T.G.W.U.* [1973] A.C. 15, H.L.).

Short cause. To qualify for inclusion in the Short Cause List (see *Practice Direction* [1981] 1 W.L.R. 1296, replacing the *Practice Direction* [1958] 1 W.L.R. 1291) the estimated time required for the case to be heard must not exceed four hours (*Practice Direction* [1977] 1 W.L.R. 1067).

Shorthold. A special form of tenancy

granted for a term certain of not less than one year and not more than five years, not containing any provisions for the earlier termination of the tenancy by the landlord (other than re-entry or forfeiture for unpaid rent or breach of some obligation of the tenancy) and certain other conditions (Housing Act 1980, s. 52(1)). A notice indicating that this special form of tenancy is intended must be given by the landlord to the tenant before it is created (s. 52(1)(*b*)). The statute confers on the tenant certain rights to early termination (s. 53), of sub-letting and assigning (s. 54), and security of tenure (s. 55).

Sickness benefit. By way of addition to the system a scheme of statutory sick pay has been introduced under which employers pay the equivalent of several weeks' benefit and recover a proportion of the sum in question (see the Social Security and Housing Benefits Act 1982, ss. 5(5), 6(1), 26(1), 97, and S.I. 1982 No. 894 (as amended by S.I. 1984 No. 385)).

Signature R.S.C. Ord. 62, App. 2, Part I, Item 2, has been renumbered Ord. 62, App. 2, Part VII, Item 2 (see S.I. 1979 No. 35). An alternative procedure is followed when counsel is not readily available, when the head of his chambers may certify receipt of the fees (*Practice Direction* [1973] 1 W.L.R. 983).

The conclusion of ordinary contracts by a trading company without the use of a seal is regulated by the Corporate Bodies' Contracts Act 1960.

Singular. The Interpretation Act 1889, s. 1, has been repealed and replaced by the Interpretation Act 1978, s. 6(c), without change of effect.

Sittings. The dates related to Whit Sunday have been amended so that they are linked to the "spring holiday," which is the bank holiday which falls on the last Monday in May (S.I. 1972 No. 1194).

The Supreme Court Offices (Hours of Business) Order 1963, has been revoked and replaced by the Supreme Court Offices (Hours of Business) Order 1969.

The Courts Act 1971, s. 2, has been repealed and replaced by the Supreme Court Act 1981, s. 71, with minor variation.

Slum clearance. The Housing Act 1957, ss. 44–46, 51, 53, 54, have been repealed by the Housing Act 1974, s. 130(4), Sched. 15; associated provisions of the 1974 Act included Part IV (ss. 36–49, which dealt with housing action areas (*q.v.*)) and Part VI (ss. 52–55, which dealt with priority neighbourhoods (*q.v.*)).

Small bankruptcy. The limit for the summary administration of a bankrupt's estate has been raised from £300 to £4,000 (Bankruptcy Act 1914, s. 127; Insolvency Act 1976, s. 1, Sched. 1, Part I).

Small dwellings. The Housing Act 1964, s. 57, has been repealed by the Housing Act 1974, s. 130(4), Sched. 15, on account of the new provision made by that Act (ss. 56–104) for financial assistance towards improvements (including compulsory improvements), repairs and conversion. Further amendments to this part of the law have been occasioned by the introduction of a scheme to assist tenants to buy their homes (see RIGHT TO BUY) by the Housing Act 1980, Part I.

Smoke. It is the production (rather than the consumption) of dark smoke which is proscribed by the legislation.

For the abolition of Clean Air Councils see the Local Government, Planning and Land Act 1980, s. 189.

Smuggling. The Customs and Excise Act 1952, s. 45, has been repealed and replaced by the Customs and Excise Management Act 1979, s. 50.

Snow. The Highways Act 1959, s. 129, has been repealed and replaced by the Highways Act 1980, s. 150, without change of effect.

Snuff. The Customs and Excise Act 1952, ss. 173, 176, 191, have been repealed by the Finance Act 1973, s. 3, Sched. 9, Part II. The Finance Act 1976, ss. 4–8, introduced tobacco products duty in the place of the former customs and excise duties, and the subject is now regulated by the Tobacco Products Duty Act 1979.

Social Security. The Employment Protection Act 1975, ss.111(2), 112, 113, have been repealed by the Supplementary Benefits Act 1976, s. 35(3), Sched. 8, the Employment Protection (Consolidation) Act 1978, s. 159(3), Sched. 17, and the Social Security (Miscellaneous Provisions) Act 1977, s. 24(6), Sched. 2, respectively.

Further amendments to the principal provisions of the scheme for social security benefits are contained in the National

Insurance Surcharge Act 1976; the Supplementary Benefits Act 1976 (which consolidates the previous legislation with certain amendments); the Social Security (Miscellaneous Provisions) Act 1977; the Social Security Act 1979; the Pensioners' Payments and Social Security Act 1979; the Pneumoconiosis, etc. (Workers' Compensation) Act 1979; the Social Security Act 1980; and the Social Security (No. 2) Act 1980. The administration of the scheme is subject to constant and massive amendments and commencement provisions contained in statutory instruments issued under the authority of the complex Acts which (despite their labyrinthine provisions) amount to no more than an elementary framework for the system of benefits concerned.

Societies. The Companies Act 1948, s. 19, has been repealed and replaced by the Companies Act 1981, s. 25; the new provision differs in that it is no longer necessary for the organisation to make an application for dispensation provided the requirements are met. Fewer companies will be able to qualify under the new provision.

Societies, Unlawful. The Unlawful Oaths Acts 1797 and 1812, have been repealed without replacement by the Statute Law (Repeals) Act 1981, s. 1(1), Sched. 1, Part I.

Soil. Prosecutions under the Act of 1953 require the consent or fiat of the Attorney-General for their commencement.

Soke. See LIBERTY.

Solicitation. "Kerb-crawling" in order to invite young girls to have intercourse amounts to solicitation (despite the decision in *Crook* v. *Edmondson* [1966] 2 Q.B. 81) and is therefore an offence by virtue of the Sexual Offences Act 1956, ss. 6(1), 32 (*R.* v. *Dodd* (*David*) (1977) 66 Cr.App.Rep. 87, C.A.).

Solicitor. The provisions of the Solicitors Act 1974, s. 22(2) (which permit barristers to conduct conveyancing work) have been expanded in the Rules for Employed Barristers (rr.5–9) promulgated by the Senate of the Inns of Court and of the Bar on March 31, 1980.

The Solicitors Remuneration Order 1882 was revoked by the Solicitors Remuneration Order 1972 (S.I. 1972 No. 1139).

The rule about costs in *R.* v. *Smith* (*Martin*) [1975] Q.B. 531, has been reversed by the addition of a right of appeal provision for this purpose (Solicitors Act 1974, s. 50(3), added by the Supreme Court Act 1981, s. 147).

The directions relating to solicitors' rights of audience in the Crown Court are *Practice Directions* [1972] 1 W.L.R. 5 and 307.

Despite the privilege attaching to communications between a solicitor and his client it is thought that the statutory provision requiring disclosure contained in the Finance Act 1974, s. 47, Sched. 10, para. 4, prevails.

The rule in *Rondel* v. *Worsley* [1969] 1 A.C. 191, H.L., has been restricted by the decision of the House of Lords in *Saif Ali* v. *Sydney Mitchell & Co.* [1980] A.C. 198, where the immunity formerly enjoyed by counsel was withdrawn from pre-court work; the same reduction of immunity probably also affects solicitors. The former rule in *Groom* v. *Crocker* [1939] 1 K.B. 194, C.A., to the effect that a solicitor could not be sued by his client in the tort of negligence has been condemned and not followed in view of the extension of liability in negligence (*q.v.*) to other professional groups (*Midland Bank Trust Co. Ltd.* v. *Hett, Stubbs & Kemp* [1979] Ch. 384; *Ross* v. *Caunters* [1980] Ch. 297).

Solicitor-General. The salary of the Solicitor-General is revised from time to time (see, *e.g.*, S.I. 1979 No. 905).

Solomon Islands. The Solomon Islands Act 1978, provides for the establishment of this former protectorate as an independent dominion within the Commonwealth.

Southern Rhodesia. See RHODESIA and ZIMBABWE.

Sovereign power or **Sovereignty.** Special provisions govern the relationship of the English legal system to foreign sovereign powers (State Immunity Act 1978).

Speaker. The salary of the Speaker is revised from time to time (see, *e.g.* S.I. 1979 No. 905).

The House of Commons Offices Act 1846, s. 5, has been repealed and replaced by the House of Commons (Administration) Act 1979, s. 1, Sched. 1, para. 3(1), without change of effect.

Special case. The procedure under R.S.C. Ord. 33, r. 3, is no longer restricted to dealing with questions of fact; the court may order any question or issue arising in any cause or matter, whether of fact or of law or partly of fact and partly of law, whether raised by the pleadings or otherwise, to be tried at, before or after the trial of the cause or matter, and give directions as to the manner in which the question or issue is to be stated. The practice of pursuing appeals with a view to determining a question of law before making an attempt to determine any facts has been deprecated as tending to increase the costs of litigation unnecessarily (*Tilling* v. *Whiteman* [1980] A.C. 1, H.L.).

Special hospital. The Mental Health Act 1959, ss. 97–99, have been repealed and replaced by the Mental Health Act 1983, s. 145(1), continuing the four hospitals as special hospitals maintained under the National Health Service Act 1977, s. 4.

Special notice. The Companies Act 1948, s. 160, has been repealed and replaced by the Companies Act 1976, s. 15, which effectively repeats the 1948 provision with additions which subject the appointment and removal of auditors to more stringent control.

Special Paper. The *Practice Direction* [1958] 1 W.L.R. 1291, has been revoked and replaced by the *Practice Direction* [1981] 1 W.L.R. 1296; the Special Paper List has disappeared as a result of the revision of the listing procedures.

Special Paper days. The *Practice Direction* [1958] 1 W.L.R. 1291, has been revoked and replaced by the *Practice Direction* [1981] 1 W.L.R. 1296; the Special Paper List has disappeared as a result of the revision of the listing procedures.

Special personal representatives. The Law of Property Act 1925, s. 16, has been repealed by the Finance Act 1975, s. 59(5), Sched. 13, Part I, in connection with the replacement of estate duty (*q.v.*) by capital transfer tax (*q.v.*). Equivalent provision was then made by the Act of 1975, s. 25(5)(*b*), now repealed and replaced by the Capital Transfer Tax Act 1984, s. 200(1)(*b*), (3), without change of effect.

When an application is made for the rectification of a will (under the Administration of Justice Act 1982, s. 20; see RECTIFICATION; RECTIFY), the six month time limit will not commence to run merely on the appointment of special personal representatives unless there is a co-existent grant of representation to the remainder of the estate (Act of 1982, s. 20(4)).

Special procedure list. Certain undefended petitions for divorce (*q.v.*) or for judicial separation (*q.v.*) or for decrees of nullity (*q.v.*) come within the provisions (Matrimonial Causes Rules 1977 (S.I. 1977 No. 344), rr. 33(3), 48), which enable the pronouncement of the decree nisi in open court to be made in the absence of the parties after the petition has been determined on affidavit evidence. Originally restricted to comparatively few causes, the procedure has been extended to include the vast majority of all the petitions presented so that the name of the procedure conceals its true nature (see *Day* v. *Day* [1980] Fam. 29, C.A.).

Special reasons. The basis of the special reasons procedure has been modified by the Transport Act 1981, s. 19. When evidence is put forward to avoid disqualification under the provisions in respect of repeated offences (see TOTTING-UP PROCEDURE), no account will be taken of circumstances alleged to make the (current) offence or any previous offence(s) not serious; nor of any other than exceptional hardship; nor of any circumstances which, in the three years preceding the conviction, have been taken into account in ordering a reduced period of disqualification or in not ordering any disqualification (Transport Act 1981, s. 19(6)).

Special roads. These roads are normally known simply as "motorways" (*q.v.*). The Highways Act 1959, ss. 11–20 and associated legislation have been repealed and replaced by the Highways Act 1980, ss. 16–20, without change of effect.

Specialty debts. The Limitation Act 1939, s. 1, has been repealed and replaced by the Limitation Act 1980, s. 8(1), without change of effect.

Specific goods. The Sale of Goods Act 1893, ss. 62, 11(1)(c) (as amended), have been repealed and replaced by the Sale of Goods Act 1979, ss. 61, 11(4), without change of effect.

Specific performance. The Sale of Goods Act 1893, s. 52, has been repealed and replaced by the Sale of Goods Act 1979, s. 51, without change of effect.

Decrees for the specific performance of contracts of employment are subject to statutory restrictions (Trade Union and

Labour Relations Act 1974, ss. 16, 17); see INJUNCTION.

Where the plaintiff has sought and obtained a decree of specific perfomance but the defendant fails to obey the order, the plaintiff may be at liberty to restore the case in order to seek an alternative judgment sounding in damages (*q.v.*) (see *Johnson* v. *Agnew* [1980] A.C. 367, H.L.).

The jurisdiction of county courts under the County Courts Act 1959, s. 52(1)(*d*), was extended so that cases involving up to £15,000 might be determined in those courts (County Courts Jurisdiction Order 1977 (S.I. 1977 No. 600)). The jurisdiction was further increased in 1981 to a limit of £30,000 (County Courts Jurisdiction Order 1981 (S.I. 1981 No. 1123)). The Act of 1959, s. 52(1)(*d*), has now been repealed and replaced (without change of effect) by the County Courts Act 1984, s. 23(*d*), where the term "specific performance" is retained (contrast the Supreme Court provisions, below).

The Judicature Act 1925, ss. 36, 56(1), have been repealed and replaced by the Supreme Court Act 1981, ss. 49, 61(1), (3), Sched. 1, para. 1(*a*), respectively. In the Act of 1981, the jurisdiction is described as "sale, exchange or partition of land, or the raising of charges on land", omitting the words "specific performance", but without significant change of effect.

Speed limits. General speed limits of national application are now prescribed for all vehicles: on dual carriageway roads the maximum permitted speed is 70 miles per hour; on single carriageway roads it is 60 miles per hour (see S.I. 1975 No. 1895; S.I. 1976 No. 1872; and S.I. 1978 No. 502). A speed limit of 70 miles per hour is imposed on motorway traffic (S.I. 1974 No. 502). In any event these limits may be reduced in respect of specified (and marked) stretches of road under the powers contained in the Road Traffic Acts.

The penalty on summary conviction of a speeding offence was increased to £100 (Road Traffic Act 1972, s. 21, Sched. 5, Part II) and £500 on motorways (Criminal Law Act 1977, s. 31, Sched. 6), and in 1984 these levels were again increased (see FINE). The disqualification formerly imposed on a third conviction (provided each conviction was of the type which also carries an endorsement) was only imposed in certain cases (see TOTTING-UP PROCEDURE). The governing provision (Road Traffic Act 1972, s. 93(3)), has been repealed and replaced by the Transport Act 1981, s. 19, which made substantial changes in the law; see also SPECIAL REASONS.

The Road Traffic Regulation Act 1967, ss. 71–73, 74, 77, 78, 78A, 79, have been repealed and replaced by the Road Traffic Regulation Act 1984, ss. 81–91, Scheds. 6 (which contains the limits) and 7 (which contains the penalty provisions), without change of effect.

Speedometer. Subject to comparatively unimportant exceptions, every motor vehicle capable of travelling in excess of 10 miles per hour must be fitted with a speedometer which is readily visible to the driver; a margin of accuracy of plus or minus 10 per cent is permitted (Motor Vehicle (Construction and Use) Regulations 1978 (S.I. 1978 No. 1017, as variously amended), reg. 18). The instrument must be maintained in good working order, and free from obstruction which might prevent easy visibility; if it stops working there is no offence if the defect occurs in the course of the journey when the contravention is detected, nor if, when the contravention is detected, reasonable steps have been taken to remedy the defect (reg. 98).

Spirits. The Customs and Excise Act 1952, ss. 93–115, 116–124, have been repealed and replaced by the Alcoholic Liquor Duties Act 1979, ss. 5–35, 75–80, without substantial change of effect.

Spiritualism. For the general revision of the penalties which may be imposed on summary conviction see FINE.

Splitting a cause of action. The County Courts Act 1959, s. 69, has been repealed and replaced by the County Courts Act 1984, s. 35, without change of effect.

Spring traps. All the statutory instruments noted, with the exception of S.I. 1958 No. 24, were revoked and replaced by the Spring Traps Approval Order 1975 (S.I. 1975 No. 1647, now amended by S.I. 1982 No. 153)).

Squatter. Fresh provision has been made to punish the use of violence to secure entry to premises, adverse possession of residential premises, certain types of trespass (to land) and obstruction of court officers executing process for possession against unauthorised occupiers (Criminal Law Act 1977, ss. 6–13). See FORCIBLE ENTRY.

The procedures under R.S.C. Ord. 113 (and C.C.R. Ord. 26) have been amended so as to require the use in all cases of an originating summons for which no acknowledgement of service is required (S.I. 1979 Nos. 522, 1716). Unless the applicant agrees to a suspended order being made, any judgment under R.S.C. Ord. 113, must be drawn so as to be capable of immediate execution (*Swordheath Properties Ltd.* v. *Floydd* [1978] 1 W.L.R. 551).

The Limitation Act 1939, has been repealed and replaced by the Limitation Act 1980, without significant change of effect beyond the incorporation of the additional terms of the Limitation Acts of 1963, 1975 and the Limitation Amendment Act 1980. The provisions of C.C.R. 1936, Ord. 26, have been repealed and replaced by the C.C.R. 1981 Ord. 24, rr. 1–7, without significant change of effect.

Stage carriage. The Road Traffic Act 1960, ss. 117, 118, have been repealed and replaced by the Public Passenger Vehicles Act 1981 s. 1 of the 1981 Act defines "public service vehicle"; s. 2(1)(*a*) defines stage carriage as a "public service vehicle being used in the operation of a local service"; the section then defines other main features of the revised public service vehicle provisions, *i.e.* "express carriage," "contract carriage," "local service" and "express service."

Stamp duties. The Forgery Act 1913, has been repealed and replaced by the Forgery and Counterfeiting Act 1981, s. 30, Sched., Part I, without specific replacement of the specialised provisions formerly thought necessary (see FORGERY).

State. Special provision has been made for clarifying the relationship of the English legal system to foreign states (State Immunity Act 1978). The new provisions made it possible for the United Kingdom to ratify the International Convention for the Unification of Certain Rules relating to the Immunity of State-owned Vessels 1926 (the "Brussels Conventions") (Cmd. 5672) and the European Convention on State Immunity 1972 (Cmnd. 6081).

The principle that English courts will not subject a foreign state to their jurisdiction has been most noticeably breached in *Thai-Europe Tapioca Service Ltd.* v. *Government of Pakistan (Directorate of Agricultural Supplies)* [1975] 1 W.L.R. 1485, C.A.; *Trendtex Trading Corporation* v. *Central Bank of Nigeria* [1977] Q.B. 529, C.A.; *The Phillippine Admiral* [1977] A.C. 373, P.C.; and *C. Czarnikow* v. *Centrala Handlu Zagranicznegro Rolimpex* [1979] A.C. 351, H.L.

Stateless person. The British Nationality (No. 1) Act 1964, has been repealed and replaced by the British Nationality Act 1981, s. 3 (with modifications). The Act of 1981, s. 36, Sched. 2, contain provisions specifically aimed at the reduction of statelessness.

Statement in lieu of prospectus. The Companies Act 1948, s. 48, has been repealed by the Companies Act 1980, ss. 82, 88(2), Sched. 4. The 1948 procedure for conversion from private to public company status has been repealed (Act of 1980, s. 88(2), Sched. 4) and replaced in modified form by the Companies Act 1980, s. 5; in the process the statement in lieu has disappeared.

Statement of claim. The procedural step of entering an appearance has been abolished and replaced by the requirement that the defendant send to the court office an acknowledgment of service and (if appropriate) notice of intention to defend (see S.I. 1979 No. 1716), but without otherwise affecting the timetable relating to a statement of claim.

Statement of defence. The requirement of entering an appearance has been abolished and replaced by acknowledgment of service (see STATEMENT OF CLAIM).

Stationery Office. The activities of this institution are now funded under the HMSO Trading Fund Order 1980 (S.I. 1980 No. 456).

Statute. The Statutes Revised series has been replaced by Statutes in Force (*q.v.*).

Statute barred. The Limitation Act 1939, together with the various amending Acts of 1963, 1975 and the Limitation Amendment Act 1980, have been repealed and replaced by the Limitation Act 1980, a consolidating Act.

Statute of Frauds 1677. The Sale of Goods Act 1893, s. 26, has been repealed and replaced by the Supreme Court Act 1981, s. 138, without change of effect.

Statutes in Force. A new series of volumes containing the Act of Parliament in force and showing them in their amended form. The various Acts are contained in "loose-leaf booklets" for insertion into binders, thus facilitating their arrangement in convenient groups. This series was designed to replace the earlier *Statutes Revised* and is published by Her Majesty's Stationery Office for the Statutory Publications Office.

Statutory declarations. The Interpretation Act 1889, s. 21, has been repealed and replaced by the Interpretation Act 1978, s. 5, Sched. 1, without change of effect.

Statutory joint industrial tribunals. The Employment Protection Act 1975, s. 90, Sched. 8, have been repealed and replaced by the Wages Councils Act 1979, s. 10, Sched. 4, without change of effect.

Statutory legacy. Special provision made for the distribution of the estate of an intestate; see DISTRIBUTION; WIDOW.

Statutory meeting. The Companies Act 1948, s. 130, has been repealed by the Companies Act 1980, ss. 82, 88(2), Sched. 4. The revised provisions govern the commencement of business by public companies, etc., are set out in the Act of 1980, ss. 4–6.

Statutory sick pay. See SICKNESS BENEFIT.

Stay. The Judicature Act 1925, s. 41, has been repealed and replaced by the Supreme Court Act 1981, s. 49, in modified form (s. 49(3) provides "power of the Court of Appeal or the High Court to stay any proceedings before it, where it thinks fit to do so . . . "), but without significant change of effect.

Sterling. For further derogations from the former rule requiring the use of sterling in court proceedings (*In re United Railways of Havana and Regla Warehouses Ltd.* [1971] A.C. 1007, H.L.) see FOREIGN CURRENCY.

Still. The Customs and Excise Act 1952, ss. 226–228 (as amended), have been repealed and replaced by the Alcoholic Liquor Duties Act 1979, ss. 81–83, without change of effect.

Stipendiary magistrate. The provisions of the Administration of Justice Act 1973, s. 2, and of the Magistrates' Courts Act 1952, s. 121(1), have been repealed and re-enacted (together with other appropriate legislation) in the Justices of the Peace Act 1979, ss. 13–16, without significant change of effect.

Stock. Amendments to the procedures for the transfer of stock have been required on account of the computerisation of accounting at the Stock Exchange (Stock Exchange (Completion of Bargains) Act 1976, s. 6; Stock Transfer (Addition of Forms) Order 1979 (S.I. 1979 No. 277)).

Stock Exchange. The Stock Exchange has introduced computerised accounting systems and amendments in the law to take account of the new system are contained in the Stock Exchange (Completion of Bargains) Act 1976 (which was brought into force on 12 February, 1979 (S.I. 1979 No. 55)).

The Stock Exchange and its members have been exempted from the controls of the Restrictive Trade Practices Act 1976 (Restrictive Trade Practices (Stock Exchange) Act 1984).

Stop notice. In the law of town and country planning this is a notice served in order to give special effect to an enforcement notice (*q.v.*) (Town and Country Planning Act 1971, s. 90 (as substituted by the Town and Country Planning (Amendment) Act 1977, s. 1)).

See also STOP ORDER.

Stoppage in transitu. The Sale of Goods Act 1893, ss. 44, 45, 47, 62(3), have been repealed and replaced by the Sale of Goods Act 1979, ss. 44, 45, 47, 61(4), without change of effect.

Stowaway. The Merchant Shipping Act 1894, ss. 237, 313, have been repealed and replaced by the Merchant Shipping Act 1970, s 77, with increases in the penalties for contravening the Act but otherwise without major change of effect; see also s. 78, which deals with unauthorised presence on a ship.

The Colonial Air Navigation Order 1949 (S.I. 1949 No. 2000), has been revoked; the current equivalent is the Air Navigation (Overseas Territories) Order 1977 (S.I. 1977 No. 422, as amended by S.I. 1977 No. 820 and S.I. 1978 No. 1520).

Street. The Highways Act 1959, ss. 295, 157–172, have been repealed and replaced by the Highways Act 1980, ss. 329(1), 186–202, without change of effect. The Public Health Act 1961, ss. 44, 48, have been repealed and replaced by the Highways Act 1980, ss. 287, 180, also without change of effect.

Street offences. For the general revision of the penalties which may be imposed on summary conviction and the abolition of enhanced penalties for second and subsequent offences see FINE.

Street playgrounds. The Road Traffic Regulation Act 1967, ss. 26, 26A, 27, have been repealed and replaced by the Road Traffic Regulation Act 1984, ss. 29–31, without change of effect.

Street refuge. The Highways Act 1959, s. 68, has been repealed and replaced by the Highways Act 1980, s. 68, without change of effect.

Street works. The Highways Act 1959, ss. 173–213, have been repealed and replaced by the Highways Act 1980, ss. 203–277, without change of effect.

Structure plan. This is a written statement which formulates the county planning authority's policy and general proposals relating to the development and other uses of land in its area, including measures for the improvement of the environment and traffic management, and it states the relationship of those proposals to general similar proposals in adjoining areas if they might be expected to affect the planning authority's area (see the Town and County Planning Act 1971, ss. 6 *et seq.*). Structure plans are the successors to development plans (see DEVELOPMENT), and there are comparable procedures for giving publicity to the plans, lodging and examining objections, and appeals procedures.

Subject to contract. This well-understood expression has been the subject of conflicting decisions which might well have added nothing at all to the law. In *Law* v. *Jones* [1974] Ch. 112, C.A., the use of the expression was ineffective to prevent the conclusion of a binding contract, which was enforceable by order for specific performance since the terms were adequately recorded (see CONTRACT FOR SALE OF LAND); in *Tiverton Estates Ltd.* v. *Wearwell Ltd.* [1975] Ch. 146, C.A., the decision was against upholding the alleged contract, on the ground that the Law of Property Act 1925, s. 40(1) memorandum required not only that the terms of the contract should be adequately recorded but also that there should be an acknowledgment or recognition by the signatory to the document that a contract had been entered into.

Submersible apparatus. Regulations made under the Merchant Shipping Act 1974, ss. 16, 17, include the Merchant Shipping (Diving Operations) Regulations 1975 (S.I. 1975 No. 1166), and the Merchant Shipping (Registration of Submersible Craft) Regulations 1976 (S.I. 1976 No. 940, amended by S.I. 1979 No. 1519).

Subpoena. For the amendment of the requirements relating to the service of a subpoena see the Rules of the Supreme Court (Amendment No. 2) 1980 (S.I. 1980 No. 1010).

The county court provisions have been revised: C.C.R. 1936 Ord. 20, r. 8, has been revoked and replaced by the C.C.R. 1981 Ord. 20, r. 12; the penalty is now provided for by the County Courts Act 1984, s. 55.

Subsidiary company. The Finance Act 1938, s. 50, was repealed by the Finance Act 1967, ss. 27(3), 45(8), Sched. 16, Part VII, without replacement.

Suffrance wharves. The Customs and Excise Act 1952, s. 14, has been repealed and replaced by the Customs and Excise Management Act 1979, s. 20, without change of effect. The Act of 1952 introduced the term "approved wharves" in substitution for "suffrance wharves" (last used in the Customs Consolidation Act 1876, s. 14, the predecessor to 1952, s. 14).

Sugar. The Sugar Act 1956, has been repealed by the Food Act 1984, s. 134, Sched. 11. By the Act of 1984, s. 68, British Sugar PLC (*q.v.*) has various teaching and research responsibilities.

Suit. The Judicature Act 1925, s. 225, has been repealed and replaced by the Supreme Court Act 1981, s. 151(1); the term "suit" no longer appears in the list of definitions.

Suitors' Deposit Account. The Supreme Court Funds Rules 1927, r. 73–80, have been revoked and replaced by the Supreme Court Funds Rules 1975 (S.I. 1975 No. 1803), rr. 28–37C, with alterations designed to take account of the reorganisation of the Court Funds Office.

Summary conviction. The usual definition of "summary offence" is an offence which, if committed by an adult, is triable only summarily (Criminal Law Act 1977, s. 64(1)(*b*)).

Summary judgment. Such judgments are also available in the Chancery Division under the procedure laid down in R.S.C. Ord. 86.

In county courts, where the claim exceeds £500 (the sum below which default actions are normally referred to arbitration (*q.v.*)), there is now a procedure comparable to the R.S.C. Ord. 14 expedited procedure (C.C.R. 1981 Ord. 9, r. 14).

Summary jurisdiction. The Magistrates' Courts Act 1952, s. 19, Sched. 1 (as amended and extended), have been repealed by the Criminal Law Act 1977, s. 65(5), Sched. 13. The classification of offences was modified by the Act of 1977, ss. 14–16, so that there are now only three classes of offence (those which are triable only on indictment, those which may be tried only summarily, and those which may be tried either way). The offences made triable either way (which represent an approximation to the list formerly contained in the Act of 1952, Sched. 1) were set out in the Criminal Law Act 1977, Sched. 3, which repeated the 1952 with two alterations: criminal diversion of letters (Post Office Act 1952, s. 56) and incitement to commit a summary offence became triable only summarily.

The 1977 provisions have now been repealed and replaced by the Magistrates' Courts Act 1980, s. 17, Sched. 1, without change of effect.

The Interpretation Act 1889, s. 13(1), has been repealed by the Interpretation Act 1978, s. 25(1), Sched. 3, without replacement. By the Act of 1978, s. 5, Sched. 1, the definition of "magistrates' court" in the Magistrates' Courts Act 1952, s. 124, was applied to all legislation in the absence of any indication to the contrary.

Summer time. The dates for the commencement and termination of summer time for the years to 1985 have been promulgated (Summer Time Order 1982 (S.I. 1982 No. 1673)).

Summons. Appeals in the Queen's Bench Division from a master lie to the Court of Appeal only when the master's jurisdiction was by consent of all the parties (R.S.C. Ord. 58, r. 2); in all other cases the appeal is to a judge in chambers (Ord. 58, r. 1).

Substituted service of summonses is now regulated by R.S.C. Ord. 65, r. 4.

The time allowed to a defendant to a county court default summons to give notice of intention to defend has been increased to 14 days from the service of the summons (inclusive of the day of service) (see C.C.R. 1981 Ord. 9, replacing C.C.R. 1936 Ord. 10, rr. 1, 2, 3, 4(1)).

For amendments to the procedure to be followed in wardship and certain matrimonial cases see the Rules of the Supreme Court (Amendment No. 2) 1980 (S.I. 1980 No. 1010).

Sunday. The common law rule that no judicial act might be done on a Sunday has been eroded so that an injunction may be so granted and served (*Re N.* (*Infants*) [1967] Ch. 512), and in urgent cases process (a term which includes a writ, judgment, notice, order, petition, originating or other summons or warrant) may with leave of the court be served on a Sunday (see R.S.C. Ord. 65, r. 10).

The Magistrates' Courts Act 1952, s. 102, has been repealed and replaced by the Magistrates' Courts Act 1980, s. 125; the specific authorisation of execution on a Sunday has not been repeated in the new provision.

For the general revision of the penalties which may be imposed on summary conviction see FINE.

Supervision order. The Criminal Justice Act 1967, s. 63, has been modified in its operation by the Criminal Law Act 1977, s. 65(4), Sched. 12. The Criminal Justice Act 1972, s. 12, has been repealed and replaced by the Powers of Criminal Courts Act 1973, s. 26, without change of effect.

Additional provisions include the Criminal Justice Act 1982, ss. 20, 21, which modify the Children and Young Persons Act 1969, s. 12, by the replacement of s. 12(2)–(3C) by new s. 12(2)–(3N)) and revise the text of s. 19.

Support. The Limitation Act 1939, has been repealed and replaced by the Limitation Act 1980, which consolidates the various amendments made by the Limitation Acts 1963, 1975 and the Limitation Amendment Act 1980, but otherwise without change of effect.

Supreme Court of Judicature. The Judicature Act 1925, s. 1, has been repealed and replaced by the Supreme Court Act 1981, s. 1, without significant change of effect.

Surcharge. The Local Government Act 1972, s. 161, has been repealed and replaced by the Local Government Finance Act 1982, s. 20, with minor changes. The word "surcharge" disappeared from the statutory provisions on this topic in 1972.

For cases within the financial jurisdiction of county courts, the C.C.R. 1936 Ord. 46, r. 26, procedure on appeals against surcharge has been revoked and replaced by the C.C.R. 1981 Ord. 49, r. 10, without change of effect.

Sureties of the peace and good behaviour. The Criminal Law Act 1967, s. 7(4), was repealed by the Powers of Criminal Courts Act 1973, s. 56(2), Sched. 6, without direct replacement, the power in the Justices of the Peace Act 1968, s. 1(7), being available to Crown Court and magistrates' courts alike.

See also the Magistrates' Courts Act 1980, ss. 115, 116 (replacing the Magistrates' Courts Act 1952, ss. 91, 92, without change of effect).

Surname or **Sirname.** The Matrimonial Causes (Amendment) Rules 1974, have been revoked and replaced by the Matrimonial Causes Rules 1977 (S.I. 1977 No. 344), r. 98(2), without change of effect.

Surprise. In any pleading subsequent to a statement of claim there must be pleaded expressly any matter which, if not specifically pleaded, might take the other party by surprise (R.S.C. Ord. 18, r. 8(1)(*b*)).

Survivorship. For the modification of certain survivorship rules in relation to capital transfer tax see COMMORIENTES.

Suspected person. The offence under the Vagrancy Act 1824, s. 4, was revised as to refer to persons suspected of loitering with intent to commit an arrestable offence (Criminal Law Act 1967, s. 10, Sched. 2, para. 2). In 1981, however, those parts of the Act of 1824, s. 4, which related to being a suspected person were repealed in favour of a new offence of interfering with a vehicle; see LOITERING.

Suspended sentence. The earlier legislation has been repealed and replaced by the Powers of Criminal Courts Act 1973, ss. 22–25. To come within the scheme for suspension, the sentence of imprisonment must not exceed two years; the period of suspension is such period as the court thinks fit not exceeding two years but not less than one year (s. 22(1)).

The scheme of suspended sentences (Powers of Criminal Courts Act 1973, ss. 22–27) has been supplemented by the scheme for partially suspended sentences. The Criminal Law Act 1977, s. 47, which provided for part of the sentence to be served forthwith, the remainder being held in suspense from release until the outstanding period of imprisonment has run; these provisions were brought into operation on 29 March 1983 (Criminal Law Act 1977 (Commencement No. 1) Order 1982 (S.I. 1982 No. 243)). The scheme was almost immediately heavily amended by the Criminal Justice Act 1982, ss. 30, 31, which reduced the minimum periods of suspension and changed the proportions required to be observed, thus making the sentence more readily available to magistrates' courts. It is impossible partially to suspend the operation of a suspended sentence which is just coming into operation after some part of its principal suspension has run (*R.* v. *Gow* (1983) 5 Cr.App.R.(S.) 250, C.A.).

See also SUPERVISION ORDER.

Swan. For the revision of the penalties which may be imposed on summary conviction (*e.g.* under the Game Act 1831) see FINE. The Protection of Birds Act 1954, ss. 1, 2, 6, have been repealed and replaced by the Wildlife and Countryside Act 1981, ss. 1–8, Sched. 1, Part I, with minor modifications.

Swearing. For the revision of the penalties which may be imposed on summary conviction see FINE.

Sweets. The Customs and Excise Act 1952, ss. 139–142 (as amended in 1969), have been repealed and replaced by the Alcoholic Liquor Duties Act 1979, s. 92(2), Sched. 4, Part I, without replacement. The definition of "sweets" in the Act of 1952, s. 307(1), was repealed (without replacement) by the Customs and Excise Management Act 1979, s. 177(3), Sched. 6.

Swimming baths. The Public Health Act 1936, s. 221(*b*) (which authorised the provision of swimming baths), has been repealed and replaced by the Local Government (Miscellaneous Provisions) Act 1976, s. 19(1)(*a*), which makes more extensive provision than the Act of 1936 for ancillary facilities and other recreational facilities (as well as using the new term "swimming pools").

T

Table. A revised form of Table A has been substituted into the Companies Act 1948 (Companies (Alteration of Table A, etc., Regulations 1984 (S.I. 1984 No. 1717), but the day for the operation of those regulations remained to be fixed).

Tape recordings. Tape recording is now most often used where formerly a shorthand note of the evidence given in proceedings would have been taken; see SHORTHAND-WRITERS.

For the purposes of the Civil Evidence Act 1968, Part I, a tape recording is a document and may therefore be ordered to be disclosed under the rules relating to discovery and inspection (*q.v.*) of documents (Act of 1968, s. 10(1)).

Using a tape recording in the course of proceedings without the prior consent of the court amounts to contempt, as does bringing sound recording equipment into court for use, the publication of tape recordings, or the use of recordings in contravention of any conditions imposed when leave to record is given (Contempt of Court Act 1981, s. 9(1)). Courts may forfeit the equipment or recordings (s. 9(3)). Official recordings are excepted from the operation of the Act (s. 9(4)).

Tax and Price Index. Introduced in 1979, this is designed as a supplement to the Retail Prices Index (see COST OF LIVING INDEX) especially geared to show the combined impact of tax and price changes. When first published, earlier figures from other economic indicators were used to compile tables showing the movements which would have been shown by the Index had it been in existence at those times. After a short initial period in the public gaze, it has all but disappeared.

Taxation of costs. The procedure of appealing to the judge is now available to any party who is dissatisfied with the decision of the taxing officer on review (R.S.C. Ord. 62, r. 35(1)).

The decision in *Re Jerome* [1907] 2 Ch. 145, has been given statutory expression in the Supreme Court of Judicature (Consolidation) Act 1925, s. 31(1)(*h*). That provision has now been repealed and replaced by the Supreme Court Act 1981, s. 18(1)(*f*). The Courts Act 1971, s. 26, has been repealed and replaced by the Supreme Court Act 1981, s. 89, Sched. 2, without change of effect.

The taxation of costs as between solicitor and client in any class of business is now regulated by the Solicitors Act 1974, ss. 70–72, 74.

For the taxation of costs in the county courts see C.C.R. 1981 Ord. 38 (which has displaced C.C.R. 1936 Ord. 47).

Telecommunications. The telecommunications functions of the Post Office have been separated out into a private sector corporation (British Telecommunications Act 1981 and the Telecommunications Act 1984). The former monopoly on telecommunications (Post Office Act 1969, ss. 23–27) was originally transferred to British Telecommunications (Act of 1981, s. 12), but has now been abolished (Act of 1984, s. 2).

Telephone tappings. The law of this matter, including the effect of the European Convention for the Protection of Human Rights and Fundamental Freedoms 1950 (Cmd. 8969), were considered in *Malone* v. *Metropolitan Police Commissioner* [1979] Ch. 344. The court ruled that the Convention was not part of our domestic law.

Telex. The Telex Regulations 1965 (as amended), have been revoked and replaced by the Post Office Scheme, details of which are published in the London Gazette.

Temporary housing accommodation. The Housing (Temporary Accommodation) Acts 1944, 1945, and the Housing Repairs and Rents Act 1957, ss. 2, 19, have been repealed by the Housing Finance Act 1972, s. 108(4), Sched. 11, Part II.

For an elaborate and confused statutory scheme requiring the provision of accommodation for homeless people see the Housing (Homeless Persons) Act 1977, which omits to specify whether temporary accommodation is adequate compliance with its provisions.

Tenancy in common. The Finance Act

1965, s. 22(1), has been repealed and replaced by the Capital Gains Tax Act 1979, s. 46(1), without change of effect.

Tender. The quantities of coins which are legal tender have been re-stated: cupro-nickel or silver coins of more than 20p in value, legal tender for payment of any amount not exceeding £10; cupro-nickel or silver coins of not more than 10p in value, legal tender for payment of any amount not exceeding £5; bronze coins, legal tender for payment of any amount not exceeding 20p (Coinage Act 1971, s. 2(1A)) (as substituted by the Currency Act 1983, s. 1(3)(*a*)).

Territorial army. The statutory provisions relating to this body have been repealed and consolidated into the Reserve Forces Act 1980, Part IV (ss. 88–120).

Territorial waters. British fishery limits have been extended to 200 miles (Fishing Limits Act 1976, s. 1), power being granted to the minister to make orders to allow foreign vessels of specified countries and of specified groups to come within those limits for specified purposes (s. 2).

Terrorism. See the Suppression of Terrorism Act 1978, s. 4, and the Prevention of Terrorism (Temporary Provisions) Act 1984, s. 14, Sched. 3, Part II, para. 3. Most acts of terrorism qualify for extradition (*q.v.*) proceedings.

Test case. See SELECTED ACTION and CONSOLIDATION OF ACTIONS.

Testable. The age at which a person becomes testable is now 18 years (Family Law Reform Act 1969, s 3).

Testamentary guardian. The Guardianship of Infants Act 1925, s. 5, has been repealed and replaced by the Guardianship of Minors Act 1971, s. 4, which confers equal powers of appointment of a testamentary guardian on both parents (see also the Guardianship Act 1973, s. 1). The Tenures Abolition Act 1660 (12 Car. 2, c. 24), s. 9 (which dealt with certain rights which were restricted to fathers), has been repealed by the Guardianship Act 1973, s. 9(1), Sched. 3.

Teste. Writs are no longer tested in any name, the rules and forms having been amended so as to delete what was alleged to be an anachronism (see R.S.C. Ord. 6, r. 1, and App. A, Form 1 (as amended and substituted by S.I. 1979 No. 1716)).

Thames. The actual boundaries of the Thames are varied from time to time by private Acts of Parliament promoted by the Port of London Authority, which has extensive powers of control and management over the river.

Theatre. The Theatrical Employers Registration Acts 1925 and 1928 have been repealed without replacement (Local Government (Miscellaneous Provisions) Act 1982, s. 1, Sched. 7, Part VI).

Theft. Further provisions are contained in the Theft Act 1978, which deals with offences of deception (*q.v.*). All the offences in the Theft Act 1968, which were originally classified as indictable crimes are now triable either way, with the following exceptions: (a) robbery, aggravated burglary, blackmail and assault with intent to rob; (b) burglary comprising the commission of, or an intention to commit, an offence which is triable only on indictment; (c) burglary in a dwelling if any person in the dwelling was subjected to any violence or the threat of violence (Magistrates' Courts Act 1980, s. 17, Sched. 1, para. 28, replacing the Criminal Law Act 1977, s. 16, Sched. 3, para. 28). The offences under the Act of 1978 were expressly made triable either way (s. 4(1)).

Thermal insulation. Grants have been made available for the thermal insulation of dwellings (Homes Insulation Act 1978).

Third party. The power to join a third party to legal proceedings often depends on the general law of contribution (*q.v.*) which has been amended by the Civil Liability (Contribution) Act 1978.

The Judicature Act 1925, s. 39, has been repealed by the Supreme Court Act 1981, s. 152(4), Sched. 7, without direct replacement. Justification for rules of court relating to third parties now rests in the words "all matters in dispute between the parties are completely and finally determined, and all multiplicity of legal proceedings with respect to any of those matters is avoided" (Act of 1981, s. 49(2)).

In county courts the conduct of third party and subsequent proceedings is regulated by C.C.R. 1981 Ord. 12.

The Torts (Interference with Goods) Act 1977, s. 8(1), entitles a defendant to proceedings for wrongful interference with goods to show that a third party has a better right than the plaintiff as respects all or any part of the interest claimed by the plaintiff, or in right of which he sues. Rules of court to give effect to the statutory provisions have been made to regulate the introduction of such a defence (R.S.C. Ord. 15, r. 10A).

Threats. The provisions of the Patents Act 1949, s. 65, are repeated (with slight addition) by the Patents Act 1977, s. 70, so as to provide the same protection for patents which come within the 1977 domestic patent provisions.

Ticket. Many of the public and general Act provisions in relation to tickets, fares, etc. have been effectively superseded by private legislation (see, *e.g.* the British Railways Act 1981 (c. xxiii), which deals with, amongst other things, travelling with intent to avoid payment of the fare).

Timber. The Finance Act 1975, Sched. 9, provisions relating to capital transfer tax have been repealed and replaced by the Capital Transfer Tax Act 1984, Part V, Chapter III (ss. 125–130), without significant change of effect.

Time. The Statutes (Definition of Time) Act 1880, has been repealed and replaced by the Interpretation Act 1978, s. 9, without significant change of effect. The Sale of Goods Act 1893, s. 10, has been repealed and replaced by the Sale of Goods Act 1979, s. 10, without change of effect.

Tithes. Tithe rentcharge annuities under the Tithe Acts 1936 and 1951 have been abolished following a double payment on 1 October 1977 (Finance Act 1977, s. 56); appropriate portions of the 1936 and 1951 Acts have been repealed (Act of 1977, s. 59, Sched. 9, Part V).

Title-deeds. The Forgery Act 1913, s. 18(1), has been repealed by the Forgery and Counterfeiting Act 1981, s. 30. Sched., Part I. The specific earlier provisions have not been repeated since the behaviour in question falls within the new general provisions for forgery. (*q.v.*).

Tobacco. The Customs and Excise Act 1952, ss. 173–194 (as amended), have been repealed by the Finance Act 1977, s. 3 Sched. 9. Duty is now charged on finished products; see TOBACCO PRODUCTS DUTY.

For the general revision of the penalties which may be imposed on summary conviction see FINE.

Tobacco products duty. Introduced by the Finance Act 1976, ss. 4–8, this is now regulated by the Tobacco Products Duty Act 1979. For former excise duties see TOBACCO.

Tobago and Trinidad. These islands have become a republic within the Commonwealth (Trinidad and Tobago Republic Act 1976).

Token. For credit tokens see CREDIT CARDS.

Toll. The County Courts Act 1959, s. 39(1)(*b*), has been repealed and replaced by the County Courts Act 1984, s. 15(2)(*b*), without change of effect.

Tomlin order. A form of order drafted by Tomlin J., for use when an action is stayed by consent of the parties and on terms scheduled to the order. The wording of the order is as follows: "AND the Plaintiff and the Defendant having agreed to the terms set forth in the Schedule hereto IT IS ORDERED that all further proceedings in this action be stayed except for the purpose of carrying those terms into effect LIBERTY to apply as to carrying those terms into effect" (*Practice Note* [1927] W.N. 290). Not being a judgment, no interest (*q.v.*) will be attracted by any money payment due under the scheduled terms unless specifically provided for. The judge will not normally inquire into the terms of the agreement (see *Noel* v. *Becker* (*Practice Note*) [1971] 1 W.L.R. 355, C.A.).

Tonnage. The Customs and Excise Act 1952, ss. 143–145, have been repealed and replaced by the Alcoholic Liquor Duties Act 1979, ss. 54–61, without change of effect.

Small ships are now to be measured for length instead of tonnage (Merchant Shipping Act 1983, s. 1).

Tools. The minimum value of a bankrupt's necessary goods which are exempt from division among the creditors has been increased from £20 to £250 (Bankruptcy Act 1914, s. 38(2); Insolvency Act 1976, s. 1, Sched. 1, Part I). The limit of £50 under the Small Debts Act 1845, s. 8, has been increased: the amount of wearing apparel and bedding which is now exempt is to the value of £100 and tools up to £150 (Protection from Execution (Prescribed Value) Order 1980 (S.I. 1980 No. 26)). The County Courts Act 1959 has been repealed and replaced by the County Courts Act 1984, without significant change of effect.

Tort. The county court jurisdiction was in 1977 increased in value from £750 to £2,000 (County Courts Act 1959, s. 39; County Courts Jurisdiction Order 1977 (S.I. 1977 No. 600)); a further increase, to £5,000, was made in 1981 (County Courts Jurisdiction Order 1981 (S.I. 1981 No. 1123)). The County Courts Act 1959, ss. 39, 47, have been repealed and replaced by the County Courts Act 1984, ss. 15, 19–20, without change of effect.

The tort of detinue has been abolished and conversion has been extended to encompass the loss of goods resulting from a bailee's breach of his duty to his bailor through culpable inaction (Torts (Interference with Goods) Act 1977, s. 2).

This class of case (tort) has been held to include actions for breach of statutory duty (see *Thornton* v. *Kirklees Metropolitan Borough Council* [1979] Q.B. 626, C.A.).

Totting-up procedure. A colloquial expression referring to the terms of the Road Traffic Act 1972, s. 93(3), which required the disqualification for holding a driving licence of a person who has been convicted of an endorsable offence and who has already been so convicted on two separate occasions in the three years immediately preceding the date of the offence being dealt with.

The 1972 provision has been repealed, but the replacement provision (Transport Act 1981, s. 19) has attracted the same label to itself. A closely similar procedure is observed, an accumulation being made of the "penalty points" imposed (under the Act of 1981, Sched. 7) in the prescribed period, special reasons (*q.v.*) still being available to avoid disqualification. The most noticeable difference lies in the increasing severity of disqualification in the event of a second or subsequent disqualification (see the Act of 1981, s. 19(4)).

See also DECEPTION (for the consequence of evading disqualification, etc., by deception) and DRIVING LICENCE.

Town and country planning. The various changes of the law in this field are noted under their own headings (*e.g.* the Town and Country Planning (Minerals) Act 1981, is noted at MINERALS).

Trade, Board of. The Interpretation Act 1889, s. 12, has been repealed and replaced by the Interpretation Act 1978, s. 25(1), Sched. 3, without replacement of the definition of this expression.

Trade dispute. Amendments have been made (by the Employment Act 1982, s. 18) to the definition in the Trade Union and Labour Relations Act 1974, s. 29(1) making the following changes: (1) qualifying disputes are limited to those between workers and their (own) employer (the original expression "between employers and workers" being too wide after the restriction of picketing (*q.v.*) activities by the 1982 Act); (2) disputes between groups of workers are excluded; (3) the expression "is connected with" is replaced by "relates wholly or mainly to," in order to exclude disputes which are only marginally linked to the items (listed as (a) to (g)) of special concern. The definition of "worker" now includes both current and former employees (Act of 1982, s. 18(6)). The law relating to matters arising outside Great Britain has also been revised (s. 18(4)); the Crown may now be a liable employer (s. 18(3)).

Trade unions. The test of whether an act is done by any person in contemplation or furtherance of a trade dispute so as not to be actionable in certain circumstances (Trade Union and Labour Relations Act 1974, s. 13) was held by the courts to be a subjective one, the honest belief of the person whose acts are complained of being the determining factor (*Duport Steels Ltd.* v. *Sirs* [1980] 1 W.L.R. 142, H.L.; see also *Express Newspapers Ltd.* v. *McShane* [1979] 1 W.L.R. 390, H.L.).

The Industry Act 1975, ss. 31–33, have been repealed without replacement by the Industry Act 1980, s. 19; the Insurance Companies Act 1974, has been repealed and replaced by the Insurance Companies Act 1982, without change of effect.

The procedure for recognition of trade unions under the Employment Protection Act 1975, s. 11(2), has been abolished (see the Employment Act 1980, s. 19(*b*), repealing the Act of 1975, ss. 11–16).

The Employment Protection Act 1975, Part II (ss. 22–88), has been repealed and replaced by the Employment Protection (Consolidation) Act 1978; the Act of 1975, ss. 55–58, 59, 61 and 62, 63–69, have been re-enacted in the Act of 1978, ss. 23–26, 29, 31–32 and 152, 121–127, without significant change of effect.

TRADE

The Employment Act 1980, ss. 1–3 (see also BALLOT) affect unions. Unreasonable exclusion or expulsion from a trade union is prohibited by the Act of 1980, s. 4(2); the remedy is a complaint to an industrial tribunal, which is not bound to accept the union's rules as a measure of reasonableness (s. 4(5)). Appeals lie to the Employment Appeals Tribunal (*q.v.*) (s. 4(8)). Compensation may be awarded for unreasonable exclusion or expulsion (s. 5).

Various activities to compel union membership were excluded from the protection of the Trade Union and Labour Relations Act 1974, s. 13, (Employment Act 1980, s. 18).

Tort immunity has again been legislated for (Employment Act 1982, s. 15), the Act of 1974, s. 14, being repealed; liability of a union has therefore been assimilated to that of an ordinary individual, special provision being made for the liability of a union for the acts of its officials, general secretary, and others. Certain limits (based on the membership size of the union involved) have been imposed on the damages which may be awarded (other than those for personal injuries resulting from negligence, nuisance or breach of statutory duty) (s. 16); the limits are subject to variation by the Secretary of State (s. 16(4)).

Traffic Commissioners. The Road Traffic Act 1960, s. 120, has been repealed and replaced by the Public Passenger Vehicles Act 1981, ss. 4–5, without significant change of effect.

Traffic signs. The Road Traffic Regulation Act 1967, ss. 54–68, 75, have been repealed and replaced by the Road Traffic Regulation Act 1984, ss. 64–80, without change of effect.

Traffic wardens. The Road Traffic Regulation Act 1967, s. 81 and the Transport Act 1968, s. 131, have been repealed and replaced by the Road Traffic Regulation Act 1984, ss. 95–97, Sched. 12, without change of effect.

Trailers. The Road Traffic Act 1972, s. 65, was repealed by the Road Traffic Act 1974, s. 24(2), (3), Sched. 6, para. 16, Sched. 7. Restrictions on trailers are authorised under the Act of 1972, ss. 40 and 42.

Training Services Agency. The abolition of this body (and the Employment Service Agency) is provided for in the Employment and Training Act 1981, s. 9.

Tramways. The Ministry of Transport Act 1919, ss. 2, 5, have been repealed by the Secretary of State for the Environment Order 1970 (S.I. 1970 No. 1681) and the Statute Law (Repeals) Act 1981, s. 1(1), Sched., Part IX, respectively.

Transfer. The groups in the Chancery Division have been abolished (Rules of the Supreme Court (Amendment No. 2) 1982 (S.I. 1982 No. 1111); see CHANCERY). The former R.S.C. Ord. 4, r. 5, has been renumbered r. 4.

The transfer of proceedings between the High Court and county courts (in both directions) is now regulated by the County Courts Act 1984, ss. 40–45 (which consolidate the earlier provisions). See also REMITTED ACTION and REMOVAL.

Transire. The Customs and Excise Act 1952, s. 59, has been repealed and replaced by the Customs and Excise Management Act 1979, s. 71, without change of effect.

Transmission machinery. The Factories Act 1937, s. 13, has been repealed and replaced by the Factories Act 1961, s. 13, without change of effect.

Transport Holding Company. The power to dissolve this body (Transport Act 1968, s. 53, has been exercised (Transport Holding Company (Dissolution) Order 1973 (S.I. 1973 No. 338)).

Transport, Minister of. Functions formerly carried out by the minister have again been transferred to him from the Secretary of State for Transport (Minister of Transport Order 1979 (S.I. 1979 No. 571)).

Traversing answer; Traversing note. Applications for judgment in default of defence (R.S.C. Ord. 19, r. 7) are more commonly made on summons, particularly in the Queen's Bench Division, and are dealt with by a master, being referred to the judge in the Chancery Division if necessary.

Treachery. The Treachery Act 1940, has been repealed by the Statute Law (Repeals) Act 1973, s. 1(1), Sched. 1, Part V, without replacement.

Treasury. The salaries of various persons associated with the Treasury are increased from time to time (see, *e.g.* S.I. 1979 No. 905).

The definition contained in the Interpretation Act 1889, s. 12, has been repealed and replaced by the Interpretation Act 1978, s. 5, Sched. 1, without change of effect.

Treating. The Representation of the People Act 1949, s. 100, has been repealed and replaced by the Representation of the People Act 1983, s. 114, without change of effect.

Tree. The registration of a tree preservation order as a local land charge is now effected under the Local Land Charges Act 1975, ss. 1, 5.

The Highways Act 1959, ss. 82, 65, 123 and 134, have been repealed and replaced by the Highways Act 1980, ss. 96, 64, 141 and 154, without change of effect. The Highways Act 1971, s. 43, and the Highways (Miscellaneous Provisions) Act 1961, s. 10, have been repealed and replaced by the Highways Act 1980, ss. 141–142, 154, also without change of effect.

Minor changes in the tree preservation orders scheme were made by the Local Government, Planning and Land Act 1980, s. 90, Sched. 15, paras. 13, 14; associated amendments to the regulations were made by S.I. 1981 No. 14.

Trespass. In cases of trespass to goods, *jus tertii* may be pleaded in cases which come within the Torts (Interference with Goods) Act 1977, s. 8(1); see THIRD PARTY.

Trial. The order of speeches in a High Court civil case is provided for in R.S.C. Ord. 35, r. 7. The Administration of Justice (Miscellaneous Provisions) Act 1933, s. 6, has been repealed and replaced by the Supreme Court Act 1981, s. 69, without change of effect; the Judicature Act 1925, s. 30, has been repealed and replaced by the Act of 1981, s. 17, also without change of effect.

Trials before official referees are now regulated by R.S.C. Ord. 36, rr. 1–8 (as amended by the Rules of the Supreme Court (Amendment No. 2) 1980 (S.I. 1982 No. 1111)); hearings before special referees are conducted under Ord. 36, r. 10, and those before masters under Ord. 36, r. 11 and Ord. 14, r. 6(2).

The expedited hearing arrangements in *Practice Direction* [1974] 1 W.L.R. 1219, are still in operation.

The determination of the mode of trial when a criminal case comes before a magistrates' court is governed by the Magistrates' Courts Act 1980, ss. 18 *et seq.* (replacing the Criminal Law Act 1977, ss. 19–23). The order of speeches on the summary trial of an information or complaint is governed by the Magistrates' Courts Rules 1981, rr. 13, 14, respectively (replacing the like-named rules of 1968).

Triers; Triors. The Criminal Justice Act 1948, s. 35, has been repealed and replaced by the Juries Act 1974, s. 12(1)(*b*), which imposes on the judge the duty of trying any challenge for cause.

Trinidad and Tobago. These islands have become a republic within the Commonwealth (Trinidad and Tobago Republic Act 1976).

Trinity House. The establishment of the Pilotage Commission (*q.v.*) has not deprived the Trinity House of its rights and duties in respect of pilotage (see the Pilotage Act 1983, ss. 1–10 replacing the Merchant Shipping Act 1979, ss. 1–13). The Pilotage Act 1913, has been repealed and replaced by the Pilotage Act 1983; further provision for the Trinity House is made by the Act of 1983, ss. 27–29 and 61.

Trinity House outport district. The Pilotage Act 1913, s. 52(1), has been repealed and replaced by the Pilotage Act 1983, s. 27, without change of effect.

Trinity sittings. These now begin on the second Tuesday after the spring holiday (which is the bank holiday falling on the last Monday in May or its substitute) (R.S.C. Ord. 64, r. 1 (as amended by S.I. 1972 No. 1194)).

Trolley vehicle. The Road Traffic Act 1930, s. 131, and the Road Traffic Regulation Act 1967, s. 104, have been repealed and replaced by the Road Traffic Regulation Act 1984, s. 141(5), without change of effect.

Trover. Detinue (*q.v.*) has been abolished.

Trunk roads. The Highways Act 1959, ss. 1, 7–10, have been repealed and replaced by the Highways Act 1980, ss. 1, 2, 4, 6, 10–11, 14, 19, without change of effect.

Trust. A beneficiary's interest under a trust is now capable of being the subject of a charging order (Charging Orders Act 1979, s. 2(1)(*a*)(iii)).

The repeal and replacement of the Mental Health Act 1959 by the Mental Health Act 1983 does not affect the operation of the Trustee Act 1925, ss. 36, 41.

The Judicature Act 1925, s. 160(1), has been repealed and replaced by the Supreme Court Act 1981, s. 114; the law has been changed so that two trustees will normally be appointed, but power is reserved to the court to appoint a sole administrator when "it appears to the court to be expedient in all the circumstances to appoint an individual as sole administrator" (s. 114(2)).

Trust corporation. The Public Trustee (Custodian Trustee) Rules 1926 (S.R.& O. 1926 No. 1423) were revoked and replaced by the Public Trustee (Custodian Trustee) Rules 1971 (S.I. 1971 No. 1894), which have in turn been revoked and replaced by the Public Trustee (Custodian Trustee) Rules 1976 (S.I. 1976 No. 1189, amended by S.I. 1976 No. 836 and S.I. 1981 No. 358). See also the Public Trustee Rules 1912 (S.R.& O. 1912 No. 348), r. 30.

Trust for sale. The Trustee Act 1893, s. 14, has been repealed and replaced by the Trustee Act 1925, ss. 14, 17, without change of effect.

Trust funds. The County Courts Act 1959, s. 168, was one of the few sections not repealed in the consolidation effected by the County Courts Act 1984.

Trustee. When a trustee is also a beneficiary, his liability to suffer recovery of money or assets wrongfully retained or distributed, etc. is now limited to the excess over his proper share, but only if he acted honestly and reasonably in making the distribution (Limitation Act 1980, s. 21(2) (consolidating the amendment made by the Limitation Amendment Act 1980, s. 5)).

Twelve-day writ. This procedure is the origin of the modern provisions for summary judgment (*q.v.*) under R.S.C. Ord. 14,

Twelvemonth. The definition of "month" in the Law of Property Act 1925, s. 61, has been repeated (without modification or repeal) in the Interpretation Act 1978, s. 5, Sched. 1.

U

Unclaimed property. The Supreme Court Funds Rules 1927, r. 97, has been revoked and replaced by the Supreme Court Funds Rules 1975 (S.I. 1975 No. 1803), r. 56, without change of effect. By r. 56A (added by S.I. 1978 No. 751), the Accountant General has power to dispose of unclaimed effects in court in certain cases. The Limitation Act 1939 (as variously amended), has been repealed and replaced by the Limitation Act 1980.

See also LOST PROPERTY.

Under-lease. The Limitation Act 1939 (as variously amended), has been repealed and replaced by the Limitation Act 1980.

Undischarged bankrupt. The credit limit available to an undischarged bankrupt has been increased from £10 to £50 (Bankruptcy Act 1914, s. 155; Insolvency Act 1976, s. 1, Sched. 1, Part I).

Undue influence. Bankers have now been added to the list of persons who may be considered to wield undue influence (*Lloyds Bank Ltd.* v.*Bundy* [1975] Q.B. 326, C.A.), but they are not considered as normally coming within the scope of the undue influence rules (*National Westminster Bank PLC* v. *Morgan* [1983] 3 All E.R. 85, C.A.).

When a contract has been concluded as a result of undue influence, it may happen that it is impossible to restore the parties to their original position (*restitutio in integrum*); in such cases the court will adjust affairs between the parties as seems most just (*O'Sullivan* v. *Management Agency Ltd.* [1984] 3 W.L.R. 448, C.A.).

Unfair contract terms. The Unfair Contract Terms Act 1977, sets out further restrictions on the extent to which civil liability for breach of contract, or for negligence or other breaches of duty may be avoided by contractual terms or otherwise.

Liability for causing the death or personal injury of any person by negligence may not be excluded or restricted by contract or by notices (s. 2(1)); in the case of other forms of loss or damage, the exclusion of liability may be effected by such terms or by notice only if the exclusion satisfies the statutory requirement of reasonableness

(s. 2(2)). Liability for loss or damage which results from negligence in the manufacture or distribution of consumer goods may not be reduced or excluded by any terms in a "guarantee" of the goods (s. 5). A consumer, or a person who deals with another on the other's standard terms of contract, has the benefit of a statutory "reasonableness test" when any other form of exclusion or restriction of liability for loss or damage resulting from negligence is relied on by the other person (ss. 3, 4).

The statutory "reasonableness test" requires any term which it governs to be fair and reasonable in the circumstances which were, or ought reasonably to have been, known or in the contemplation of the parties when the contract was made (s. 11(1)); a list of matters to which attention is to be paid is set out in the Act (s. 11(2), Sched. 2). In relation to (non-contractual) notices, the reasonableness test requires that it should be fair and reasonable to allow reliance on a notice, having regard to all the circumstances obtaining when the liability arose or (but for the notice) would have arisen (s. 11(3)). The onus of proof of reasonableness lies on the party who relies on the term or notice which is subject to the requirement of reasonableness (s. 11(5)). The same considerations as to reasonableness are imported into the Misrepresentation Act 1967, s. 3 (as substituted by the Act of 1977, s. 8); see MISREPRESENTATION; RESCISSION.

Unfair dismissal. The dismissal of an employee by an employer who is unable to show that the dismissal was fair (see the Employment Protection (Consolidation) Act 1978, Part V (ss. 54–80)). The right not to be unfairly dismissed (conferred by s. 54(1)) is enjoyed by every employee with more than 52 weeks (see S.I. 1979 No. 959) of employment with the employer in question, though the right is excluded (by ss. 54(2), 141–149) in certain cases (*e.g.* mariners, dock workers, and those working under fixed term contracts, as well as in the cases dealt with by the Employment Act 1980, s. 8). The Act of 1978 contains a complex definition of the term "dismissal" (see s. 55).

There is a statutory presumption in favour of employees, so that once a dismissal is alleged by the employee to be unfair and the appropriate related facts have been proved to the satisfaction of the tribunal, it is incumbent on the employer to show that the dismissal is outside the proscribed range (s. 57). Specific provision is made for dismissals relating to trade union membership (s. 58), those grounded on redundancy (s. 59) or on pregnancy (s. 60), and in connection with a lock-out or other industrial action (s. 61). Failure to permit a woman to return to work after confinement normally amounts to a dismissal (s. 56). The fact that an employer is or has been under pressure to effect a dismissal which is in fact unfair does not constitute a defence to proceedings in respect of that unfair dismissal (s. 63).

Claims based on allegations of unfair dismissal (contrast wrongful dismissals (*q.v.*)) are determined by industrial tribunals (*q.v.*); they are commenced by filing an originating application. In normal cases the application must be received by the tribunal before the expiration of three months beginning with the effective date of termination of the contract of employment (as defined in the Act of 1978, ss. 55(4), 153(1)), or such longer period as the tribunal considers reasonable provided it is satisfied that it was not reasonably practicable to present the complaint within the normal period (s. 67(1), (2)). A substantial body of case law has accumulated on the question of when the time limit may properly be extended.

The remedies available to a person who successfully presents a complaint of unfair dismissal to a tribunal include reinstatement (*q.v.*), re-engagement (*q.v.*) and a compensatory (money) award (see ss. 72–76). The statute contains formulae for the determination of the amount which is due, and there is a limit which is prescribed under s. 75(1) (currently being £8,000; see S.I. 1984 No. 2020)) and which is adjusted from time to time (under s. 75(2)).

The Employment Act 1980, ss. 6–10, futher modified this already complex body of law. Section 6 modified the provisions relating to the test of an employer's reasonableness in acting on what is claimed to be the ground for dismissal. Section 7 contained detailed amendments to the provisions for dismissal relating to trade union membership, introducing balloting provisions (Employment Protection (Consolidation) Act 1978, s. 58A) in relation to union membership agreements (see CLOSED SHOP). Further amendments were made to the method (contained in the Act of 1978, s. 73) of assessing the "basic award" (s. 9).

The Employment Act 1982, s. 2, Sched. 2, gave the Secretary of State a discretionary power to compensate individuals who were dismissed for failure to conform to requirements of union membership agreements. The same Act modified (again) the assessment (Act of 1978, s. 72; Act of 1982, s. 4) of the "basic award" and added a new "special award" (Act of 1978, s. 75A; Act of 1982, s. 5).

Uniformity, Acts of. The observance prescribed by the Acts has been extensively modified by the Prayer Book (Alternative and other Services) Measure 1965, under which a number of modern forms of service have been promulgated.

Union. The Interpretation Act 1889, s. 16, has been repealed and replaced by the Interpretation Act 1978, s. 25(1), Sched. 1, without replacement.

Union membership agreement. See CLOSED SHOP.

Unit trusts. The Finance Act 1972, ss. 112, 113, and the Finance (No. 2) Act 1975, ss. 63, 64, have been repealed and replaced by the Capital Gains Tax Act 1979, ss. 92–98, where the provisions relating to that tax in respect of unit trusts were consolidated.

United Reformed Church. See the United Reformed Church Acts 1972 (c. xviii) and 1981 (c. xxiv). The Act of 1972 has been extended to the Isle of Man (S.I. 1977 No. 979). See also DISSENTERS.

University. The Court of Appeal has declined to undertake the functions of a university visitor (*Patel* v. *University of Bradford Senate* [1979] 1 W.L.R. 1066).

University courts. The Judicature Act 1925, s. 209, has been repealed without specific replacement by the Supreme Court Act 1981, s. 152(4), Sched. 7.

Unlawful assembly. The decision in *Kamara* v. *D.P.P.* [1974] A.C. 104, has been modified by fresh provision for offences relating to entering and remaining of property (Criminal Law Act 1977, ss. 6–13); see FORCIBLE ENTRY.

Unoccupied property. For the repeal of the Community Land Act 1975, see the Local Government, Planning and Land Act 1980, ss. 101, 194, Scheds. 17, 34. The Act of 1980, s. 42, also provides for the revision of the system of rates on unoccupied property. The Secretary of State was given power to terminate the operation of the General Rate Act 1967, ss. 17A, 17B (Act of 1980, s. 41(1)), and (more startlingly) a power to reintroduce them (s. 42(2)).

Unseaworthy ships. The Merchant Shipping Act 1894, ss. 463, 483, have been (prospectively) repealed by the Merchant Shipping Act 1970, s. 100(3), Sched. 5. The Merchant Shipping Act 1894, s. 457, has been repealed and replaced by the Merchant Shipping Act 1979, s. 44, which makes it an offence (both by the master and by the owner) to have a dangerously unsafe ship in a port in the United Kingdom or such a ship registered in the United Kingdom and which is in any other port. The defence allowed under the Act of 1894 has been re-enacted in the new provision.

Unsolicited goods and services. For the general revision of the penalties which may be imposed on summary conviction and the abolition of enhanced penalties for second and subsequent convictions see FINE.

Unsound food. The Food and Drugs Act 1955, ss. 8–11, and the Local Goverment Act 1972 s. 198, have been repealed and replaced by the Food Act 1984, ss. 8–11, 71, without change of effect.

Unsworn statement from the dock. The right of the defendant to make such a statement in criminal proceedings has been abolished (Criminal Justice Act 1982, s. 72).

Unus nullus rule. In the law of affiliation, corroboration is required by the statute when the mother of the child whose paternity is in question gives evidence; if for some reason the case can be complete without her evidence, corroboration is not required (Affiliation Proceedings Act 1957, s. 4(2)). The Affiliation Proceedings (Amendment) Act 1972, s. 1(1), inserted a new text of s. 4(1) into the 1957 Act, avoiding the original statutory requirement that the mother should give evidence. The rule about corroboration has been retained, but only when the mother gives evidence.

Usury. The Clergy Discipline Act 1892, was repealed by the Ecclesiastical Jurisdiction Measure 1963, s. 87, Sched. 5, without specific replacement.

Utter. The Forgery Act 1913, s. 6, has been repealed by the Forgery and Counterfeiting Act 1981, s. 30, Sched., Part I. Although the conduct in question is still prohibited, the term "utter" no longer appears, the terms "pass" and "tender" being used instead. The general provisions of the Act of 1981 have replaced the many specific provisions of 1913, though without significant change of effect. See FORGERY.

V

Vacation. The date related to Whit Sunday has been amended to read "spring holiday," which is the bank holiday which falls on the last Monday in May (S.I. 1972 No. 1194).

The arrangements which have been made for dealing with court business in the Long Vacation (now officially called "the month of August") are published in the major periodicals and law reports some time before the end of the Trinity sittings.

Vaccination. The National Health Service Act 1948, s. 26, has been repealed and replaced by the National Health Service Act 1977, s. 52, without significant change of effect, although the new provision refers to vaccination or immunisation against diseases in very general terms.

Vaccine damage. Under the Vaccine Damage Payments Act 1979, s. 1, any person who is severely disabled as a result of vaccination for diphtheria, tetanus, whooping cough, poliomyelitis, measles, rubella, tuberculosis, smallpox, or any other disease prescribed under the Act, is entitled to £10,000 compensation provided the claimant can satisfy the Secretary of State that his disablement results from the vaccination and that he fulfils certain other conditions (s. 2). Claims rejected by the Secretary of State may be reviewed by tribunals (s. 4) which consider the extent of causation or disablement, according to the requirements of each case; the tribunals are under the supervision of the Council on Tribunals (Tribunals and Inquiries (Vaccine Damage Tribunals) Order 1979 (S.I. 1979 No. 659)). The administration of the scheme is regulated by the Vaccine Damage Payments Regulations 1979 (S.I. 1979 No. 432).

Vagrancy. The offence under the Vagrancy Act 1824, s. 4, was revised as to refer to persons suspected of loitering with intent to commit an arrestable offence (Criminal Law Act 1967, s. 10, Sched. 2, para. 2). That part of the Vagrancy Act 1824, s. 4, which related to this loitering has been repealed by the Criminal Attempts Act 1981. The 1981 Act, s. 9, introduced a new, summary offence of interfering with vehicles, the essence of which (s. 9(2)) is interference intending that there shall be committed the theft of the vehicle in question (or any associated trailer or any part of it), the theft of anything in or on the vehicle or trailer, or an offence of taking and driving away (under the Theft Act 1968, s. 12). The maximum penalty (s. 9(3)) is three months' imprisonment or a fine not exceeding £500 (now £1,000; see FINE) or both. Arrest without warrant by a constable is authorised against a person who is or whom the constable reasonably suspects of committing an offence (s. 9(4)).

The Magistrates' Courts Act 1952, s. 27(3), has been repealed and replaced by the Magistrates' Courts Act 1980, s. 34(3), subject to an increase in the maximum sum which may be imposed.

The power to imprison (under the Act of 1824, ss. 3, 4) has been removed (Act of 1982, s. 70), and the procedure for and the consequence of deeming person to be an incorrigible rogue have been modified (Act of 1982, ss. 70(2), 77, Sched. 12, para. 1).

Valuation list. The General Rate Act 1975, has been repealed by the Local Government, Planning and Land Act 1980, s. 194, Sched. 34, Part IX. The requirement of revision of the list has been modified from the original five years, allowing a revision to be ordered when thought needed (Act of 1967, s. 68).

Value added tax. The turnover figure of

£5,000 is increased from time to time; see, *e.g.* the Value Added Tax (Increase of Registration Limits) Order 1983 (S.I. 1983 No. 401, by which the registration limit was increased to £18,000 per year). The general provisions for the tax have been consolidated into the Value Added Tax Act 1983.

Valuer. Since a mutually-appointed valuer is not acting in an arbitral or quasi-arbitral capacity, he may be liable in the tort of negligence (*Arenson* v. *Arenson* [1977] A.C. 405, H.L.).

Venue. The question of the proper venue for commencement of proceedings is important and is provided for in some detail for county courts (see C.C.R. 1981 Ord. 4, replacing C.C.R. 1936 Ord. 2).

Verdict. The provisions of the Criminal Justice Act 1967, s. 13(1), (2), have been repealed and replaced by the Juries Act 1974, s. 17(1), (3), without change of effect. Likewise the Courts Act 1971, s. 39, has been repealed and replaced by the Juries Act 1974, s. 17. The practice in cases where a majority verdict is under consideration has been amplified in *Practice Direction* [1970] 1 W.L.R. 916.

The very strict view of compliance with the terms of the 1967 Practice Direction taken in *R.* v. *Reynolds* (1981) 73 Cr.App.R. 324, C.A., followed in *R.* v. *Pigg* (1982) 74 Cr.App.R. 352, C.A., was overruled in *R.* v. *Pigg* (1983) 76 Cr.App.R. 79, H.L.; provided the foreman of the jury makes it clear (from the viewpoint of an ordinary person) how the jury was divided, the precise form of words does not matter.

Vermin. The Housing Act 1957, s. 44(7), has been repealed by the Housing Act 1974, s. 130(4), Sched. 15, without replacement.

Vesting declaration. The Town and Country Planning Act 1968, s. 30, Sched. 1, have been repealed and replaced by the Compulsory Purchase (Vesting Declarations) Act 1981, without significant change of effect. The Secretary of State has power to make vesting declarations in relation to "right to buy" (*q.v.*) cases (Housing Act 1980, s. 24).

Vestments. The Vestures of Ministers Measure 1964, has been repealed without specific replacement by the Church of England (Worship and Doctrine) Measure 1974, s. 6(3), Sched. 2.

Veterinary surgeon. The Diseases of Animals Act 1950, has been repealed and replaced by the Animal Health Act 1981, without change of effect (see particularly s. 84).

Vexatious actions. The Judicature Act 1925, s. 51, has been repealed and replaced by the Supreme Court Act 1981, s. 42. The new provision contains an amendment to allow a restriction on the institution of proceedings to be imposed for a specified period as an alternative to an unrestricted order. The Act of 1959, has been incorporated in the 1981 Act, s. 42(1)(i), which provides that an order to that effect may be made; the ban is no longer automatic.

Vicar. The Incumbents Act 1868, has been repealed by the Statute Law (Repeals) Act 1977, s. 1(1), Sched. 1, Part V.

Vicarage. The Incumbents Act 1868, has been repealed by the Statute Law (Repeals) Act 1977, s. 1(1), Sched. 1, Part V.

Vice-Chancellor. The Administration of Justice Act 1970, s. 5, has been repealed and replaced by the Supreme Court Act 1981, ss. 2(1)(*g*) (making the Vice-Chancellor an *ex-officio* member of the Court of Appeal), 4(1)(*d*) (which makes him a member of the High Court), and 5(1) (which designates him the vice-president of the Chancery Division). The Act of 1981, s. 10(1), makes this a Royal appointment for the first time.

Vice-consul. The Interpretation Act 1889, s. 12(20), has been repealed by the Interpretation Act 1978 s. 25(1), Sched. 1, without replacement. The Act of 1978 defines "consul" by reference to the meaning set out in Art. 1 of the Vienna Convention (set out in the Consular Relations Act 1968, Sched. 1) (Act of 1978, s. 5, Sched. 1).

Vice-president. The Judicature Act 1925, s. 6(4), has been repealed and replaced by the Supreme Court Act 1981, s. 3(3), which allows of the appointment of a vice-president for each (*i.e.* the Criminal and the Civil) of the Divisions of the Court of Appeal.

Video recordings. See the Video Recordings Act 1984, for (prospective) provisions for the regulation of such recordings and dealings, etc. The Act defines these new forms of information and entertainment (s. 1(3)) thus: "any disc or magnetic tape containing information by the use of which the whole of a part of a video work may be produced"; "video work" means any series of visual images (with or without sound) —(a) produced electromagnetically by the use of information contained on any disc or magnetic tape; and (b) shown as a moving picture (s. 1(2)).

View. It is well established that any view of a public place should take place in the presence of the parties and their legal advisers or with their knowledge and consent so as to avoid any misunderstandings on account of changed circumstances.

For the matters to be taken into account in connection with a judicial view outside the jurisdiction see *Tito* v. *Waddell* [1975] W.L.R. 1313, which lead to the notable visit of Megarry J. to Ocean Island (for the subsequent proceedings see *Tito* v. *Waddell* (*No. 2*) [1977] Ch. 106, Megarry V.-C).

Vintners Company. The Customs and Excise Act 1952, s. 166, has been repealed and replaced by the Alcoholic Liquor Duties Act 1979, s. 89, without change of effect.

Vir et uxor censentur in lege una persona. This argument has been used to resist a civil claim involving conspiracy, but without success (*Midland Bank Trust Co. Ltd.* v. *Green* (*No. 3*) [1979] Ch. 496).

Visitation. For the refusal of the courts to undertake the task of visitation in respect of universities see *Patel* v. *University of Bradford Senate* [1979] 1 W.L.R. 1066. The Judicature Act 1925, s. 19(5), has been repealed without replacement by the Supreme Court Act 1981, s. 152(4), Sched. 7.

Volenti non fit injuria. By the Unfair Contract Terms Act 1977, s. 2(3), it is provided that where a contract term or notice purports to exclude or restrict liability for negligence, a person's agreement to or awareness of it is not of itself to be taken as indicating his voluntary acceptance of any risk.

Volunteers. The Reserve Forces Act 1966, has been repealed and replaced by the Reserve Forces Act 1980 (which is a consolidating Act), without change of effect.

Vouch; Voucher. The taking of an account and "vouching" of an account in Chancery Chambers are now regulated by R.S.C. Ord. 43, rr. 2–4. It is usual to agree as many items as possible, leaving only the disputed matters to be adjudicated upon by the court.

Cash vouchers (*q.v.*) have been subjected to further taxation provisions (Finance Act 1976, s. 71).

W

Wages. The Merchant Shipping Act 1894, s. 157, has been repealed and replaced by the Merchant Shipping Act 1970, ss. 7 *et seq.* The Act of 1894, s. 167, has been repealed and replaced by the Merchant Shipping Act 1970, s. 18, without change of effect. The Administration of Justice Act 1956, ss. 1(1)(*o*), 3, 5, have been repealed and replaced by the Supreme Court Act 1981, ss. 20(1)(*o*), 21, 24, with only slight modifications.

The restriction imposed by the Wages Attachment Abolition Act 1870, must be read subject to the powers of the courts to attach earnings under the Attachment of Earnings Act 1971; see ATTACHMENT.

The jurisdiction of county courts to hear actions for the recovery of wages by a minor was in 1977 increased from £750 to £2,000 (County Courts Jurisdiction Order 1977 (S.I. 1977 No. 600)); a further increase, to £5,000 was made in 1981 (County Courts Jurisdiction Order 1981 (S.I. 1981) No. 1123)). The County Courts Act 1959, s. 80, which was the basis of the jurisdiction to recover wages, has been repealed and replaced by the County Courts Act 1984, s. 47, without change of effect.

The Factories Act 1961, s. 135, has been affected by the Factories Act 1961 Enforcement of s. 135) Regulations 1974 (S.I. 1974 No. 1776); s. 136 of the 1961 Act has been repealed (Factories Act 1961 (Repeals) Regulations 1975 (S.I. 1975 No. 1012)).

Wages councils. The Wages Councils Act 1959 (as amended), has been repealed and replaced by the Wages Councils Act 1979, without change of effect; the provisions of the Employment Protection Act 1975, s. 90, have been re-enacted in the Act of 1979,

s. 10, Sched. 4 (see STATUTORY JOINT INDUSTRIAL COUNCILS).

Wake. The Public Health Act 1936, s. 165, has been repealed and replaced by the Public Health (Control of Diseases) Act 1984, s. 45; the new section contains a revised penalty provision ("level 1 on the standard scale," raised to £50 by S.I. 1984 No. 447; see FINE).

Wales. The Wales and Berwick Act 1746, and the Welsh Language Act 1967, s. 4, have been repealed and replaced by the Interpretation Act 1978, s. 5 Sched. 1, by virtue of which "Wales" now means the area consisting of the counties established by the Local Government Act 1972, s. 20. The pre-1974 and pre-1967 definitions are preserved by the Act of 1978, Sched. 2, para. 5(a).

For the abortive legislation to establish a Welsh government see DEVOLUTION.

Walkways. The Highways Act 1971, s. 18, has been repealed and replaced by the Highways Act 1980, s. 35, without change of effect. See also the Walkways Regulations 1973 (S.I. 1973 No. 686, amended by S.I. 1974 No. 735).

War charities. For the general revision of the penalties which may be imposed on summary conviction see FINE.

War damage. The War Damage Act 1943, together with the War Damage (Public Utility Undertakings) Act 1949, the War Damage (Clearance Payments) Act 1960 and the War Damage Act 1964, were all repealed without replacement by the Statute Law (Repeals) Act 1981, s. 1(1), Sched. 1 Part XI.

War memorials. The Parish Councils Act 1967, ss. 8(2)(a), 15, have been repealed by the Local Government Act 1972, s. 272, Sched. 30; the Act of 1957, Sched. 2, has been repealed by the Statute Law (Repeals) Act 1974, s. 1, Sched., Part XI.

War risks insurance. The War Risks Insurance Act 1939, and the War Damage (Amendment) Act 1942, were repealed without replacement by the Statute Law (Repeals) Act 1981, s. 1(1), Sched. 1, Part XI.

War-time leases. The Validation of War-time Leases Act 1944, has ben repealed by the Statute Law (Repeals) Act 1976, s. 1(1), Sched. 1, Part XX, without replacement.

Ward; Wardship. The jurisdiction of the High Court in all matters of wardship is now exercised by the Family Division (*q.v.*) (Supreme Court Act 1981, s. 61(1), (3), Sched. 1, para. 3(*b*)(i), replacing the Administration of Justice Act 1970, s. 1(2), Sched. 1). Proceedings for the appointment of a guardian of a minor's estate continue to be proper to the Chancery Division (Supreme Court Act 1981, s. 61(1), (3), Sched. 1, para. 1(*j*), replacing the Supreme Court of Judicature (Consolidation) Act 1925, s. 56(1); Administration of Justice Act 1970, s. 1(6), Sched. 2, para. 8). The Law Reform (Miscellaneous Provisions) Act 1949, s. 9, has been repealed and replaced by the Act of 1981, s. 41; the protection afforded by the section comes into operation as soon as the application is made.

The Mental Health Act 1959, s. 58, has been repealed and replaced by the Mental Health Act 1983, ss. 29, 33, without significant change of effect.

Payments under the Family Law Reform Act 1969, s. 6, may now be ordered to be made to the ward himself, no longer being restricted to payment to the court (Administration of Justice Act 1982, s. 50, amending the Act of 1969, s. 6(2)(b)).

Warehouse. The Customs and Excise Act 1952, s. 80, has been repealed and replaced by the Customs and Excise Management Act 1979, s. 92, without change of effect. See also QUEEN'S WAREHOUSES.

Warrant. The Magistrates' Courts Act 1952, ss. 1, 15, 47, 77, have been repealed and replaced by the Magistrates' Courts Act 1980, ss. 1, 13, 55, 97, without significant change of effect.

Warrant of attorney. The Debtors Act 1869, ss. 24–28, have been repealed by the Administration of Justice Act 1956, ss. 16, 57(2), without replacement. Since a warrant of attorney was directly linked to the procedure for entering an appearance, the device is obsolete (see APPEARANCE).

Warranty. The Sale of Goods Act 1893, ss. 11(1)(b), 12, 62(1), have been repealed and replaced by the Sale of Goods Act 1979, ss. 11(3), 12, 61, without change of effect.

In the law of contract the distinction between warranties and conditions is a matter for the court and cannot be determined by the parties (*Wickman Machine Tools Sales Ltd.* v. *L. Schuler A.G.* [1974]

A.C. 235, H.L.).

Wasting assets. For special provision for such assets see the Capital Gains Tax Act 1979, ss. 37–39, 127, which consolidate earlier provisions.

Water. The National Water Council has been dissolved (S.I. 1983 No. 1927), together with the Water Space Amenity Commission (Water Act 1983, s. 3). The constitution of water authorities has been revised (Water Act 1973, s. 3 (as substituted by the Act of 1983, s. 1)). Fresh provision has been made for the representation of consumers' interests in water authorities' schemes of management (1973, s. 23A (added by the Act of 1983, s. 7)).

Water Space Amenity Commission. This body has been abolished (Water Act 1983, s. 3).

Way. The Highways Act 1959, ss. 34, 36, have been repealed and replaced by the Highways Act 1980, ss. 31, 33, without change of effect.

Wedding presents. These are exempted from capital transfer tax (*q.v.*) (Finance Act 1975, s. 29, Sched. 6, paras. 6, 7.

Weights and measures. Further amendments to the Weights and Measures Act 1963, have been effected by the Weights and Measures Act 1977 (all of which is now in force, except Part IV (part) and Part V), and the Weights and Measures Act 1979, which includes provisions establishing the Metrological Co-ordinating Unit (*q.v.*).

Wharf. The Customs and Excise Act 1952, s. 14 (as amended), has been repealed and replaced by the Customs and Excise Management Act 1979, s. 20, without change of effect.

Whip. The salaries of whips are revised from time to time (see, *e.g.* S.I. 1979 No. 905).

Widow. The statutory legacy in favour of a surviving spouse allocated under the Intestates' Estates Act 1952 (as amended), was increased from £15,000 to £25,000 where the estate was survived by issue, and from £40,000 to £55,000 in the event of there being no surviving issue (but certain other close relatives) (Family Provision (Intestate Succession) Order 1977 (S.I. 1977 No. 415)). These sums were again increased (to £85,000 and £40,000, respectively) in 1981 (S.I. 1981 No. 255). The rate of interest payable on statutory legacies was increased from four per cent to seven per cent (Intestate Succession (Interest and Capitalisation) Order 1977 (S.I. 1977 No. 1491)) and then reduced to six per cent (Intestate Succession (Interest and Capitalisation) Order 1983 (S.I. 1983 No. 1374)).

Wild birds. The Protection of Birds Act 1954 and associated legislation have been repealed and replaced by the Wildlife and Countryside Act 1981, ss. 1–8, Scheds. 1–4, without significant change of effect.

Will. The deposit of wills is also regulated by the Wills (Deposit for Safe Custody) Regulations 1978 (S.I. 1978 No. 1724)). The Judicature Act 1925, s. 172, and the Administration of Justice Act 1928, s. 11, have been repealed and replaced by the Supreme Court Act 1981, s. 126, with modifications. See DEPOSIT OF WILLS.

The Mental Health Act 1959, s. 103(1)(*dd*), has been repealed and replaced by the Mental Health Act 1983, s. 96(1)(*e*), without change of effect.

The attestation provisions for wills (Wills Act 1837, s. 9) have been amended (Administration of Justice Act 1982, s. 17): see ATTESTATION CLAUSE.

The effect of divorce and matrimonial proceedings bringing a marriage to an end has been modified (Wills Act 1837, ss. 18, 18A, substituted and added by the Administration of Justice Act 1982, s. 18); see REVOCATION. The Law of Property Act 1925, s. 177, has therefore been repealed without replacement (Act of 1982, s. 75(1), Sched. 9, Part I).

The text of the Wills Act 1837, s. 33, has been modified (by the Administration of Justice Act 1982, s. 19), and the Family Law Reform Act 1969, s. 16 repealed (1982, s. 75(1), Sched. 9, Part I)); see LAPSE.

A new presumption has been enacted in relation to gifts by will to a spouse: in the absence of evidence to the contrary, a testator who makes what appears to be an absolute gift to a spouse, but by the same instrument purports to give his issue an interest in the same property, the gift to the spouse is absolute notwithstanding the purported gift to the issue (Administration of Justice Act 1982, s. 22).

The Forgery Act 1913, s. 2(1), has been repealed and replaced by the Forgery and Counterfeiting Act 1981, s. 30, Sched., Part I, without specific replacement. The general provisions of the Act of 1981 (see FORGERY) suffice to cover the offences for which specific provision was formerly made. The maximum penalty has been reduced to 10 years' imprisonment (Act of 1981, s. 6(2), (3)).

In the event of slips and clerical errors in a will the court now has power (under the Administration of Justice Act 1982, ss. 20, 21) to rectify the instrument (see RECTIFICATION; RECTIFY).

Window cleaning. For the general revision of the penalties which may be imposed on summary conviction see FINE.

Wine. The Customs and Excise Act 1952, ss. 143–145, have been repealed and replaced by the Alcoholic Liquor Duties Act 1979, s. 92(2), Sched. 4, Part I. For the customs regulation of wine and the import of wine see the Act of 1979, ss. 54–61. The Food and Drugs Act 1955, has been repealed and replaced by the Food Act 1984.

Withdrawal. For the abolition of the procedure for entering an appearance and its replacement by an acknowledgment of service see APPEARANCE.

Withdrawal of a juror. For the discharge of a juror under the Juries Act 1974, s. 16, see also JURY.

Witness. A witness is no longer required to show any reason for preferring to affirm, being entitled to take this alternative course if he wishes (Oaths Act 1978, s. 5).

The witnesses to be called and the order in which they are to be called is a matter solely for the party who calls them (*Briscoe* v. *Briscoe* [1968] P. 501).

Woman. The Interpretation Act 1889, s. 1, has been repealed and replaced by the Interpretation Act 1978, s. 6, with the addition that words importing the feminine also import the masculine (see FEMININE). See also MATERNITY PAY.

Worker. In employment law this term is often used in the main statutory sense when its meaning is as follows: an individual regarded in whichever (if any) of the following capacities is applicable to him, *i.e.*, a person who works or normally works or seeks to work otherwise than in police service (a) under a contract of employment; or (b) under any other contract (whether express or implied, and, if express, whether oral or in writing) whereby he undertakes to do or to perform personally any work or services for another party to the contract who is not a professional client of his; or (c) in employment under or for the purposes of a government department (otherwise than as a member of the naval, military or air forces of the Crown or of any women's service administered by the Defence Council) in so far as any such employment does not fall within the previous classes (Trade Union and Labour Relations Act 1974, s. 30(1)). There are special provisions for the position of those (such as pharmacists, dentists and ophthalmic opticians) who work in connection with health authorities (Act of 1974, s. 30(3)).

In the definition of "trade dispute" the word "worker" has a specialised meaning, recently revised (see the Act of 1974, s. 29, and TRADE DISPUTE).

See also EMPLOYER.

Workless day; Workless period. See GUARANTEE PAYMENT.

Worship, Place of. The Council for Places of Worship (formerly called the Council for the Care of Churches) has various duties in connection with petitions for faculties, especially when a faculty is sought to authorise the disposal of any article which the judge considers is, or might be, of historic or architectural interest (see the Faculty Jurisdiction Order 1967 (S.I. 1967 No. 1002), r. 5A).

Wort. For the use of worts in determining the charge to excise duty for beer see the Alcoholic Liquor Duties Act 1979, ss. 37, 38.

Wreck. The Merchant Shipping Act 1894, s. 157, and the Merchant Shipping (Labour Conventions) Act 1925, s. 1, have been repealed and replaced by the Merchant Shipping Act 1970, s. 15, which deals with the right (or loss of right) to wages in certain circumstances, including wreck.

Wreck commissioners. For the (prospective) repeal of the Merchant Shipping Act 1894, Part VI (ss. 464–491), see the Merchant Shipping Act 1970, s. 100(3), Sched. 5. For the new provisions for the appointment and remuneration of wreck commissioners see the Act of 1970, ss. 82, 83.

Writ. The Administration of Justice (Miscellaneous Provisions) Act 1938, s. 7, has been repealed and replaced by the Supreme Court Act 1981, ss. 29–30, without significant change of effect.

Writ of summons. The mandatory part of a writ of summons now requires the defendant to acknowledge service of the writ and to send notice of intention to defend (if that be the case) to the court office (see S.I. 1979 No. 1716). The teste (*q.v.*) has been abolished.

Indorsements of service (*q.v.*) have been abolished.

The form of a writ of summons is set out in R.S.C. App. A, Form 1 (the forms previously numbered 1–5 having been revoked) (S.I. 1979 No. 1716).

The requirement (under R.S.C. Ord. 76, r. 2) of endorsement of a probate writ by a Chancery master before issue has been abolished (Rules of the Supreme Court (Amendment) 1984 (S.I. 1984 No. 1051)).

The extension of validity for service of a writ (Ord. 6, r. 8) is not fixed at a six months' renewal, the court having power to extend the validity for such period as it thinks fit provided it does not exceed an additional twelve months from the expiration of the validity of the writ

Writing. The Interpretation Act 1889, s. 20, has been repealed and replaced by the Interpretation Act 1978, s. 5, Sched. 1, without change of effect.

Wrong. The Limitation Act 1939, and associated legislation, have been repealed and consolidated into the Limitation Act 1980.

Wrongful dismissal. This term is used to designate the common law rules relating to dismissal. Statutory intervention in this field has been most extensive and centres on the purely statutory concept of unfair dismissal (*q.v.*). The two classes of civil wrong must be kept carefully distinct, although industrial tribunals (*q.v.*) may determine both classes of case.

Y

Yacht. The exemption from compulsory pilotage has been terminated (Merchant Shipping Act 1979, s. 8); see also PILOTAGE; PILOTAGE COMMISSION. The rules relating to limitation of liability (*q.v.*) are in the process of amendment. The Customs and Excise Act 1952, s. 68, has been repealed and replaced by the Customs and Excise Management Act 1979, s. 81, without change of effect.

The Merchant Shipping Act 1894, s. 3(1), has been modified so as to exclude from registration those ships which do not exceed 13.7 metres in length (Merchant Shipping Act 1983, s. 4). See also TONNAGE.

Year. The Interpretation Act 1889, s. 22, has been repealed and replaced by the Interpretation Act 1978, s. 5, Sched. 1, without change of effect.

In any cause or matter (other than matrimonial proceedings: Matrimonial Causes Rules 1977 (S.I. 1977 No. 344), r. 125), in which no step has been taken for a year, a party who wishes to proceed is required to give one month's notice of his intention to do so (R.S.C. Ord. 3, r. 6).

Young person. For the (prospective) repeal of the Merchant Shipping (International Labour Conventions) Act 1925, with minor exceptions, see the Merchant Shipping Act 1970, s. 100(3), Sched. 5.

For the revisions of the punishments which may be imposed on young persons see DETENTION CENTRE and YOUTH CUSTODY.

Youth custody. Imprisonment is now prohibited in the case of defendants under 21 years of age (Criminal Justice Act 1982, s. 1(1)).

In place of the abolished Borstal institutions (*q.v.*), the Criminal Justice Act 1982, ss. 6–7, have introduced this form of detention for offenders who are under 21 but not less than 15 years of age who are convicted of an offence which, in the case of an offender over 21, is punishable with imprisonment (s. 6(1)(*a*)). The court must be satisfied that no other method of dealing with the offender is adequate and must state the reason(s) in open court (s. 6(1)(*c*)). An age differential applies to female offenders (s. 6(4)), the minimum age for them being

17 instead of 15 (this being essentially a question of lack of institutions for the girls).

This form of detention differs principally from its predecessor in two ways: (1) it is possible for a magistrates' court to order such a punishment, subject to the usual limitations on the cumulative total of custodial sentences (Magistrates' Courts Act 1980, ss. 30, 31, 133); and (2) it is provided that "the usual term of youth custody is a term exceeding four months" (Criminal Justice Act 1982, s. 7(5)).

Judicial regret has been expressed at the impossibility of imposing a suspended sentence of youth custody (which would run directly contrary to the underlying rationale of the Act of 1982, s. 1(4)): for a discussion of the principles to be observed see *R.* v. *Dobbs*; *R.* v. *Hitchings* (1983) 5 Cr.App.R.(S.) 328 C.A.

Z

Zimbabwe. Formerly called Southern Rhodesia, after a long period of illegal and unilaterally declared independence (see the Southern Rhodesia Act 1965), this country was granted fully responsible status as a republic by the Zimbabwe Act 1979. An amnesty has been provided (s. 3) in respect of a wide range of acts and omissions for the period from 11 November 1965, until 20 December 1979 (when the Act came into force), and special provision has been made for Zimbabwe to join the Commonwealth should she so wish (s. 5). See also RHODESIA.

Several old debts arising under loans to the Colony of Rhodesia and the Federation of Southern Rhodesia and Nyasaland and which have been attributed to the new state have been written off (Miscellaneous Financial Provisions Act 1983, s. 3).

Zoo. Local authorities have powers of control over zoos since it is unlawful to operate a zoo without the statutory licence from the local authority (Zoo Licensing Act 1981, s. 1(1)). Conditions may be attached to a licence (s. 5), which will normally last for six years (s. 5(2)) after an initial four year licence (s. 5(1)). There are also powers to inspect (ss. 10–12) and special provision for local authority establishments (s. 13) and dispensations may be made for particular zoos (s. 14).

An aggrieved person may appeal against the refusal of a licence, or against any conditions attached or against any variation or cancellation of a condition; the appeal lies to the magistrates' court for the area where the zoo is situated (s. 18). The Act was brought into operation on 30 April 1984 (Zoo Licensing Act 1981 (Commencement) Order 1984 (S.I. 1984 No. 423)).

Zoonoses. The Agriculture (Miscellaneous Provisions) Act 1972, s. 1, has been repealed and replaced by the Animal Health Act 1981, s. 29(1), without change of effect.